# THE WRATH OF FANTÔMAS

INSPIRED BY THE FANTÔMAS NOVELS BY PIERRE SOUVESTRE AND MARCEL ALLAIN

Writer : Olivier Bocquet

Art & Colors : Julie Rocheleau

# THE WRATH OF FANTÔMAS

### Writer
Olivier Bocquet

### Art & Colors
Julie Rocheleau

Inspired by the FANTÔMAS novels by
Pierre Souvestre and Marcel Allain

| | |
|---|---|
| TRANSLATED BY<br>EDWARD GAUVIN | EDITOR<br>JONATHAN STEVENSON |

## TITAN COMICS

| | |
|---|---|
| DESIGNER<br>WILFRIED TSHIKANA-EKUTSHU | COMICS BRAND MANAGER<br>CHRIS THOMPSON |
| ART ASSISTANT<br>DAN BOULTWOOD | PUBLICIST<br>IMOGEN HARRIS |
| MANAGING & LAUNCH EDITOR<br>ANDREW JAMES | ADS & MARKETING ASSISTANT<br>BELLA HOY |
| ART DIRECTOR<br>OZ BROWNE | DIRECT SALES & MARKETING MANAGER<br>RICKY CLAYDON |
| SENIOR PRODUCTION CONTROLLER<br>JACKIE FLOOK | COMMERCIAL MANAGER<br>MICHELLE FAIRLAMB |
| PRODUCTION CONTROLLER<br>PETER JAMES | PUBLISHING MANAGER<br>DARRYL TOTHILL |
| PRODUCTION ASSISTANT<br>RHIANNON ROY | PUBLISHING DIRECTOR<br>CHRIS TEATHER |
| SENIOR SALES MANAGER<br>STEVE TOTHILL | OPERATIONS DIRECTOR<br>LEIGH BAULCH |
| CIRCULATION EXECUTIVE<br>FRANCES HALLAM | EXECUTIVE DIRECTOR<br>VIVIAN CHEUNG |
| PRESS OFFICER<br>WILL O'MULLANE | PUBLISHER<br>NICK LANDAU |

THE WRATH OF FANTÔMAS

9781785868863

Published by Titan Comics
A division of Titan Publishing Group Ltd.
144 Southwark St., London, SE1 0UP.
Titan Comics is a registered trademark of Titan Publishing Group, Ltd.
All rights reserved.

Originally published in French as La Colére De Fantômas © DARGAUD 2017 Bocquet/Rocheleau

No part of this publication may be reproduced, stored in a retrieval system, or transmitted, in any
form or by any means, without the prior written permission of the publisher. Names, characters,
places and incidents featured in this publication are either the product of the author's imagination
or used fictitiously. Any resemblance to actual persons, living or dead (except for satirical
purposes), is entirely coincidental.

A CIP catalogue record for this title is available from the
British Library

10 9 8 7 6 5 4 3 2 1
First Published January 2019
Printed in China.
Titan Comics.

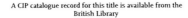

# INTRODUCTION BY OLIVIER BOCQUET

On February 10, 2011, Fantômas turned 100.

Created by Pierre Souvestre and Marcel Allain, and initially intended for a popular readership, this best-selling series of serialized novels ended up reaching every stratum of society.

The Surrealists seized upon it; intellectuals, artists, writers, journalists, and psychoanalysts waxed eloquent about its imagination, its themes, its politics, its stylistic and dramatic inventions… Adaptations, homages, copies, parodies, and perversions number in the hundreds, likely thousands, across all media.

Marcel Allain said of *Fantômas* that it sold more copies than the Bible. This was doubtless an exaggeration. On the other hand, for a few decades, *Fantômas* was perhaps more widely *read* than the Bible. Millions of readers all over the world followed the archvillain's adventures over the course of the thirty-two novels that featured him.

However, though the name "Fantômas" still lives today, his memory is dying out. To many, this first terrorist of the modern era; the man who put all Europe to the sword, held kings hostage and toppled entire nations; the man who killed, tortured, mutilated, burned, and pillaged; the man who spread epidemics and raised an army of criminals, the Master of Crime, the Prince of Terror, is but a blue-faced jester, pursued by a clown, aboard a flying Citroën from the '50s.

But those in the know patiently await their hour. They know that Fantômas will not let himself be forgotten. They know that Fantômas always returns. They also know that, in reality, Fantômas never left.

And for a very simple reason: he is the first superhero in History. All the masked men and women who splatter the pages of American comic books and movie screens are his illegitimate children. The blood of Fantômas courses through the veins of every last one of them.

Twenty-five years after Fantômas was born, the first masked superhero made his appearance in a comic strip. The word "superhero" had not yet been coined. The year was 1936: two years before Superman, three before Batman. He wore black tights, a black hood, and a black domino mask, and his name was… The Phantom.

For those who still harbor the slightest doubt: yes, the father of all superheroes was a supervillain.

Now, in a fitting reversal, it is his turn to invade the comics page.

O.

# FOREWORD BY JAMES LOVEGROVE

Who is Fantômas?

If you've picked up this book, chances are you already know the answer. Either that or you've been enticed by that haunting, spectacular cover – and who could blame you?

Fantômas was the creation of two jobbing French writers, Marcel Allain and Pierre Souvestre. Over the course of thirty-two months, from 1911 to 1913, the pair produced thirty-two Fantômas novels together. Yes, that's one book per month. Even though they divided up the burden by writing alternate chapters, it's still a phenomenal work rate. I'm breaking out in a cold sweat just thinking about it.

The Fantômas series was a hit from the outset, with five million copies sold during its heyday. All across France, from Calais to Carcassonne, Brest to Belfort, fans in their droves plonked down their centimes, eager to read the latest misadventures of the villainous protagonist who routinely carried out acts of robbery, murder, and sabotage while forever staying one step ahead of his policeman nemesis, the dogged Inspector Juve.

Souvestre died in the Spanish 'flu epidemic of 1918, and Allain resumed the series for a further eleven volumes beginning in 1925, having married Souvestre's widow in the interim (a move some might regard as taking co-authorship a step too far). There were also five immensely successful Fantômas films directed by Louis Feuillade between 1913 and 1914, and various later screen adaptations, including an American silent serial. For a while, France – and the wider world – was in the grip of Fantômas fever. The source material was lauded by Jean Cocteau for its "absurd and magnificent lyricism" and fascinated the Surrealists, including Magritte, whose painting "The Menaced Assassin" explicitly evokes elements from the books.
But who is Fantômas?

Fantômas himself is a mystery. His origins, his motivations, even his face remain unknown – blurry, indefinable. He may be British by birth, or French. He may have aristocratic blood in his veins. He goes by many aliases but his real name is never revealed.

What is certain is that he is an elusive master of disguise and a ruthless sociopath who will stop at nothing to realise his nefarious plans. He is no jaunty gentleman thief like his direct literary forebear, Maurice Leblanc's Arsène Lupin, or Lupin's equivalent across the Channel, E.W. Hornung's A.J. Raffles. He is a creature of pure, cold malevolence and doesn't care what happens to those who get in his way. Even his own children aren't immune to his evildoing; they are just bit players in the drama of his life, to be pushed around and manipulated according to whim.

His exploits are often the stuff of pure Grand Guignol. In the very first Fantômas novel, he dupes a hapless actor into taking his place on the guillotine, just one of many patsies who end up paying the price for his crimes. Elsewhere, he scares a captive woman to death by blindfolding her and pretending to slice her arm open with a knife. He scalps another woman by trapping her long hair in the workings of an automatic washing-machine. He arranges for a transatlantic passenger steamer to sink mid-voyage, and unleashes a horde of plague rats on another ocean liner, resulting in the deaths of all aboard.

Fantômas commits atrocity after atrocity, audacious heist after audacious heist, stashing away a vast fortune in ill-gotten gains at his secret lair in Mexico. Yet, with his uncanny ability to pass himself off as anyone and no one, he is never captured. He is never brought to justice for his crimes. He is a Moriarty whom Sherlock Holmes fails to send hurtling over the Reichenbach Falls. He is a Blofeld against whom James Bond's licence to kill proves useless. He is an avatar of his era, that period in the run-up to the First World War when Europe was in turmoil, the continent's inhabitants as powerlessly fretful as cattle being led to the gates of the abattoir. The times, it seems, demanded an anonymous antihero who made a mockery of the establishment and the rule of law. Fantômas fit the bill perfectly.

And now, with The Wrath of Fantômas, Olivier Bocquet and Julie Rocheleau have resurrected the unkillable character in the graphic novel medium. This is the same figure from a century ago, in his customary milieu, but in the hands of these talented creators he seems fresh and utterly, chillingly relevant to our age of terrorism, amorality, and dread. Bocquet's terse script plunders the original novels like a burglar cracking a safe full of jewels, its pace and breathless style mimicking Allain and Souvestre's to a T. Rocheleau's richly-coloured impressionistic artwork swirls across the pages, so redolent of early-twentieth-century Paris it seems steeped in absinthe. It is a grisly triumph.

Who is Fantômas?

By the time you've finished reading this book, you will know. But, for your peace of mind's sake, you may not be glad you did.

James Lovegrove

BOOK I

# THE GUILLOTINE

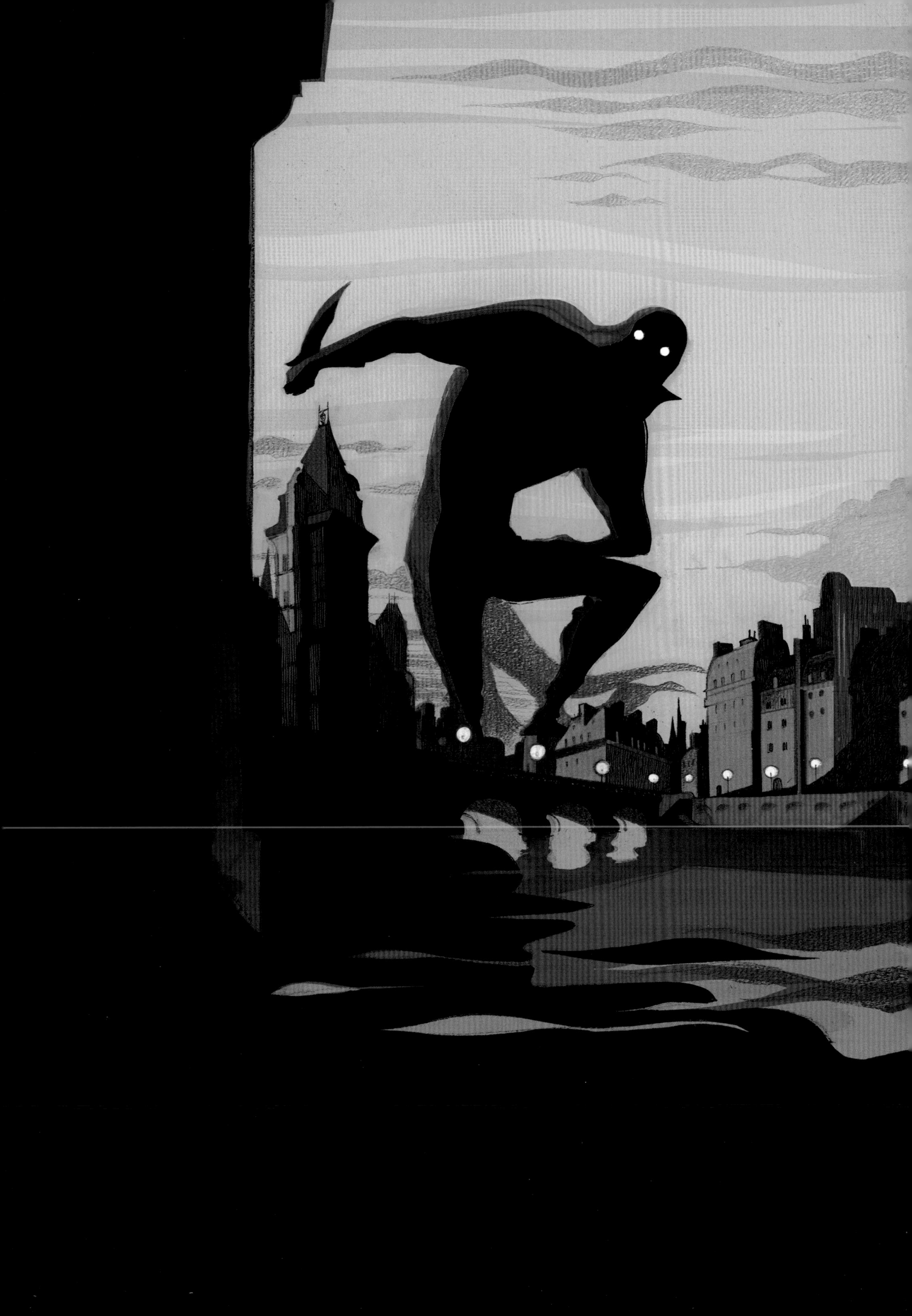

# PROLOGUE

In which
it is observed that nothing stands in the way of progress,
sundry characters are introduced, for whom fame shall come calling,
an imponderable event disturbs festive proceedings,
and first blood is drawn.

Saturday, December 28, 1895

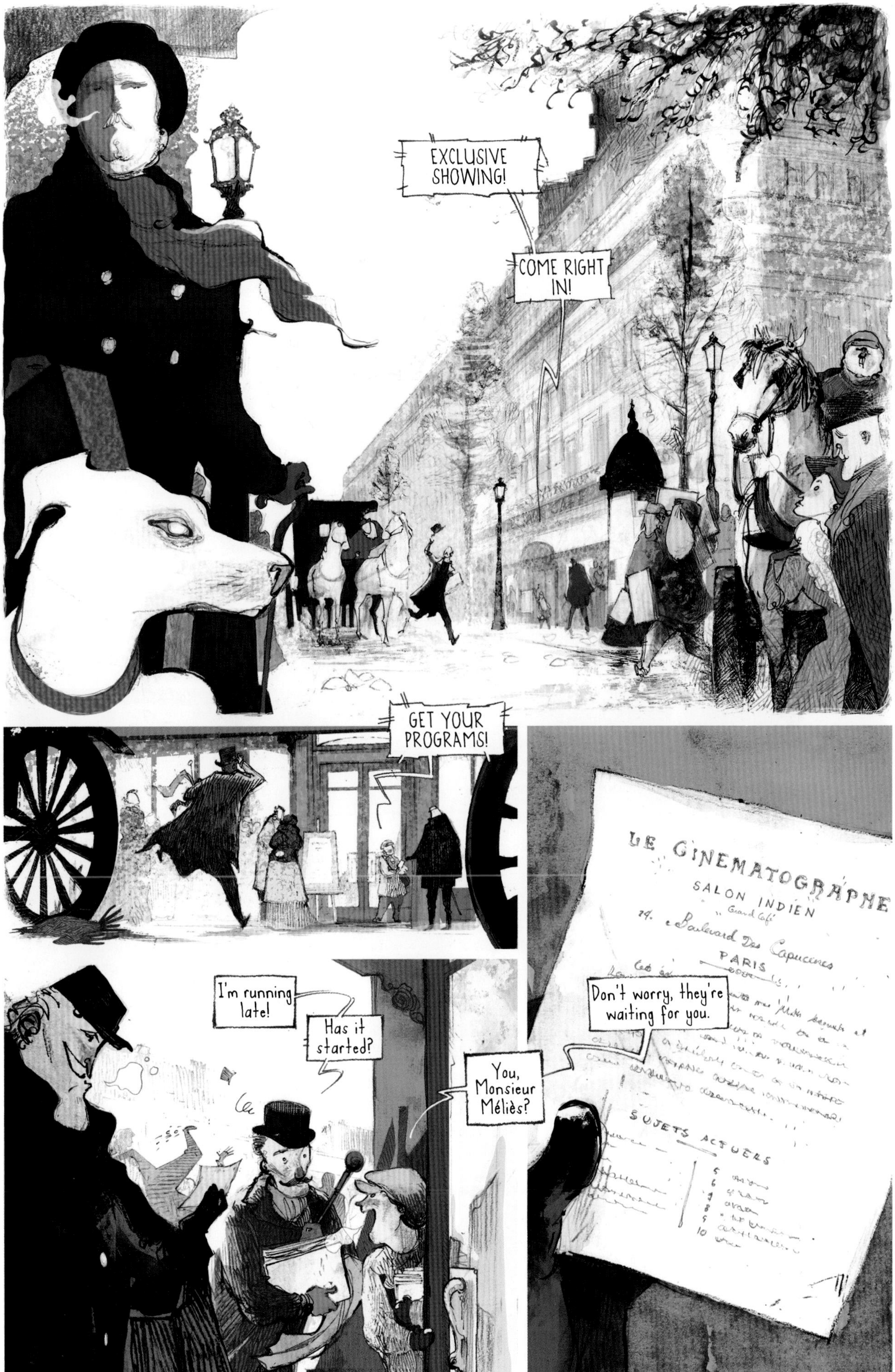
EXCLUSIVE SHOWING!
COME RIGHT IN!
GET YOUR PROGRAMS!
LE CINEMATOGRAPHE
SALON INDIEN
Grand Café
Boulevard Des Capucines
PARIS
SUJETS ACTUELS
I'm running late!
Has it started?
You, Monsieur Méliès?
Don't worry, they're waiting for you.

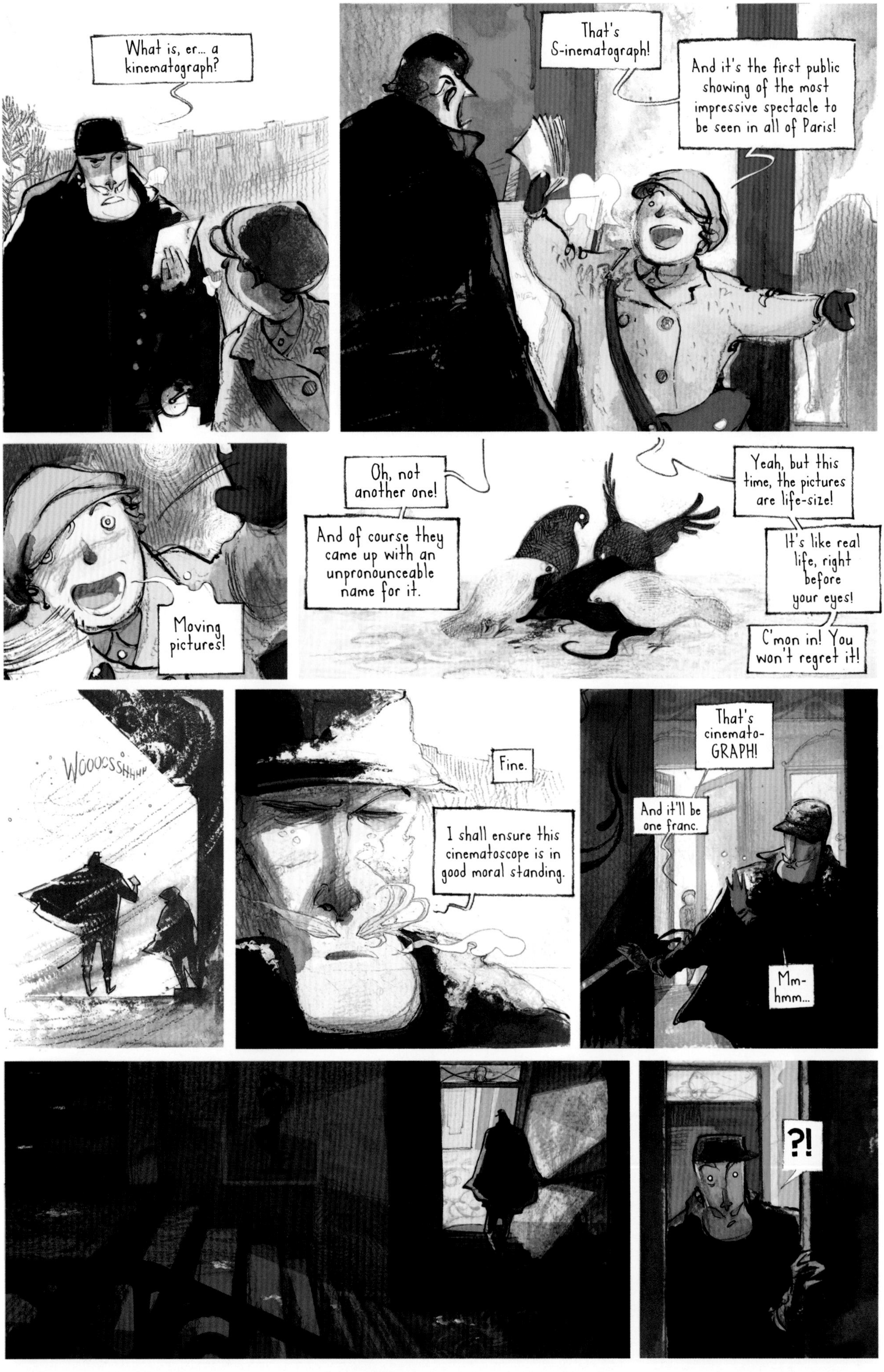
What is, er... a kinematograph?
That's S-inematograph!
And it's the first public showing of the most impressive spectacle to be seen in all of Paris!
Moving pictures!
Oh, not another one!
And of course they came up with an unpronounceable name for it.
Yeah, but this time, the pictures are life-size!
It's like real life, right before your eyes!
C'mon in! You won't regret it!
WOOOSSHHHH
Fine.
I shall ensure this cinematoscope is in good moral standing.
That's cinemato-GRAPH!
And it'll be one franc.
Mm-hmm...
?!

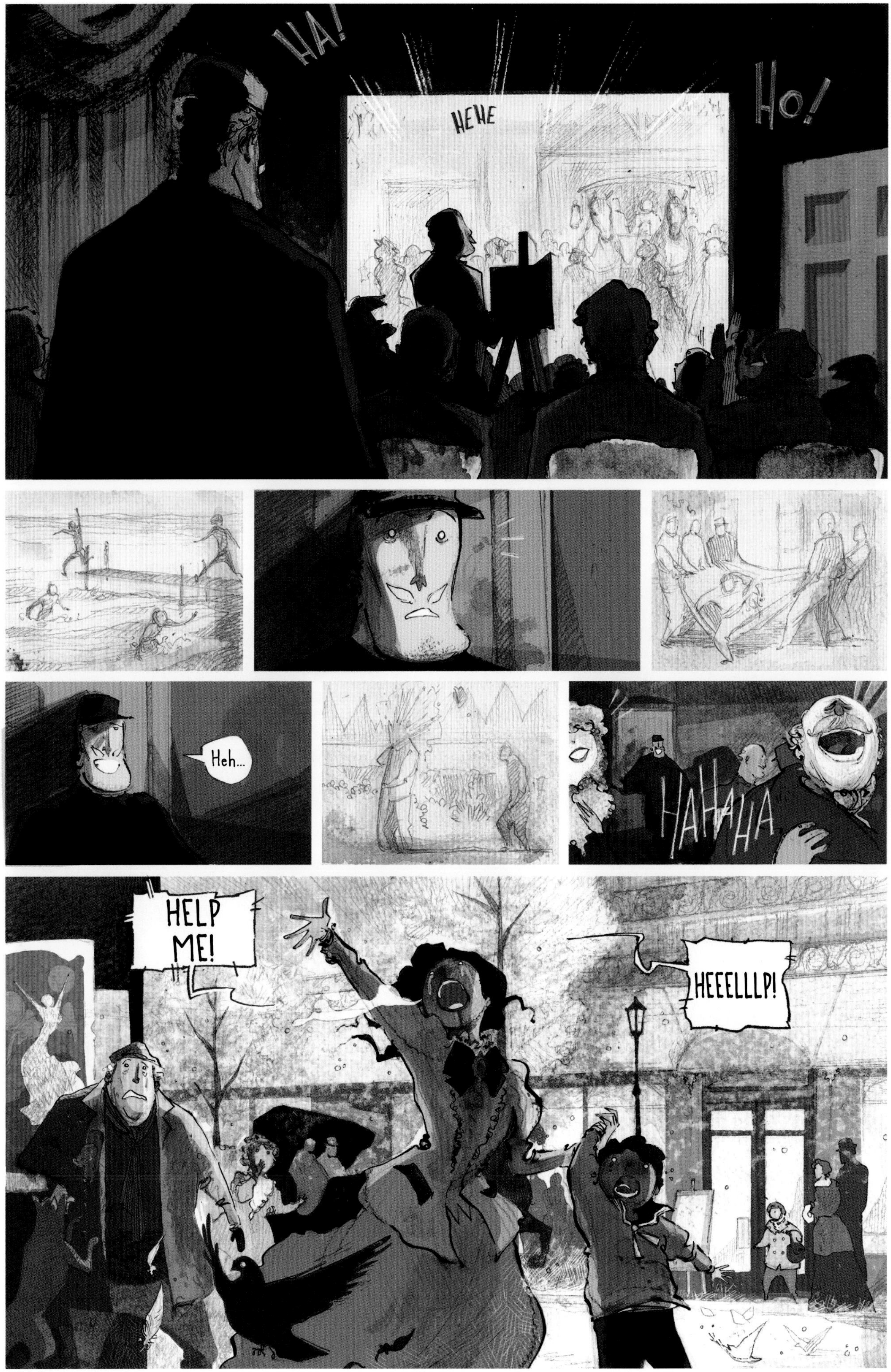
HA!
HEHE
HO!
Heh...
HAHAHA
HELP ME!
HEEELLLP!

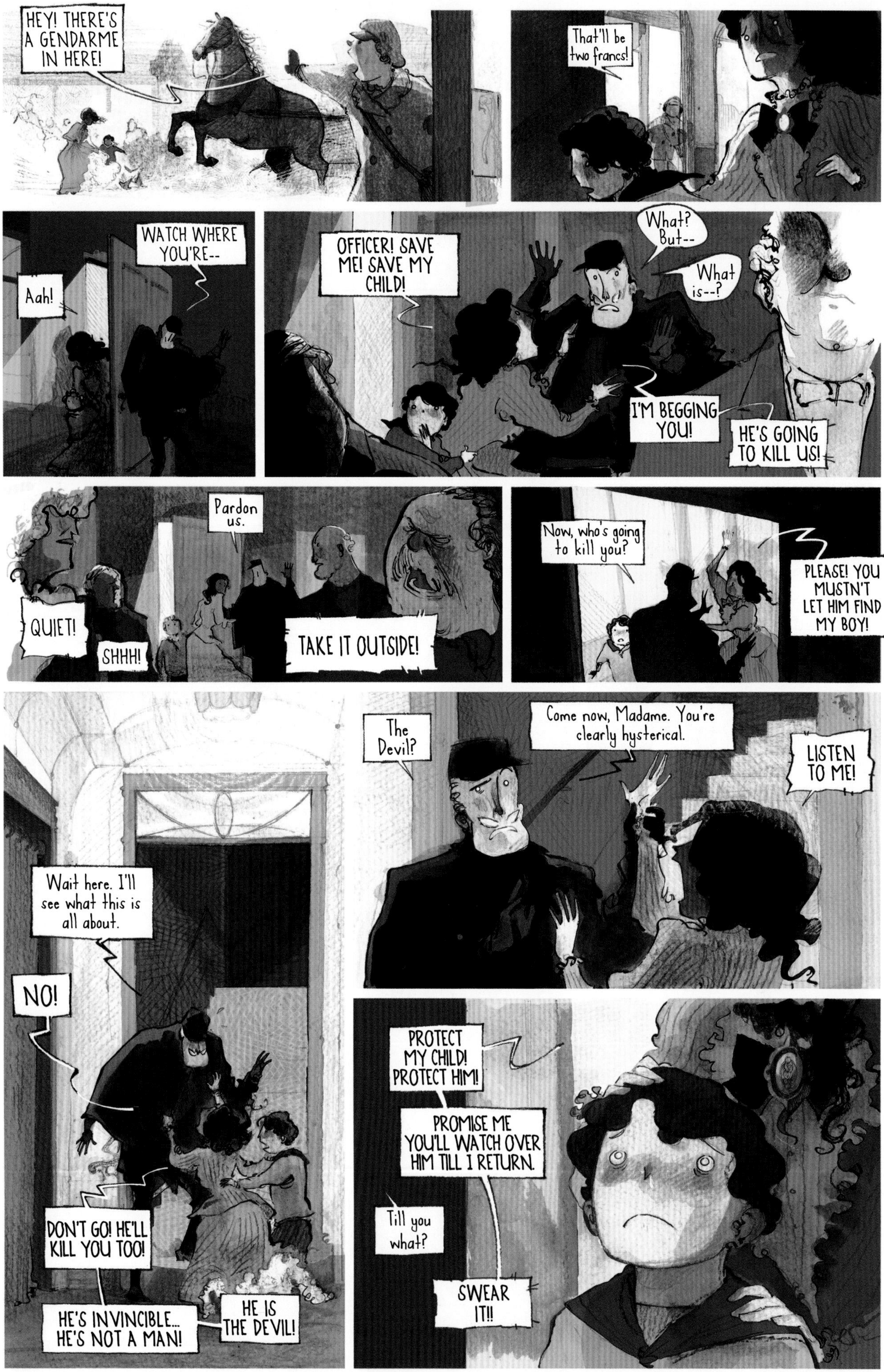
HEY! THERE'S A GENDARME IN HERE!
That'll be two francs!
WATCH WHERE YOU'RE--
Aah!
OFFICER! SAVE ME! SAVE MY CHILD!
What? But--
What is--?
I'M BEGGING YOU!
HE'S GOING TO KILL US!
Pardon us.
QUIET!
SHHH!
TAKE IT OUTSIDE!
Now, who's going to kill you?
PLEASE! YOU MUSTN'T LET HIM FIND MY BOY!
Wait here. I'll see what this is all about.
NO!
DON'T GO! HE'LL KILL YOU TOO!
HE'S INVINCIBLE... HE'S NOT A MAN!
HE IS THE DEVIL!
The Devil?
Come now, Madame. You're clearly hysterical.
LISTEN TO ME!
PROTECT MY CHILD! PROTECT HIM!
PROMISE ME YOU'LL WATCH OVER HIM TILL I RETURN.
Till you what?
SWEAR IT!!

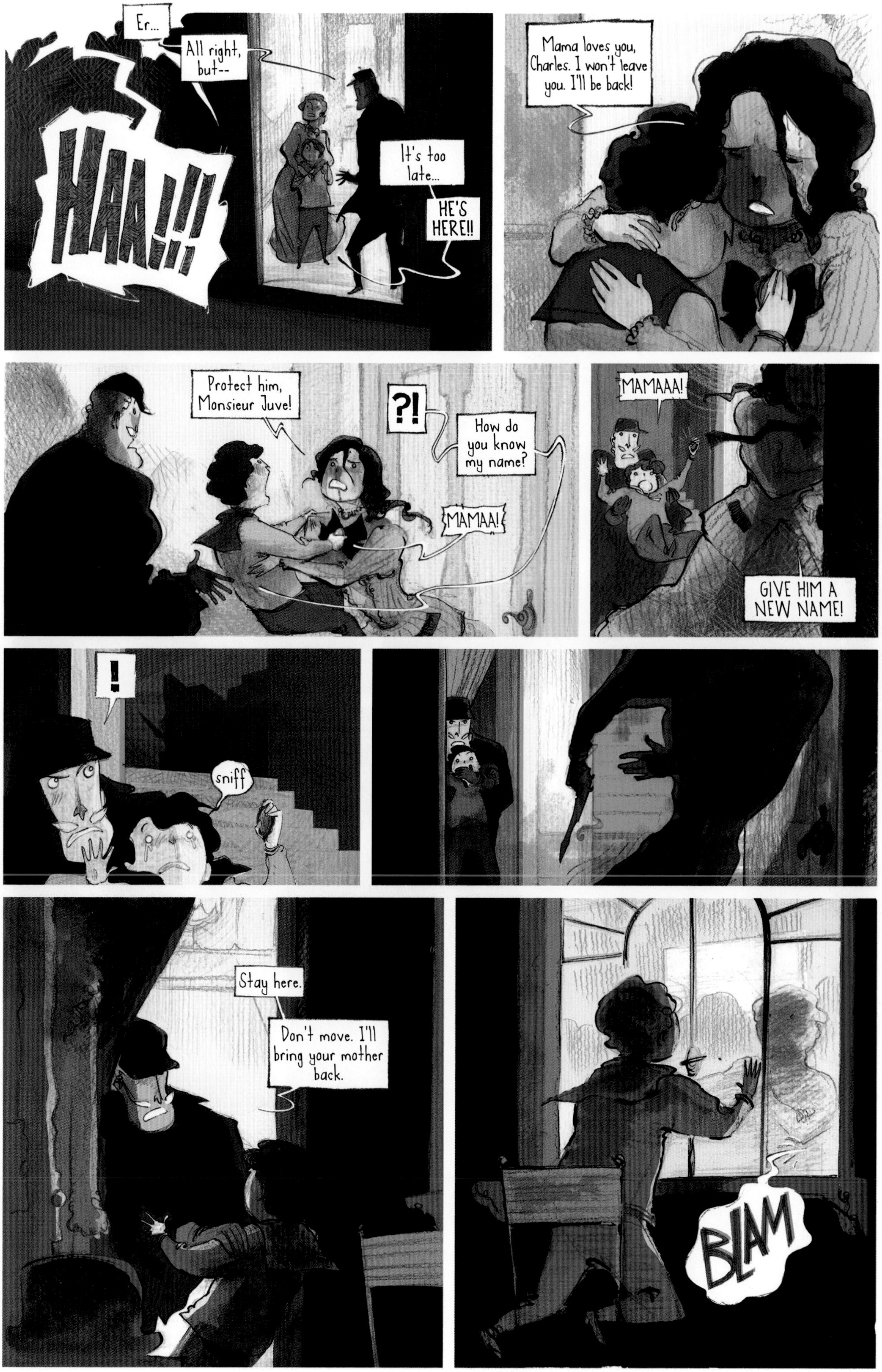

Er...
All right, but--
HAA!!!
It's too late...
HE'S HERE!!
Mama loves you, Charles. I won't leave you. I'll be back!
Protect him, Monsieur Juve!
?!
How do you know my name?
MAMAA!
MAMAAA!
GIVE HIM A NEW NAME!
!
sniff
Stay here.
Don't move. I'll bring your mother back.
BLAM

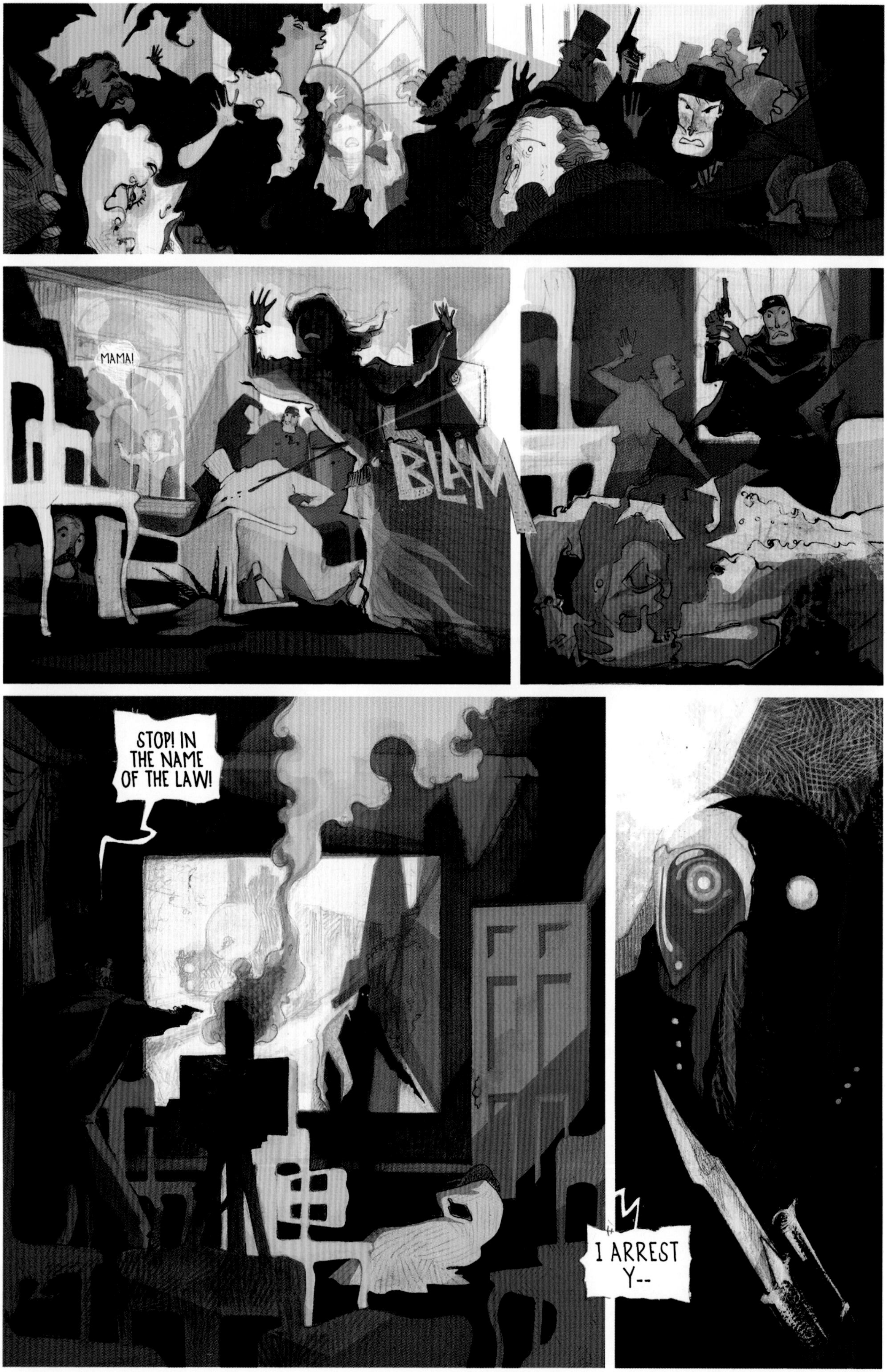
MAMA!
BLAM
STOP! IN THE NAME OF THE LAW!
I ARREST Y--

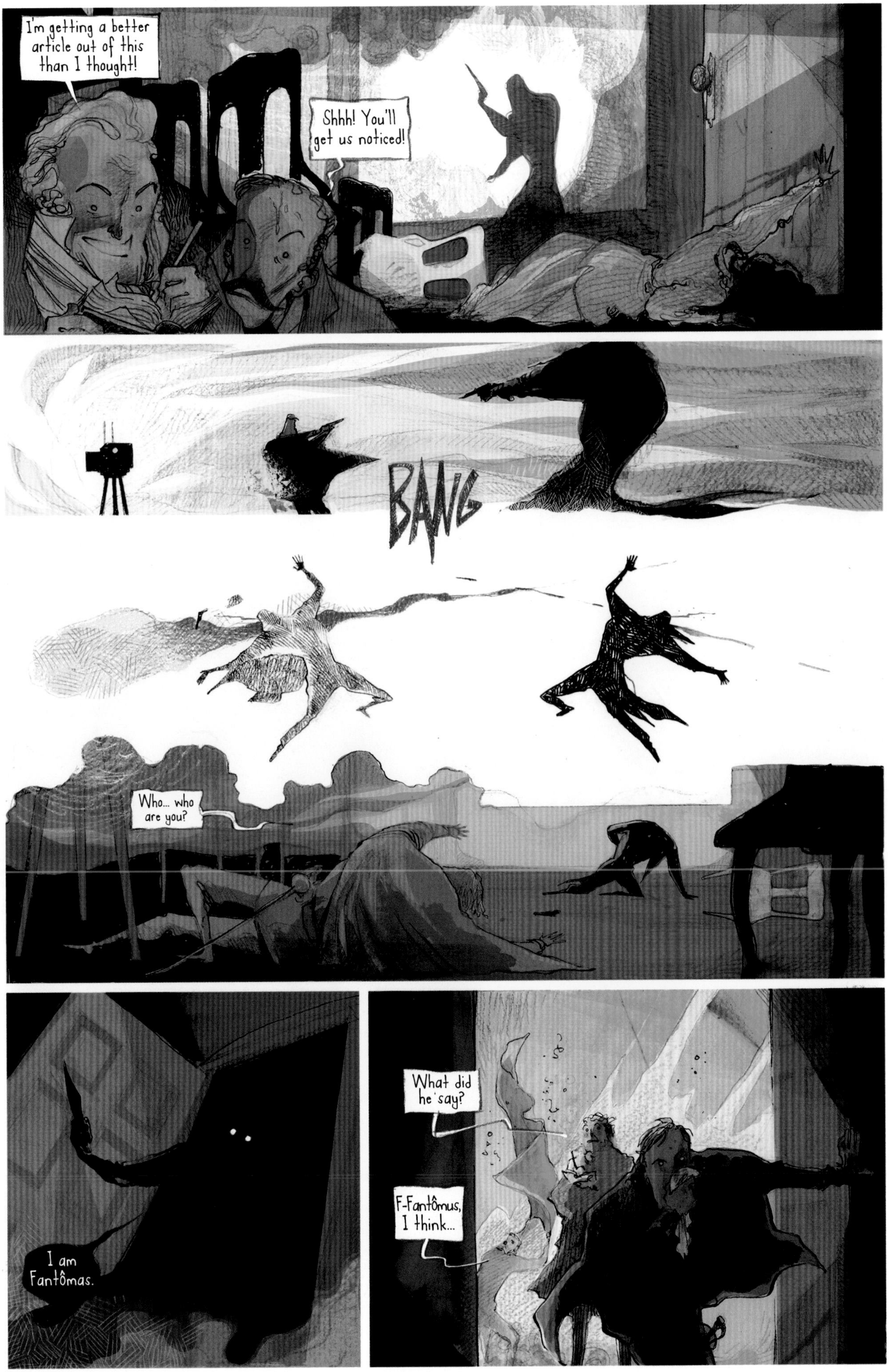
I'm getting a better article out of this than I thought!
Shhh! You'll get us noticed!
BANG
Who... who are you?
I am Fantômas.
What did he say?
F-Fantômus, I think...

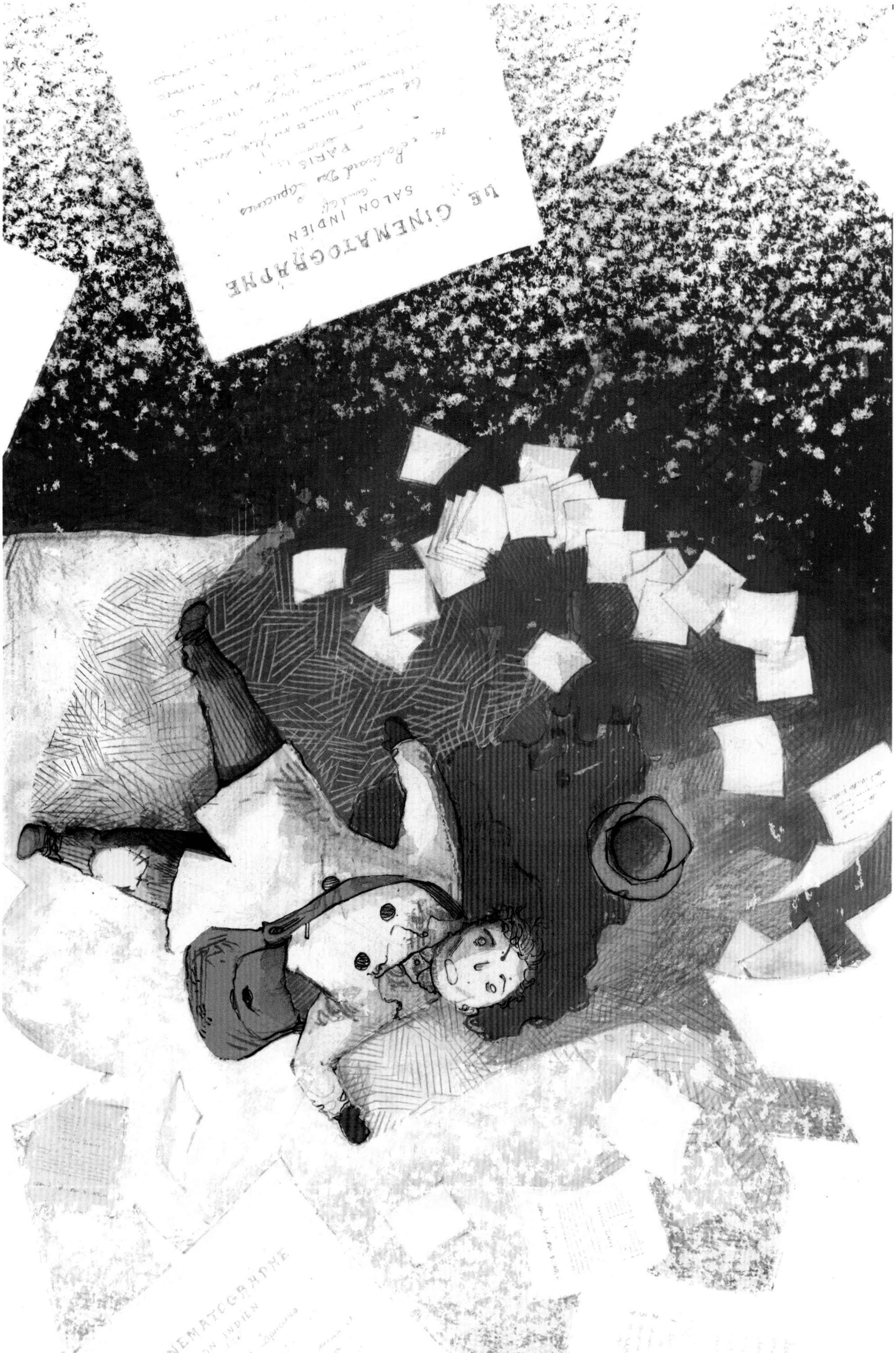
LE CINEMATOGRAPHE
SALON INDIEN
PARIS

# THE GUILLOTINE

In which
an unfortunate misunderstanding occurs,
an enigmatic smile vanishes,
a suicide fails to take,
and vengeance is afoot.

Monday, August 21, 1911.
Sixteen years later...

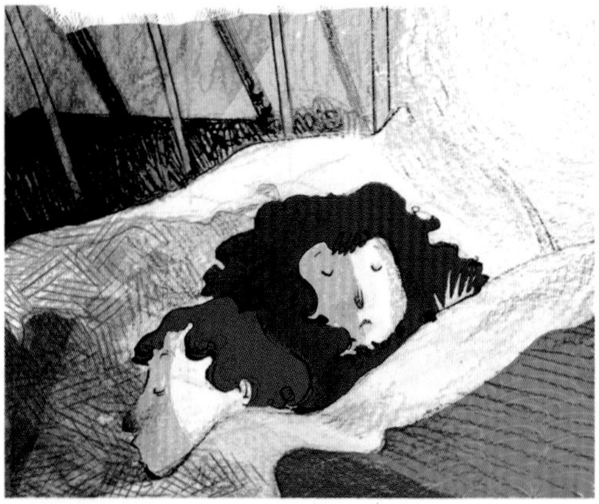

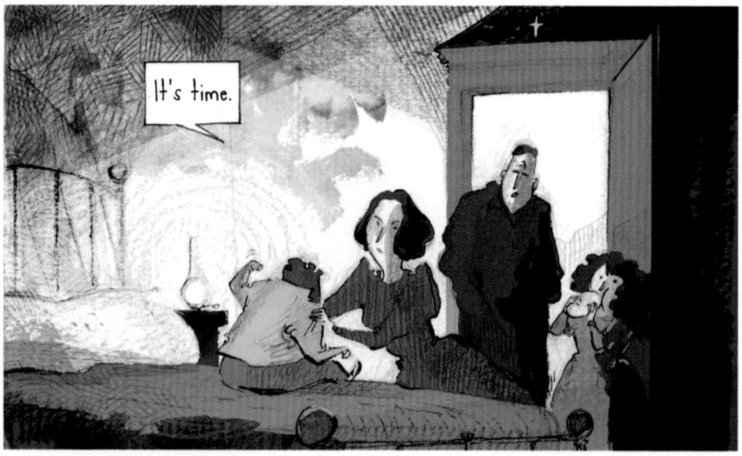
It's time.

Tomorrow morning at 5, in front of La Santé Prison, Anatole Deibler, Executioner for the Republic, will stretch Fantômas out on the guillotine.

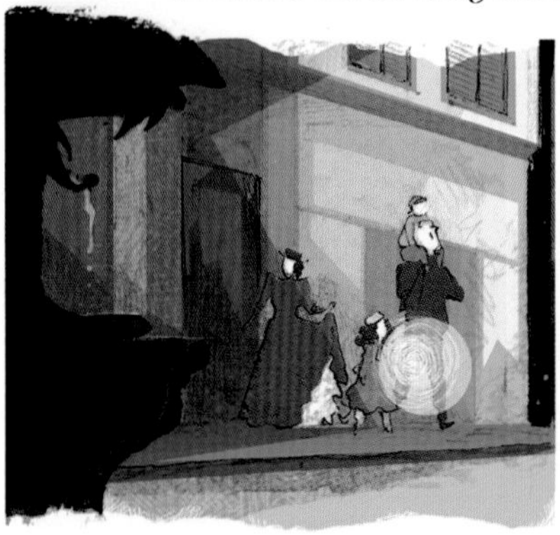

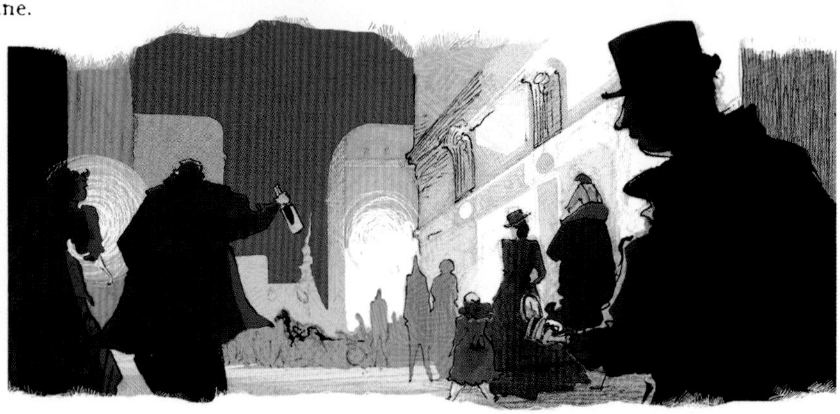

With one swift stroke, he shall free the good Dr. Guillotine's lead-weighted blade, and the most dangerous criminal in history will cease to be.

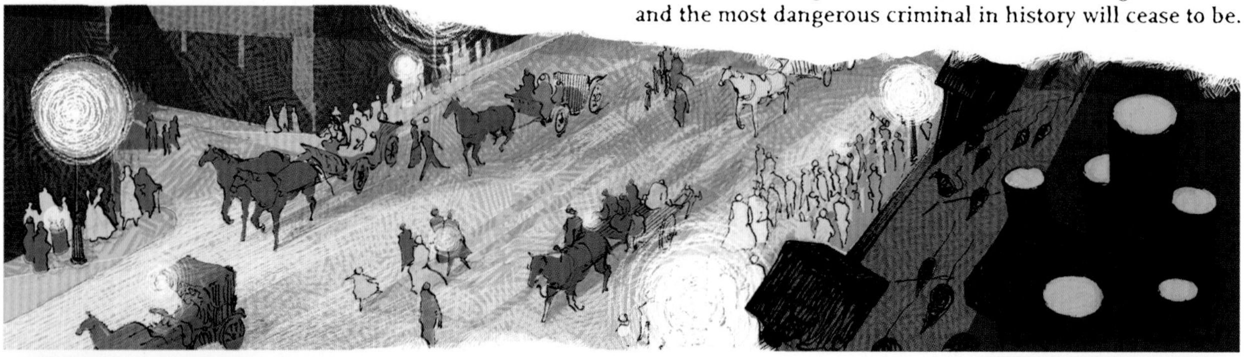

Beheaded, like a common fish.

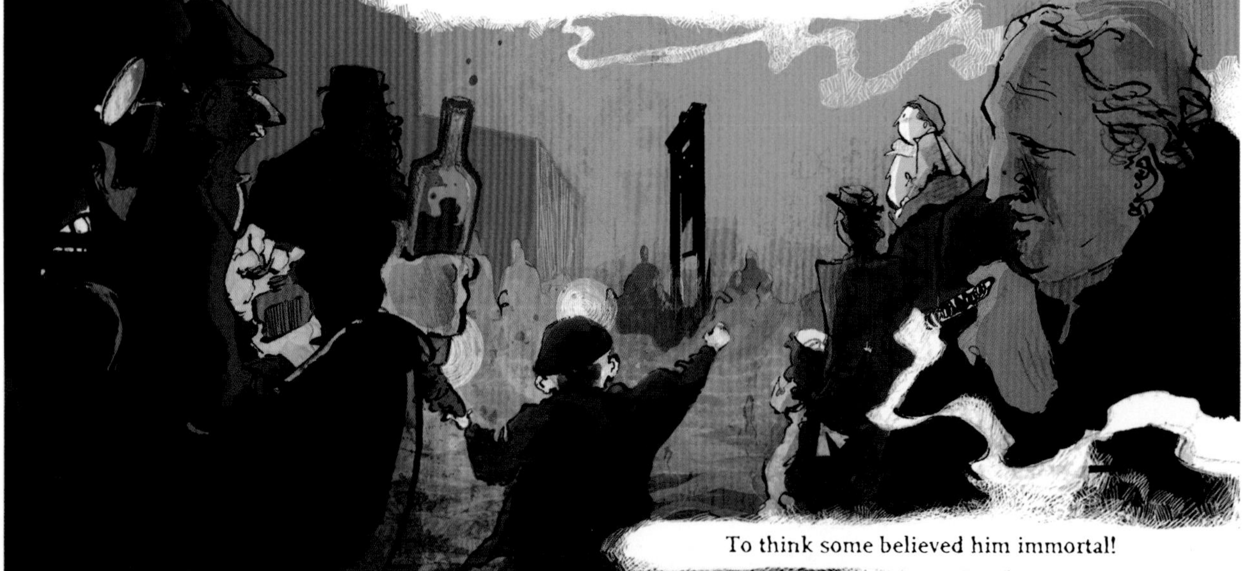
To think some believed him immortal!

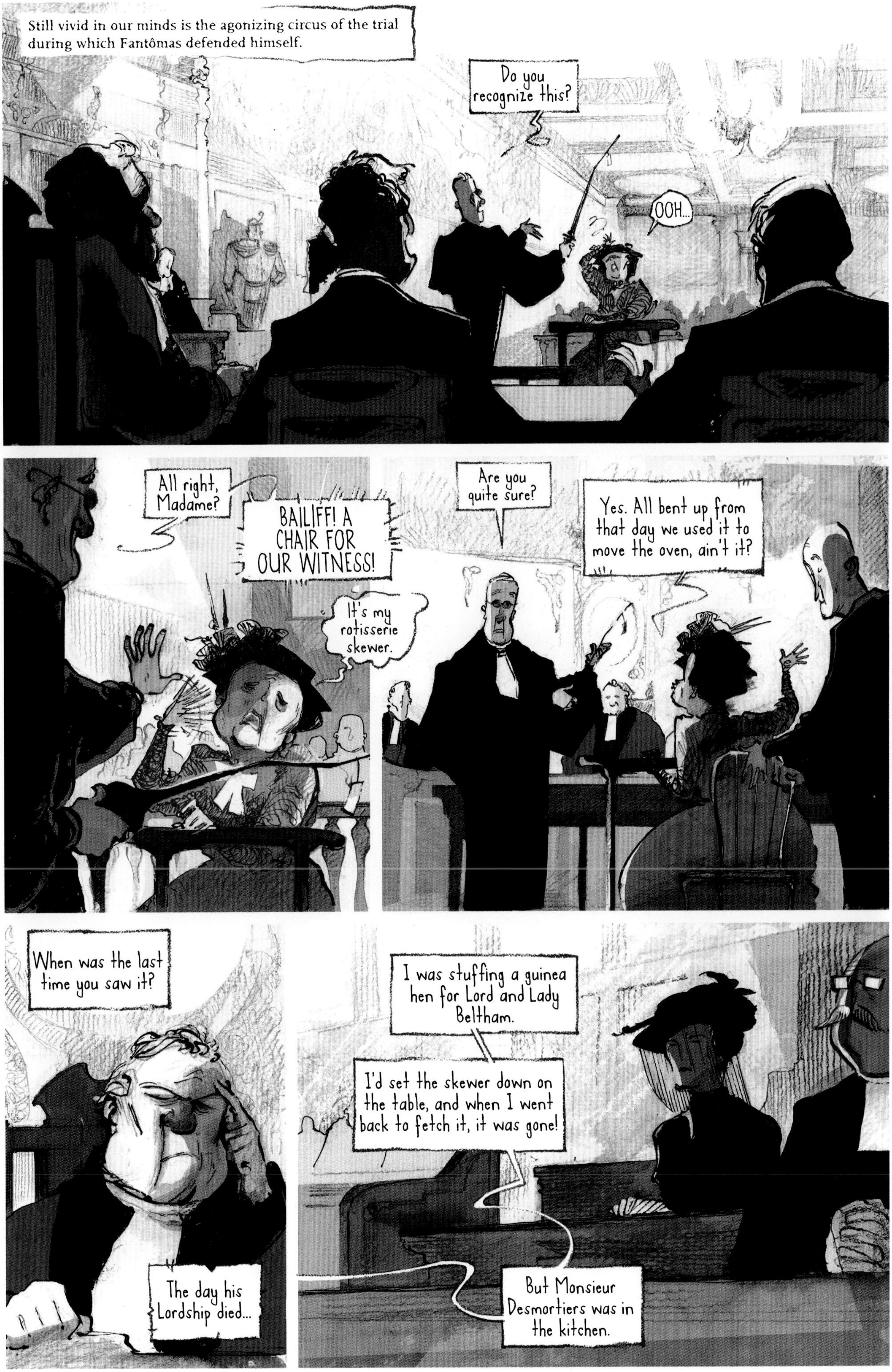
Still vivid in our minds is the agonizing circus of the trial during which Fantômas defended himself.
Do you recognize this?
OOH...
All right, Madame?
BAILIFF! A CHAIR FOR OUR WITNESS!
It's my rotisserie skewer.
Are you quite sure?
Yes. All bent up from that day we used it to move the oven, ain't it?
When was the last time you saw it?
The day his Lordship died...
I was stuffing a guinea hen for Lord and Lady Beltham.
I'd set the skewer down on the table, and when I went back to fetch it, it was gone!
But Monsieur Desmortiers was in the kitchen.

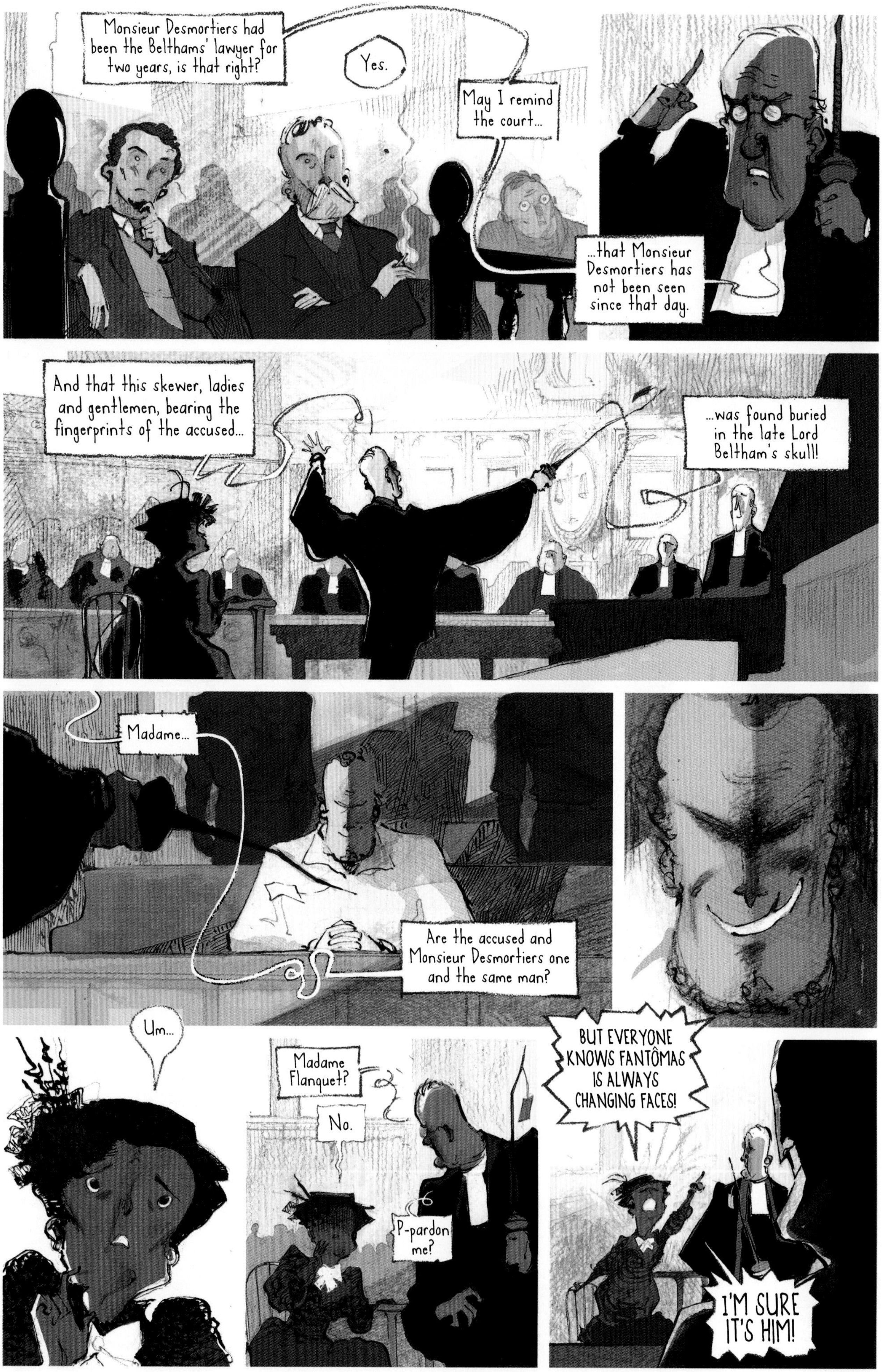
Monsieur Desmortiers had been the Belthams' lawyer for two years, is that right?
Yes.
May I remind the court...
...that Monsieur Desmortiers has not been seen since that day.
And that this skewer, ladies and gentlemen, bearing the fingerprints of the accused...
...was found buried in the late Lord Beltham's skull!
Madame...
Are the accused and Monsieur Desmortiers one and the same man?
Um...
Madame Flanquet?
No.
P-pardon me?
BUT EVERYONE KNOWS FANTÔMAS IS ALWAYS CHANGING FACES!
I'M SURE IT'S HIM!

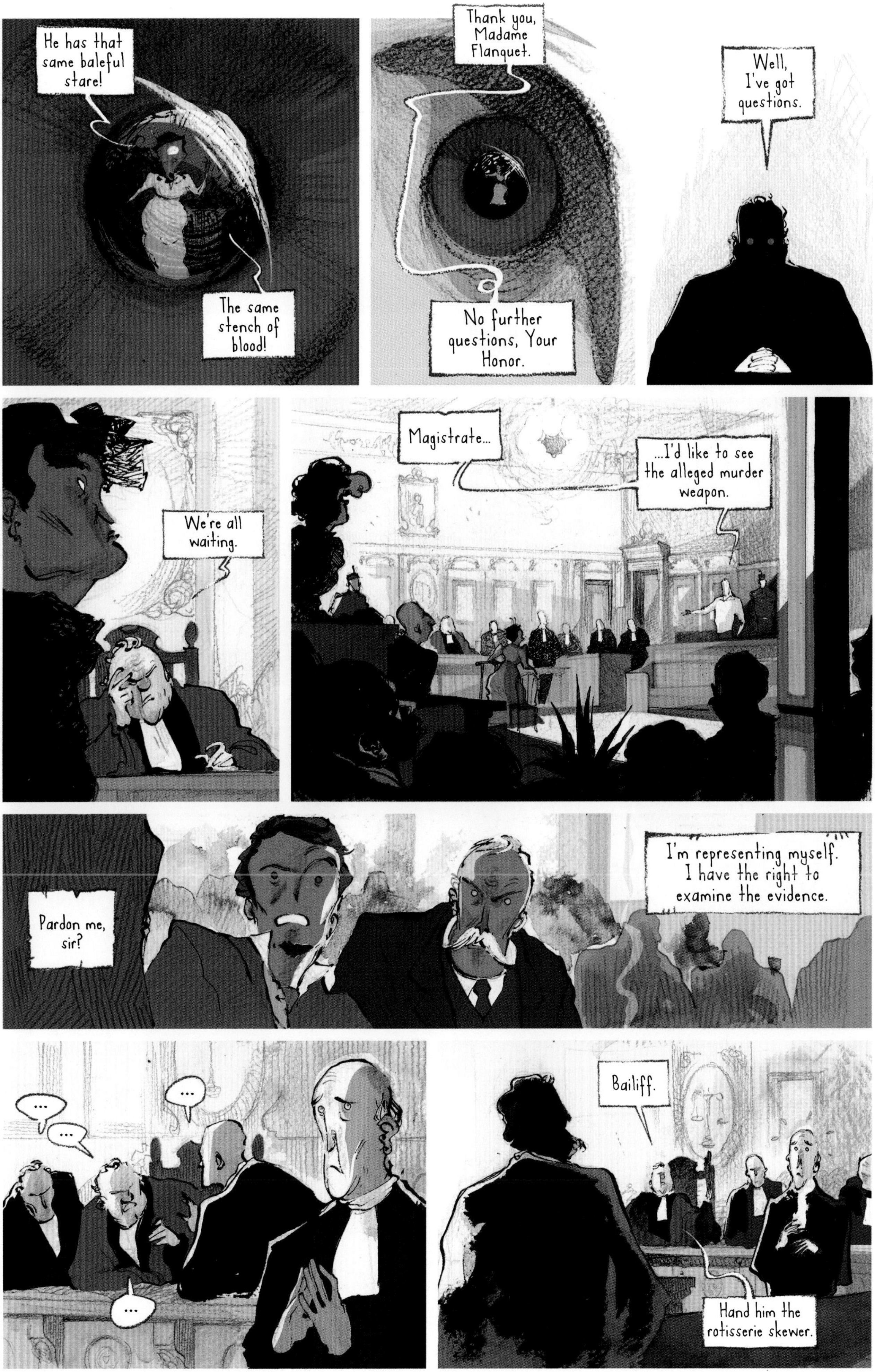
He has that same baleful stare!
The same stench of blood!
Thank you, Madame Flanquet.
No further questions, Your Honor.
Well, I've got questions.
We're all waiting.
Magistrate...
...I'd like to see the alleged murder weapon.
Pardon me, sir?
I'm representing myself. I have the right to examine the evidence.
...
...
...
...
Bailiff.
Hand him the rotisserie skewer.

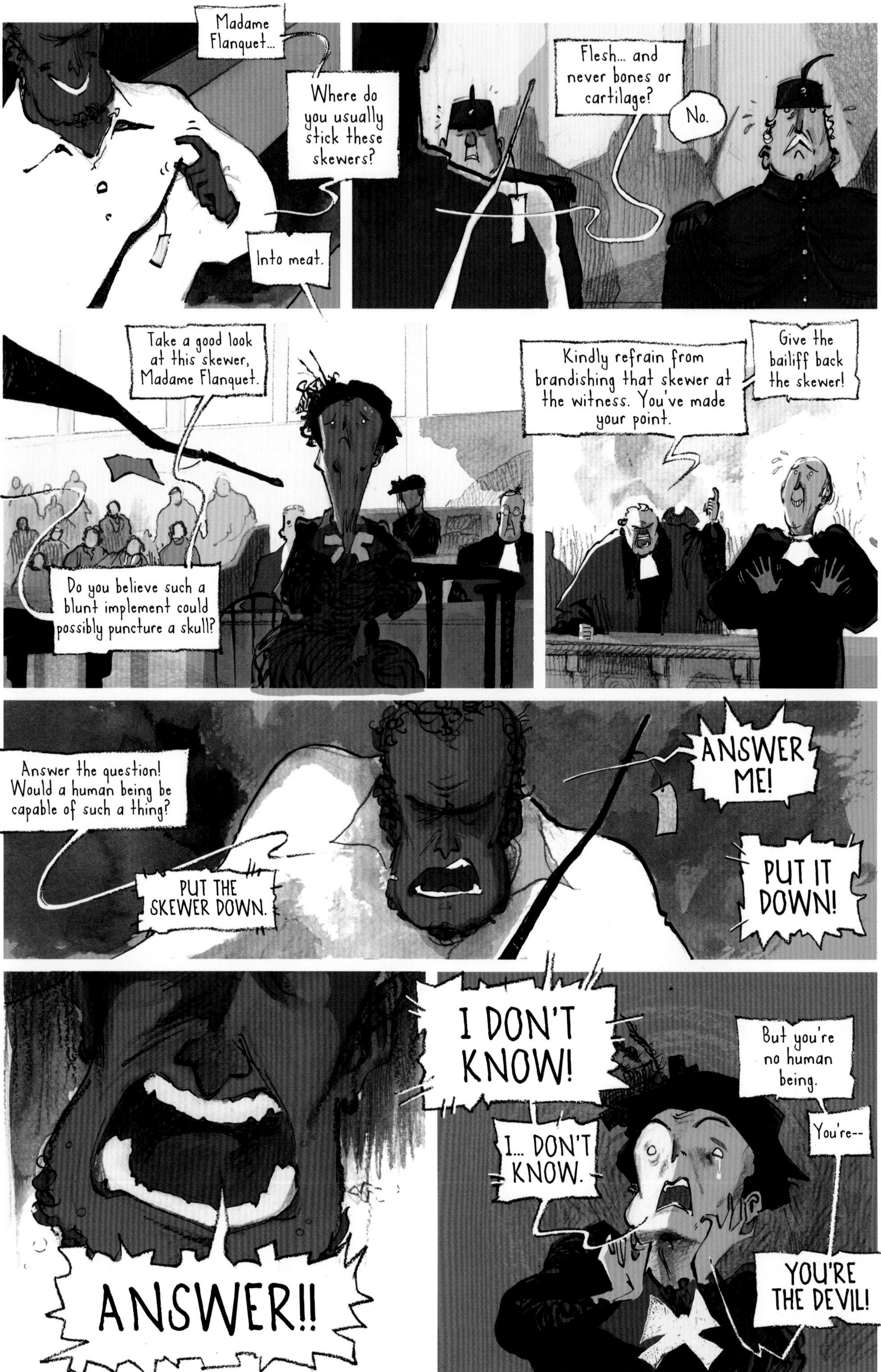
Madame Flanquet...
Where do you usually stick these skewers?
Into meat.
Flesh... and never bones or cartilage?
No.
Take a good look at this skewer, Madame Flanquet.
Do you believe such a blunt implement could possibly puncture a skull?
Kindly refrain from brandishing that skewer at the witness. You've made your point.
Give the bailiff back the skewer!
Answer the question! Would a human being be capable of such a thing?
PUT THE SKEWER DOWN.
ANSWER ME!
PUT IT DOWN!
ANSWER!!
I DON'T KNOW!
I... DON'T KNOW.
But you're no human being.
You're--
YOU'RE THE DEVIL!

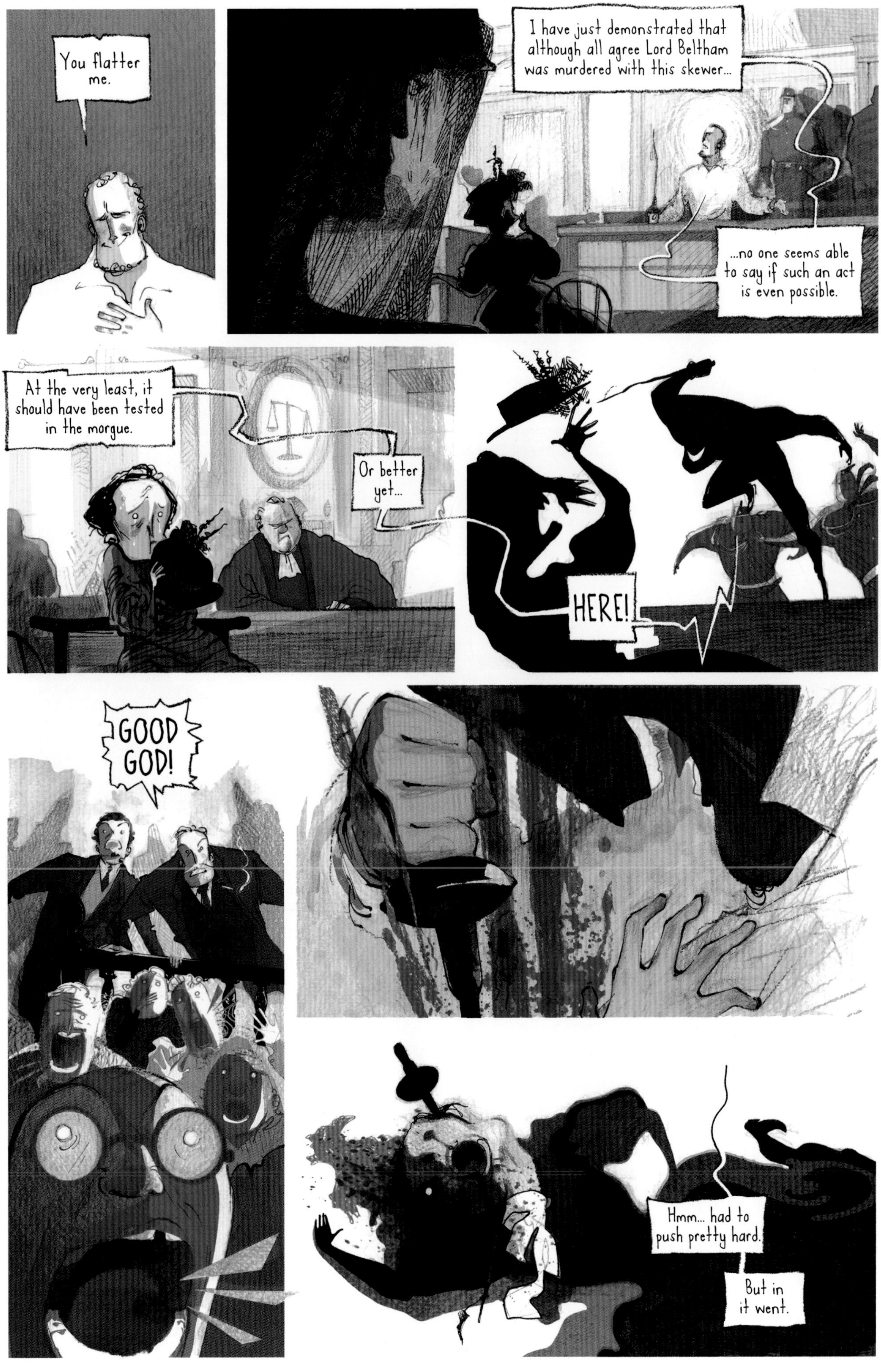

You flatter me.
I have just demonstrated that although all agree Lord Beltham was murdered with this skewer...
...no one seems able to say if such an act is even possible.
At the very least, it should have been tested in the morgue.
Or better yet...
HERE!
GOOD GOD!
Hmm... had to push pretty hard.
But in it went.

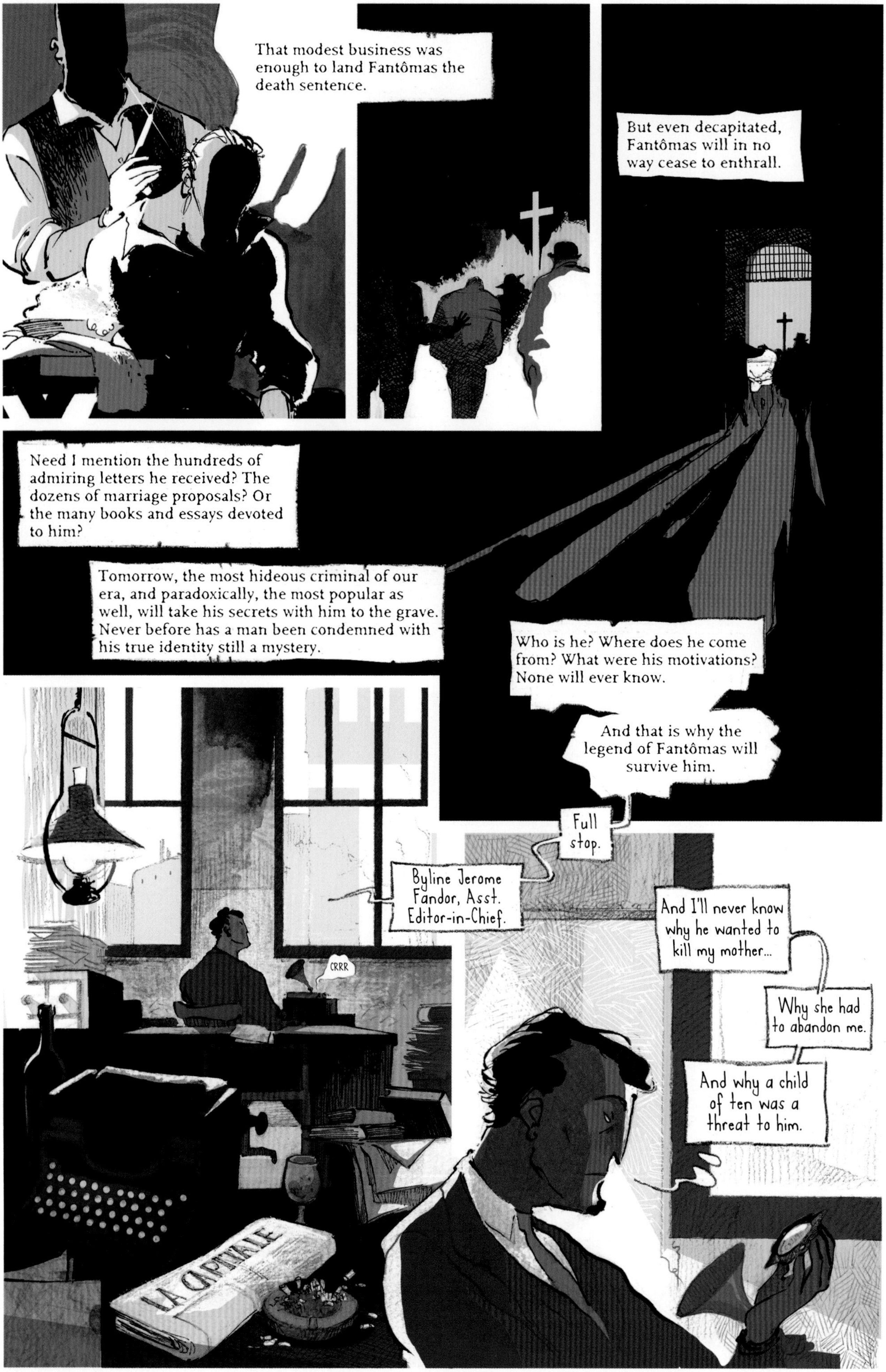
That modest business was enough to land Fantômas the death sentence.
But even decapitated, Fantômas will in no way cease to enthrall.
Need I mention the hundreds of admiring letters he received? The dozens of marriage proposals? Or the many books and essays devoted to him?
Tomorrow, the most hideous criminal of our era, and paradoxically, the most popular as well, will take his secrets with him to the grave. Never before has a man been condemned with his true identity still a mystery.
Who is he? Where does he come from? What were his motivations? None will ever know.
And that is why the legend of Fantômas will survive him.
Full stop.
Byline Jerome Fandor, Asst. Editor-in-Chief.
CRRR
And I'll never know why he wanted to kill my mother...
Why she had to abandon me.
And why a child of ten was a threat to him.
LA CAPITALE

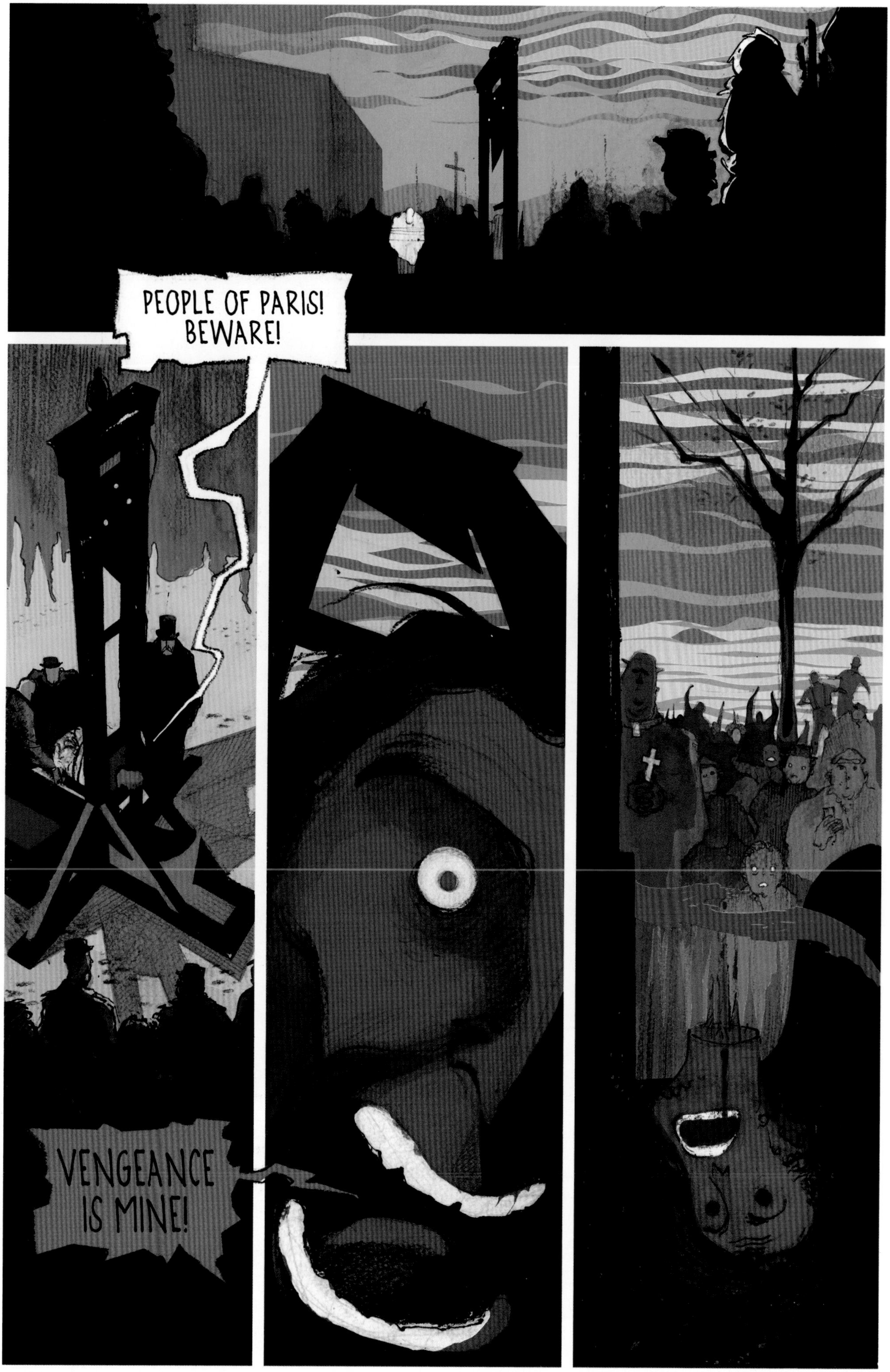
PEOPLE OF PARIS! BEWARE!
VENGEANCE IS MINE!

Tuesday, August 22, 1911.

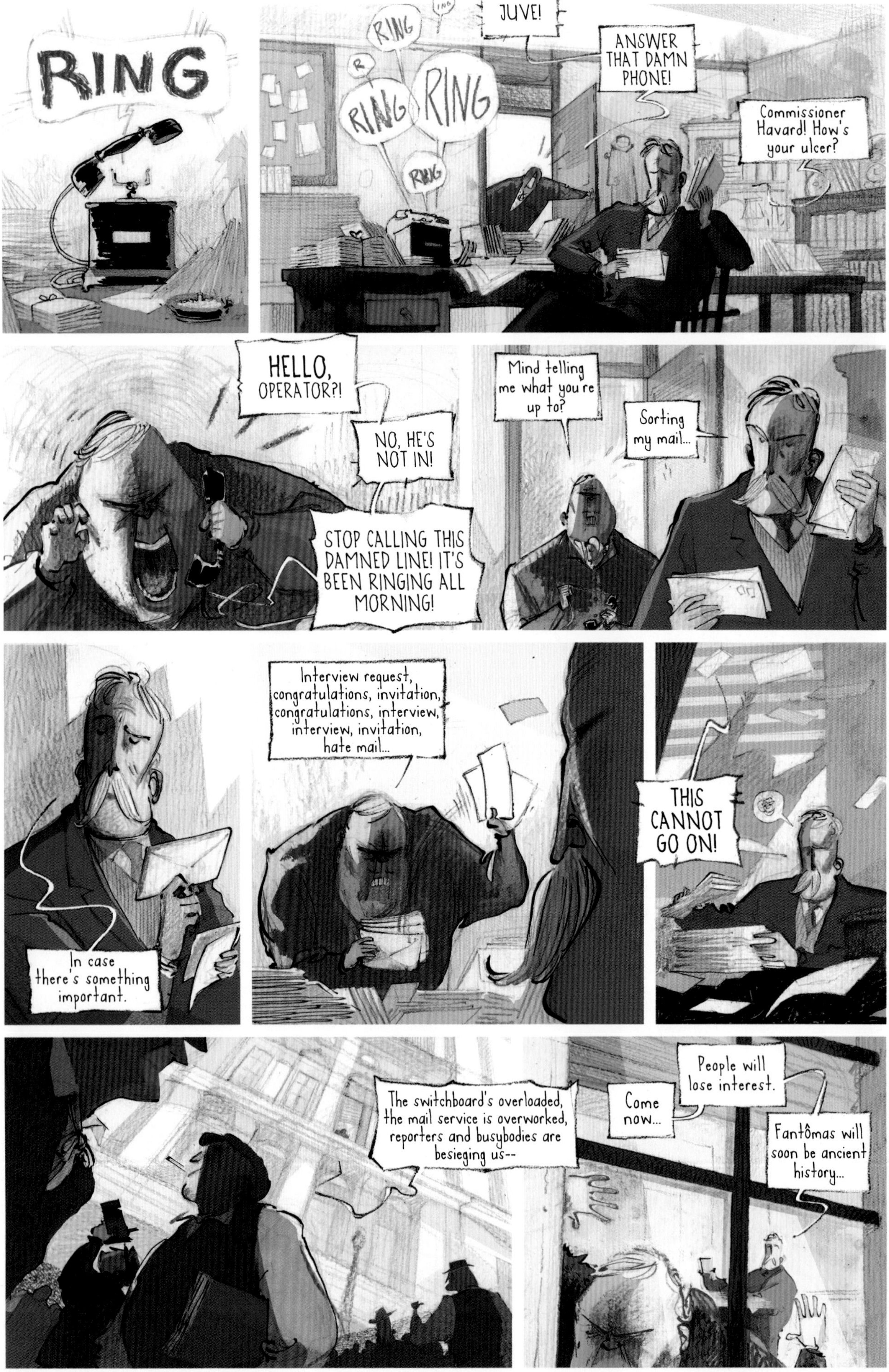
RING
RING
ING
RING RING
RING
JUVE!
ANSWER THAT DAMN PHONE!
Commissioner Havard! How's your ulcer?
HELLO, OPERATOR?!
NO, HE'S NOT IN!
STOP CALLING THIS DAMNED LINE! IT'S BEEN RINGING ALL MORNING!
Mind telling me what you're up to?
Sorting my mail...
In case there's something important.
Interview request, congratulations, invitation, congratulations, interview, interview, invitation, hate mail...
THIS CANNOT GO ON!
The switchboard's overloaded, the mail service is overworked, reporters and busybodies are besieging us--
Come now...
People will lose interest.
Fantômas will soon be ancient history...

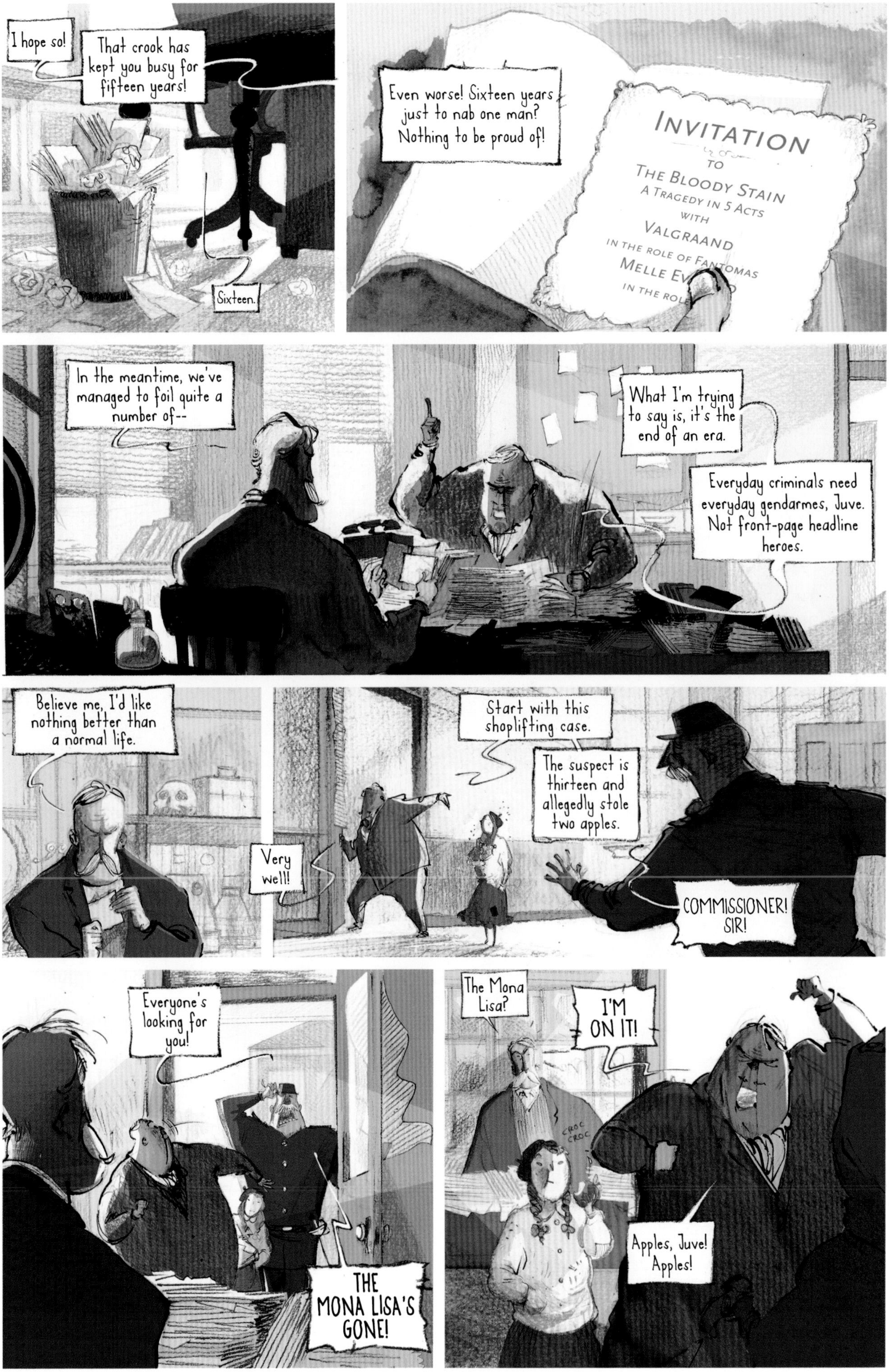
I hope so!
That crook has kept you busy for fifteen years!
Sixteen.
Even worse! Sixteen years just to nab one man? Nothing to be proud of!
INVITATION
TO
THE BLOODY STAIN
A TRAGEDY IN 5 ACTS
WITH
VALGRAAND
IN THE ROLE OF FANTOMAS
In the meantime, we've managed to foil quite a number of--
What I'm trying to say is, it's the end of an era.
Everyday criminals need everyday gendarmes, Juve. Not front-page headline heroes.
Believe me, I'd like nothing better than a normal life.
Start with this shoplifting case.
The suspect is thirteen and allegedly stole two apples.
Very well!
COMMISSIONER! SIR!
Everyone's looking for you!
THE MONA LISA'S GONE!
The Mona Lisa?
I'M ON IT!
CROC CROC
Apples, Juve! Apples!

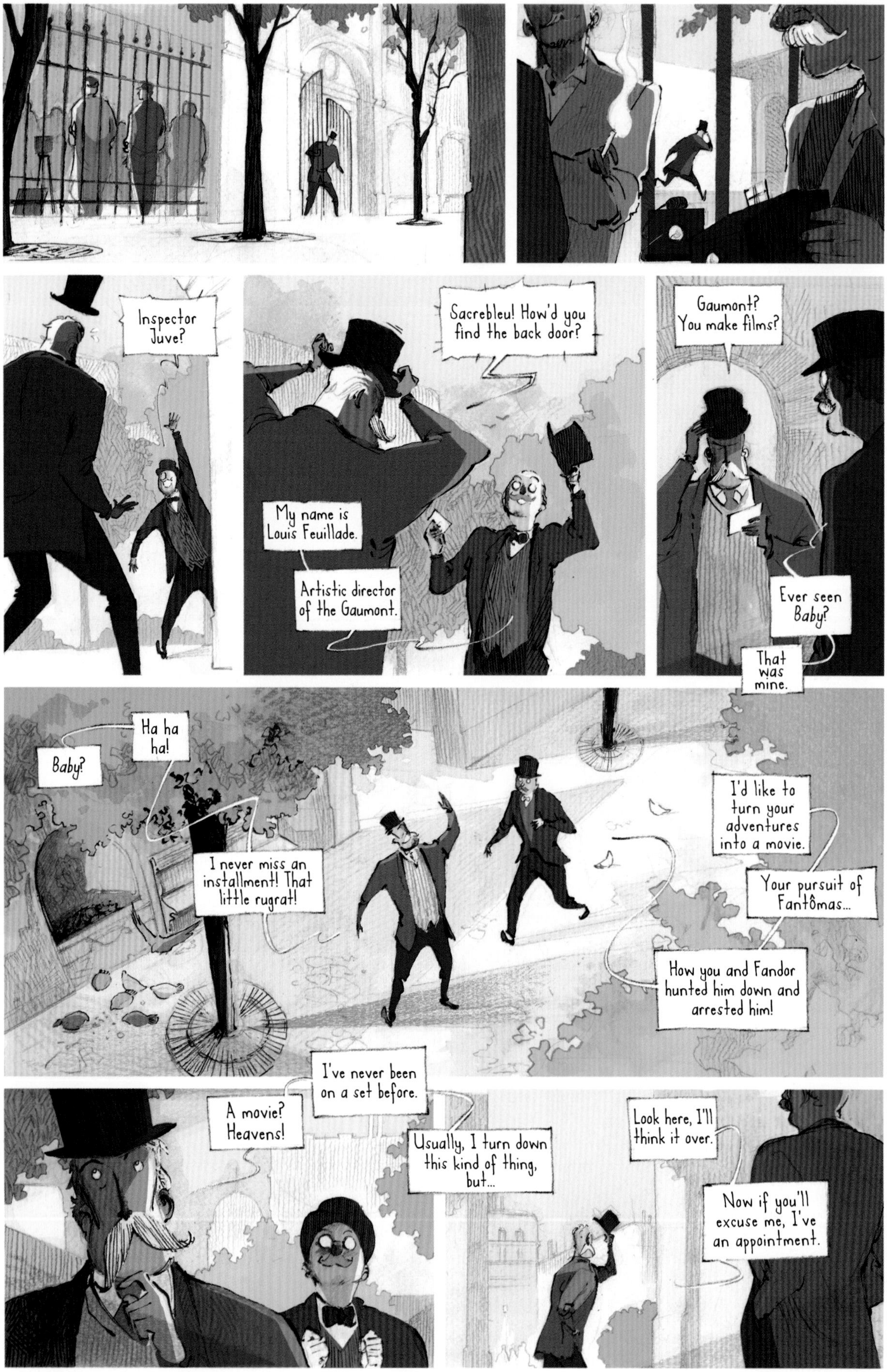
Inspector Juve?
Sacrebleu! How'd you find the back door?
My name is Louis Feuillade.
Artistic director of the Gaumont.
Gaumont? You make films?
Ever seen Baby?
That was mine.
Baby?
Ha ha ha!
I never miss an installment! That little rugrat!
I'd like to turn your adventures into a movie.
Your pursuit of Fantômas...
How you and Fandor hunted him down and arrested him!
A movie? Heavens!
I've never been on a set before.
Usually, I turn down this kind of thing, but...
Look here, I'll think it over.
Now if you'll excuse me, I've an appointment.

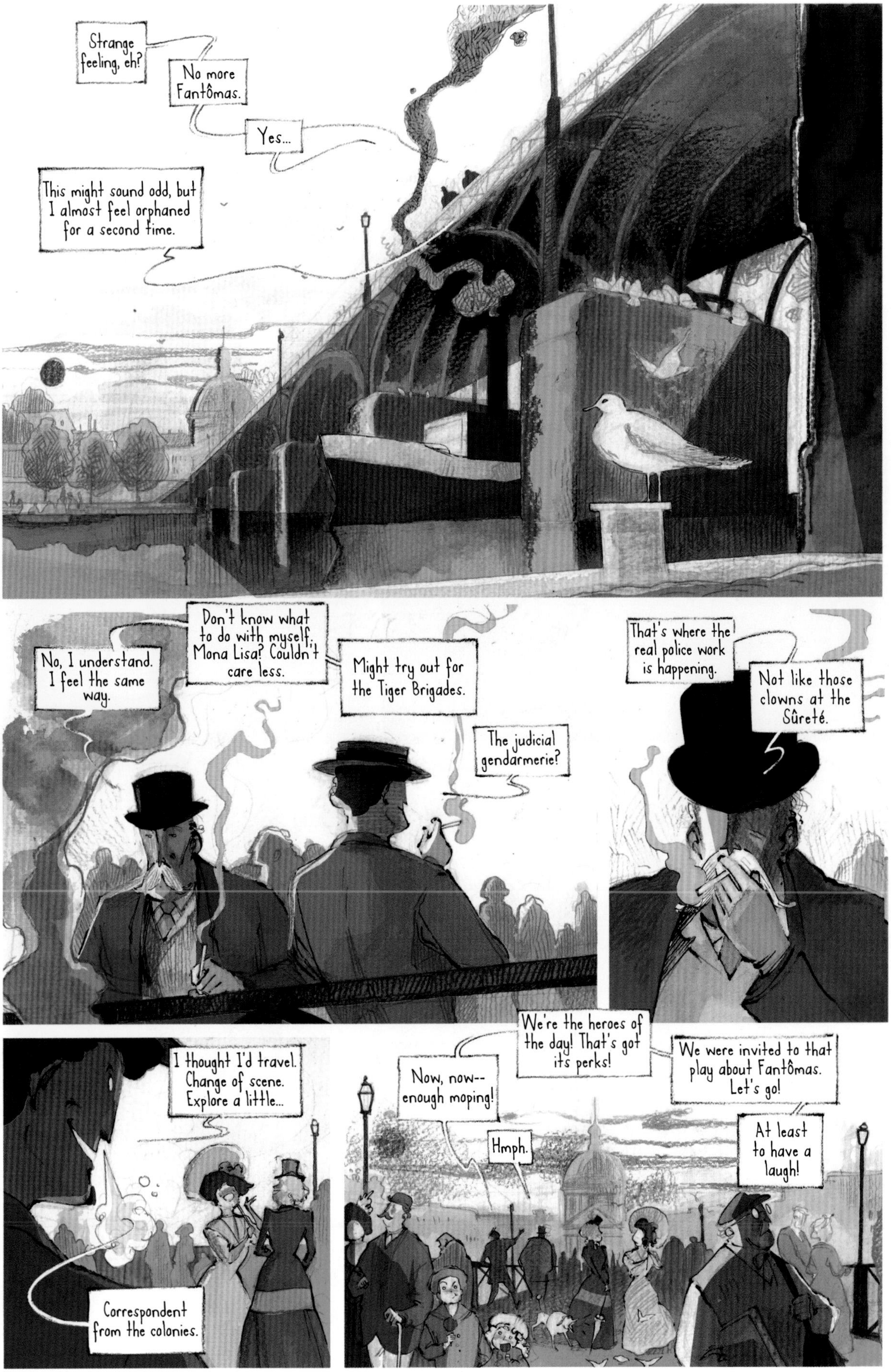
Strange feeling, eh?
No more Fantômas.
Yes...
This might sound odd, but I almost feel orphaned for a second time.
Don't know what to do with myself. Mona Lisa? Couldn't care less.
No, I understand. I feel the same way.
Might try out for the Tiger Brigades.
The judicial gendarmerie?
That's where the real police work is happening.
Not like those clowns at the Sûreté.
I thought I'd travel. Change of scene. Explore a little...
Correspondent from the colonies.
We're the heroes of the day! That's got its perks!
Now, now-- enough moping!
We were invited to that play about Fantômas. Let's go!
Hmph.
At least to have a laugh!

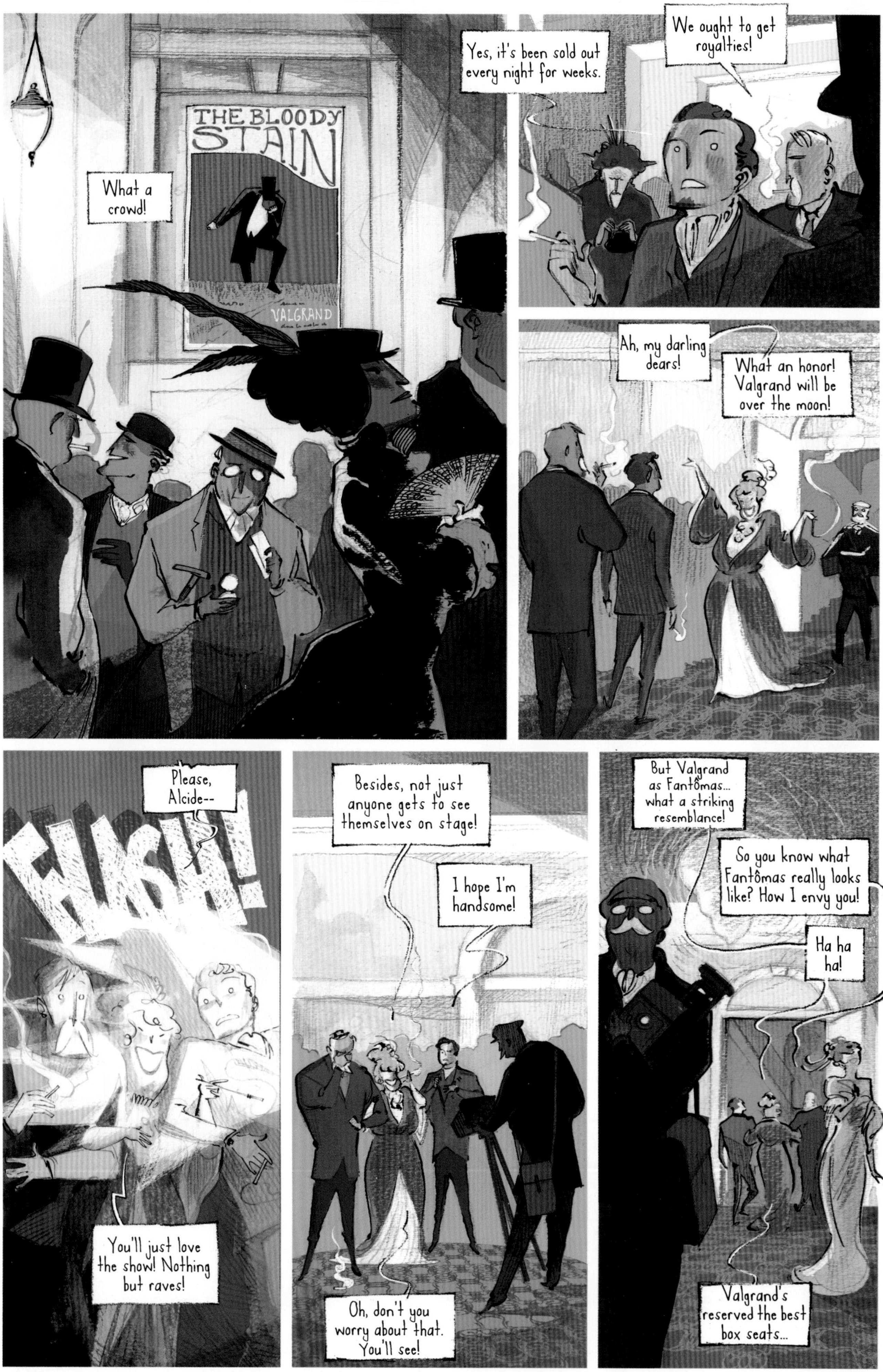
THE BLOODY STAIN
VALGRAND
What a crowd!
Yes, it's been sold out every night for weeks.
We ought to get royalties!
Ah, my darling dears!
What an honor! Valgrand will be over the moon!
Please, Alcide--
FLASH!
You'll just love the show! Nothing but raves!
Besides, not just anyone gets to see themselves on stage!
I hope I'm handsome!
Oh, don't you worry about that. You'll see!
But Valgrand as Fantômas... what a striking resemblance!
So you know what Fantômas really looks like? How I envy you!
Ha ha ha!
Valgrand's reserved the best box seats...

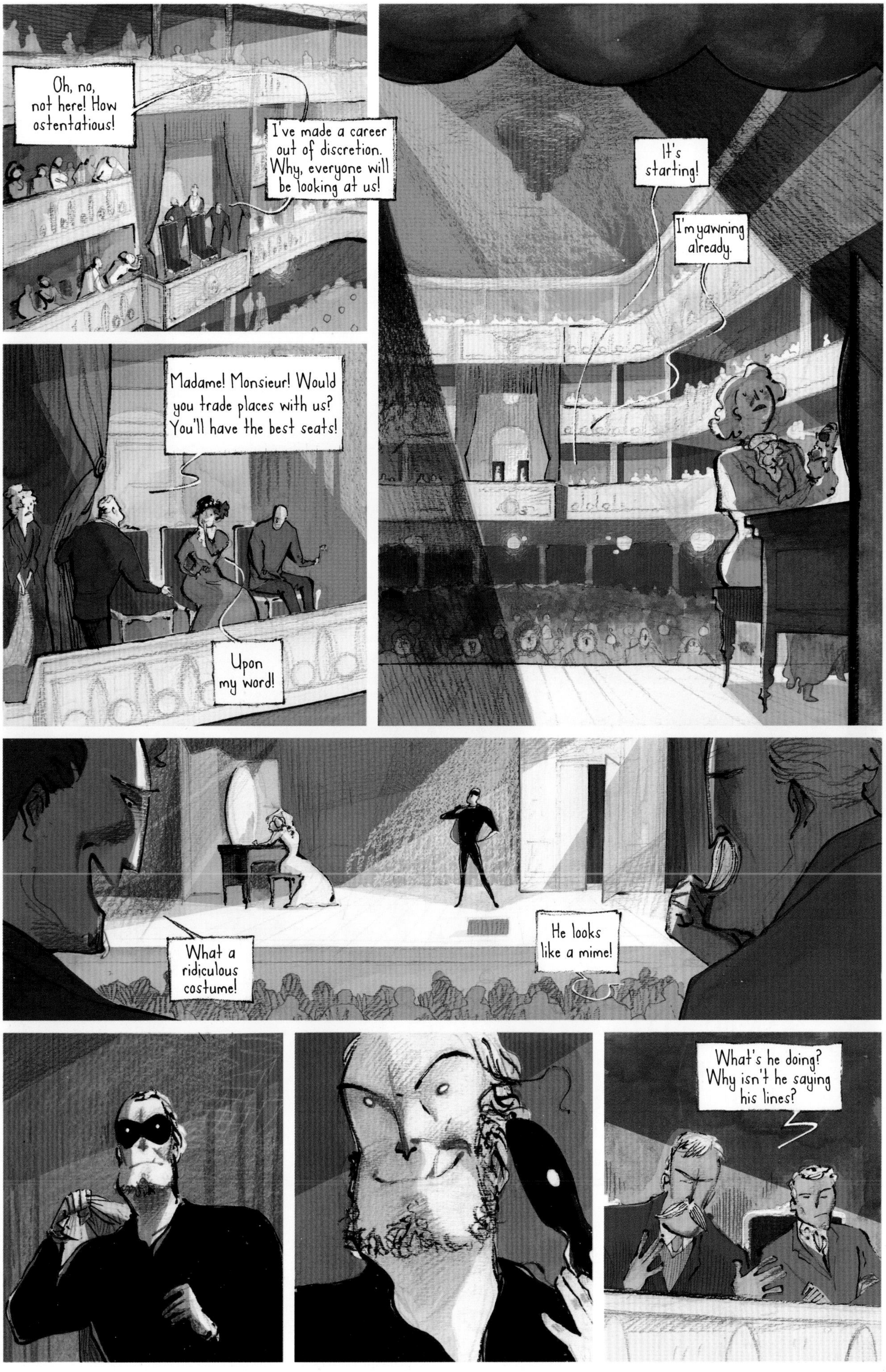
Oh, no, not here! How ostentatious!
I've made a career out of discretion. Why, everyone will be looking at us!
Madame! Monsieur! Would you trade places with us? You'll have the best seats!
Upon my word!
It's starting!
I'm yawning already.
What a ridiculous costume!
He looks like a mime!
What's he doing? Why isn't he saying his lines?

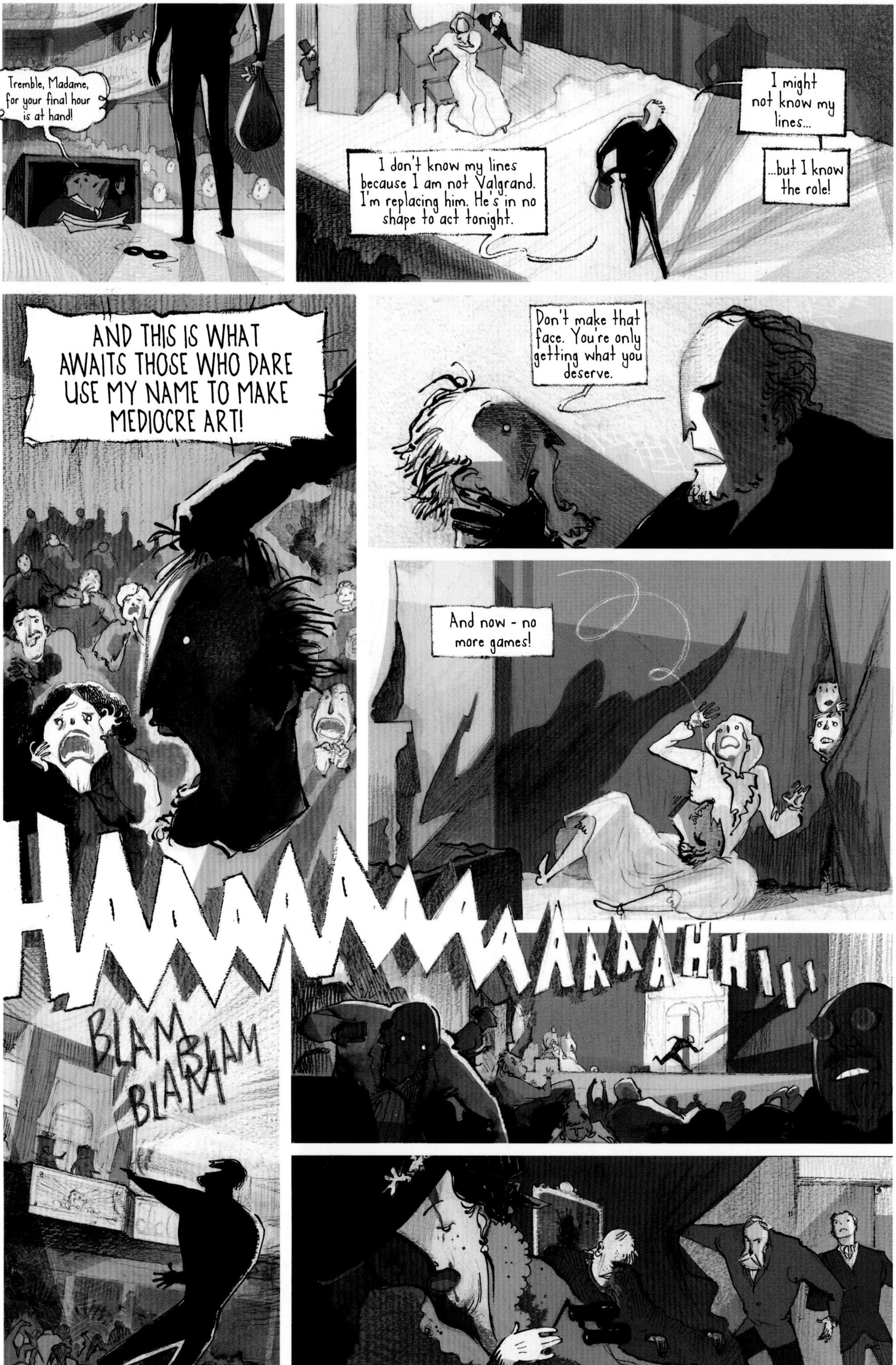
Tremble, Madame, for your final hour is at hand!
I don't know my lines because I am not Valgrand. I'm replacing him. He's in no shape to act tonight.
I might not know my lines...
...but I know the role!
AND THIS IS WHAT AWAITS THOSE WHO DARE USE MY NAME TO MAKE MEDIOCRE ART!
Don't make that face. You're only getting what you deserve.
And now - no more games!
AAAAAAAAAAAAAAHH!!!
BLAM BLAM
BLAM BLAM

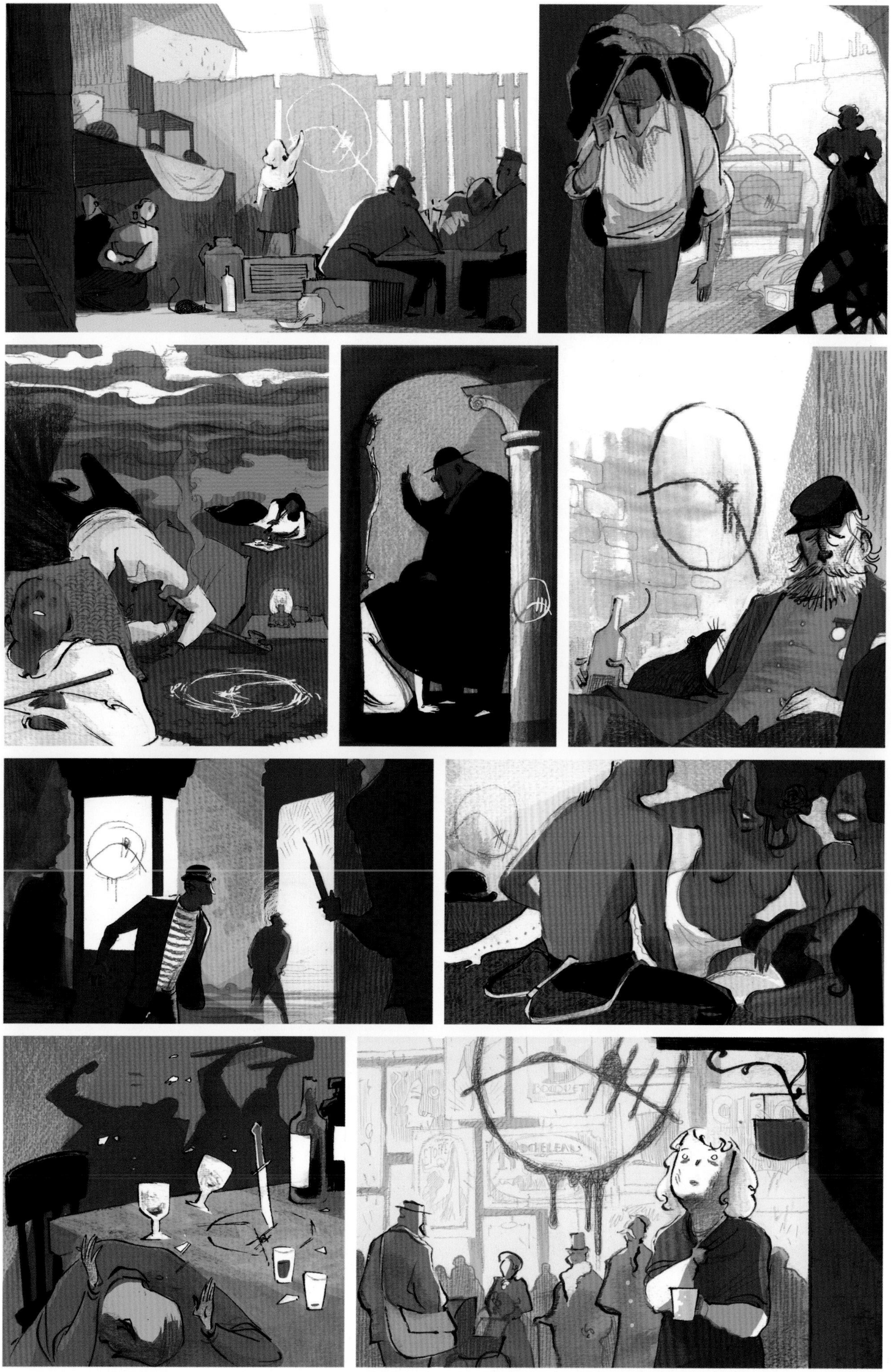

Wednesday, August 23, 1911

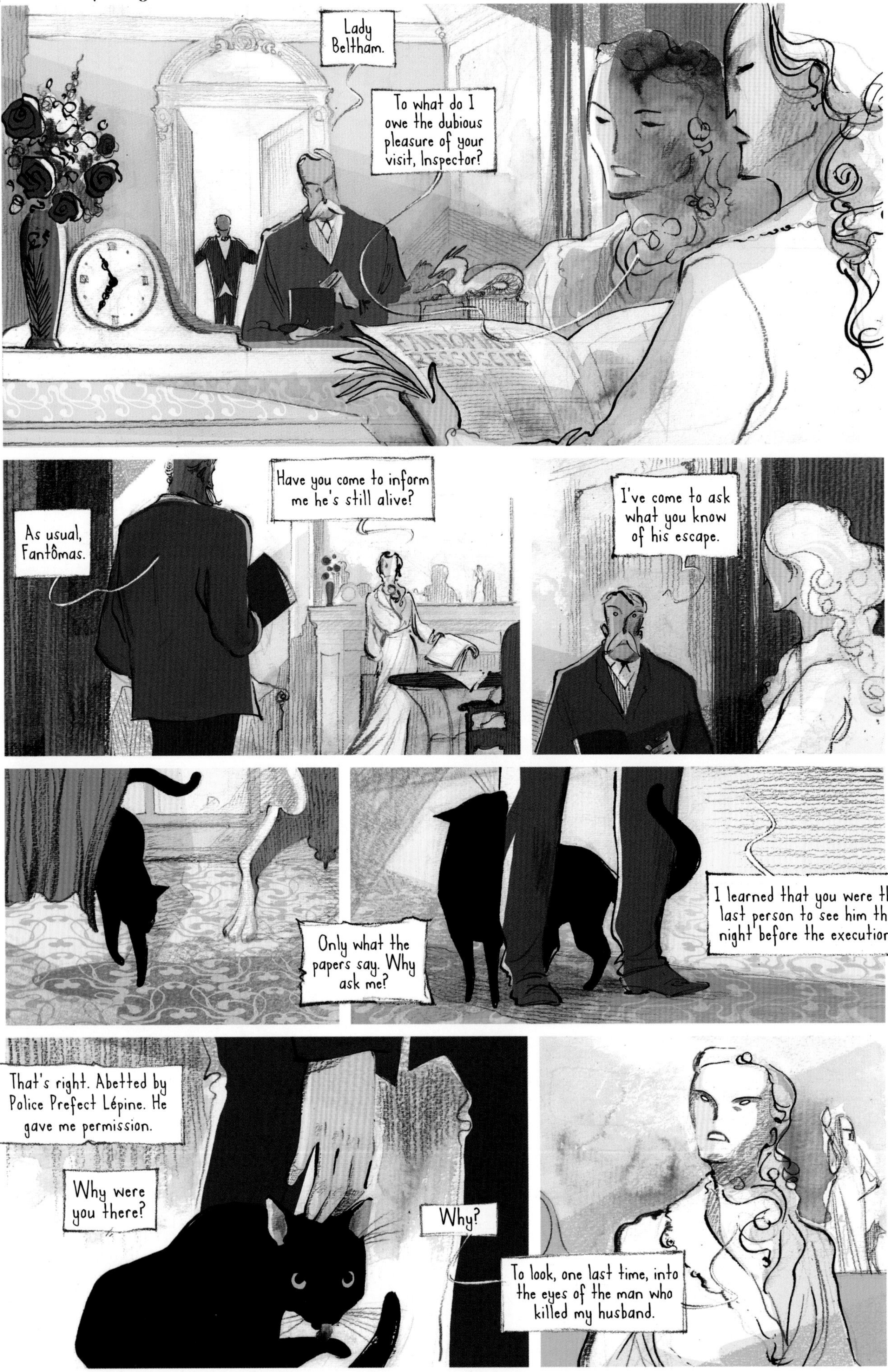
Lady Beltham.
To what do I owe the dubious pleasure of your visit, Inspector?
As usual, Fantômas.
Have you come to inform me he's still alive?
I've come to ask what you know of his escape.
Only what the papers say. Why ask me?
I learned that you were the last person to see him the night before the execution.
That's right. Abetted by Police Prefect Lépine. He gave me permission.
Why were you there?
Why?
To look, one last time, into the eyes of the man who killed my husband.

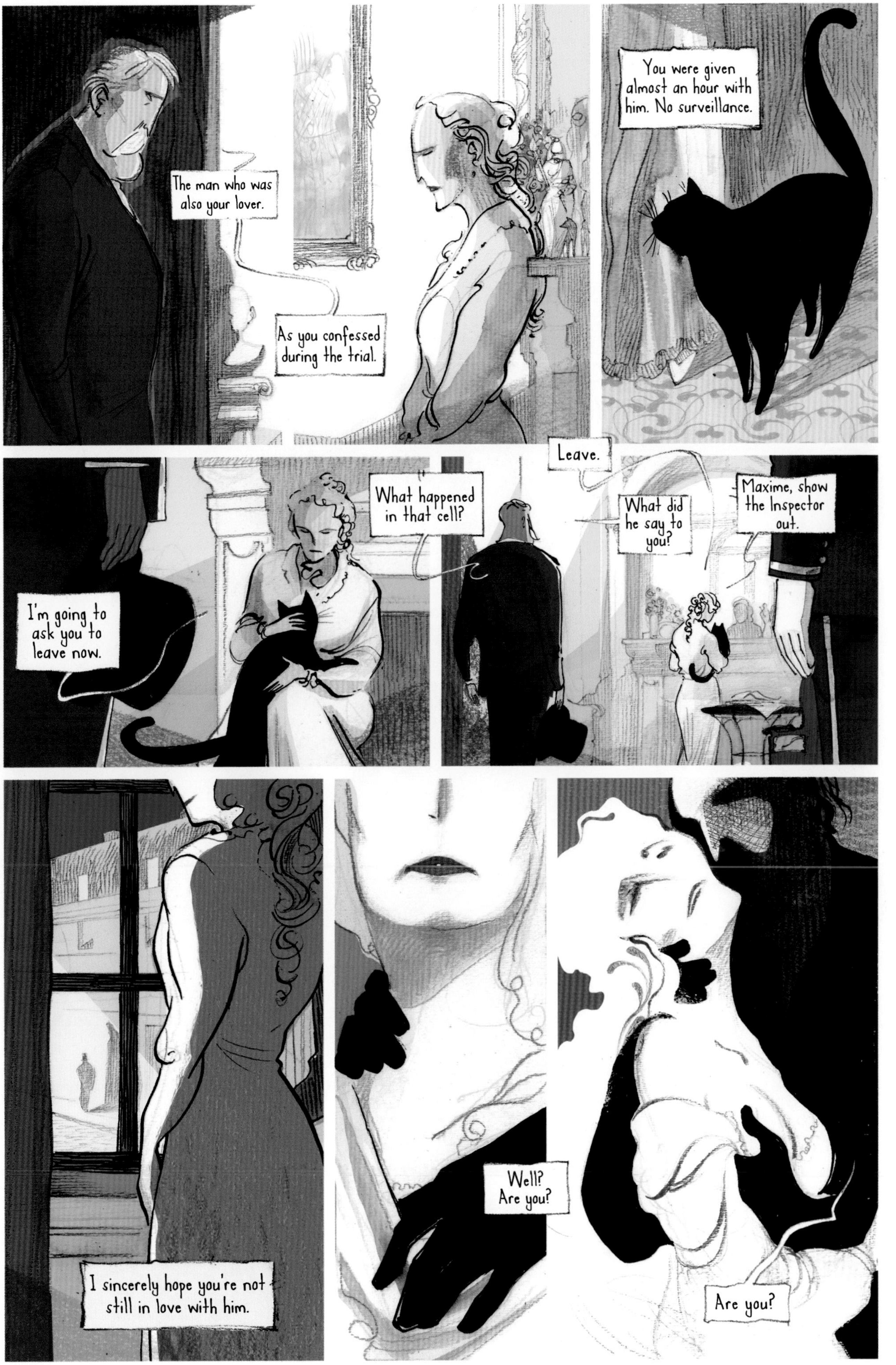
The man who was also your lover.
As you confessed during the trial.
You were given almost an hour with him. No surveillance.
I'm going to ask you to leave now.
What happened in that cell?
Leave.
What did he say to you?
Maxime, show the Inspector out.
I sincerely hope you're not still in love with him.
Well? Are you?
Are you?

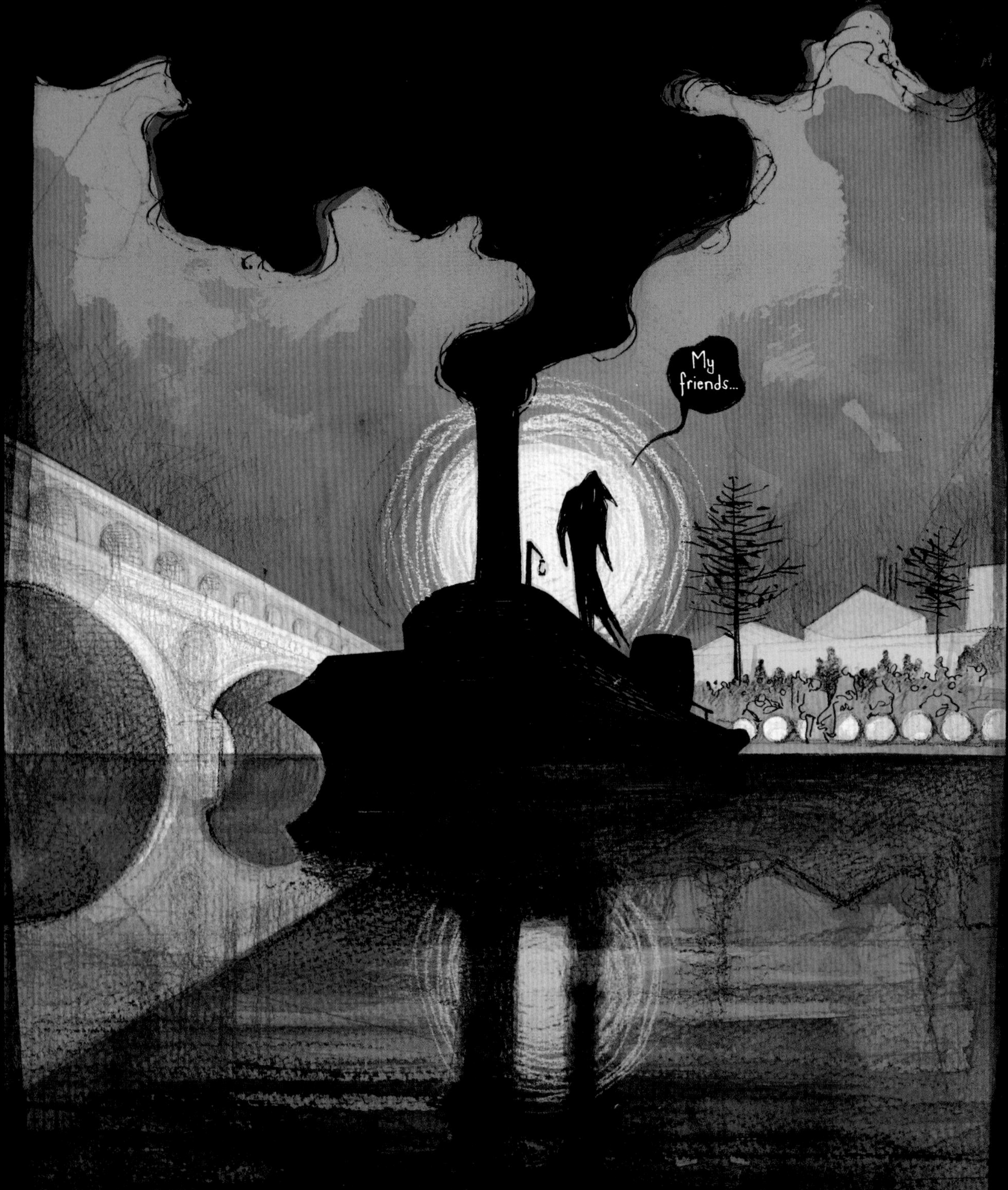
My friends...

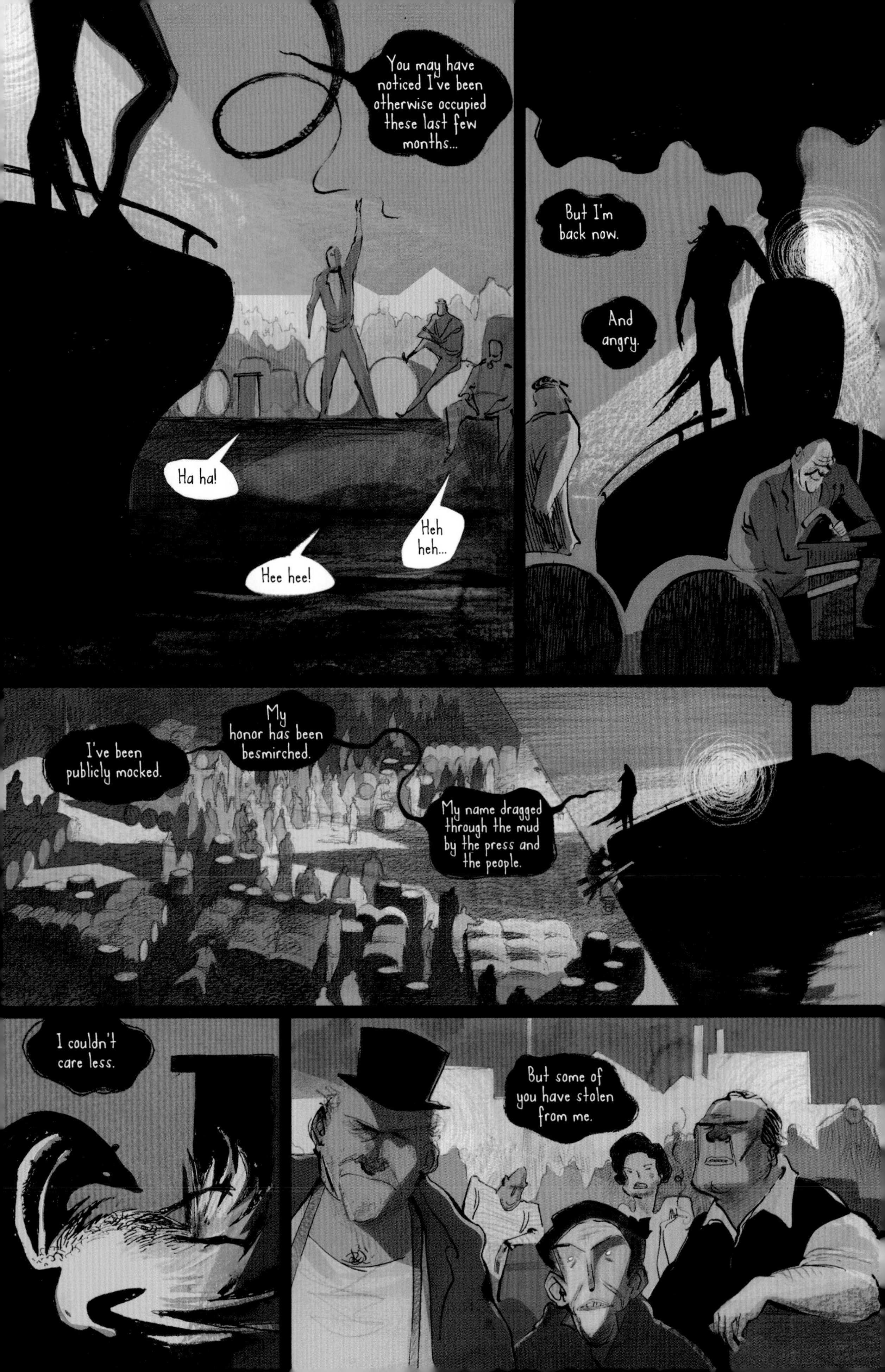
You may have noticed I've been otherwise occupied these last few months...
Ha ha!
Heh heh...
Hee hee!
But I'm back now.
And angry.
I've been publicly mocked.
My honor has been besmirched.
My name dragged through the mud by the press and the people.
I couldn't care less.
But some of you have stolen from me.

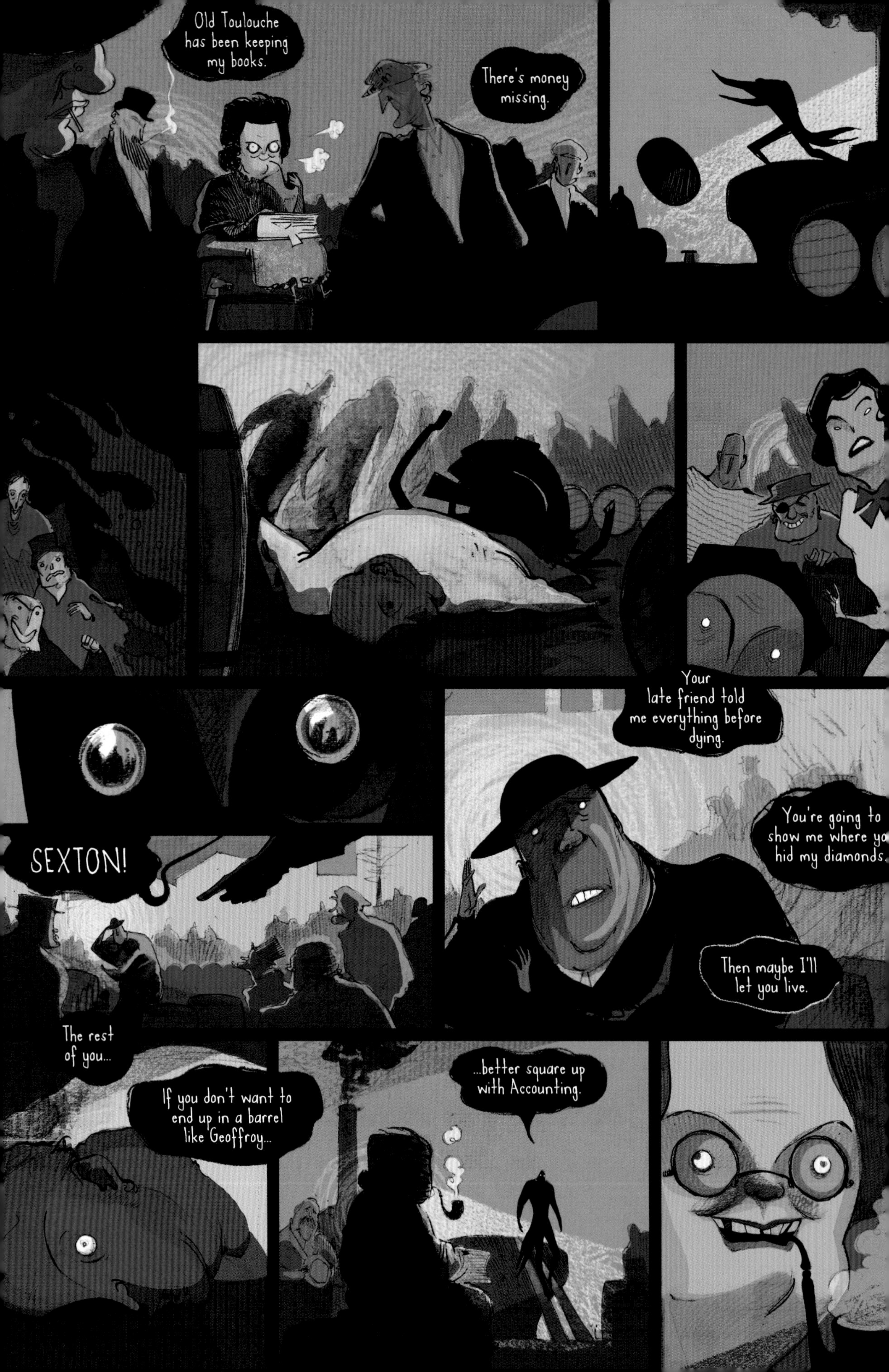
Old Toulouche has been keeping my books.
There's money missing.
Your late friend told me everything before dying.
SEXTON!
You're going to show me where yo hid my diamonds.
Then maybe I'll let you live.
The rest of you...
If you don't want to end up in a barrel like Geoffroy...
...better square up with Accounting.

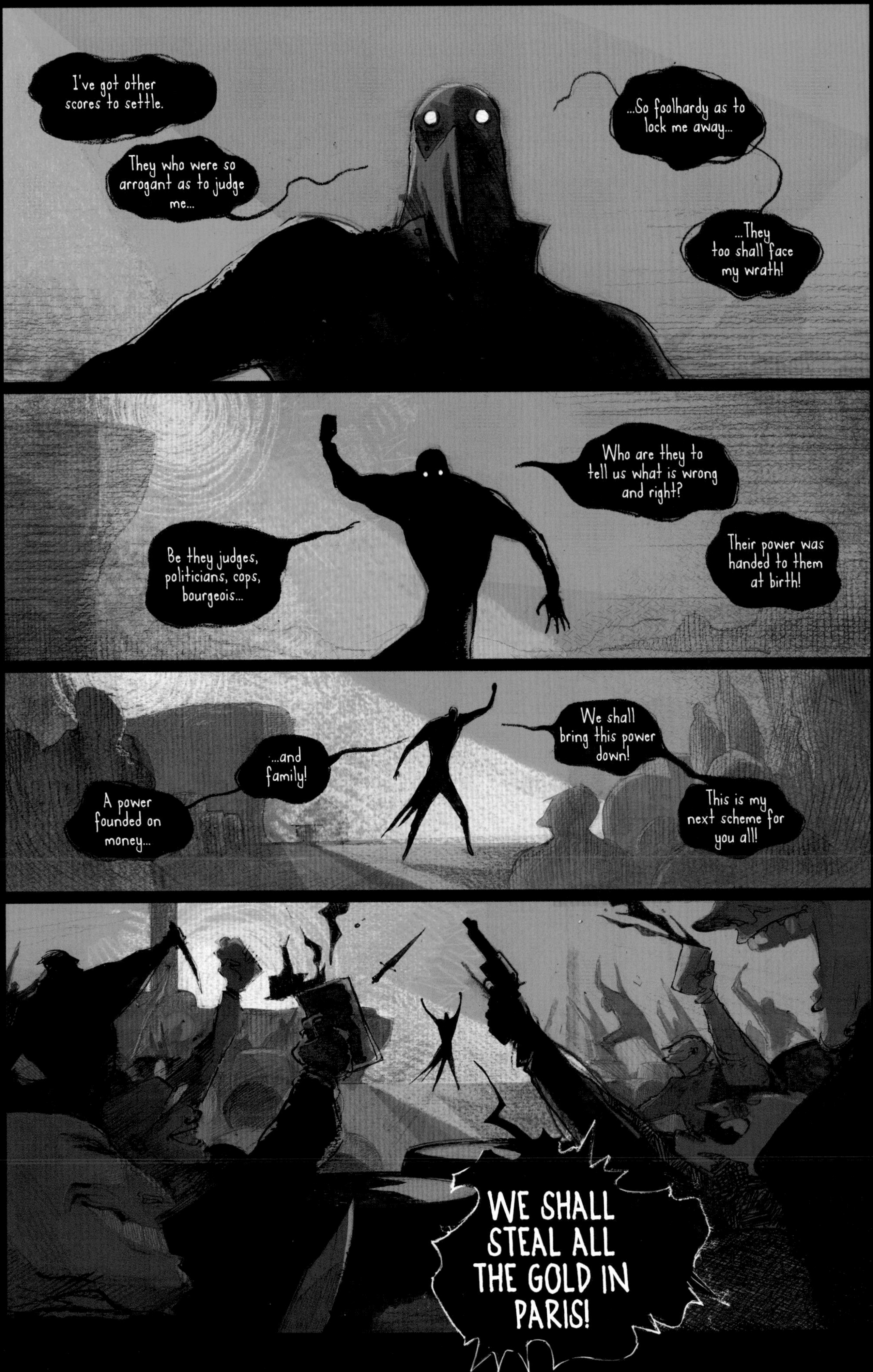
I've got other scores to settle.
They who were so arrogant as to judge me...
...So foolhardy as to lock me away...
...They too shall face my wrath!
Who are they to tell us what is wrong and right?
Be they judges, politicians, cops, bourgeois...
Their power was handed to them at birth!
A power founded on money...
...and family!
We shall bring this power down!
This is my next scheme for you all!
WE SHALL STEAL ALL THE GOLD IN PARIS!

Thursday, August 24, 1911

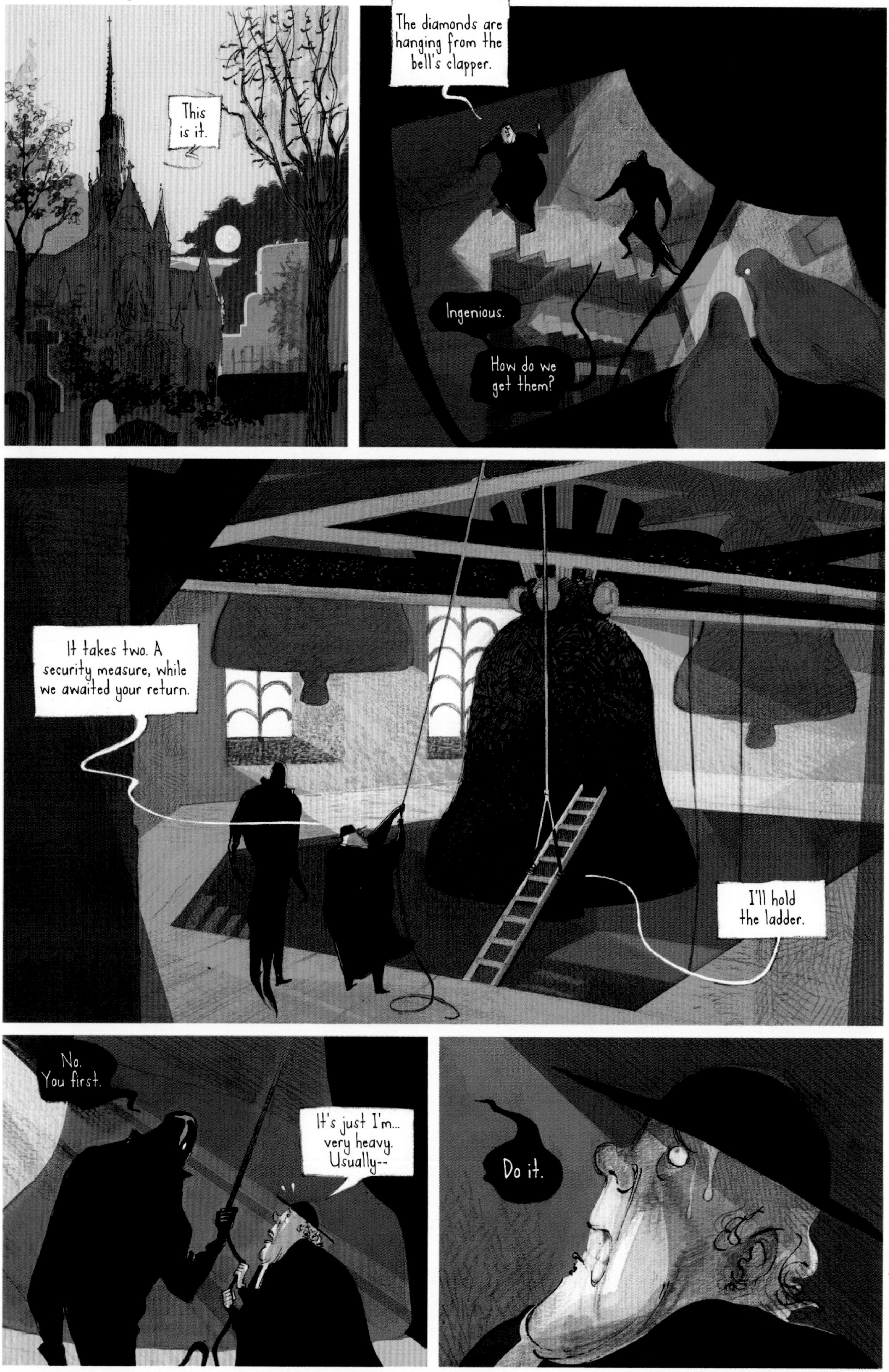
This is it.
The diamonds are hanging from the bell's clapper.
Ingenious.
How do we get them?
It takes two. A security measure, while we awaited your return.
I'll hold the ladder.
No. You first.
It's just I'm... very heavy. Usually--
Do it.

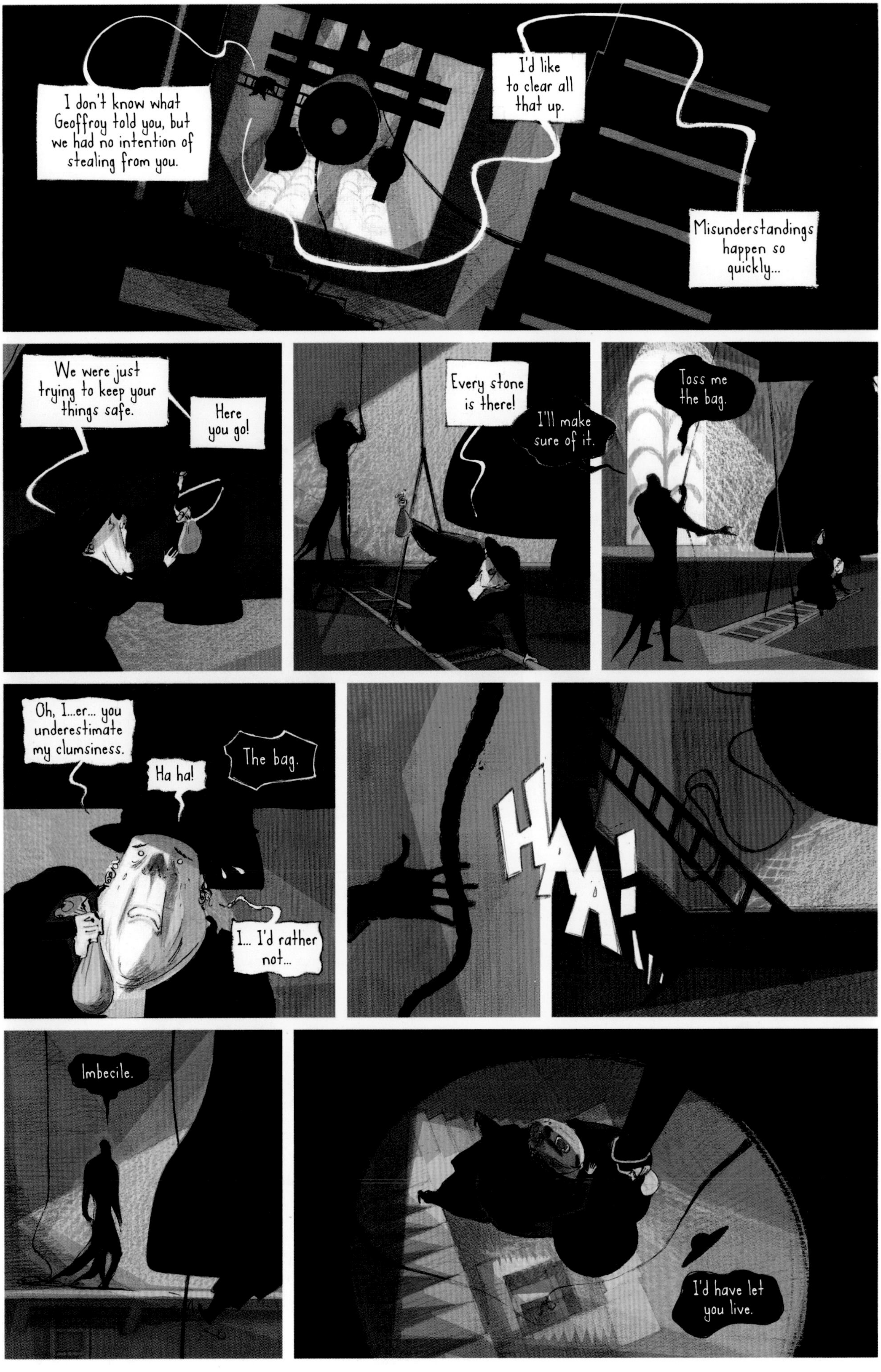

I don't know what Geoffroy told you, but we had no intention of stealing from you.
I'd like to clear all that up.
Misunderstandings happen so quickly...
We were just trying to keep your things safe.
Here you go!
Every stone is there!
I'll make sure of it.
Toss me the bag.
Oh, I...er... you underestimate my clumsiness.
Ha ha!
The bag.
I... I'd rather not...
HAAA!...
Imbecile.
I'd have let you live.

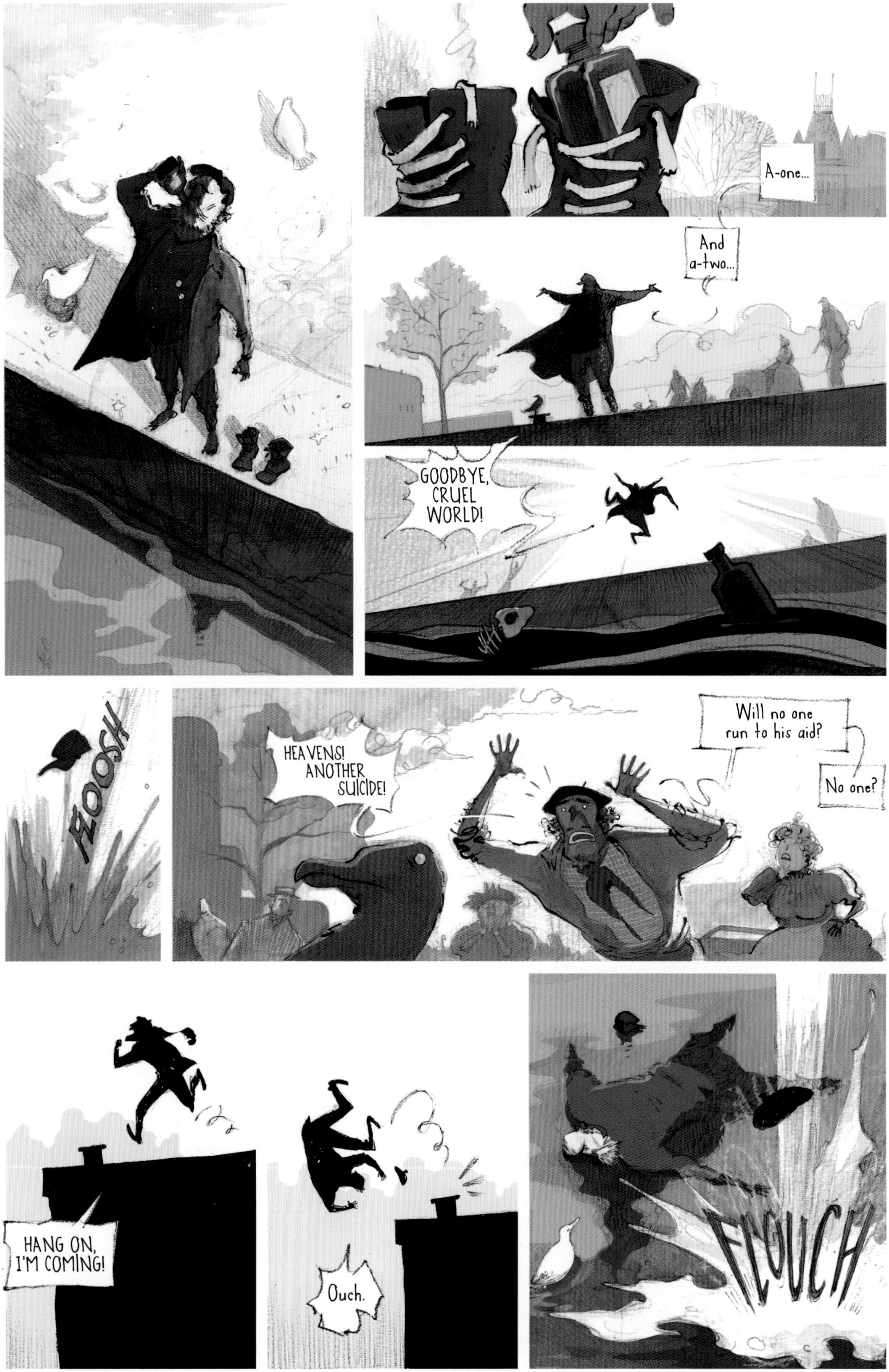
A-one...
And a-two...
GOODBYE, CRUEL WORLD!
FLOOSH
HEAVENS! ANOTHER SUICIDE!
Will no one run to his aid?
No one?
HANG ON, I'M COMING!
Ouch.
FLOUCH

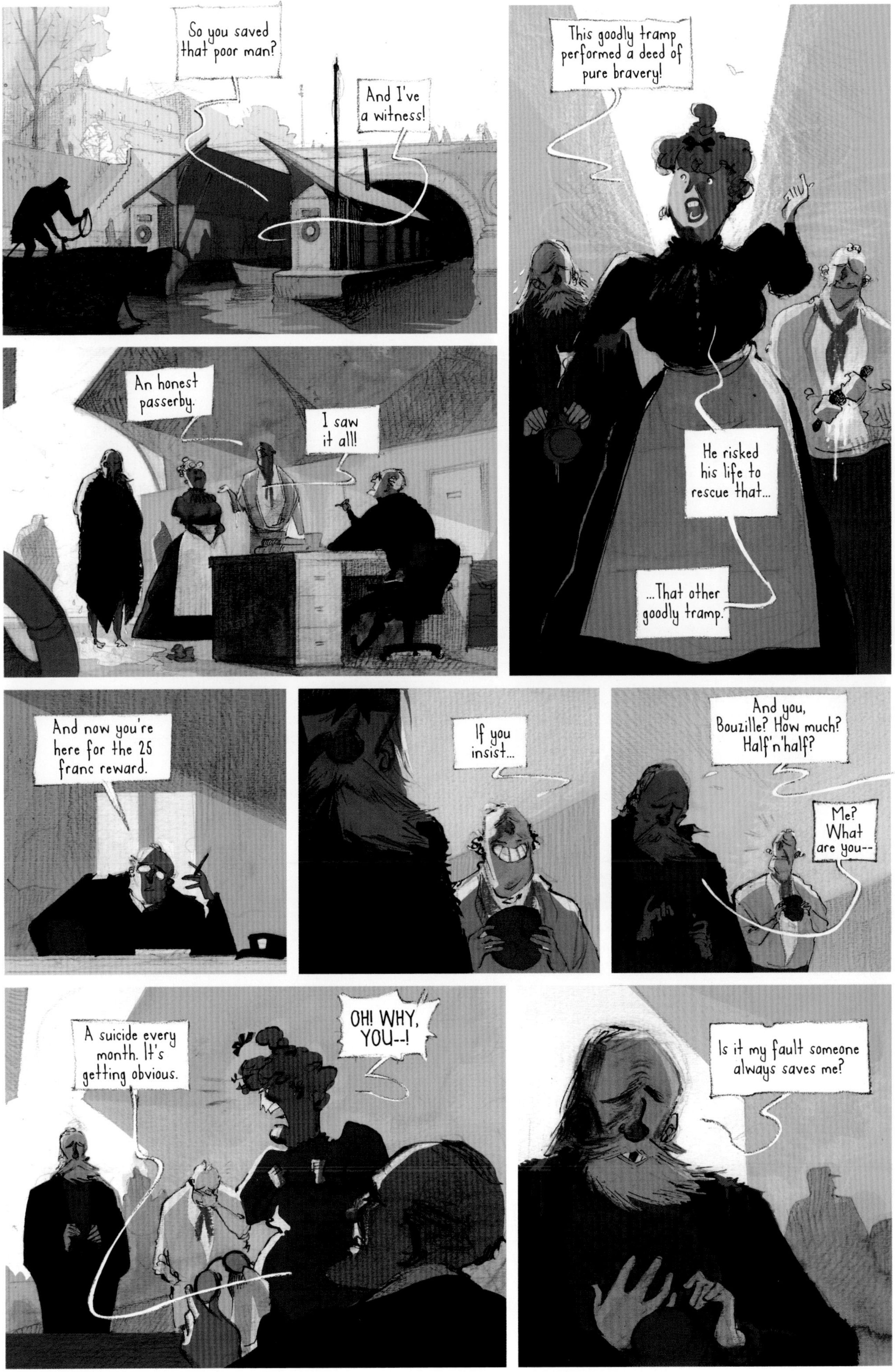
So you saved that poor man?
And I've a witness!
This goodly tramp performed a deed of pure bravery!
An honest passerby.
I saw it all!
He risked his life to rescue that...
...That other goodly tramp.
And now you're here for the 25 franc reward.
If you insist...
And you, Bouzille? How much? Half'n'half?
Me? What are you--
A suicide every month. It's getting obvious.
OH! WHY, YOU--!
Is it my fault someone always saves me?

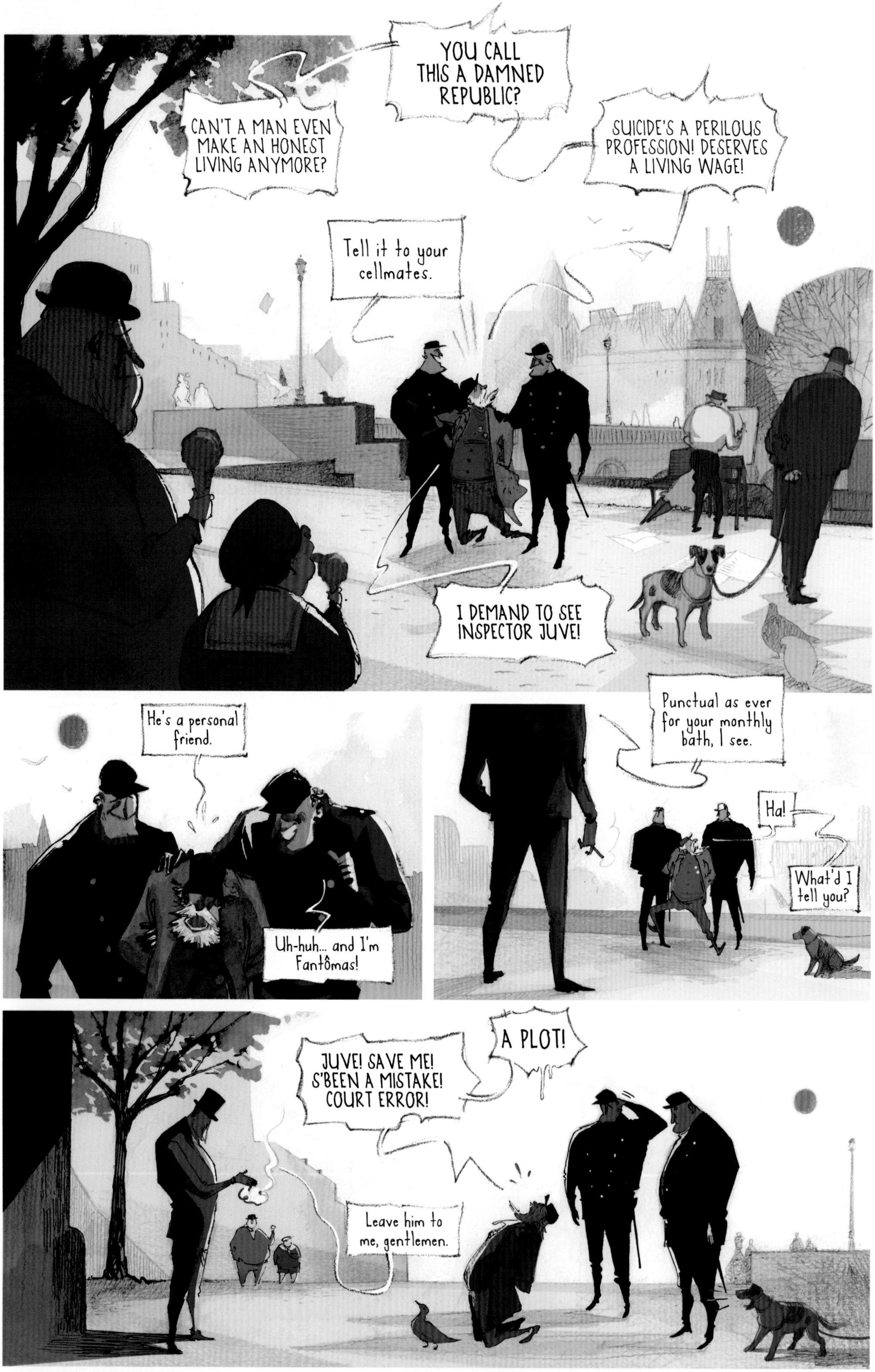
CAN'T A MAN EVEN MAKE AN HONEST LIVING ANYMORE?
YOU CALL THIS A DAMNED REPUBLIC?
SUICIDE'S A PERILOUS PROFESSION! DESERVES A LIVING WAGE!
Tell it to your cellmates.
I DEMAND TO SEE INSPECTOR JUVE!
He's a personal friend.
Uh-huh... and I'm Fantômas!
Punctual as ever for your monthly bath, I see.
Ha!
What'd I tell you?
JUVE! SAVE ME! S'BEEN A MISTAKE! COURT ERROR!
A PLOT!
Leave him to me, gentlemen.

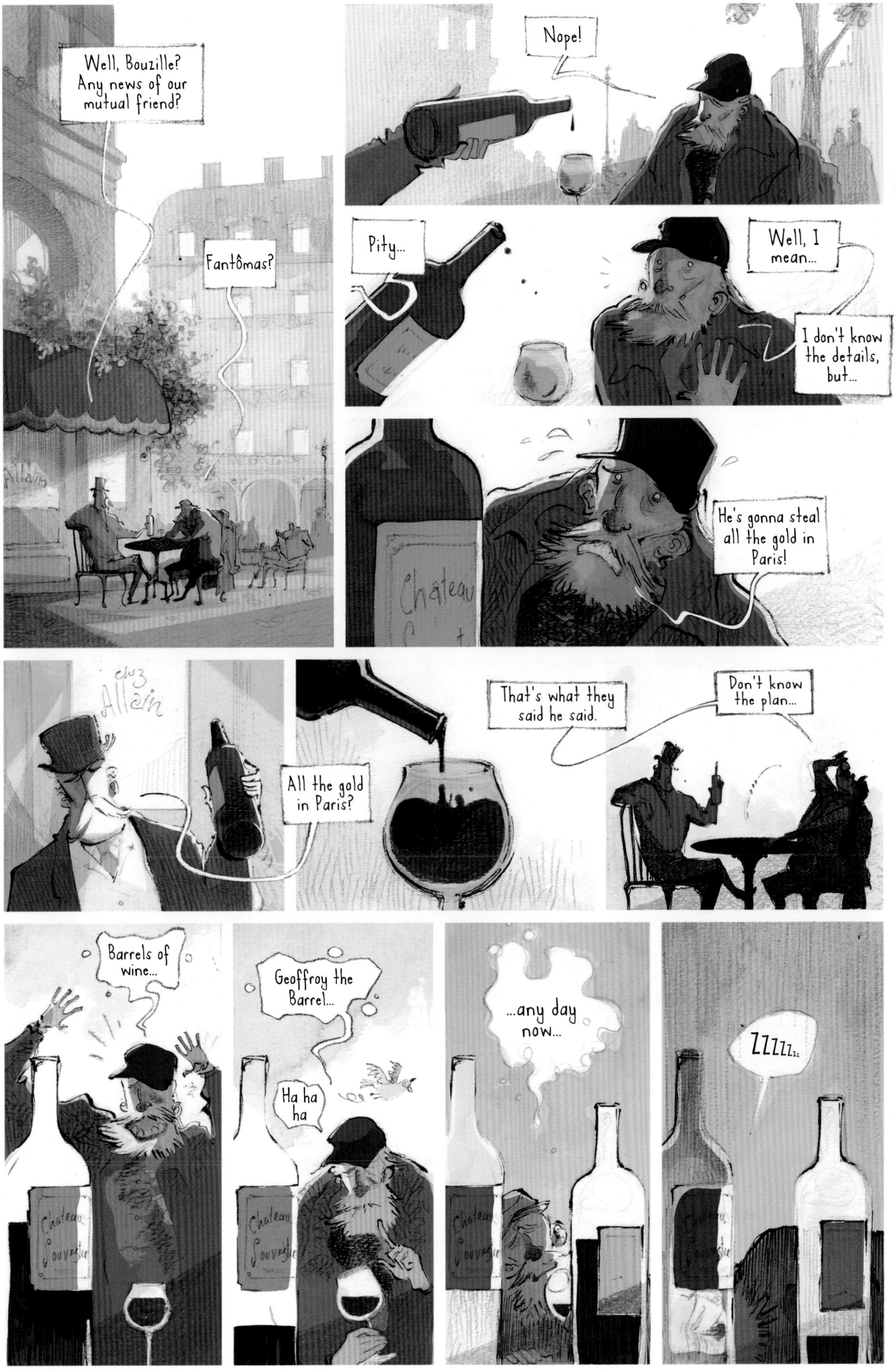
Well, Bouzille? Any news of our mutual friend?
Fantômas?
Allain
Nope!
Pity...
Well, I mean...
I don't know the details, but...
Château
He's gonna steal all the gold in Paris!
chez Allain
All the gold in Paris?
That's what they said he said.
Don't know the plan...
Barrels of wine...
Château Souvestre
Geoffroy the Barrel...
Ha ha ha
Château Souvestre
...any day now...
Château Souvestre
ZZZZzz
Château Souvestre

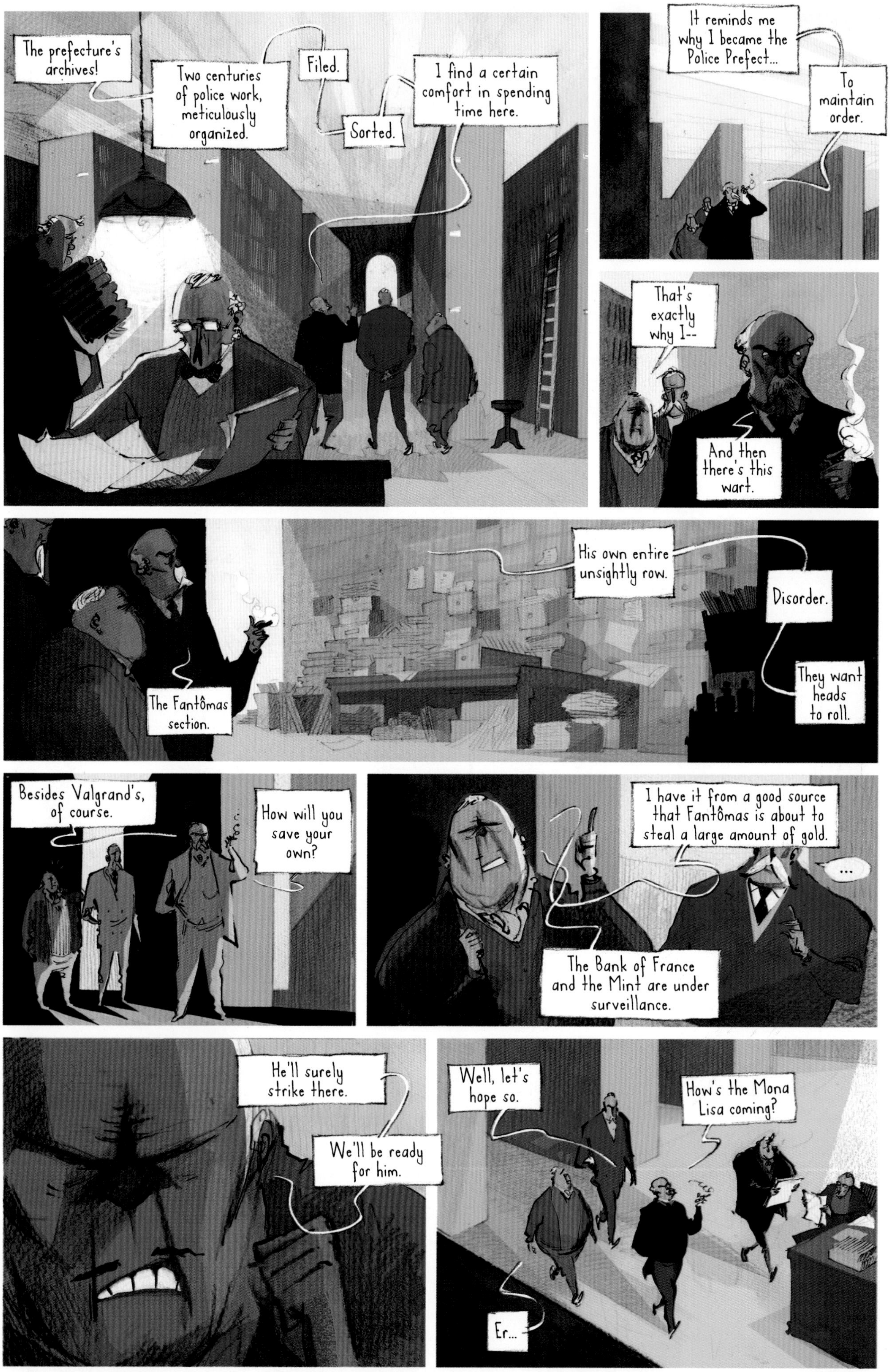
The prefecture's archives!
Two centuries of police work, meticulously organized.
Filed.
Sorted.
I find a certain comfort in spending time here.
It reminds me why I became the Police Prefect...
To maintain order.
That's exactly why I--
And then there's this wart.
The Fantômas section.
His own entire unsightly row.
Disorder.
They want heads to roll.
Besides Valgrand's, of course.
How will you save your own?
I have it from a good source that Fantômas is about to steal a large amount of gold.
...
The Bank of France and the Mint are under surveillance.
He'll surely strike there.
We'll be ready for him.
Well, let's hope so.
How's the Mona Lisa coming?
Er...

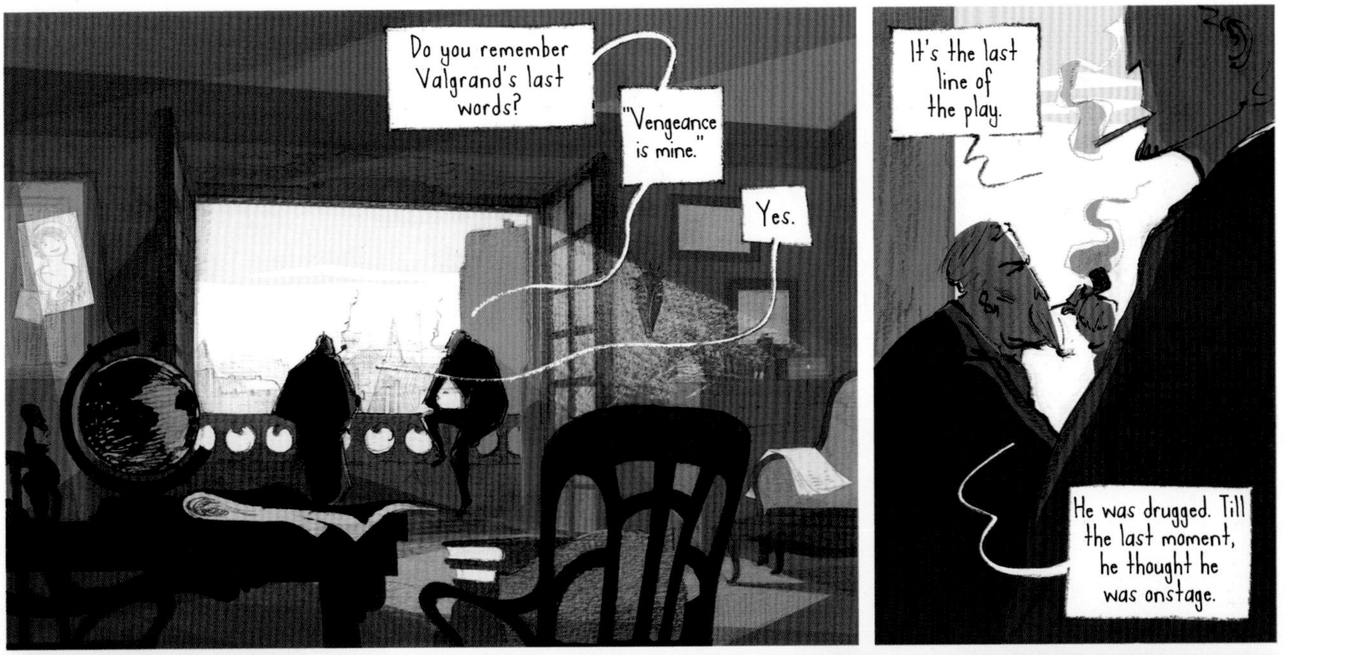
Do you remember Valgrand's last words?
"Vengeance is mine."
Yes.
It's the last line of the play.
He was drugged. Till the last moment, he thought he was onstage.

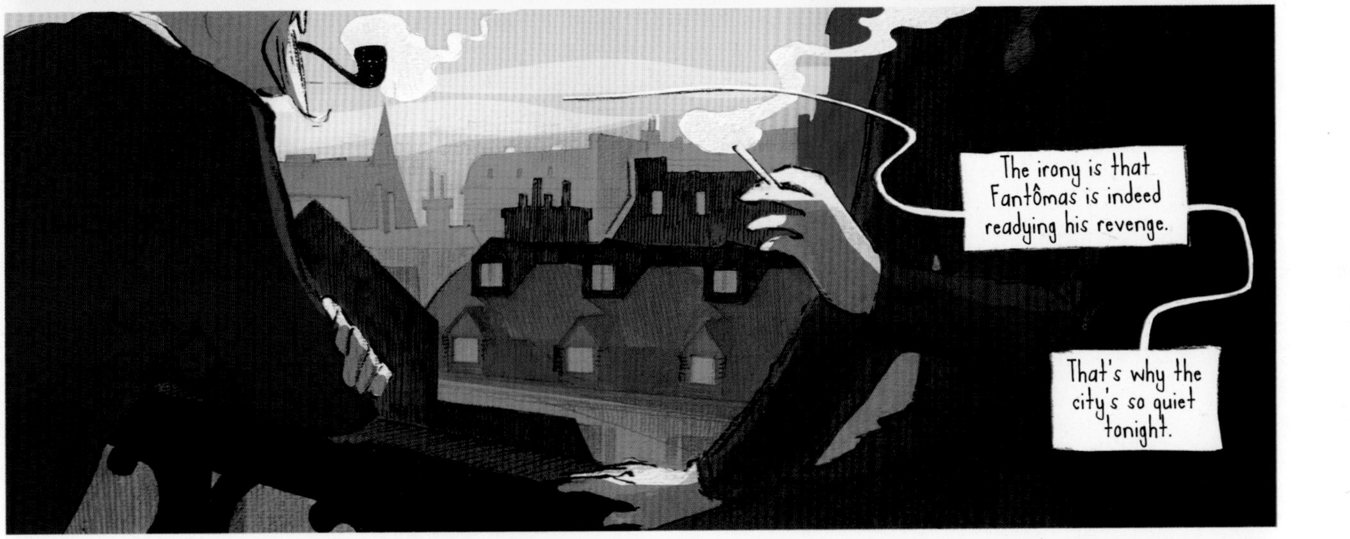
The irony is that Fantômas is indeed readying his revenge.
That's why the city's so quiet tonight.

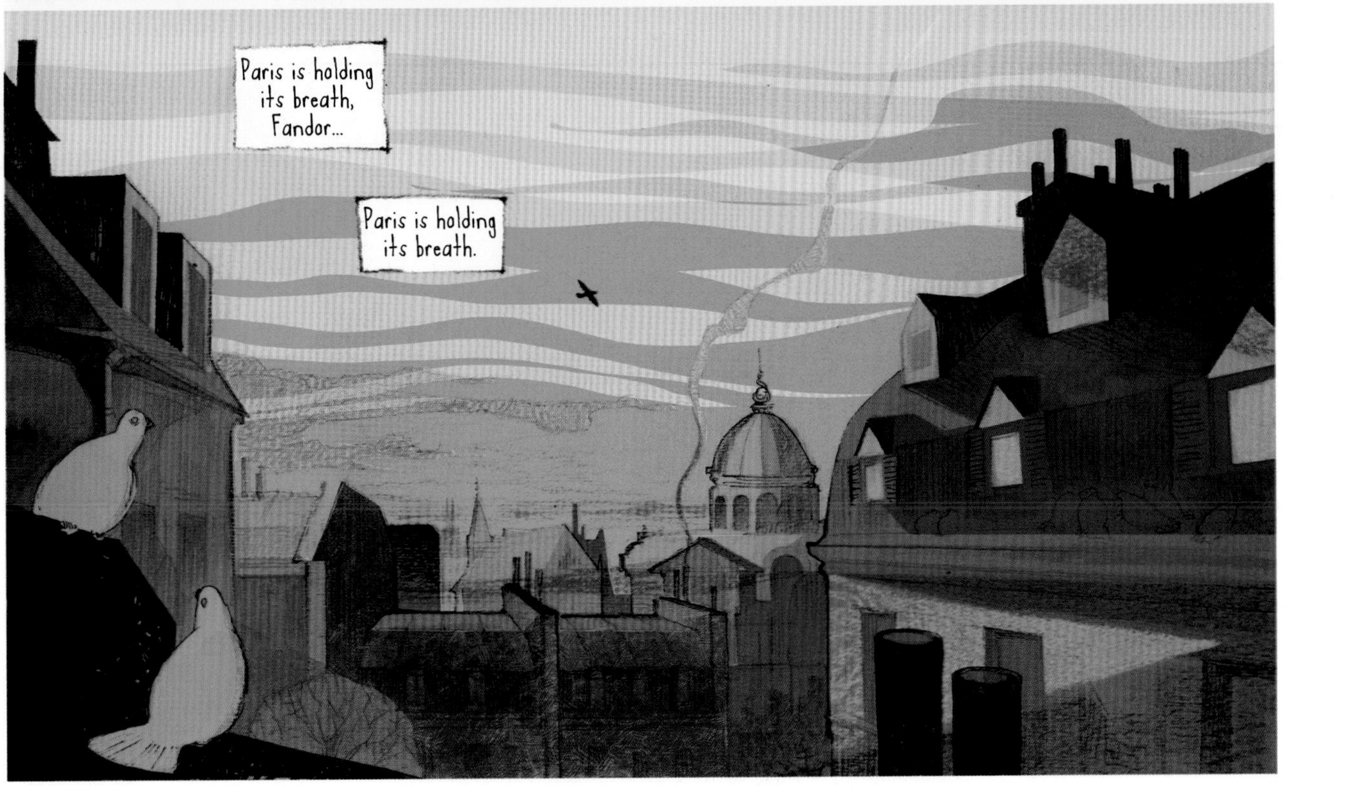
Paris is holding its breath, Fandor...
Paris is holding its breath.

Friday, August 25, 1911

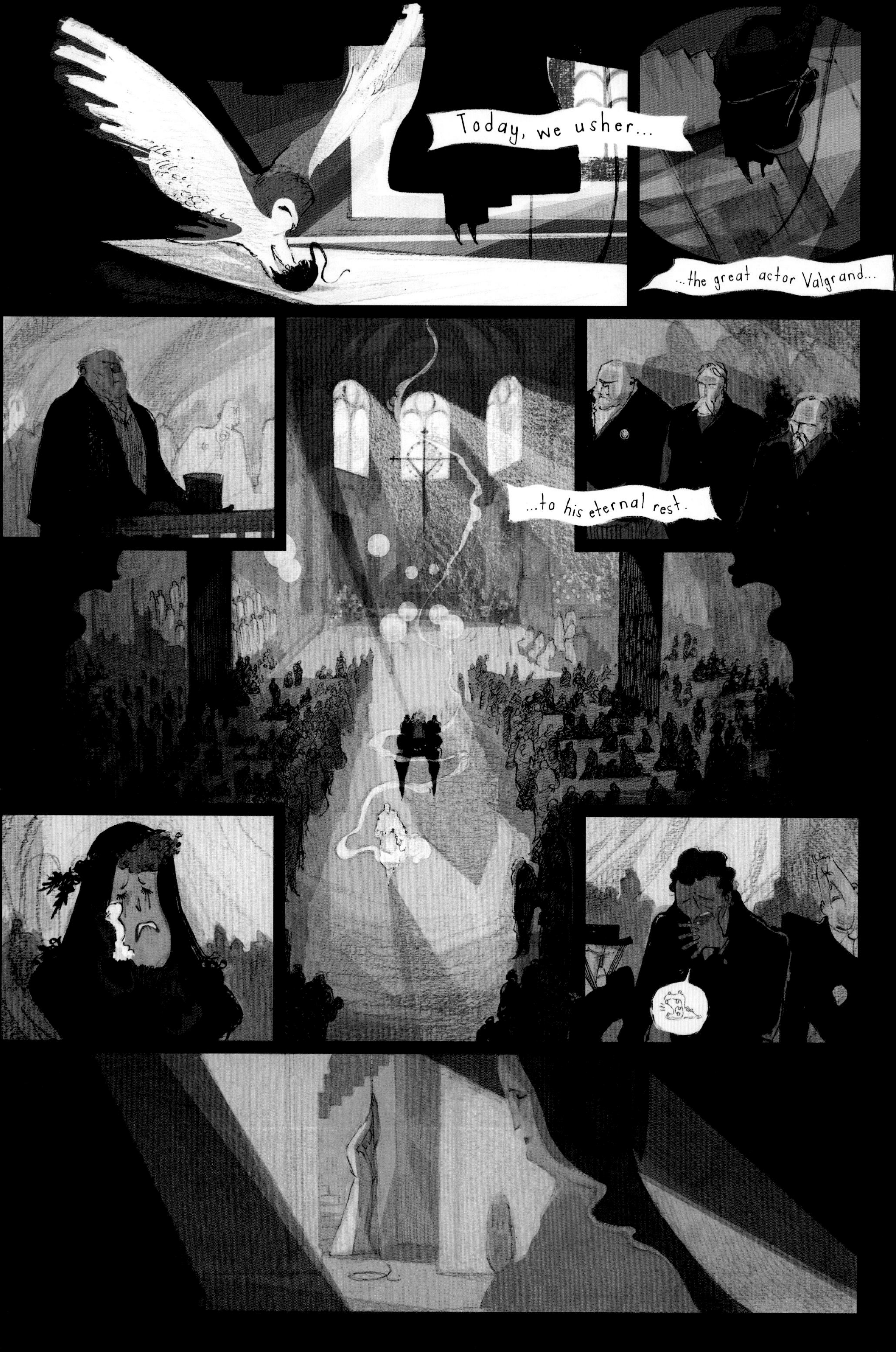
Today, we usher...
...the great actor Valgrand...
...to his eternal rest.

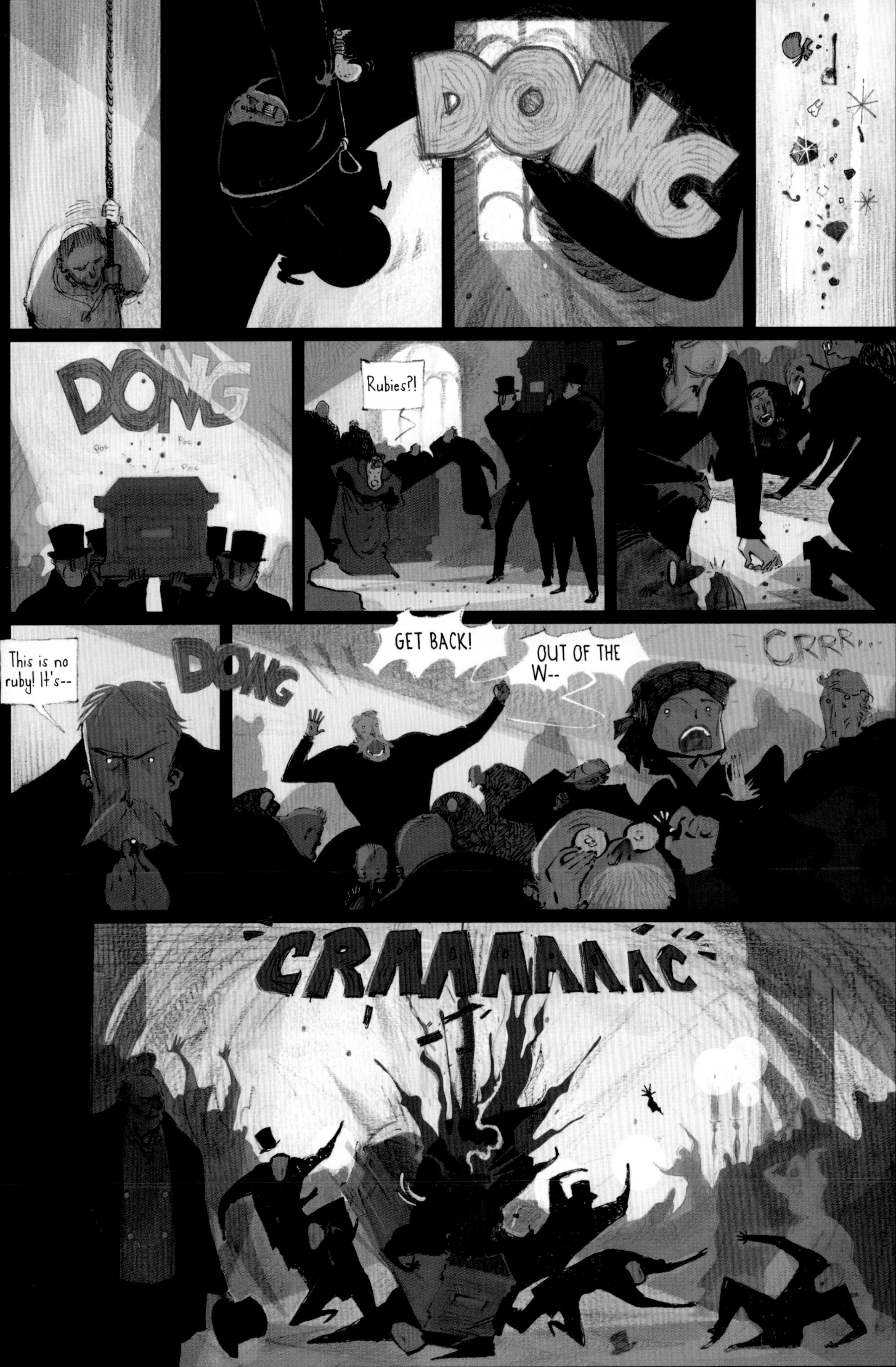
DONG
DONG
POC
POC
POC
Rubies?!
This is no ruby! It's--
DONG
GET BACK!
OUT OF THE W--
CRRR...
CRAAAAAAC

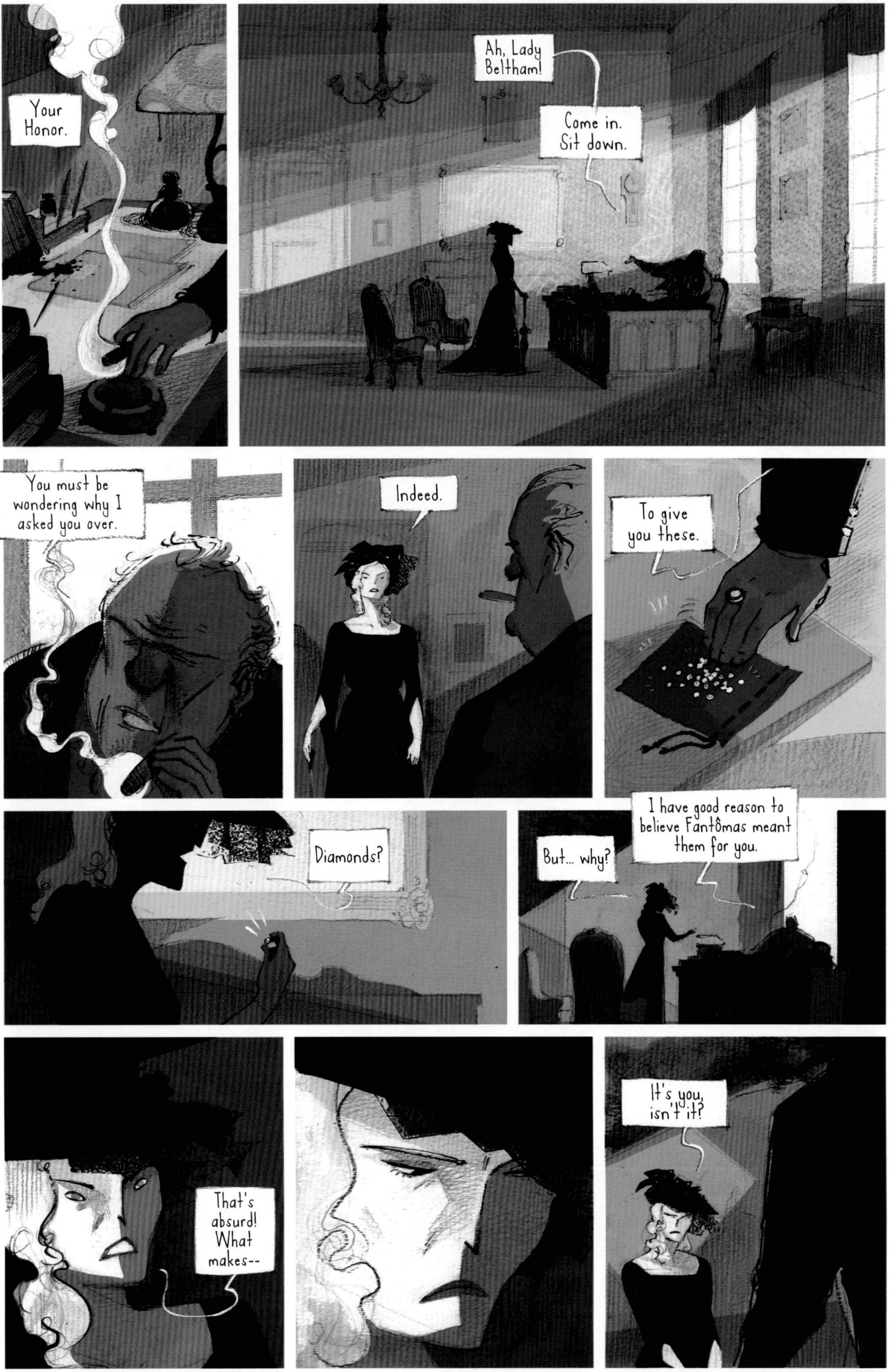
Your Honor.
Ah, Lady Beltham!
Come in. Sit down.
You must be wondering why I asked you over.
Indeed.
To give you these.
Diamonds?
But... why?
I have good reason to believe Fantômas meant them for you.
That's absurd! What makes--
It's you, isn't it?

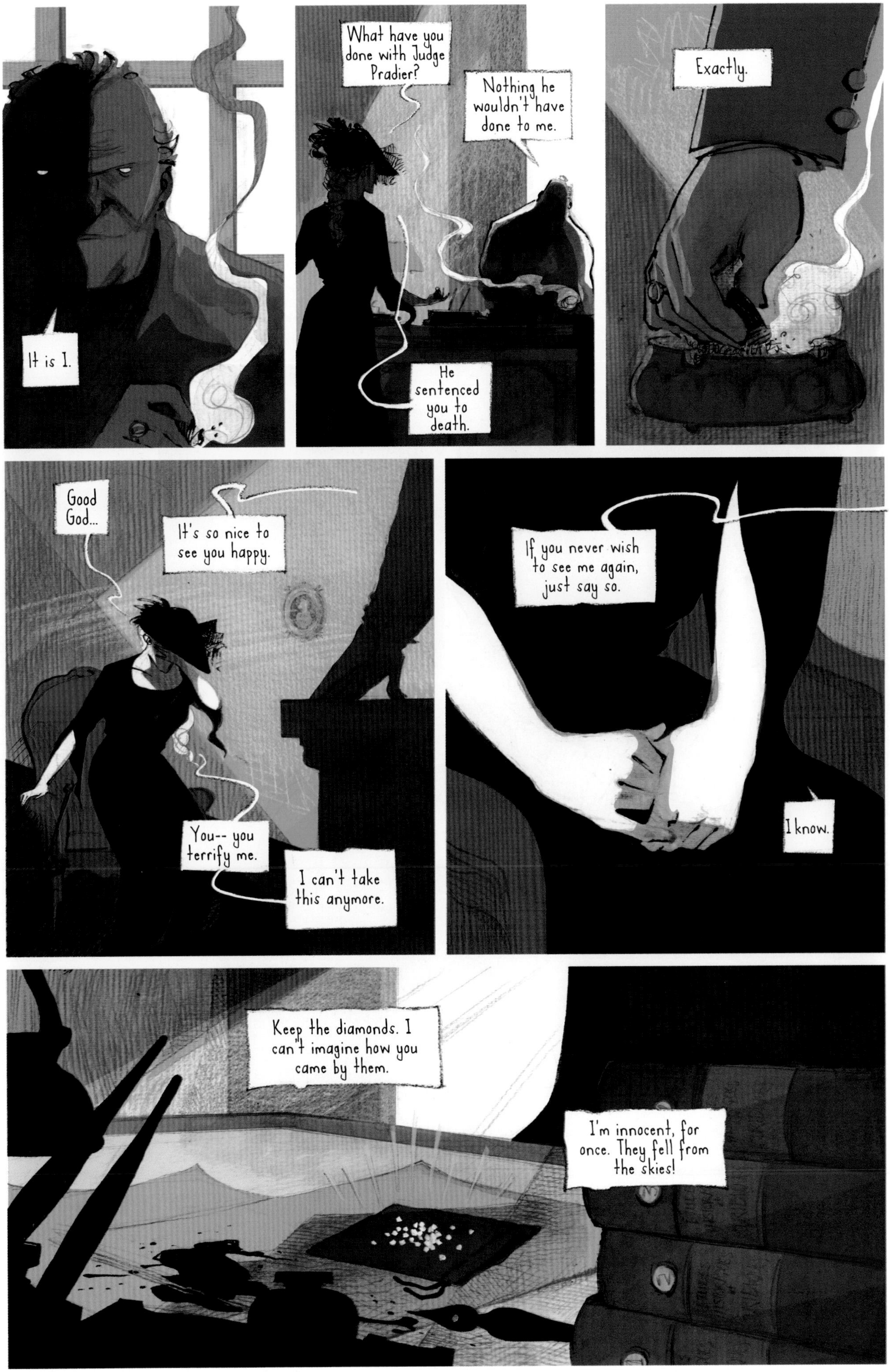
It is I.
What have you done with Judge Pradier?
Nothing he wouldn't have done to me.
He sentenced you to death.
Exactly.
Good God...
It's so nice to see you happy.
You-- you terrify me.
I can't take this anymore.
If you never wish to see me again, just say so.
I know.
Keep the diamonds. I can't imagine how you came by them.
I'm innocent, for once. They fell from the skies!

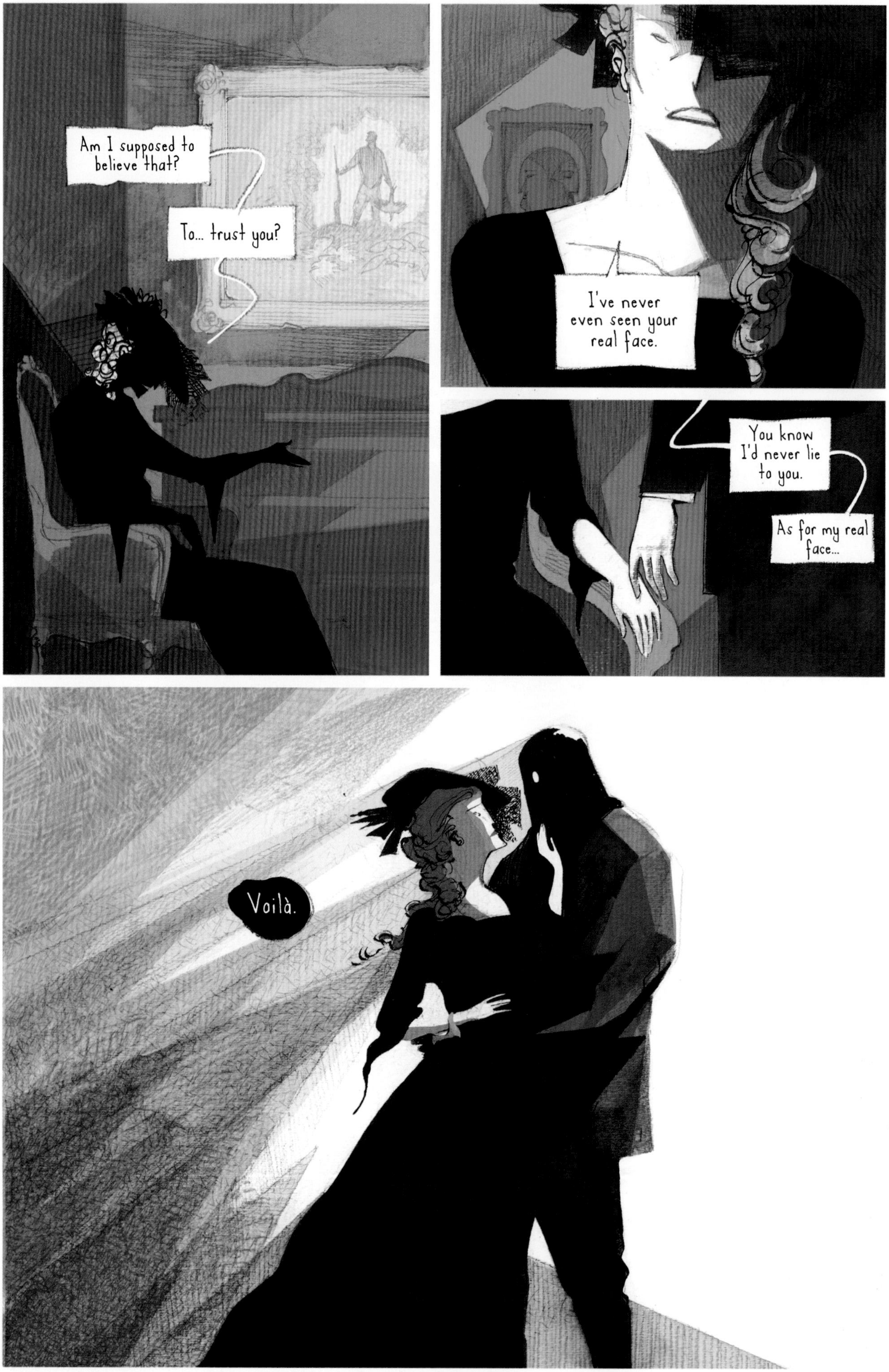
Am I supposed to believe that?
To... trust you?
I've never even seen your real face.
You know I'd never lie to you.
As for my real face...
Voilà.

Monday, September 4, 1911

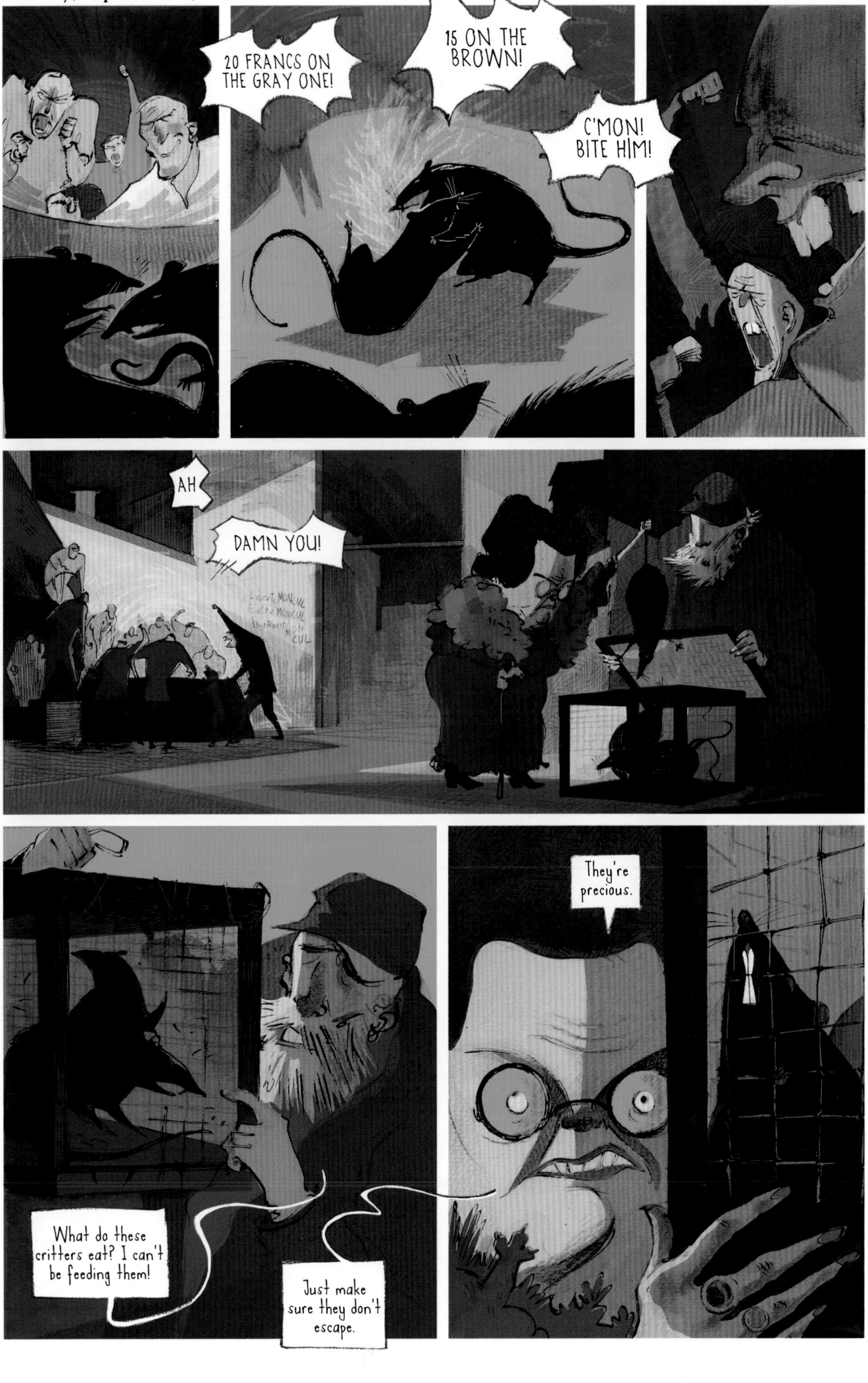
20 FRANCS ON THE GRAY ONE!
15 ON THE BROWN!
C'MON! BITE HIM!
AH
DAMN YOU!
What do these critters eat? I can't be feeding them!
Just make sure they don't escape.
They're precious.

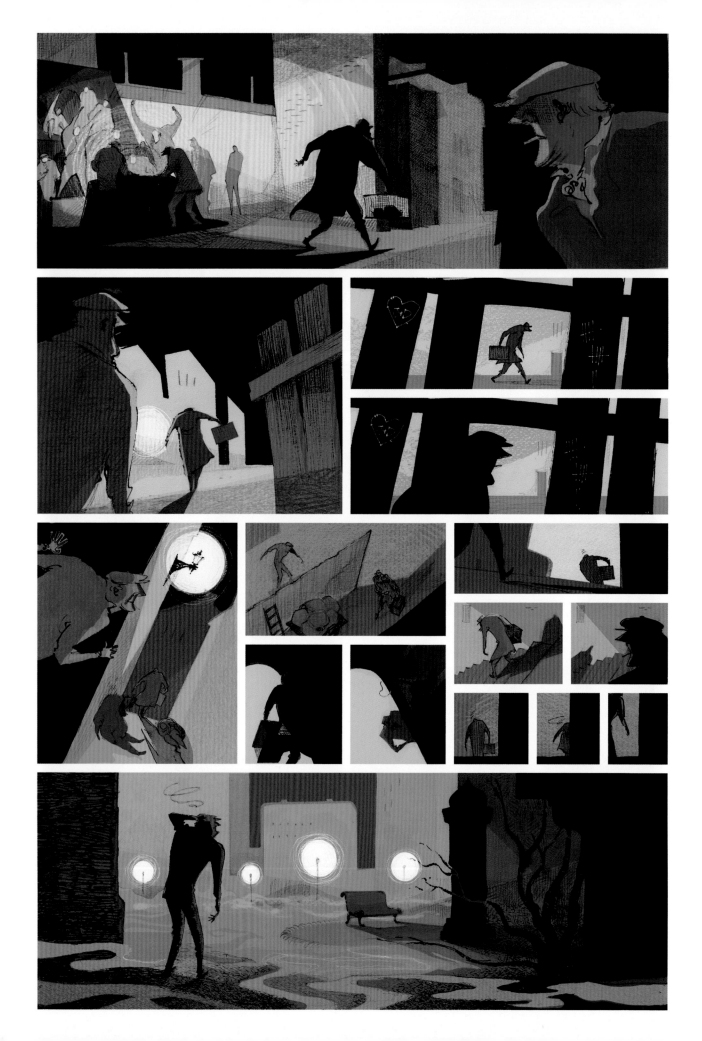

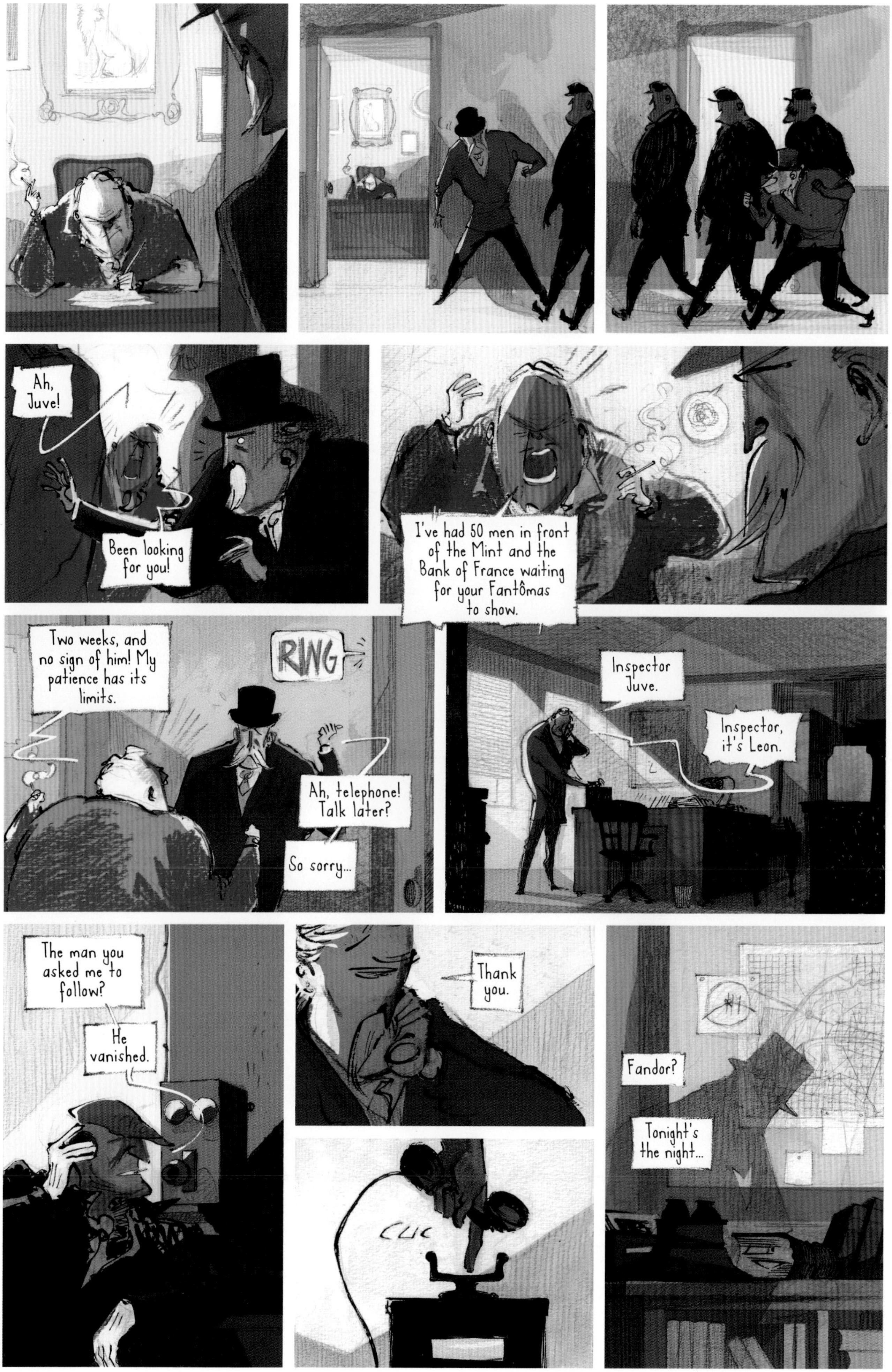
Ah, Juve!
Been looking for you!
I've had 50 men in front of the Mint and the Bank of France waiting for your Fantômas to show.
Two weeks, and no sign of him! My patience has its limits.
RING
Ah, telephone! Talk later?
So sorry...
Inspector Juve.
Inspector, it's Leon.
The man you asked me to follow?
He vanished.
Thank you.
CLIC
Fandor?
Tonight's the night...

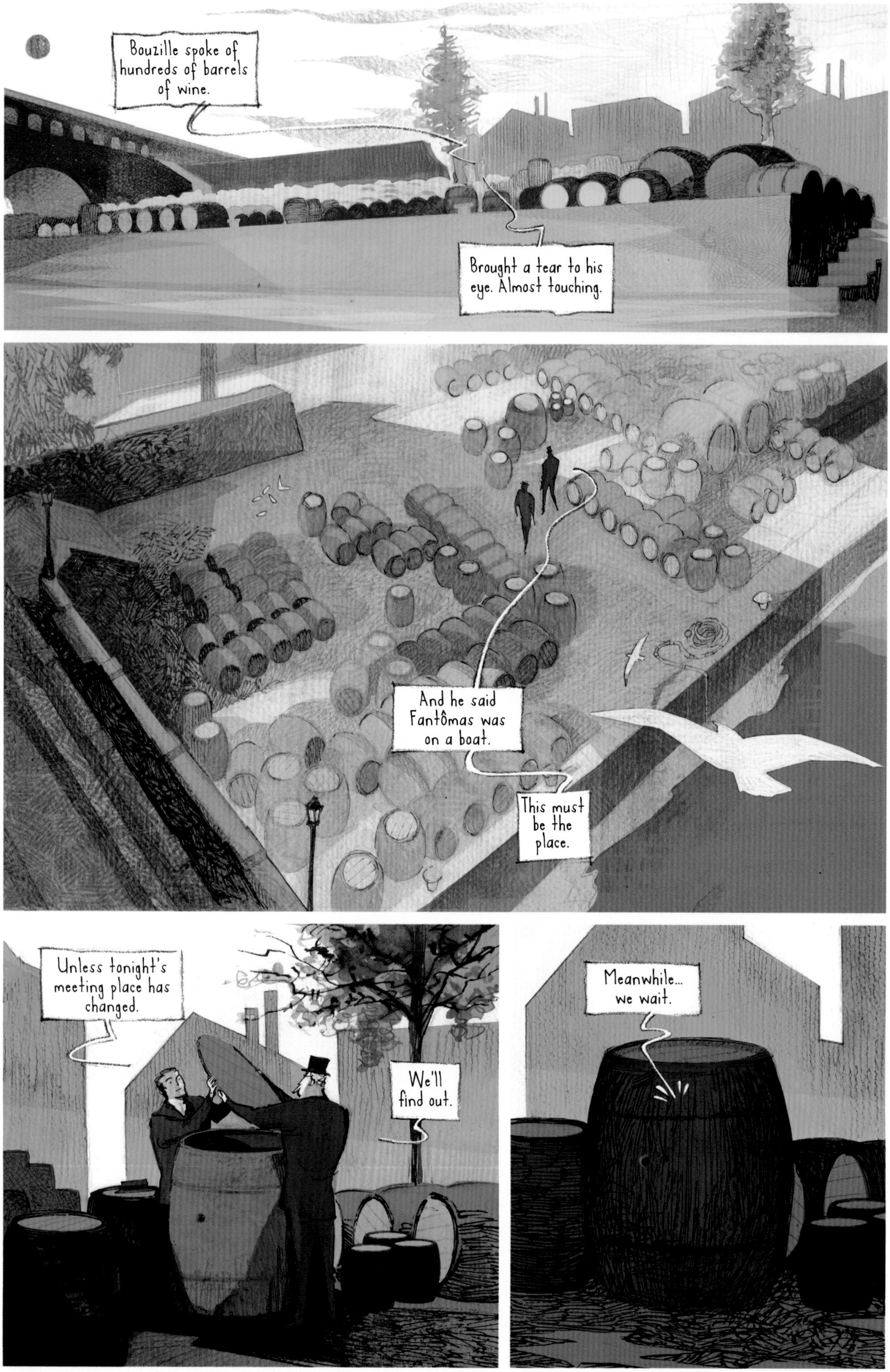
Bouzille spoke of hundreds of barrels of wine.
Brought a tear to his eye. Almost touching.
And he said Fantômas was on a boat.
This must be the place.
Unless tonight's meeting place has changed.
We'll find out.
Meanwhile... we wait.

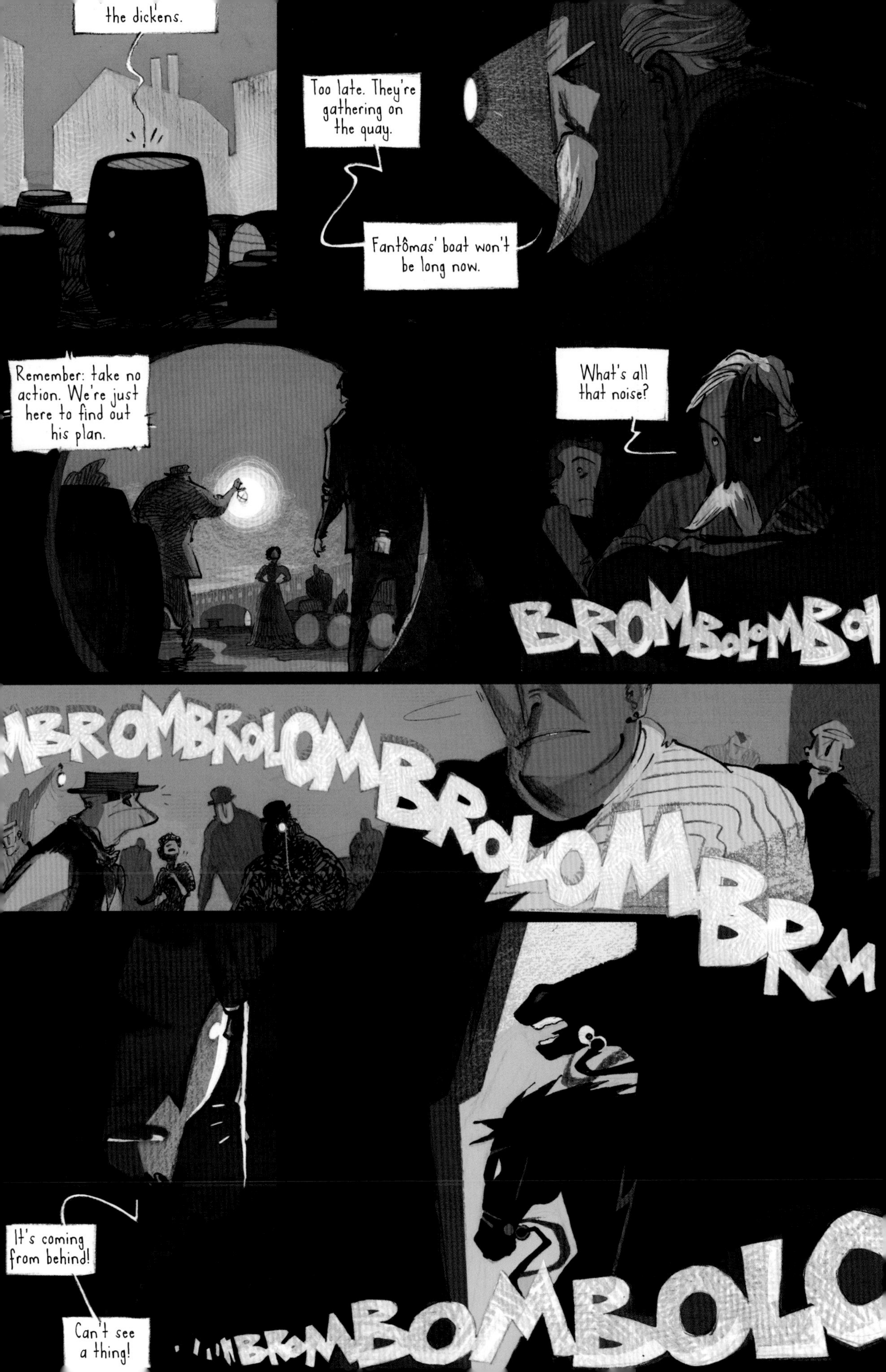
the dickens.
Too late. They're gathering on the quay.
Fantômas' boat won't be long now.
Remember: take no action. We're just here to find out his plan.
What's all that noise?
BROMBOLOMBO
MBROMBROLOMBROLOMBRM
It's coming from behind!
Can't see a thing!
BROMBOMBOLO

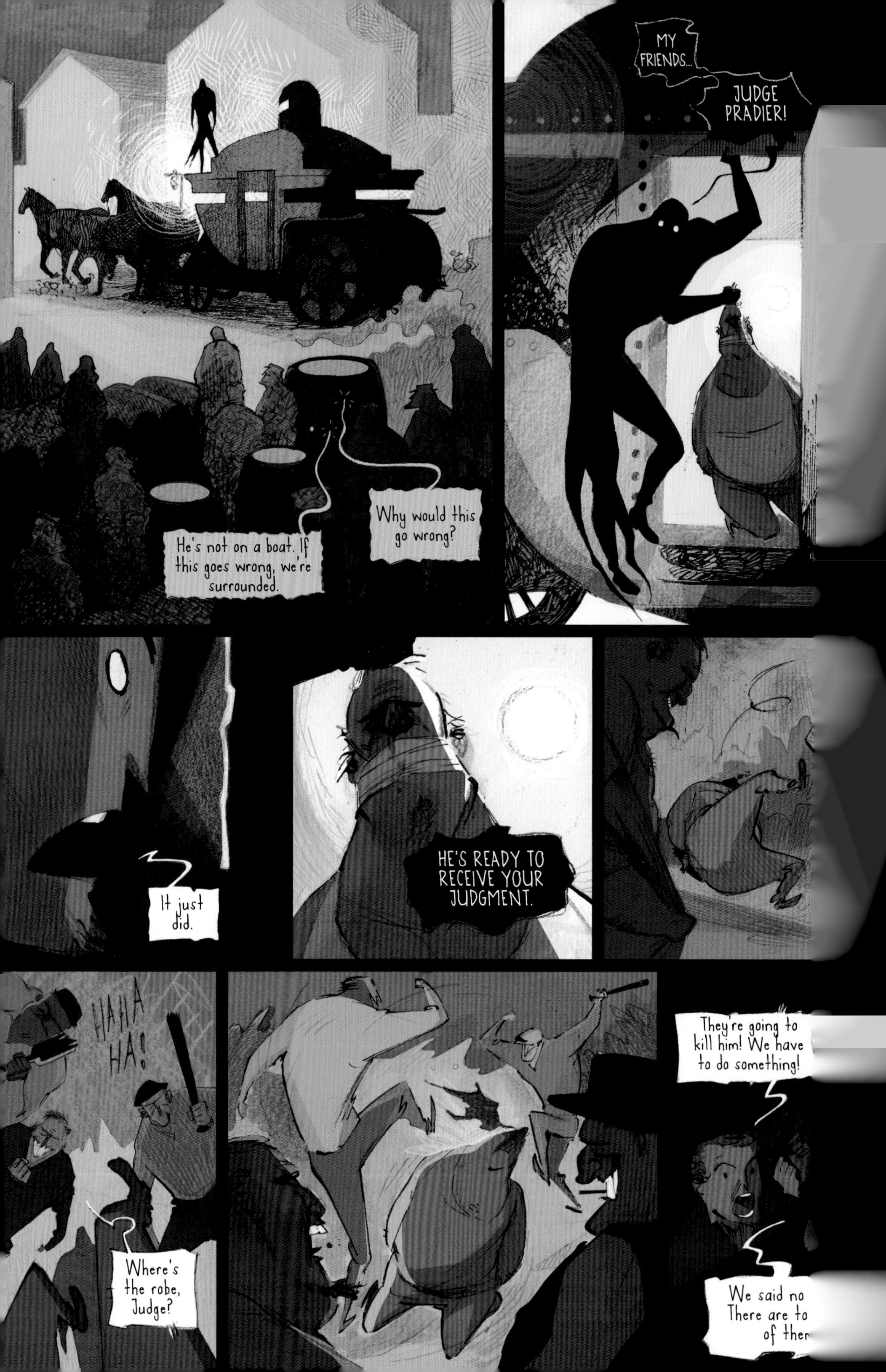

He's not on a boat. If this goes wrong, we're surrounded.
Why would this go wrong?
MY FRIENDS...
JUDGE PRADIER!
It just did.
HE'S READY TO RECEIVE YOUR JUDGMENT.
HA HA HA!
Where's the robe, Judge?
They're going to kill him! We have to do something!
We said no
There are to
of ther

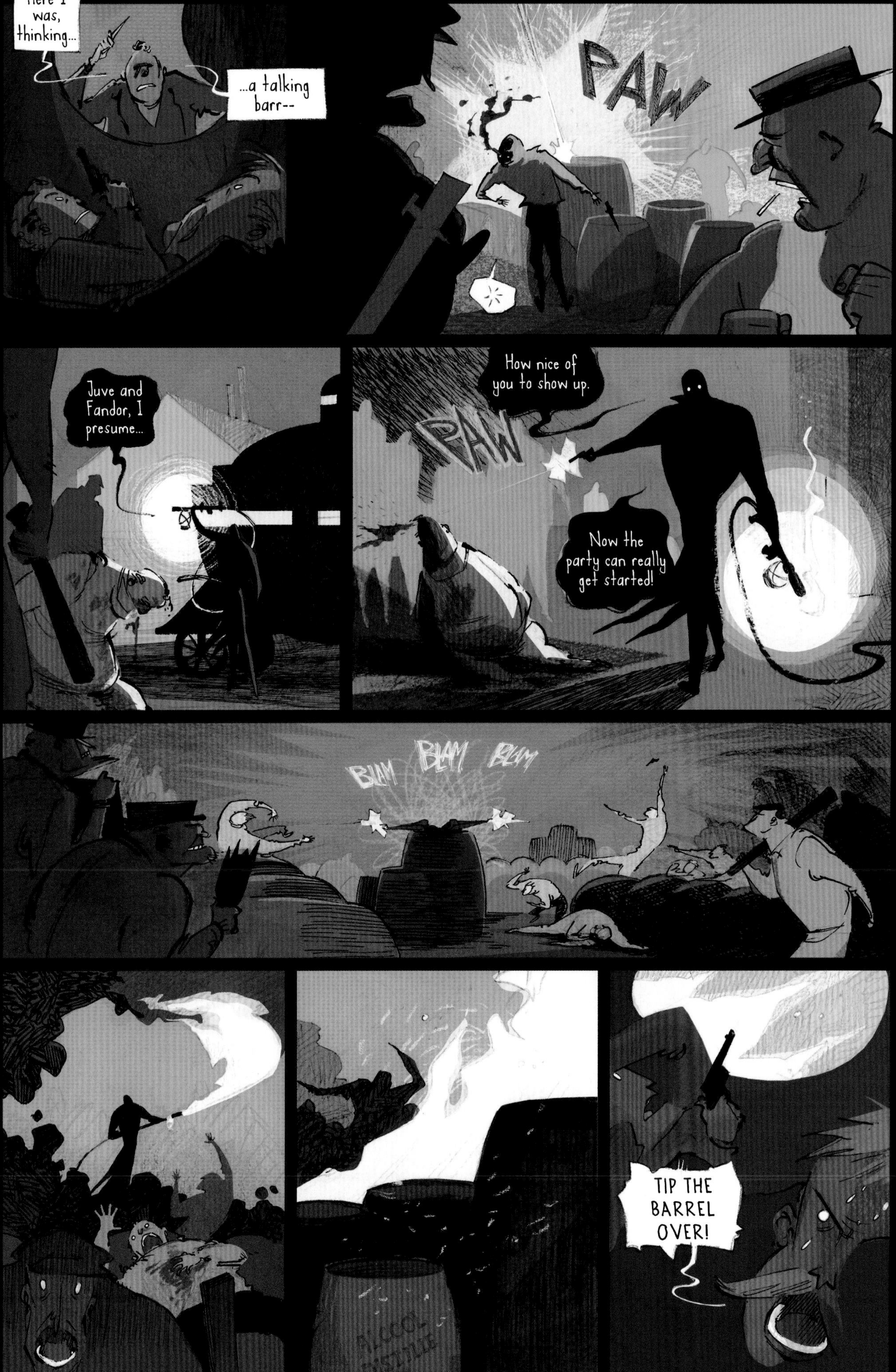
Here I was, thinking...
...a talking barr--
PAW
Juve and Fandor, I presume...
How nice of you to show up.
PAW
Now the party can really get started!
BLAM BLAM BLAM
TIP THE BARREL OVER!

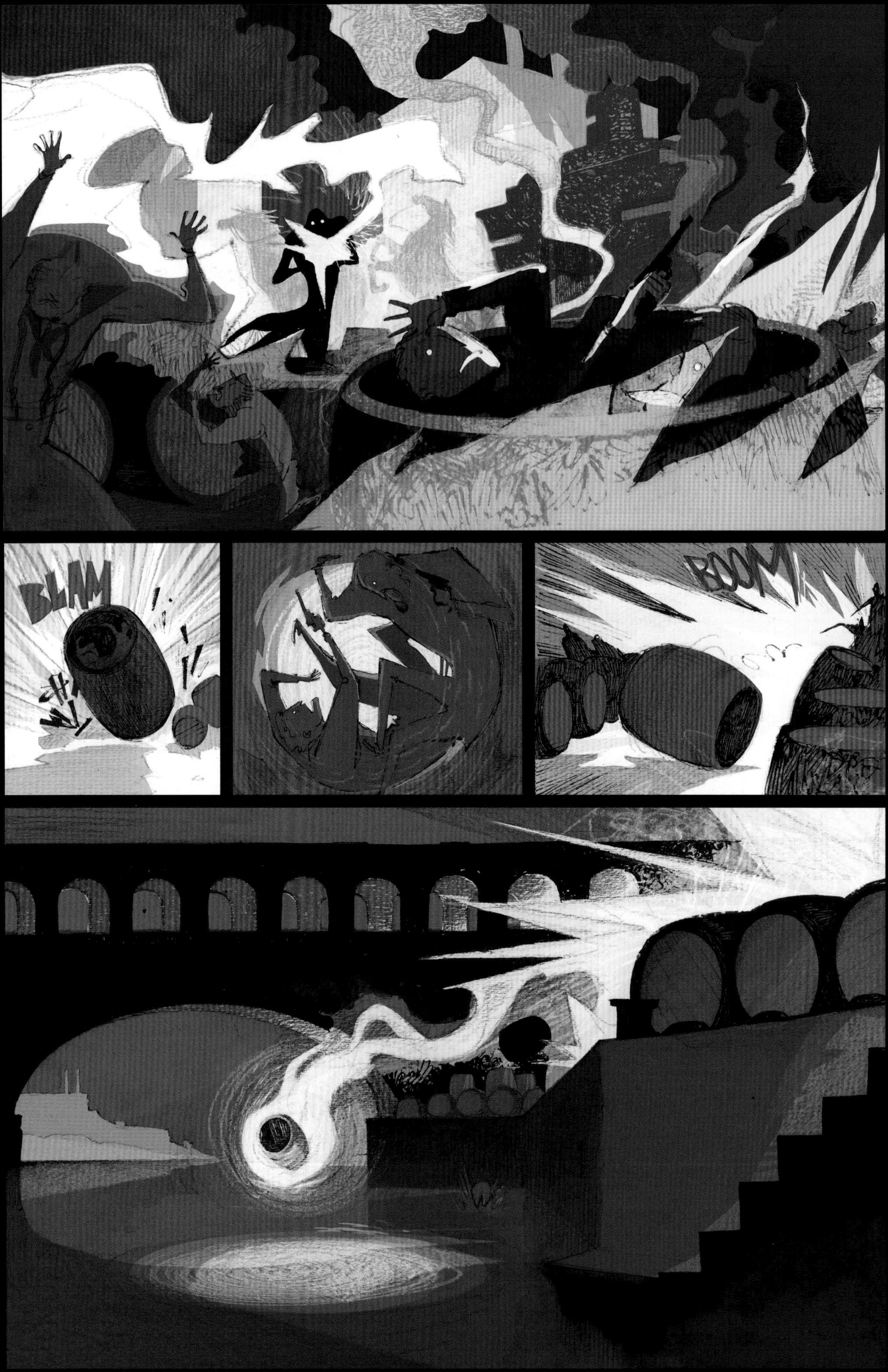
BLAM
BOOM

# BOOK II

## ALL THE GOLD IN PARIS

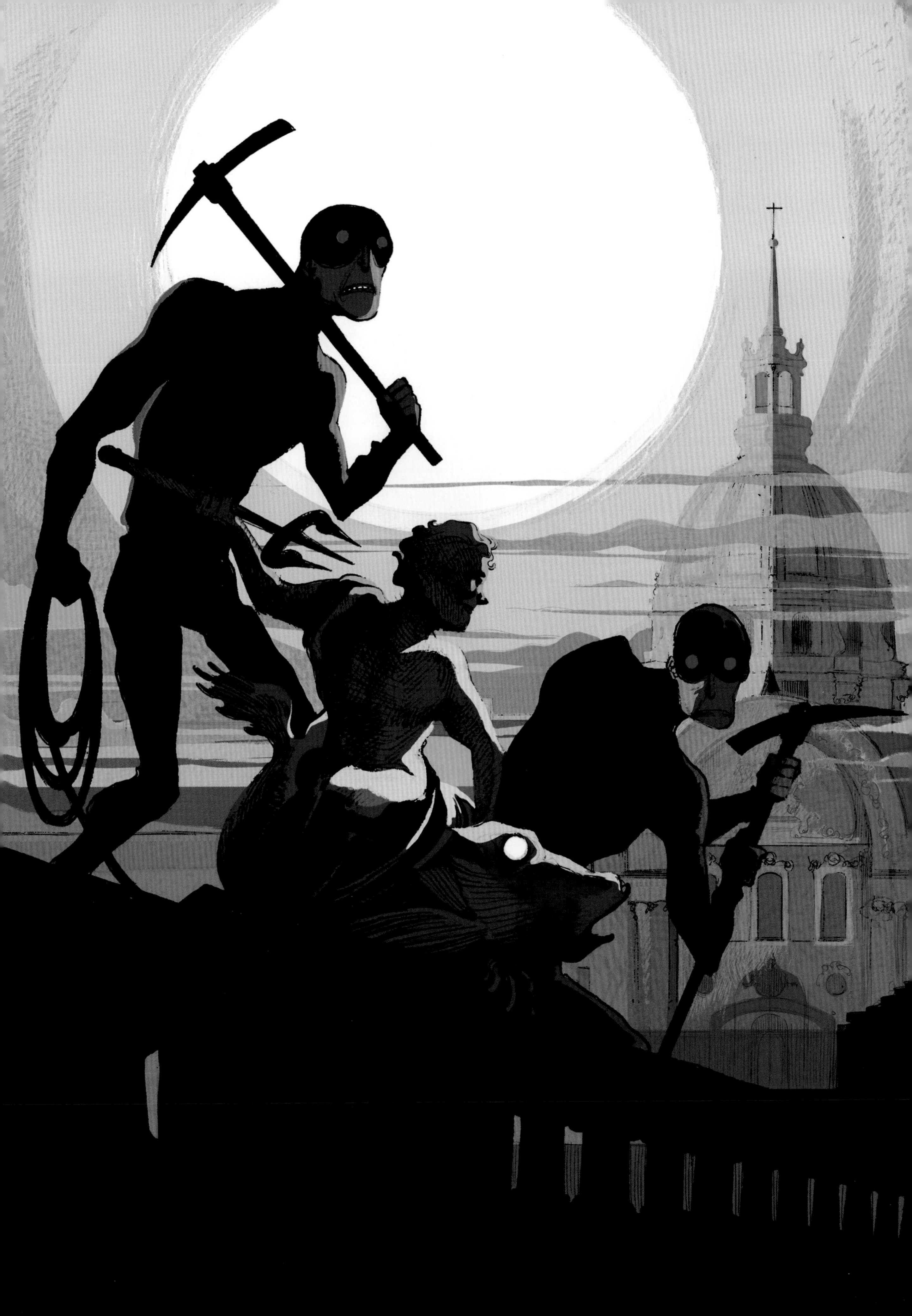

# ALL THE GOLD IN PARIS

In which
a few veterans return to active duty,
a letter arrives from the far corners of the world,
witnesses are urged to keep their silence,
and crime does not seem to pay so badly after all.

Tuesday, September 5, 1911

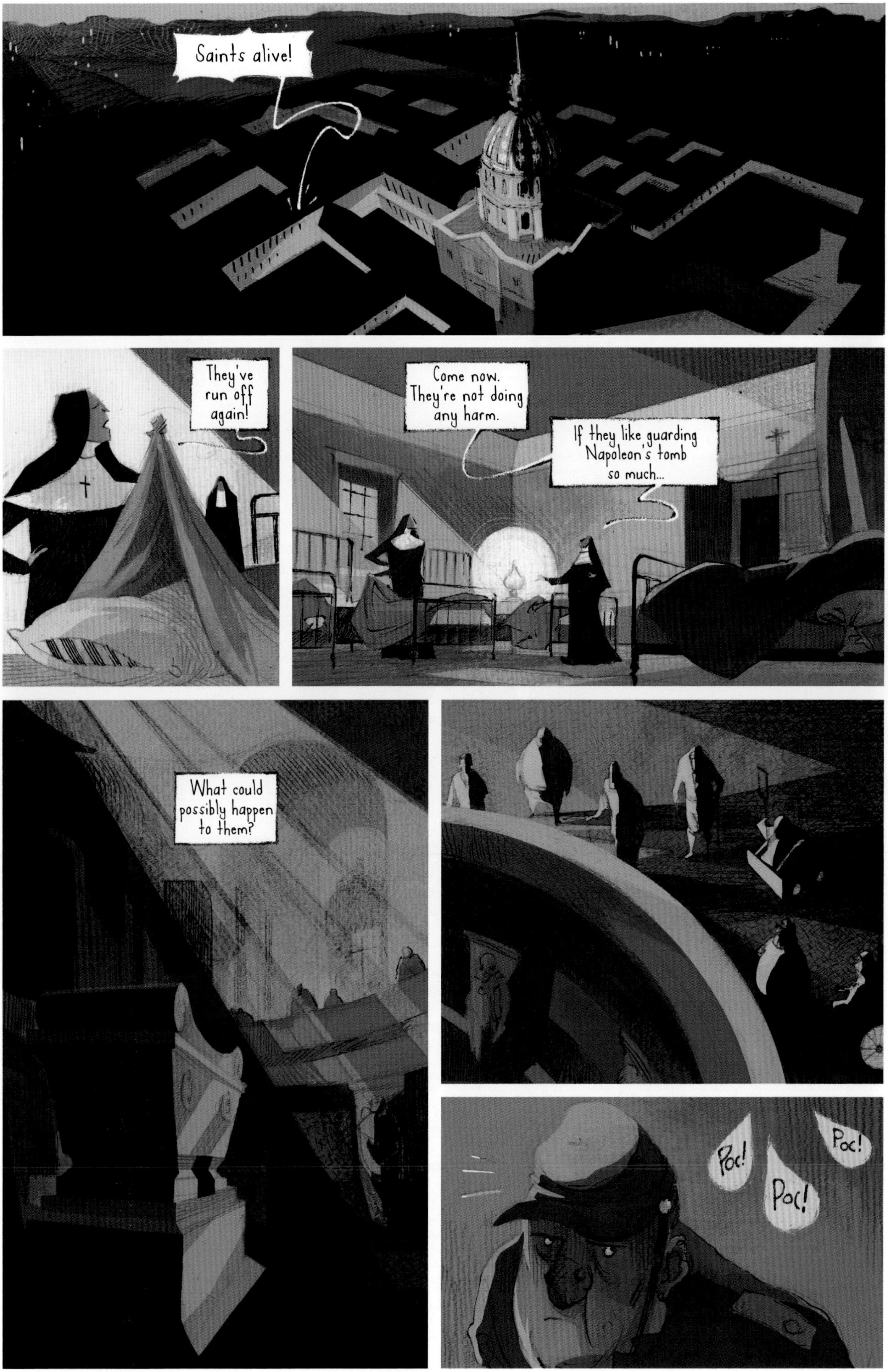
Saints alive!
They've run off again!
Come now. They're not doing any harm.
If they like guarding Napoleon's tomb so much...
What could possibly happen to them?
Poc!
Poc!
Poc!

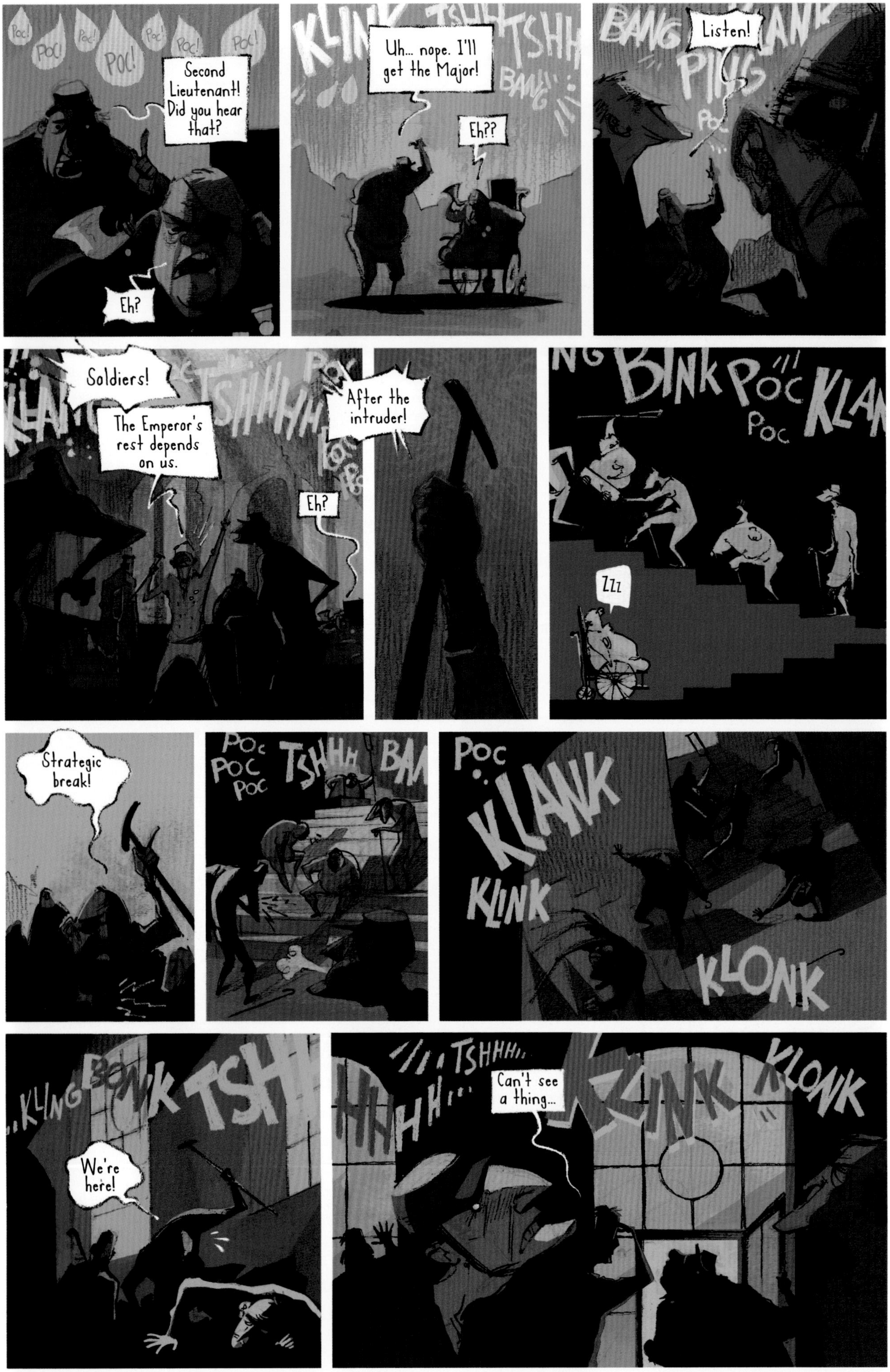
Poc! POC! Poc! POC! Poc! Poc! Poc!
Second Lieutenant! Did you hear that?
Eh?
KLINK TSHHH TSHH BANG
Uh... nope. I'll get the Major!
Eh??
BANG KLANK PING Poc
Listen!
KLANG TSHHHH POC
Soldiers!
The Emperor's rest depends on us.
Eh?
After the intruder!
BINK POC Poc KLAN
Zzz
Strategic break!
POC POC POC TSHHH BA
POC KLANK KLINK KLONK
KLING BONK TSH
We're here!
TSHHH HHHH...
Can't see a thing...
KLINK KLONK

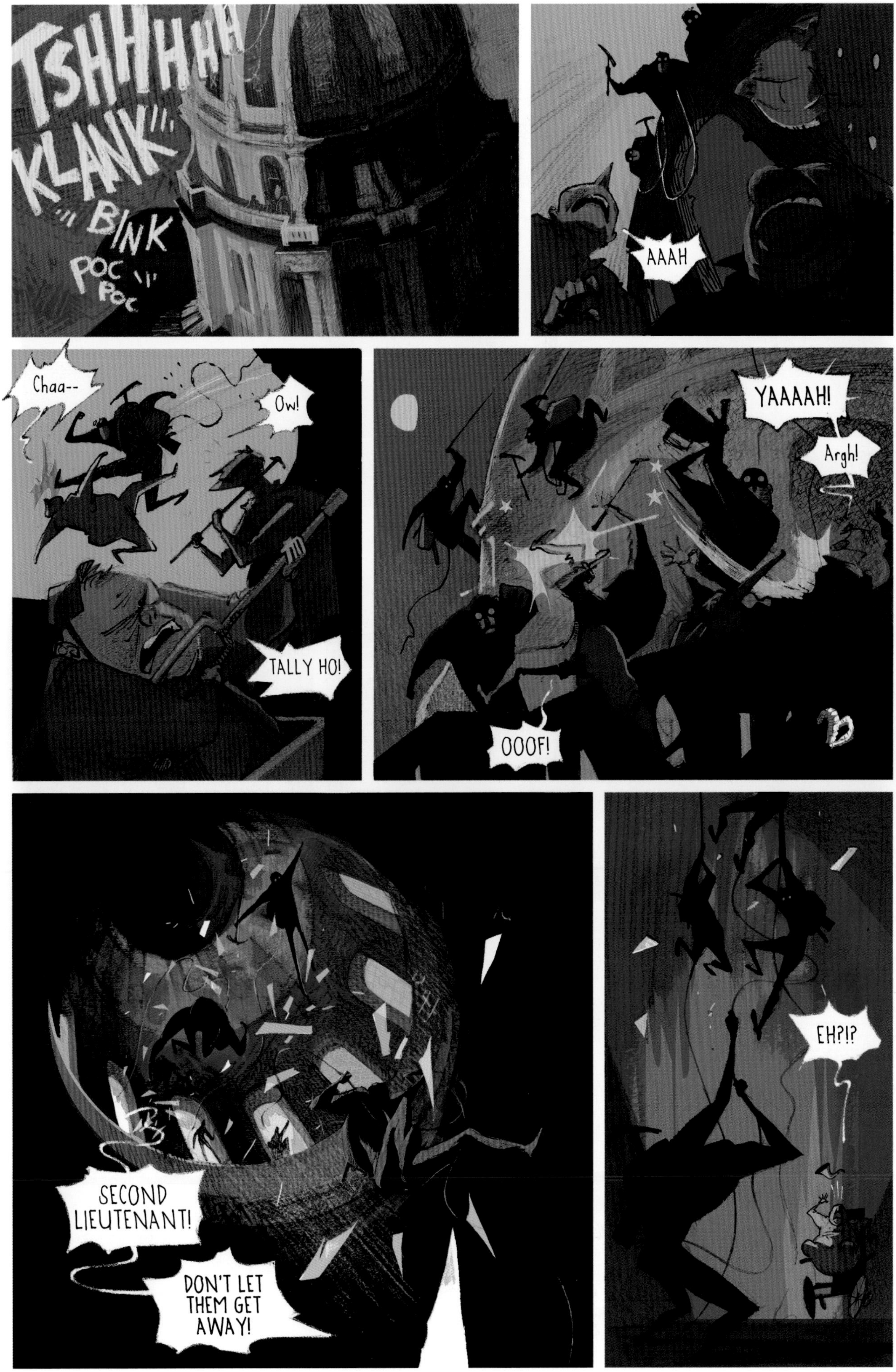
TSHHHHH
KLANK
BINK
POC
POC
AAAH
Chaa--
Ow!
TALLY HO!
YAAAAH!
Argh!
OOOF!
SECOND LIEUTENANT!
DON'T LET THEM GET AWAY!
EH?!?

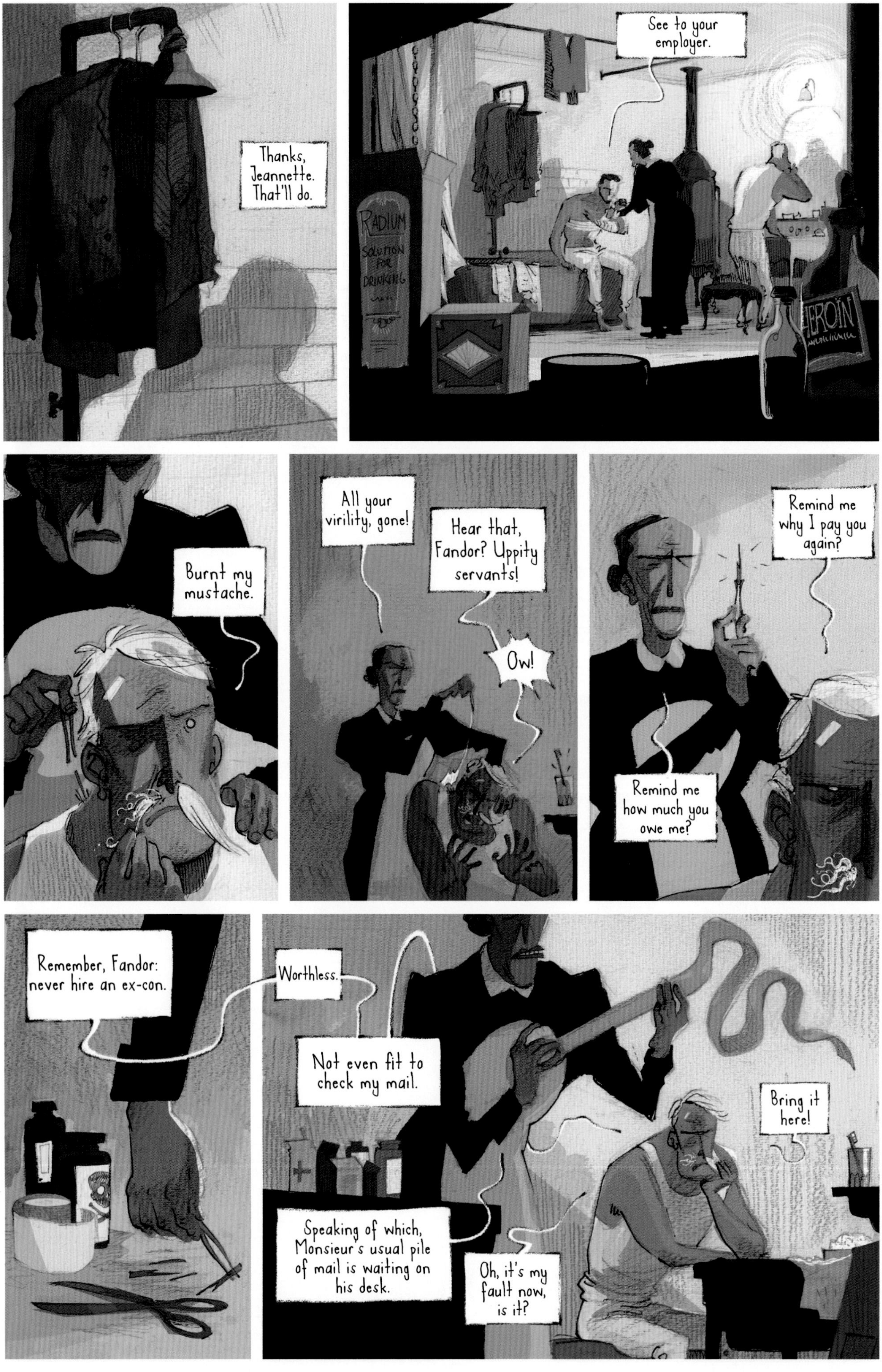
Thanks, Jeannette. That'll do.
See to your employer.
RADIUM
SOLUTION FOR DRINKING
HEROÏN
Burnt my mustache.
All your virility, gone!
Hear that, Fandor? Uppity servants!
Ow!
Remind me why I pay you again?
Remind me how much you owe me?
Remember, Fandor: never hire an ex-con.
Worthless.
Not even fit to check my mail.
Speaking of which, Monsieur's usual pile of mail is waiting on his desk.
Oh, it's my fault now, is it?
Bring it here!

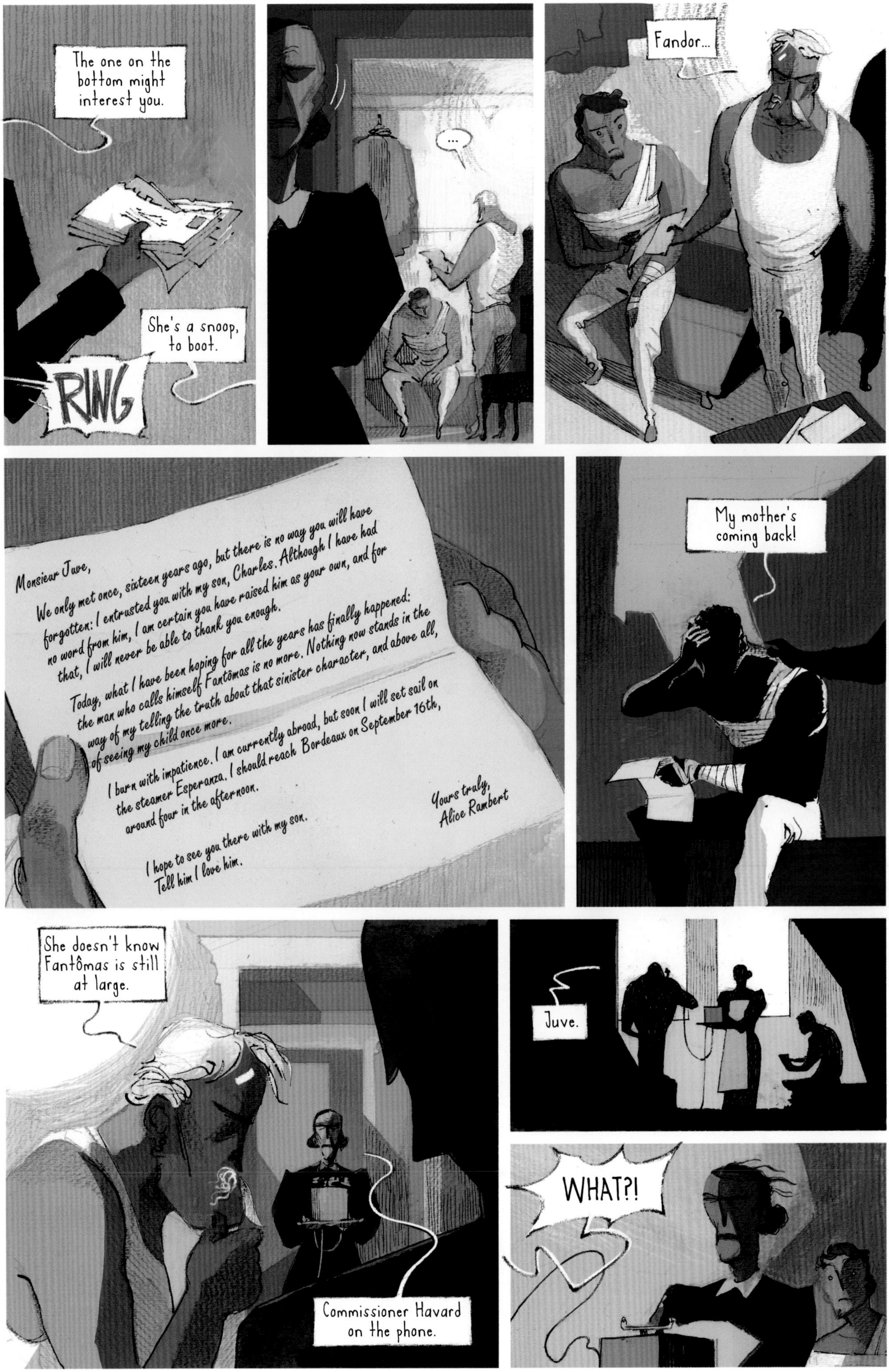
The one on the bottom might interest you.
She's a snoop, to boot.
RING
...
Fandor...
Monsieur Juve,
We only met once, sixteen years ago, but there is no way you will have forgotten: I entrusted you with my son, Charles. Although I have had no word from him, I am certain you have raised him as your own, and for that, I will never be able to thank you enough.
Today, what I have been hoping for all the years has finally happened: the man who calls himself Fantômas is no more. Nothing now stands in the way of my telling the truth about that sinister character, and above all, of seeing my child once more.
I burn with impatience. I am currently abroad, but soon I will set sail on the steamer Esperanza. I should reach Bordeaux on September 16th, around four in the afternoon.
I hope to see you there with my son.
Tell him I love him.
Yours truly,
Alice Rambert
My mother's coming back!
She doesn't know Fantômas is still at large.
Commissioner Havard on the phone.
Juve.
WHAT?!

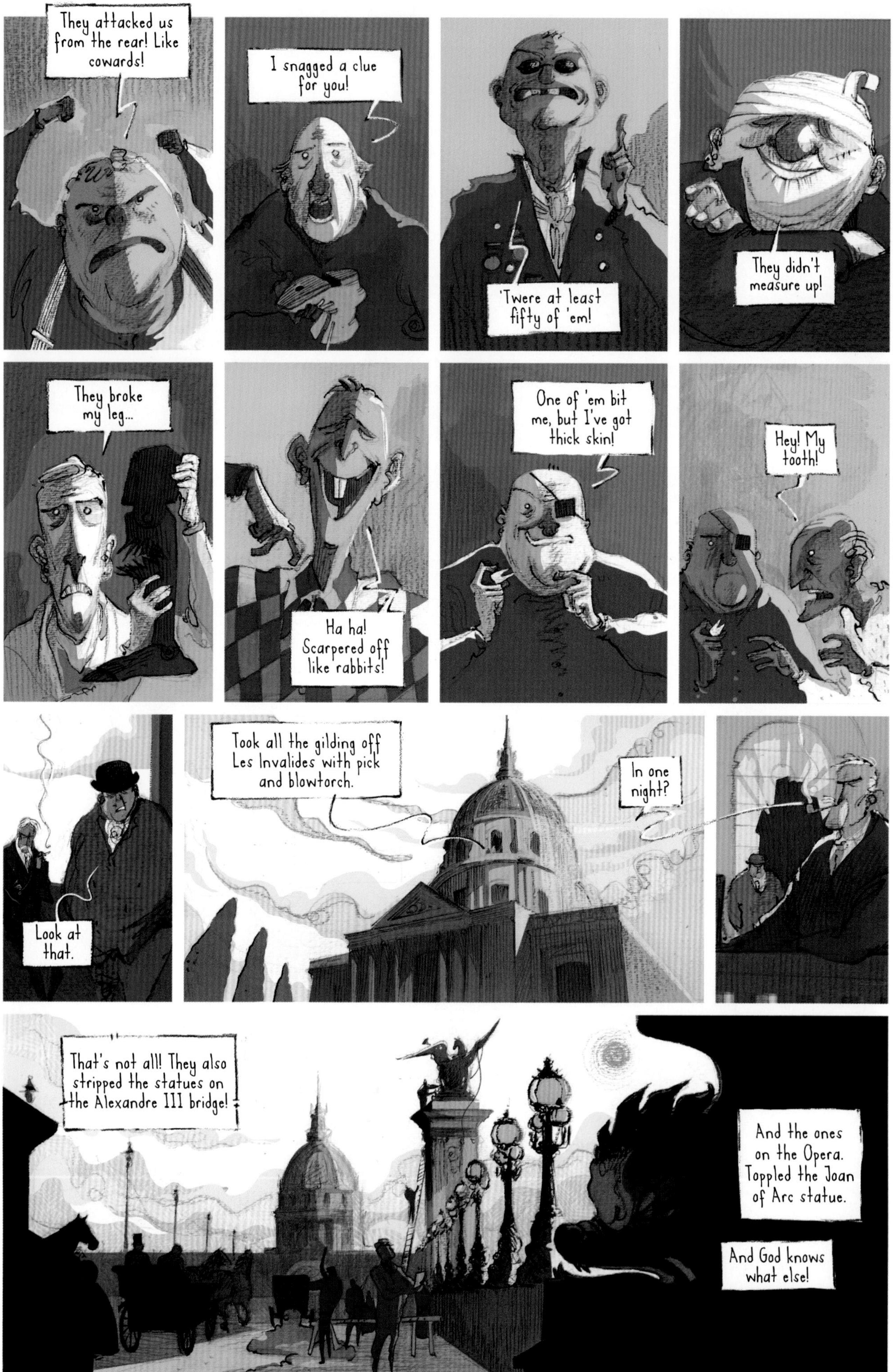
They attacked us from the rear! Like cowards!
I snagged a clue for you!
'Twere at least fifty of 'em!
They didn't measure up!
They broke my leg...
Ha ha! Scarpered off like rabbits!
One of 'em bit me, but I've got thick skin!
Hey! My tooth!
Look at that.
Took all the gilding off Les Invalides with pick and blowtorch.
In one night?
That's not all! They also stripped the statues on the Alexandre III bridge!
And the ones on the Opera. Toppled the Joan of Arc statue.
And God knows what else!

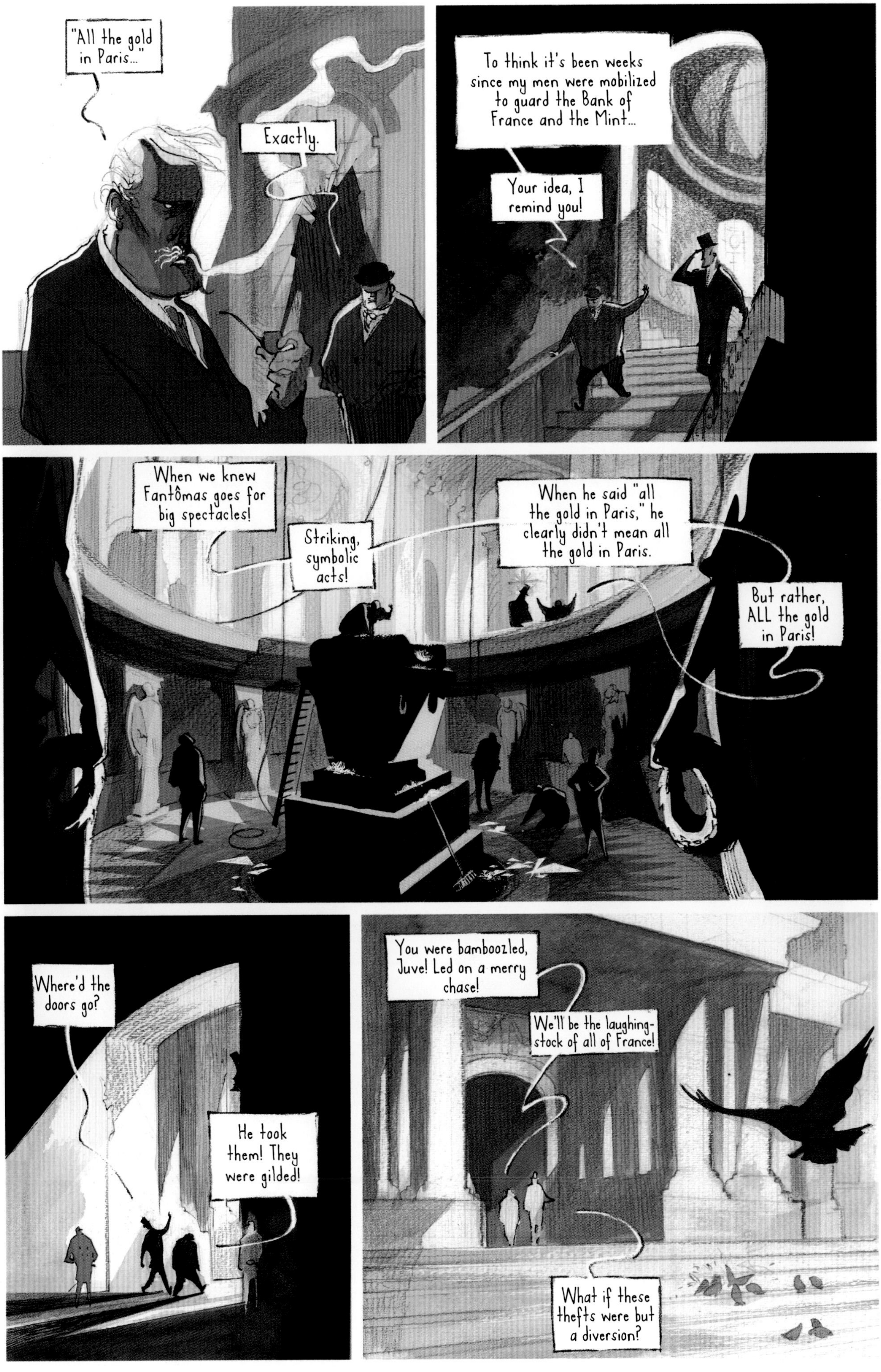
"All the gold in Paris..."
Exactly.
To think it's been weeks since my men were mobilized to guard the Bank of France and the Mint...
Your idea, I remind you!
When we knew Fantômas goes for big spectacles!
Striking, symbolic acts!
When he said "all the gold in Paris," he clearly didn't mean all the gold in Paris.
But rather, ALL the gold in Paris!
Where'd the doors go?
He took them! They were gilded!
You were bamboozled, Juve! Led on a merry chase!
We'll be the laughing-stock of all of France!
What if these thefts were but a diversion?

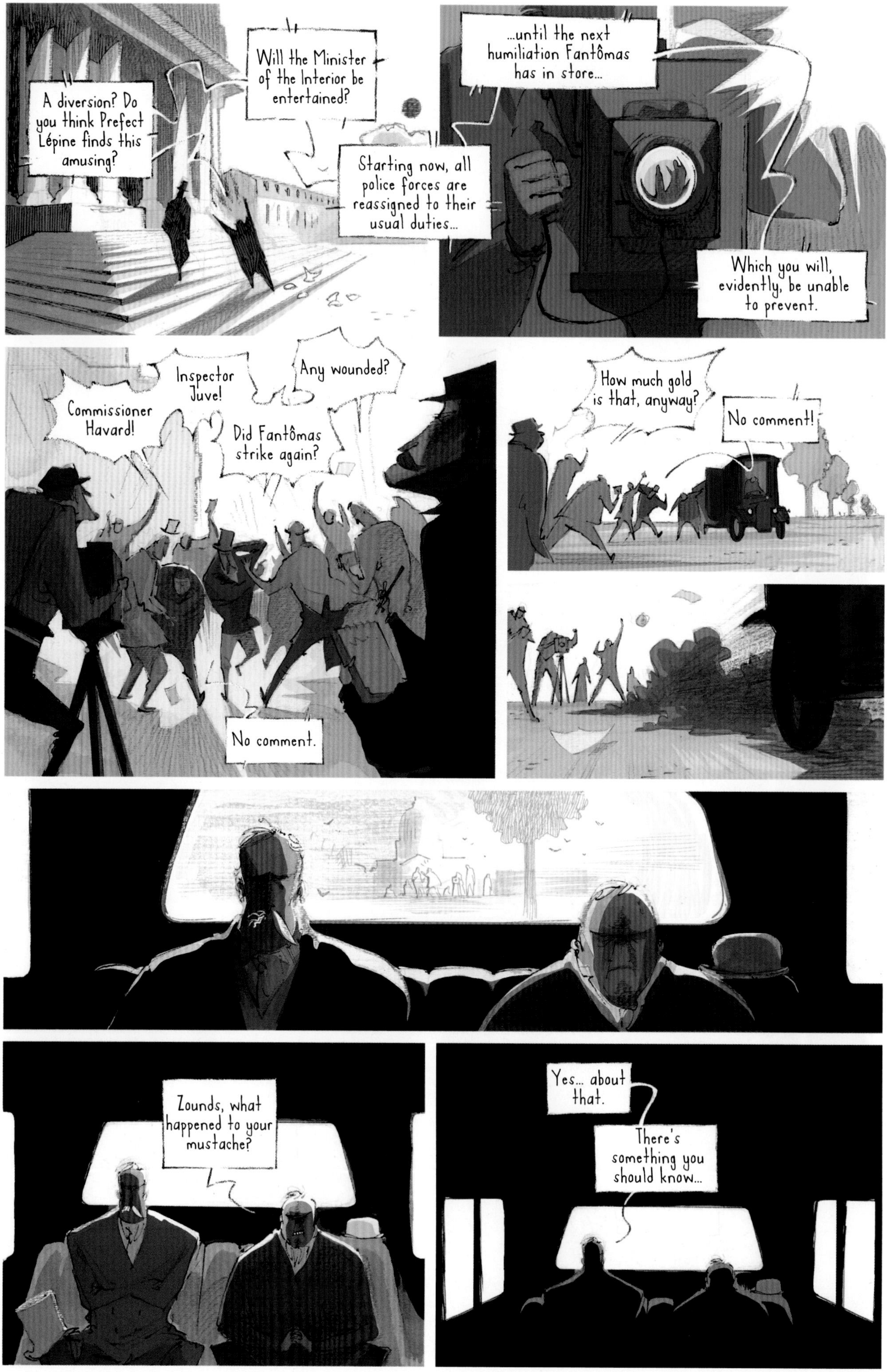
A diversion? Do you think Prefect Lépine finds this amusing?
Will the Minister of the Interior be entertained?
Starting now, all police forces are reassigned to their usual duties...
...until the next humiliation Fantômas has in store...
Which you will, evidently, be unable to prevent.
Commissioner Havard!
Inspector Juve!
Any wounded?
Did Fantômas strike again?
No comment.
How much gold is that, anyway?
No comment!
Zounds, what happened to your mustache?
Yes... about that.
There's something you should know...

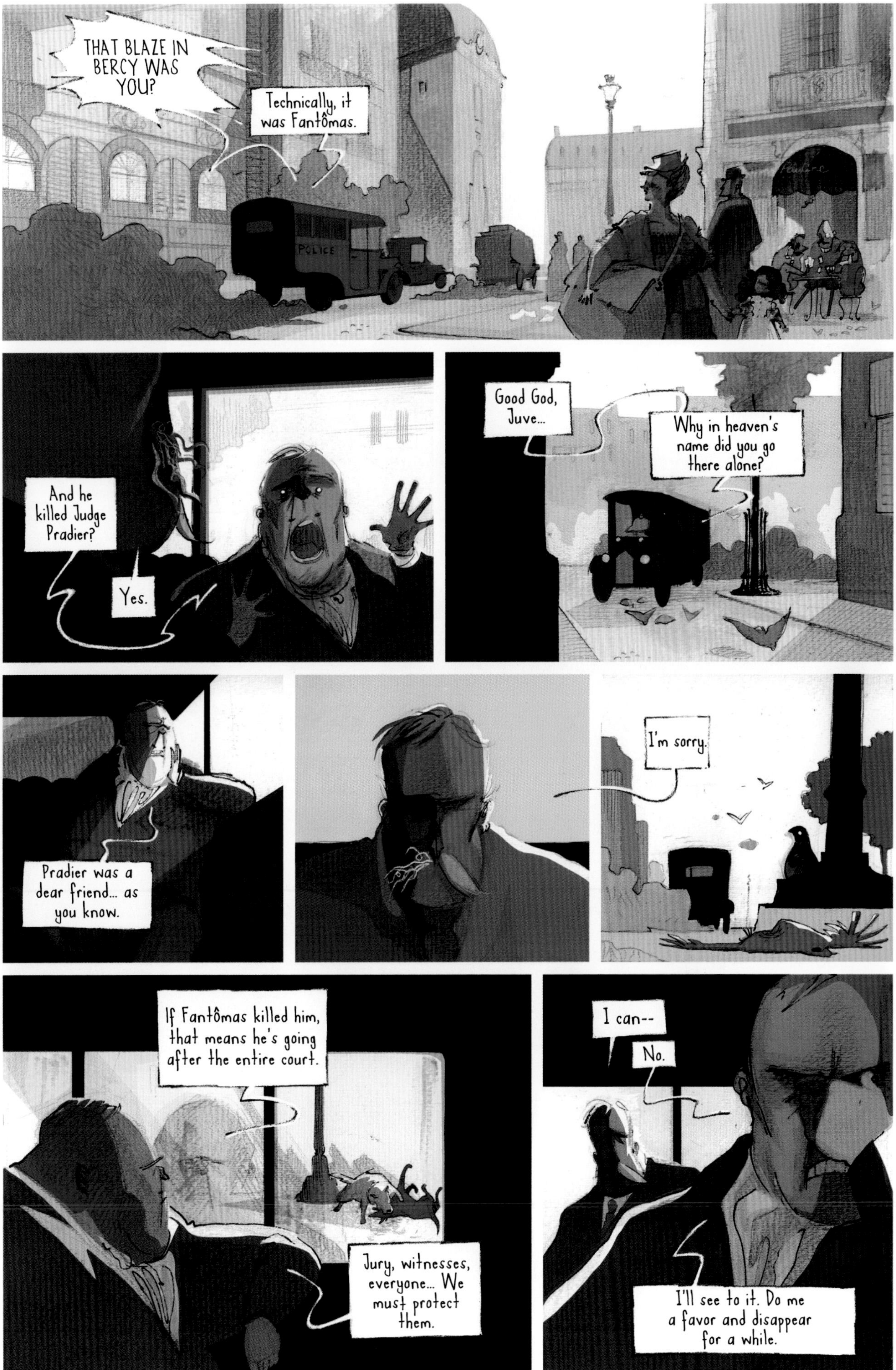
THAT BLAZE IN BERCY WAS YOU?
Technically, it was Fantômas.
POLICE
And he killed Judge Pradier?
Yes.
Good God, Juve...
Why in heaven's name did you go there alone?
Pradier was a dear friend... as you know.
I'm sorry.
If Fantômas killed him, that means he's going after the entire court.
Jury, witnesses, everyone... We must protect them.
I can--
No.
I'll see to it. Do me a favor and disappear for a while.

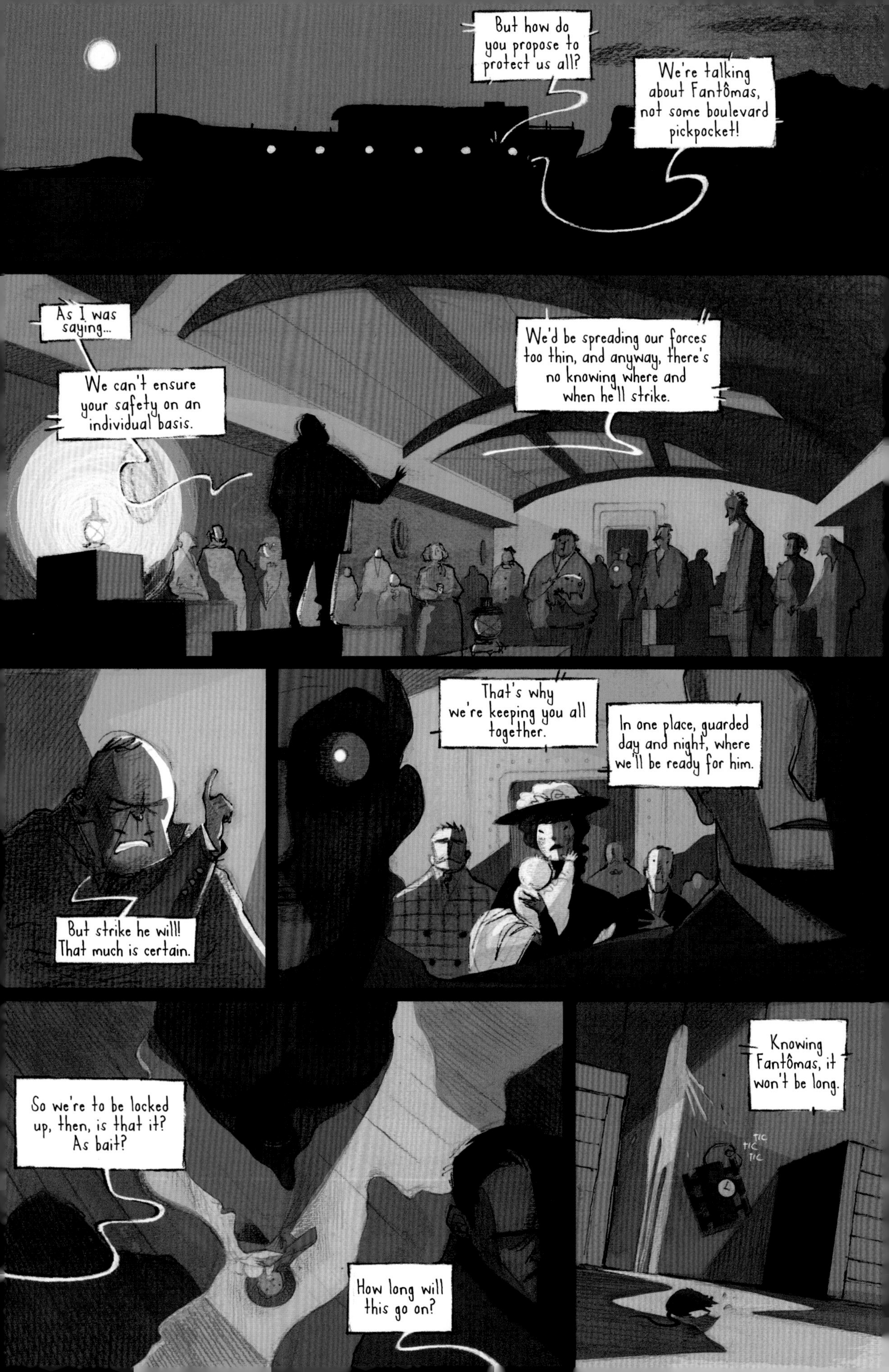
But how do you propose to protect us all?
We're talking about Fantômas, not some boulevard pickpocket!
As I was saying...
We can't ensure your safety on an individual basis.
We'd be spreading our forces too thin, and anyway, there's no knowing where and when he'll strike.
But strike he will! That much is certain.
That's why we're keeping you all together.
In one place, guarded day and night, where we'll be ready for him.
So we're to be locked up, then, is that it? As bait?
How long will this go on?
Knowing Fantômas, it won't be long.
TIC
TIC
TIC

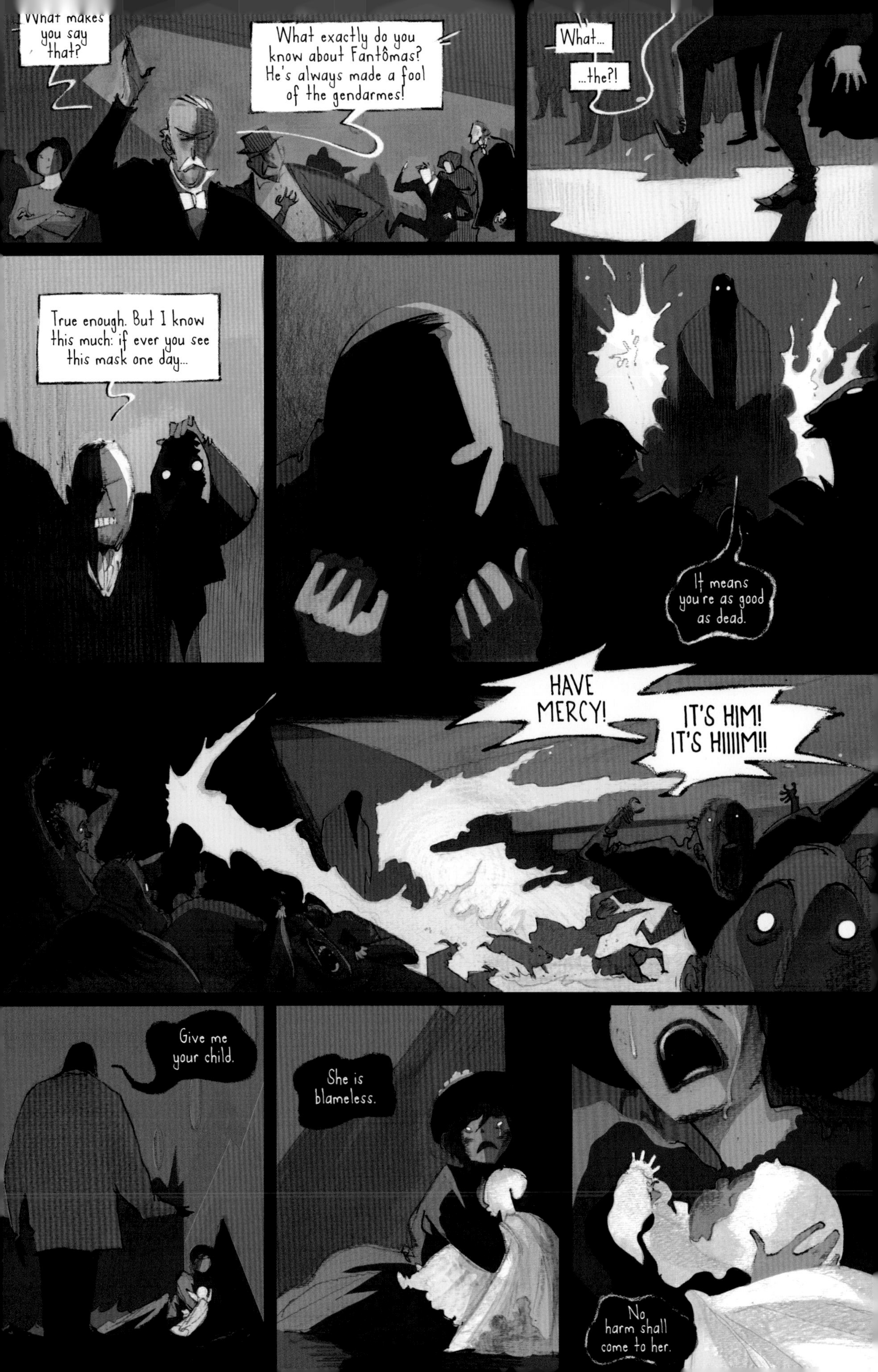
What makes you say that?
What exactly do you know about Fantômas? He's always made a fool of the gendarmes!
What...
...the?!
True enough. But I know this much: if ever you see this mask one day...
It means you're as good as dead.
HAVE MERCY!
IT'S HIM! IT'S HIIIIM!!
Give me your child.
She is blameless.
No harm shall come to her.

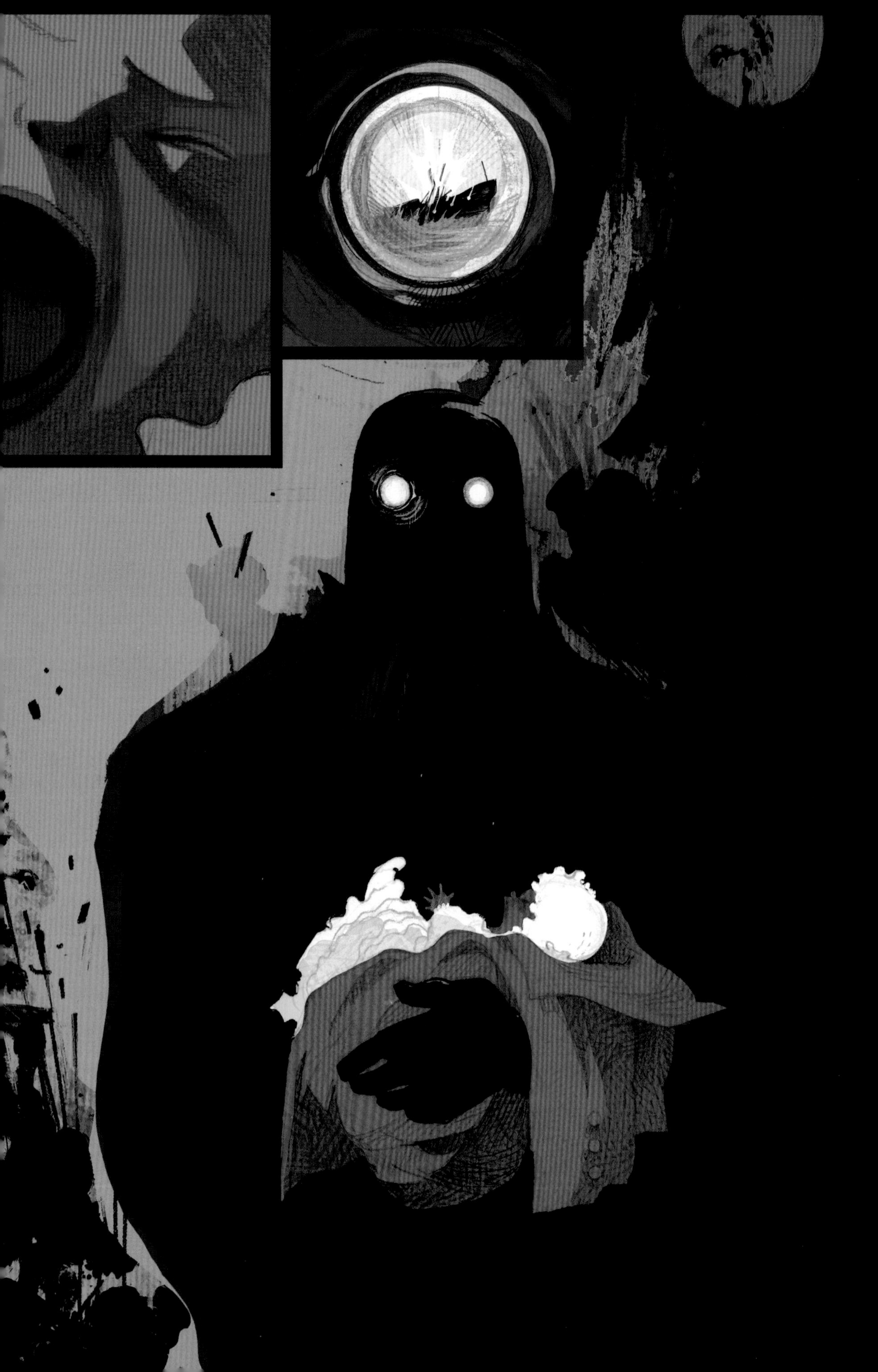

Saturday, September 9, 1911

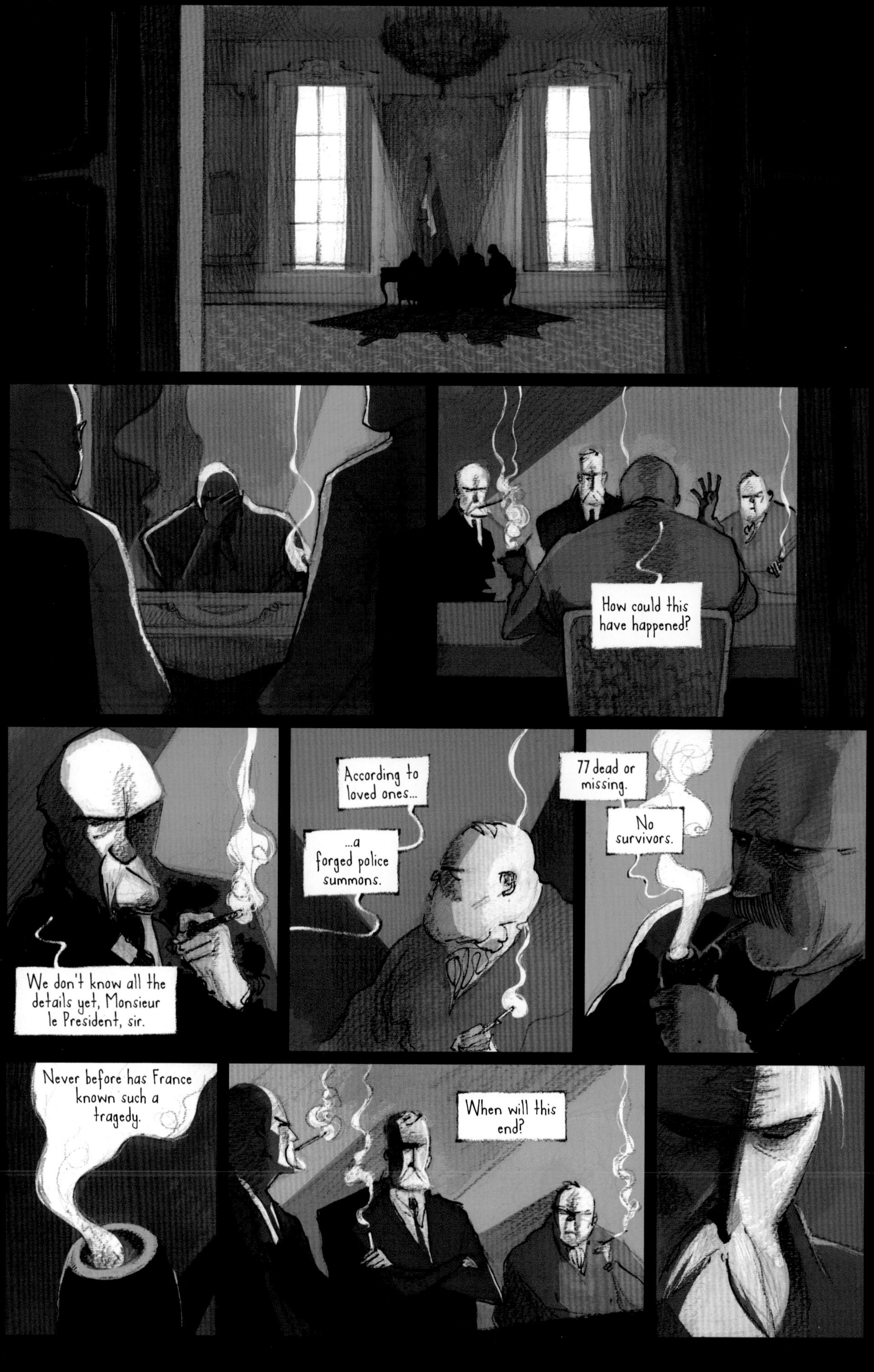
How could this have happened?
We don't know all the details yet, Monsieur le President, sir.
According to loved ones...
...a forged police summons.
77 dead or missing.
No survivors.
Never before has France known such a tragedy.
When will this end?

Sunday, September 10, 1911

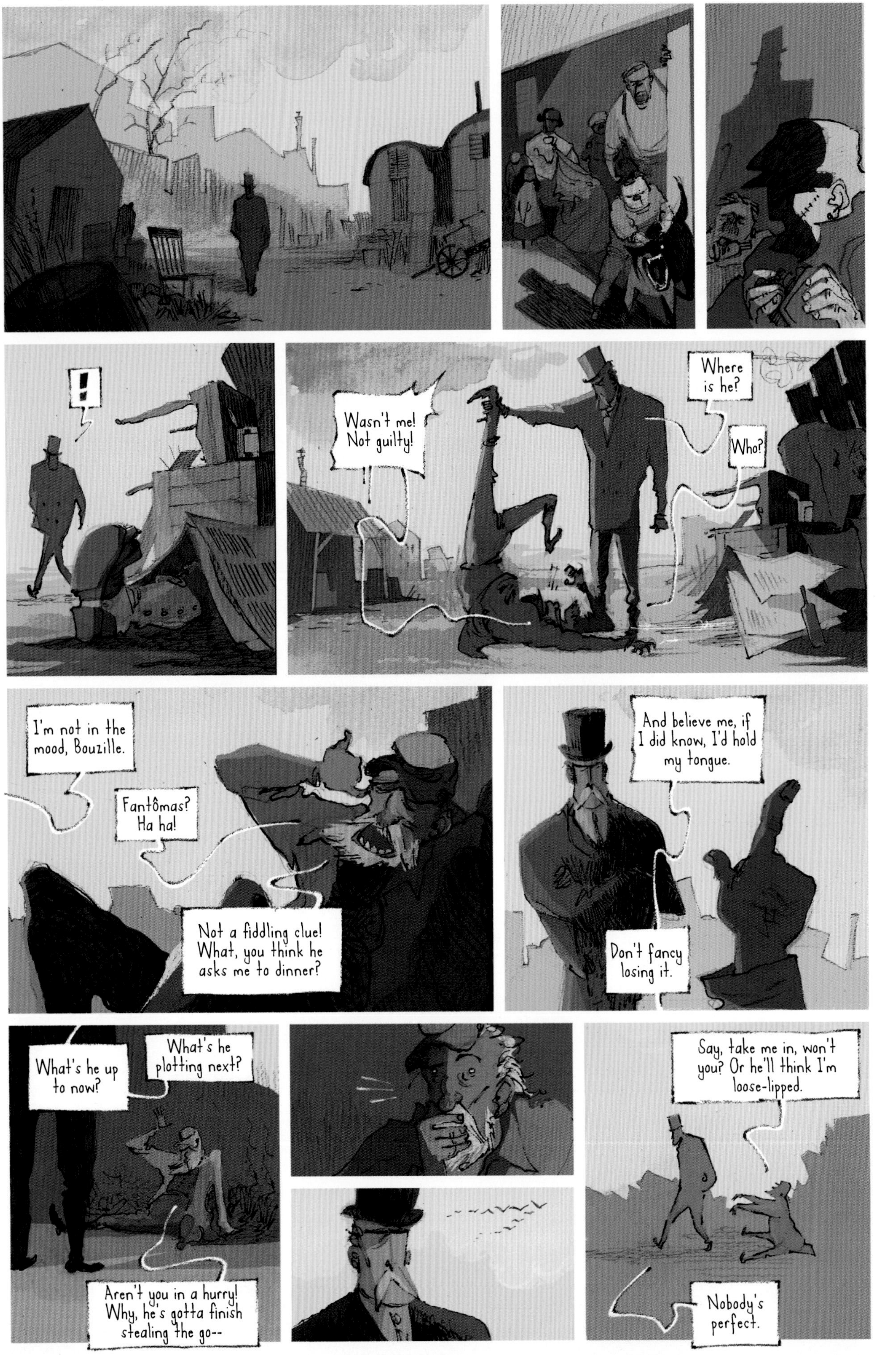
!
Wasn't me! Not guilty!
Where is he?
Who?
I'm not in the mood, Bouzille.
Fantômas? Ha ha!
Not a fiddling clue! What, you think he asks me to dinner?
And believe me, if I did know, I'd hold my tongue.
Don't fancy losing it.
What's he up to now?
What's he plotting next?
Aren't you in a hurry! Why, he's gotta finish stealing the go--
Say, take me in, won't you? Or he'll think I'm loose-lipped.
Nobody's perfect.

Monday, September 11, 1911

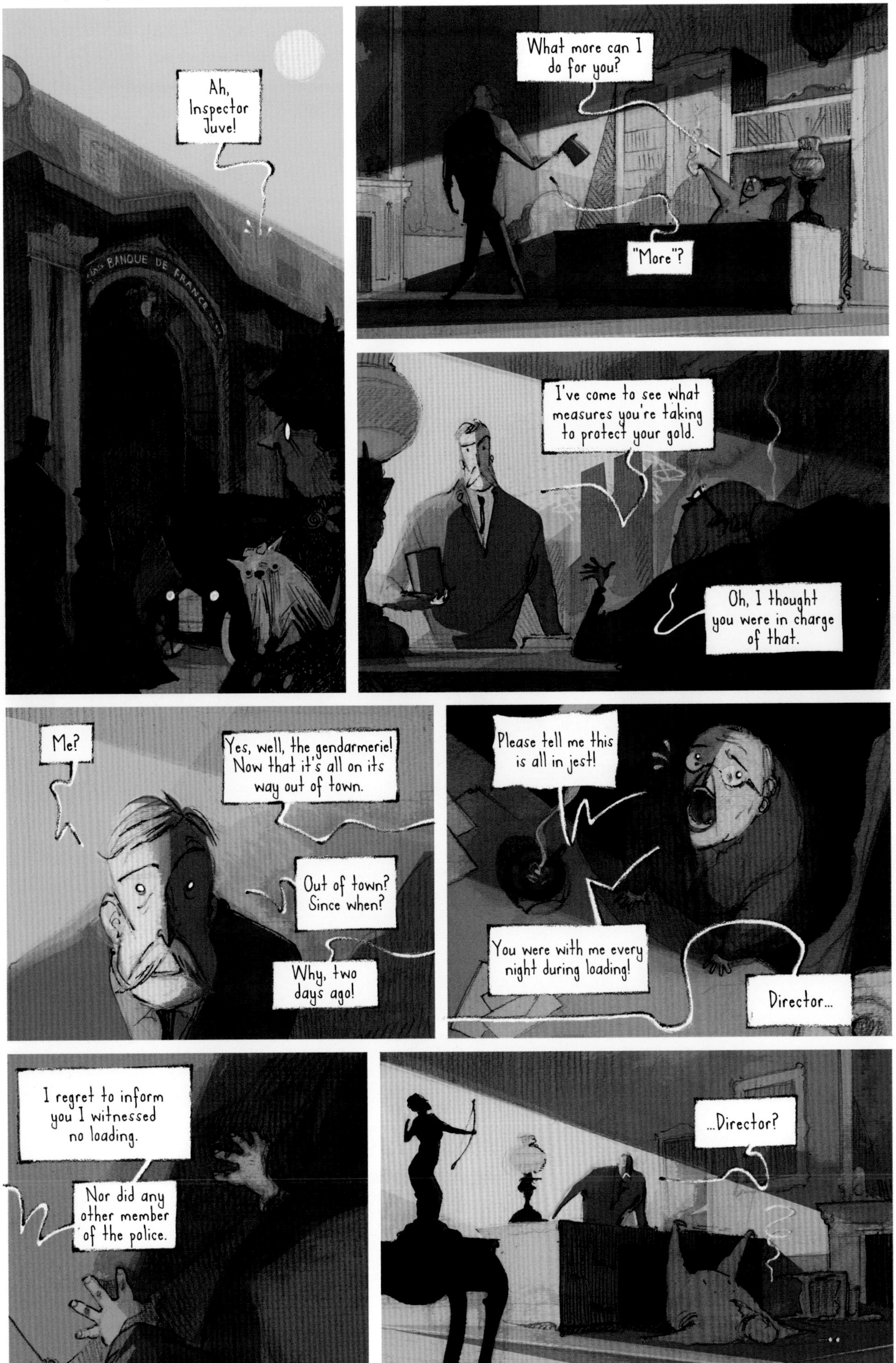
BANQUE DE FRANCE
Ah, Inspector Juve!
What more can I do for you?
"More"?
I've come to see what measures you're taking to protect your gold.
Oh, I thought you were in charge of that.
Me?
Yes, well, the gendarmerie! Now that it's all on its way out of town.
Out of town? Since when?
Why, two days ago!
Please tell me this is all in jest!
You were with me every night during loading!
Director...
I regret to inform you I witnessed no loading.
Nor did any other member of the police.
...Director?

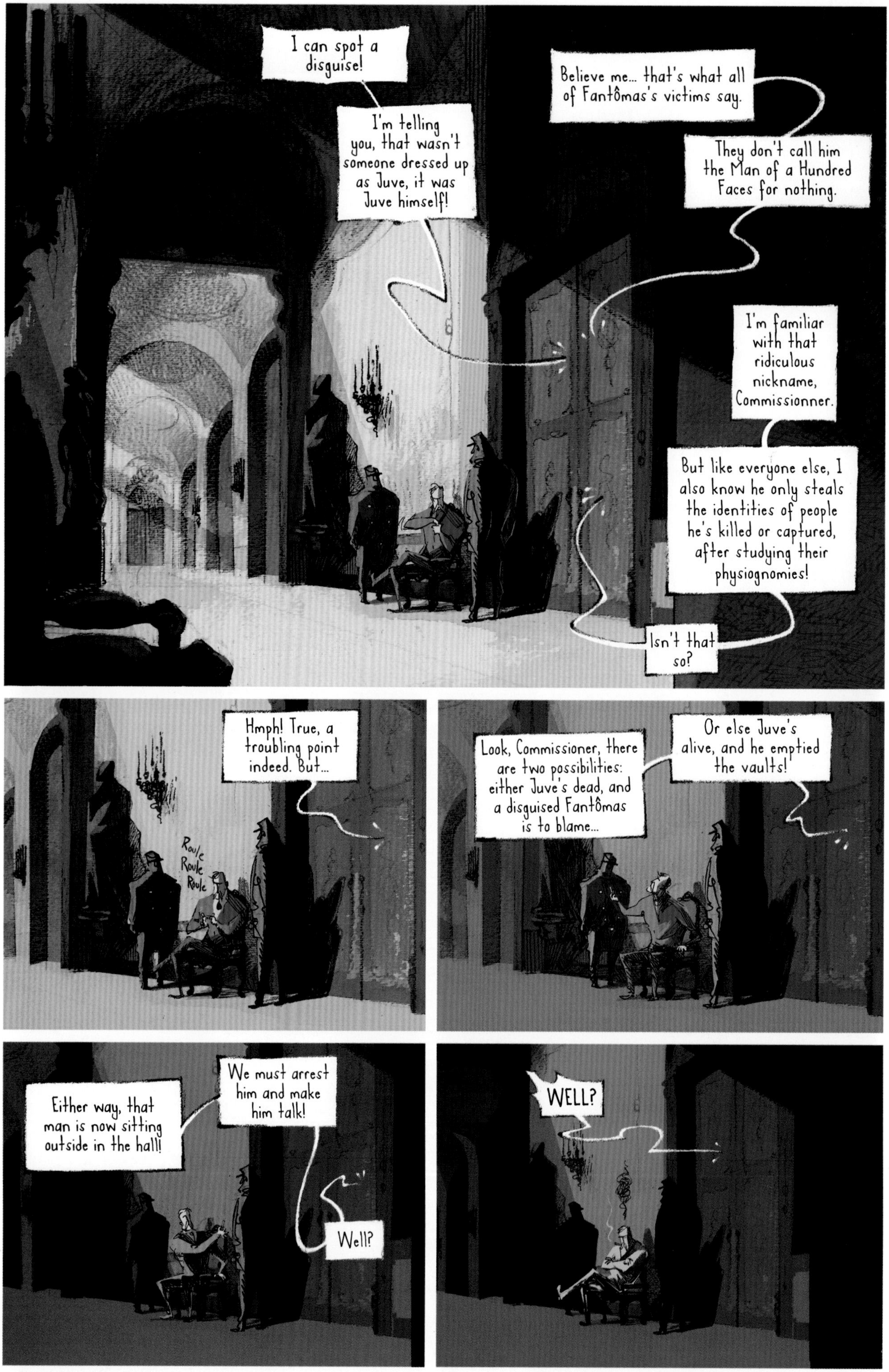
I can spot a disguise!
I'm telling you, that wasn't someone dressed up as Juve, it was Juve himself!
Believe me... that's what all of Fantômas's victims say.
They don't call him the Man of a Hundred Faces for nothing.
I'm familiar with that ridiculous nickname, Commissionner.
But like everyone else, I also know he only steals the identities of people he's killed or captured, after studying their physiognomies!
Isn't that so?
Hmph! True, a troubling point indeed. But...
Roule Roule Roule
Look, Commissioner, there are two possibilities: either Juve's dead, and a disguised Fantômas is to blame...
Or else Juve's alive, and he emptied the vaults!
Either way, that man is now sitting outside in the hall!
We must arrest him and make him talk!
Well?
WELL?

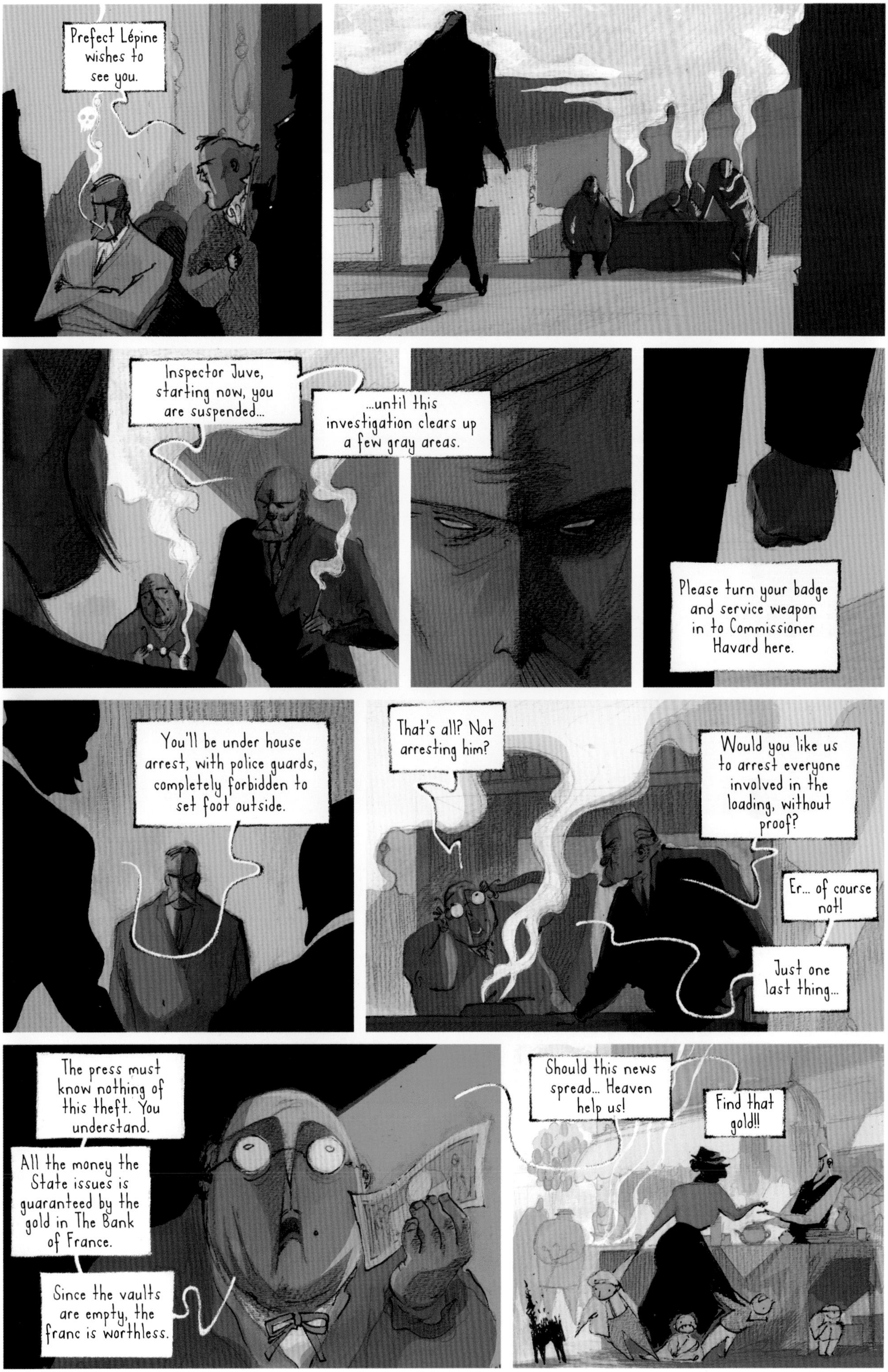

Prefect Lépine wishes to see you.
Inspector Juve, starting now, you are suspended...
...until this investigation clears up a few gray areas.
Please turn your badge and service weapon in to Commissioner Havard here.
You'll be under house arrest, with police guards, completely forbidden to set foot outside.
That's all? Not arresting him?
Would you like us to arrest everyone involved in the loading, without proof?
Er... of course not!
Just one last thing...
The press must know nothing of this theft. You understand.
All the money the State issues is guaranteed by the gold in The Bank of France.
Since the vaults are empty, the franc is worthless.
Should this news spread... Heaven help us!
Find that gold!!

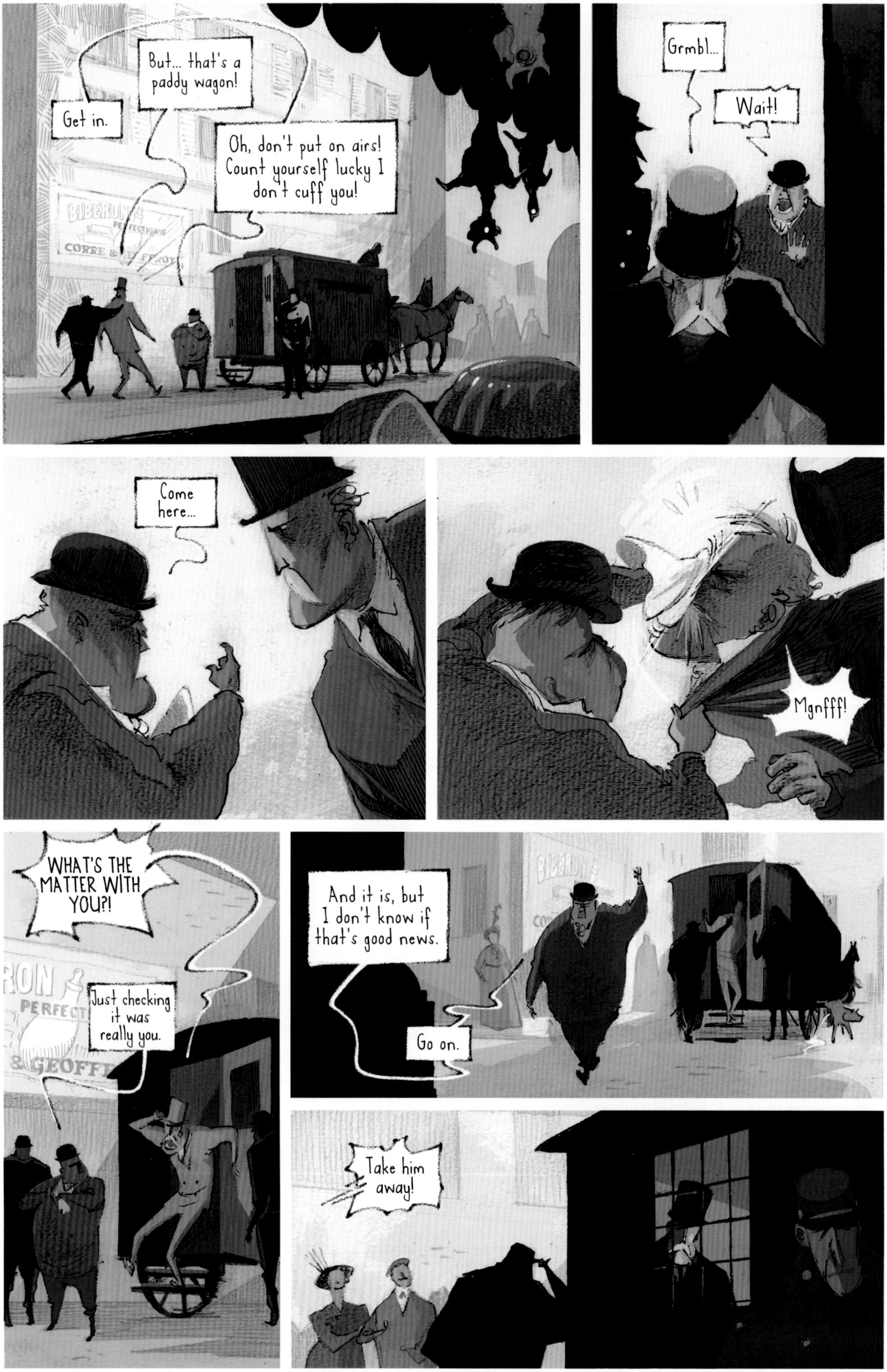

Get in.
But... that's a paddy wagon!
Oh, don't put on airs! Count yourself lucky I don't cuff you!
BIBERONS PERFECTIONNÉ CORRE & GEOFFROY
Grmbl...
Wait!
Come here...
Mgnfff!
WHAT'S THE MATTER WITH YOU?!
Just checking it was really you.
And it is, but I don't know if that's good news.
Go on.
Take him away!

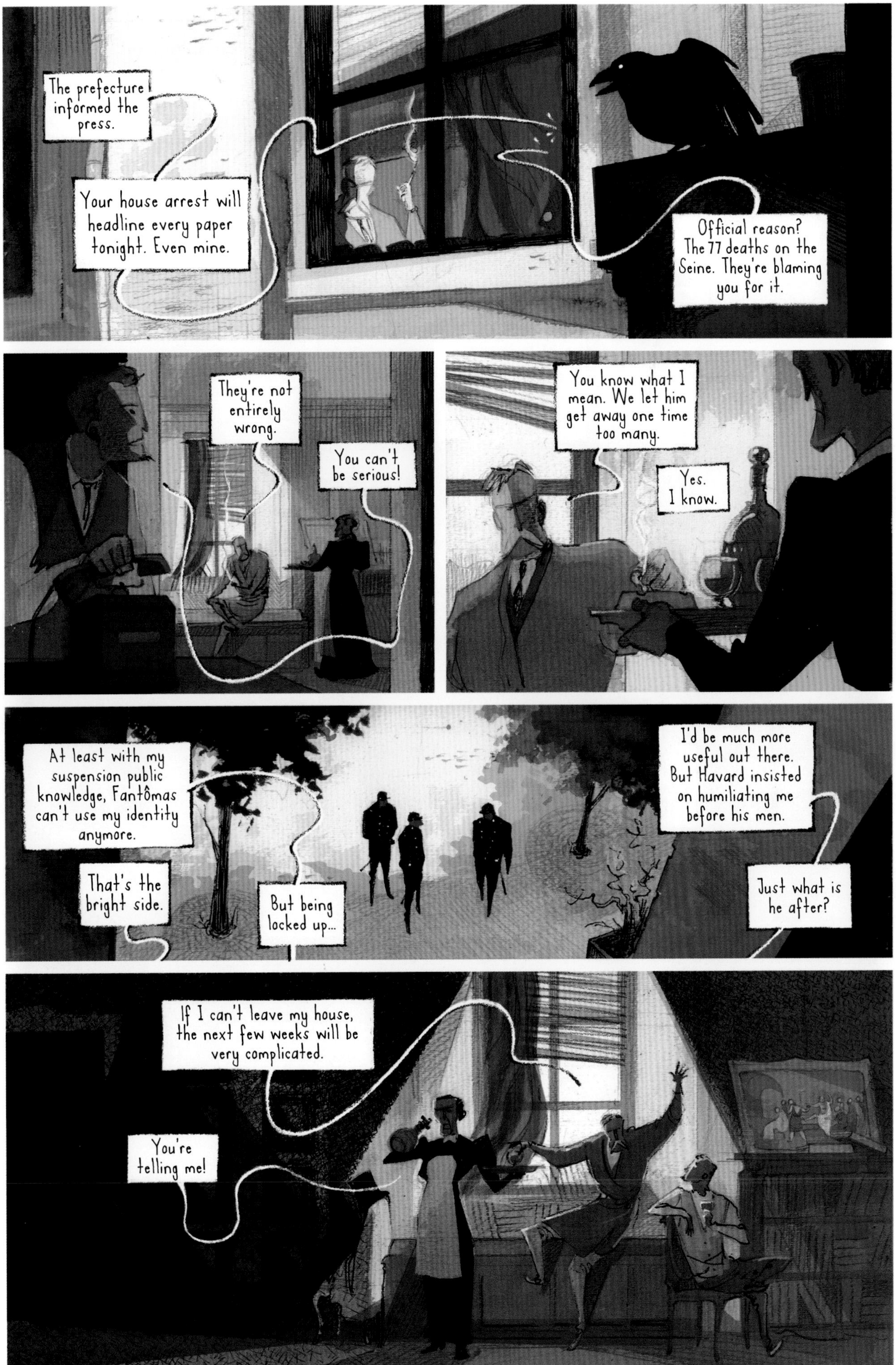
The prefecture informed the press.
Your house arrest will headline every paper tonight. Even mine.
Official reason? The 77 deaths on the Seine. They're blaming you for it.
They're not entirely wrong.
You can't be serious!
You know what I mean. We let him get away one time too many.
Yes. I know.
At least with my suspension public knowledge, Fantômas can't use my identity anymore.
That's the bright side.
But being locked up...
I'd be much more useful out there. But Havard insisted on humiliating me before his men.
Just what is he after?
If I can't leave my house, the next few weeks will be very complicated.
You're telling me!

Tuesday, September 12, 1911

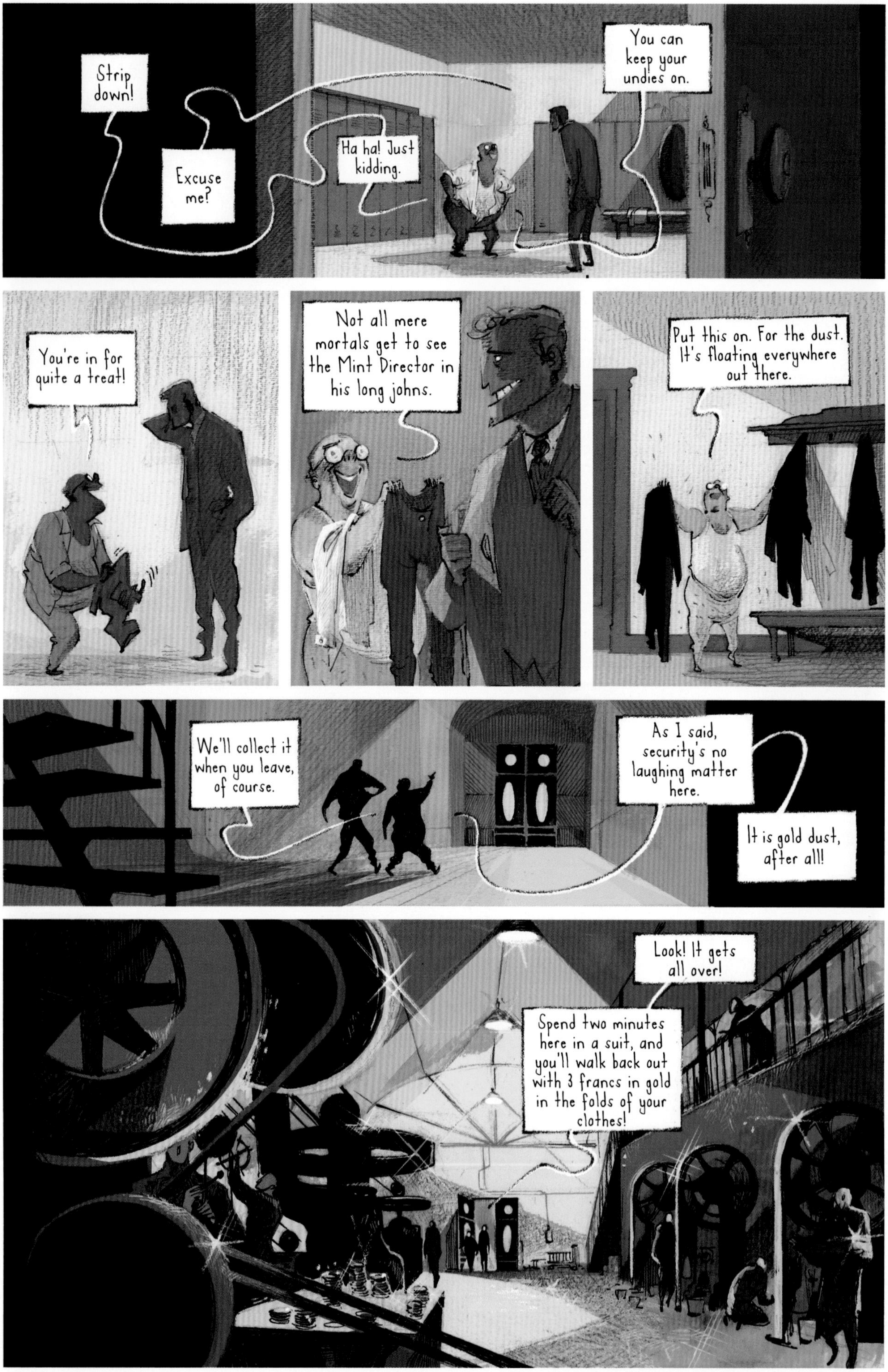

Strip down!
Excuse me?
Ha ha! Just kidding.
You can keep your undies on.
You're in for quite a treat!
Not all mere mortals get to see the Mint Director in his long johns.
Put this on. For the dust. It's floating everywhere out there.
We'll collect it when you leave, of course.
As I said, security's no laughing matter here.
It is gold dust, after all!
Look! It gets all over!
Spend two minutes here in a suit, and you'll walk back out with 3 francs in gold in the folds of your clothes!

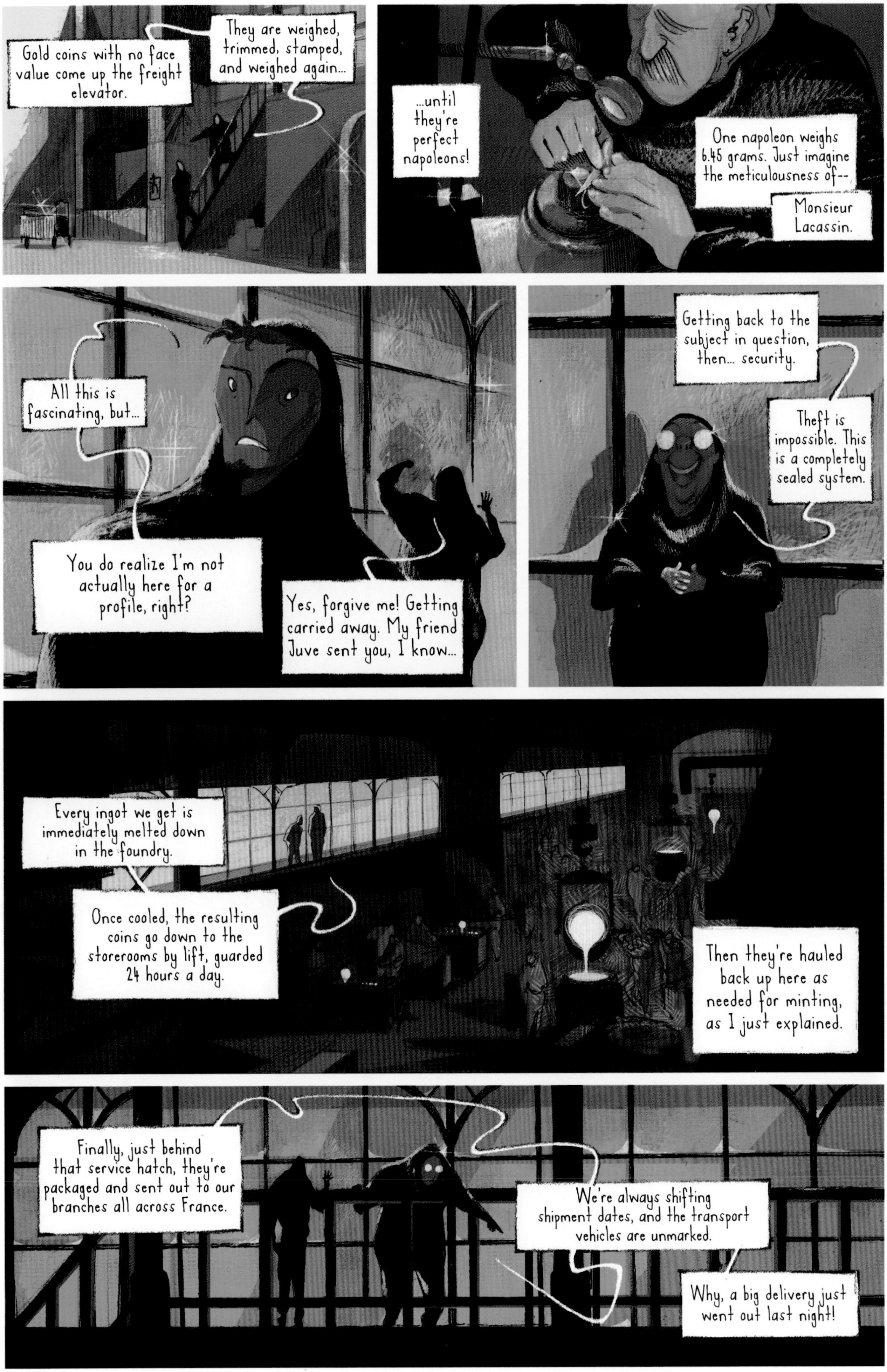
Gold coins with no face value come up the freight elevator.
They are weighed, trimmed, stamped, and weighed again...
...until they're perfect napoleons!
One napoleon weighs 6.45 grams. Just imagine the meticulousness of--
Monsieur Lacassin.
All this is fascinating, but...
You do realize I'm not actually here for a profile, right?
Yes, forgive me! Getting carried away. My friend Juve sent you, I know...
Getting back to the subject in question, then... security.
Theft is impossible. This is a completely sealed system.
Every ingot we get is immediately melted down in the foundry.
Once cooled, the resulting coins go down to the storerooms by lift, guarded 24 hours a day.
Then they're hauled back up here as needed for minting, as I just explained.
Finally, just behind that service hatch, they're packaged and sent out to our branches all across France.
We're always shifting shipment dates, and the transport vehicles are unmarked.
Why, a big delivery just went out last night!

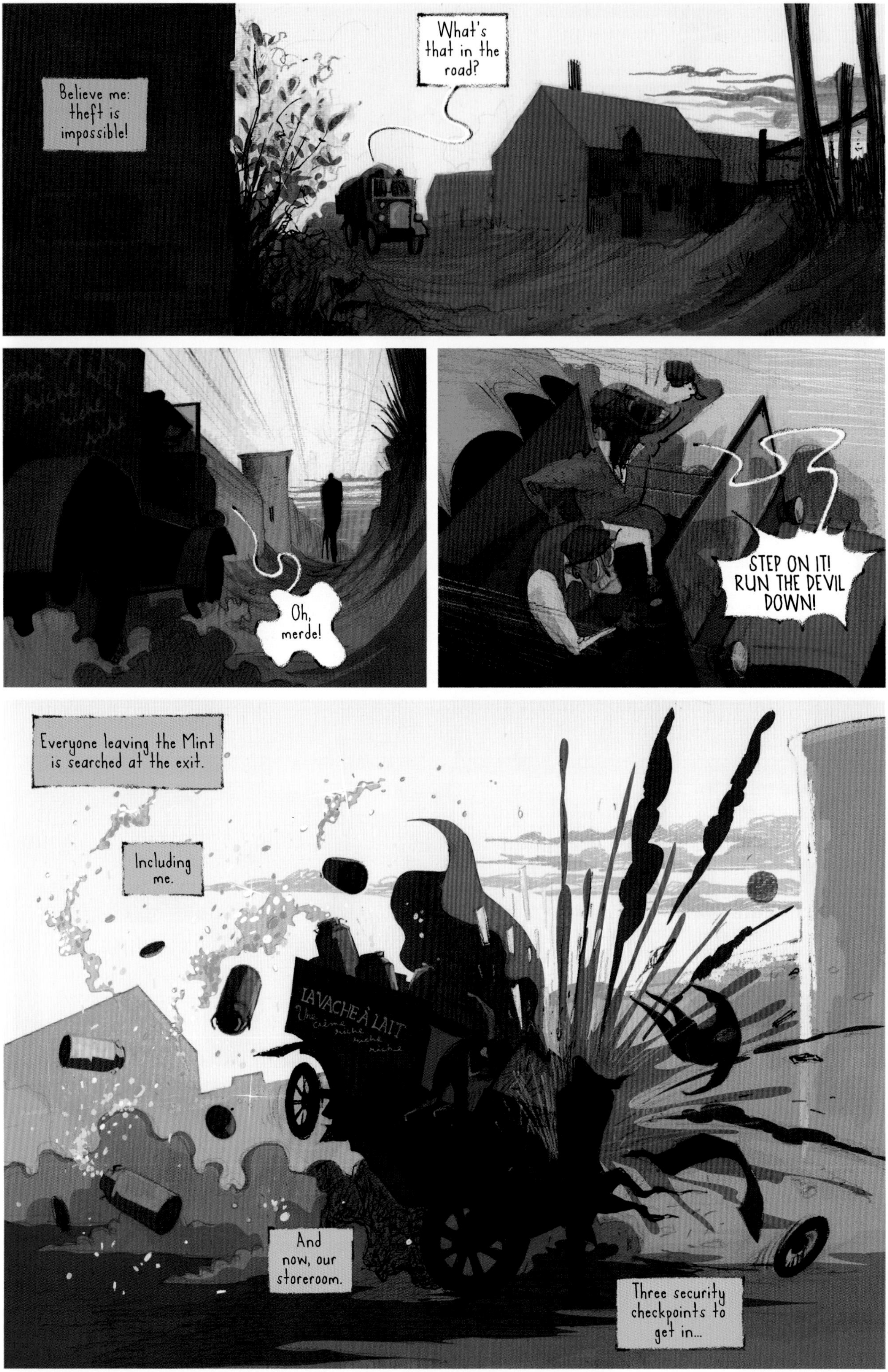
Believe me: theft is impossible!
What's that in the road?
Oh, merde!
STEP ON IT! RUN THE DEVIL DOWN!
Everyone leaving the Mint is searched at the exit.
Including me.
LA VACHE À LAIT
And now, our storeroom.
Three security checkpoints to get in...

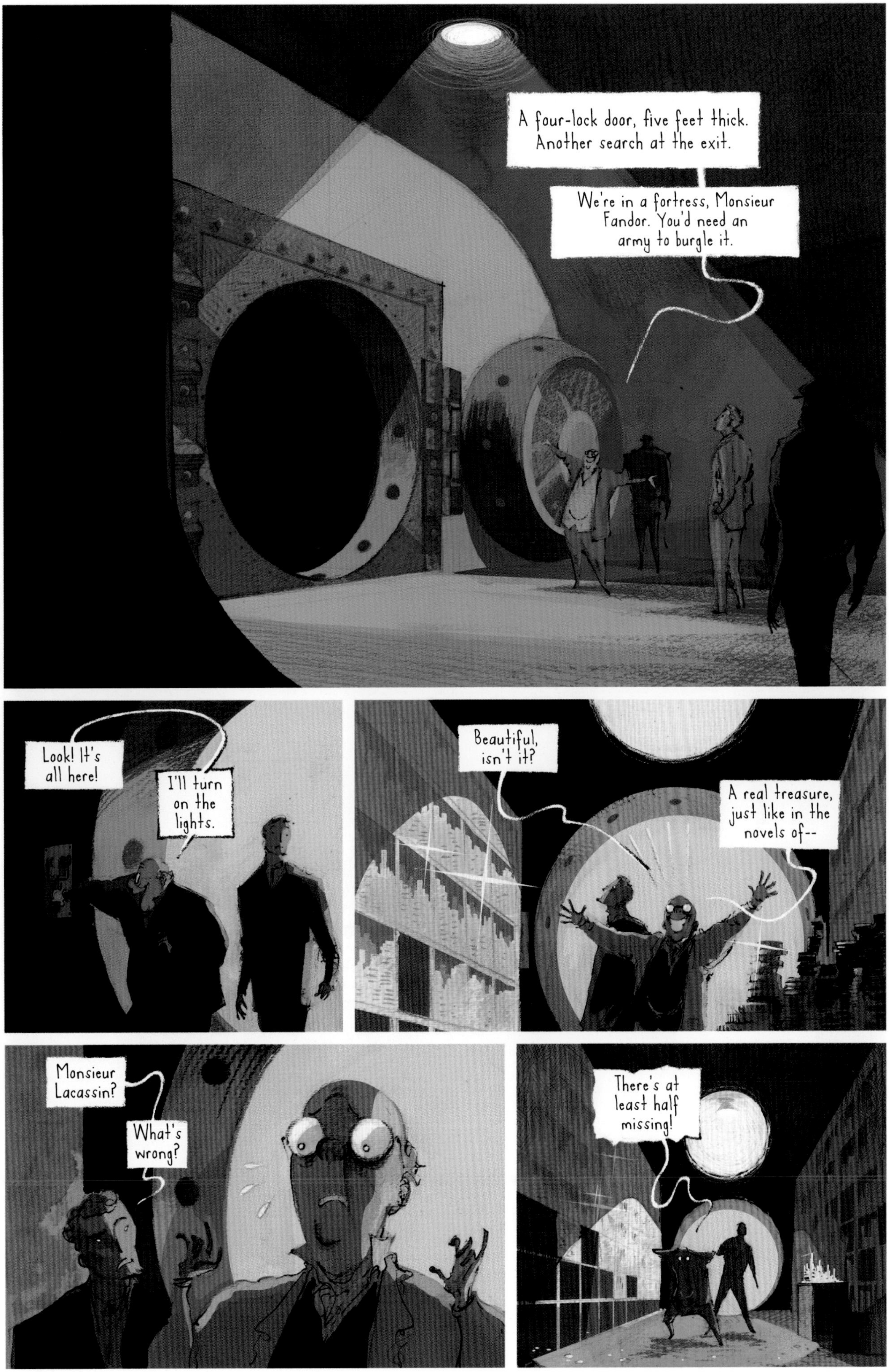

A four-lock door, five feet thick. Another search at the exit.
We're in a fortress, Monsieur Fandor. You'd need an army to burgle it.
Look! It's all here!
I'll turn on the lights.
Beautiful, isn't it?
A real treasure, just like in the novels of--
Monsieur Lacassin?
What's wrong?
There's at least half missing!

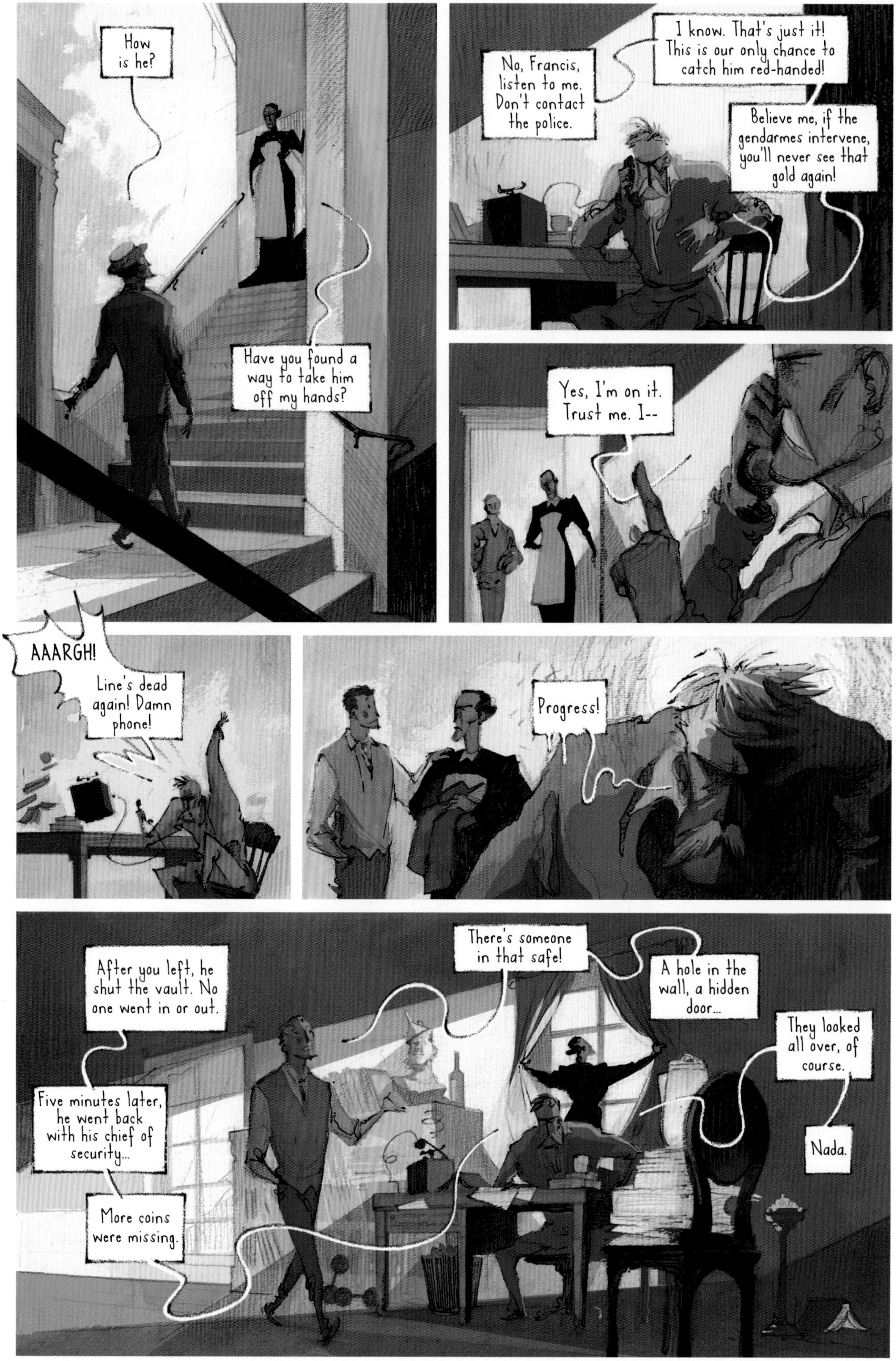
How is he?
Have you found a way to take him off my hands?
No, Francis, listen to me. Don't contact the police.
I know. That's just it! This is our only chance to catch him red-handed!
Believe me, if the gendarmes intervene, you'll never see that gold again!
Yes, I'm on it. Trust me. I--
AAARGH!
Line's dead again! Damn phone!
Progress!
After you left, he shut the vault. No one went in or out.
Five minutes later, he went back with his chief of security...
More coins were missing.
There's someone in that safe!
A hole in the wall, a hidden door...
They looked all over, of course.
Nada.

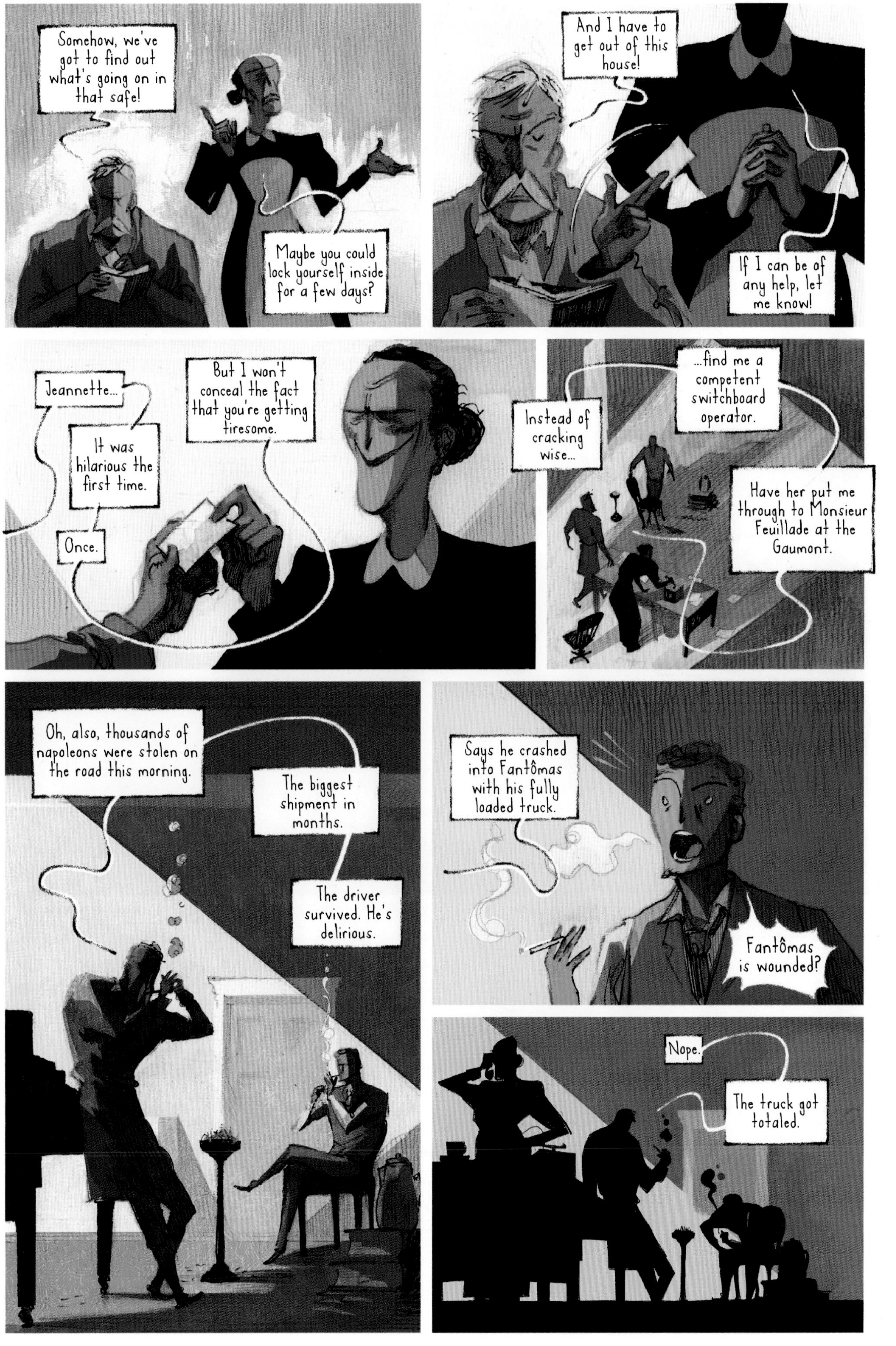
Somehow, we've got to find out what's going on in that safe!
Maybe you could lock yourself inside for a few days?
And I have to get out of this house!
If I can be of any help, let me know!
Jeannette...
It was hilarious the first time.
Once.
But I won't conceal the fact that you're getting tiresome.
Instead of cracking wise...
...find me a competent switchboard operator.
Have her put me through to Monsieur Feuillade at the Gaumont.
Oh, also, thousands of napoleons were stolen on the road this morning.
The biggest shipment in months.
The driver survived. He's delirious.
Says he crashed into Fantômas with his fully loaded truck.
Fantômas is wounded?
Nope.
The truck got totaled.

Wednesday, September 13, 1911

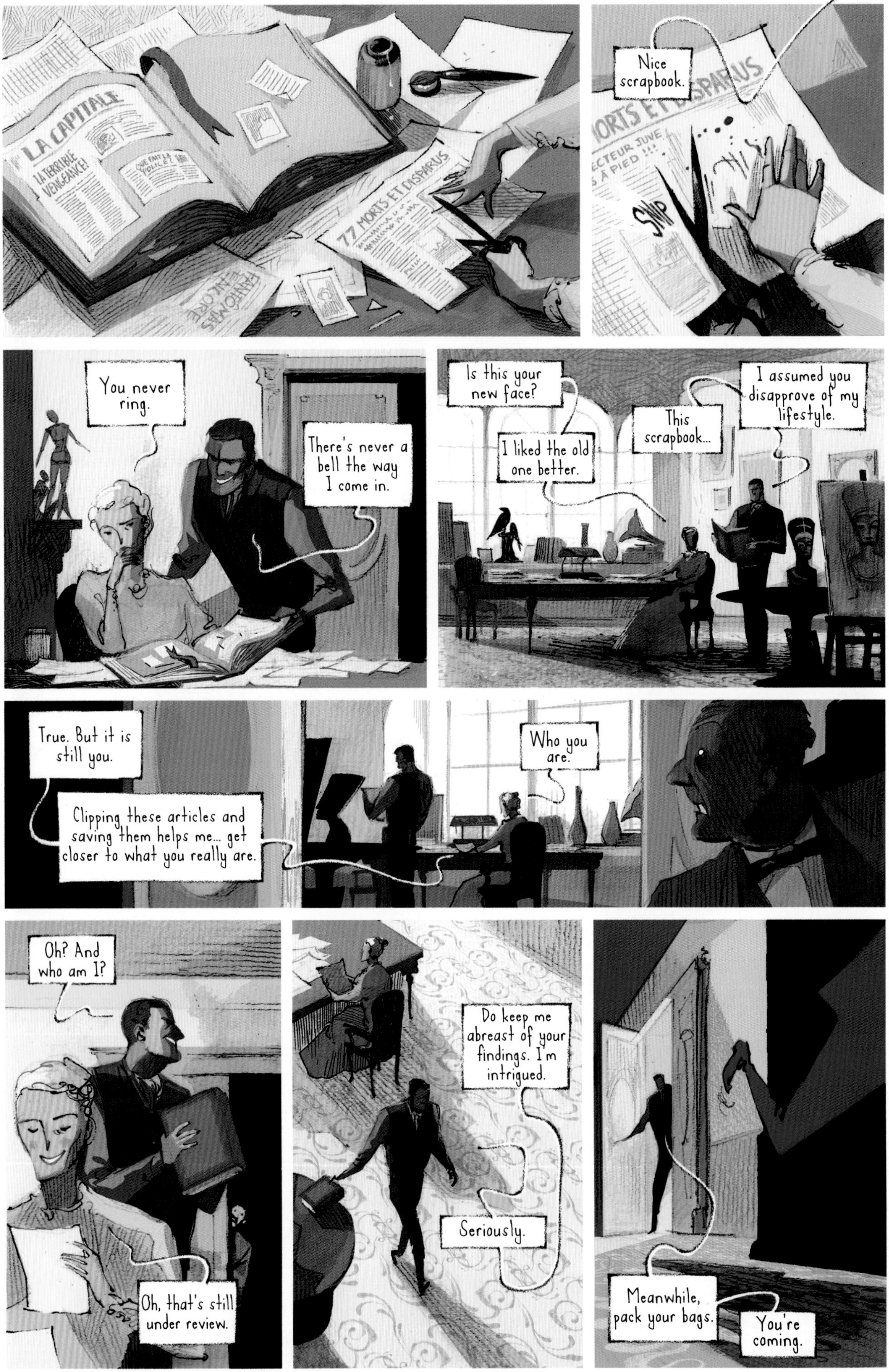

LA CAPITALE
LA TERRIBLE VENGEANCE!
QUE FAIT LA POLICE?
77 MORTS ET DISPARUS
Nice scrapbook.
SNIP
You never ring.
There's never a bell the way I come in.
Is this your new face?
I liked the old one better.
This scrapbook...
I assumed you disapprove of my lifestyle.
True. But it is still you.
Clipping these articles and saving them helps me... get closer to what you really are.
Who you are.
Oh? And who am I?
Oh, that's still under review.
Do keep me abreast of your findings. I'm intrigued.
Seriously.
Meanwhile, pack your bags.
You're coming.

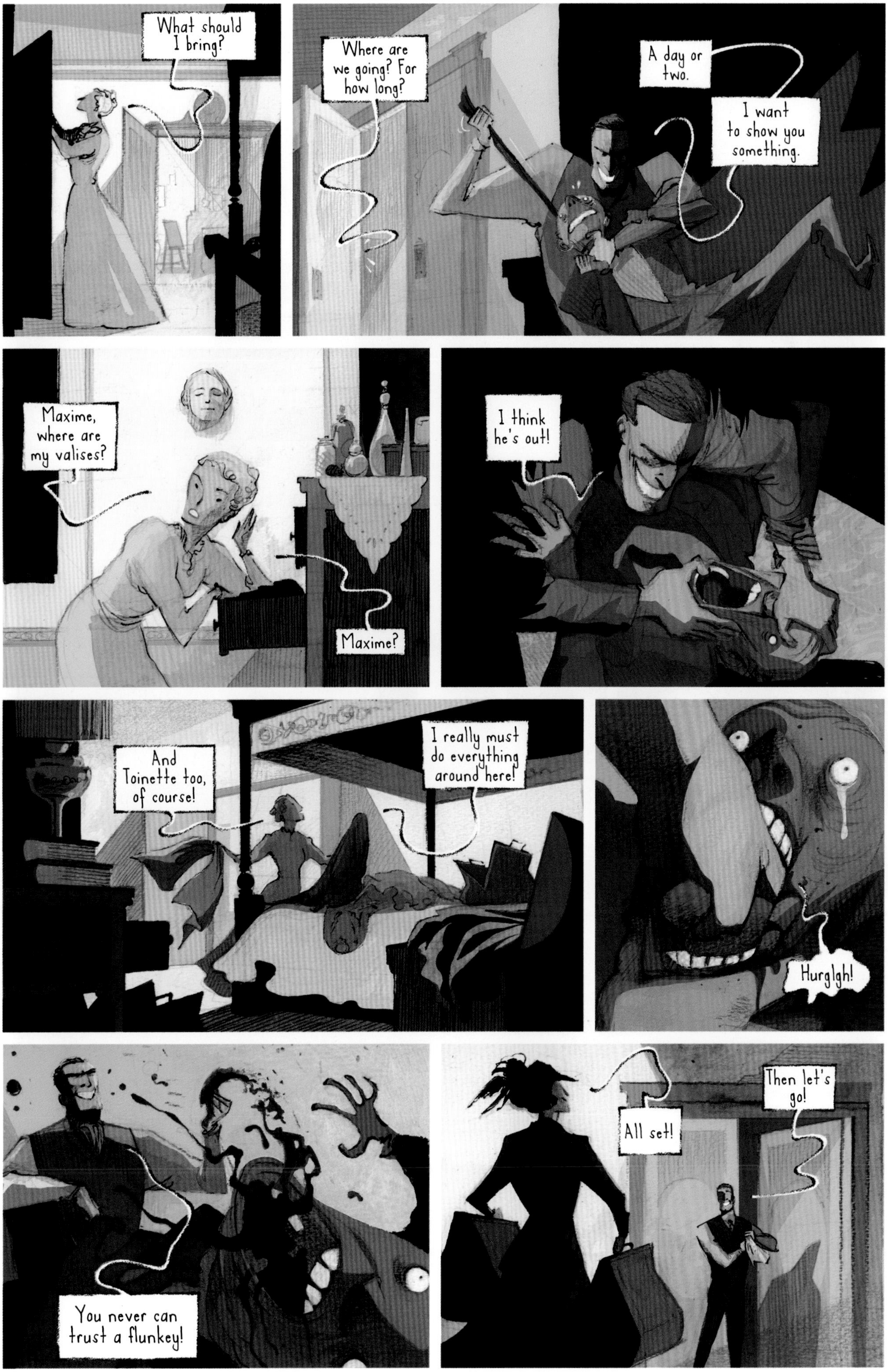
What should I bring?
Where are we going? For how long?
A day or two.
I want to show you something.
Maxime, where are my valises?
Maxime?
I think he's out!
And Toinette too, of course!
I really must do everything around here!
Hurglgh!
You never can trust a flunkey!
All set!
Then let's go!

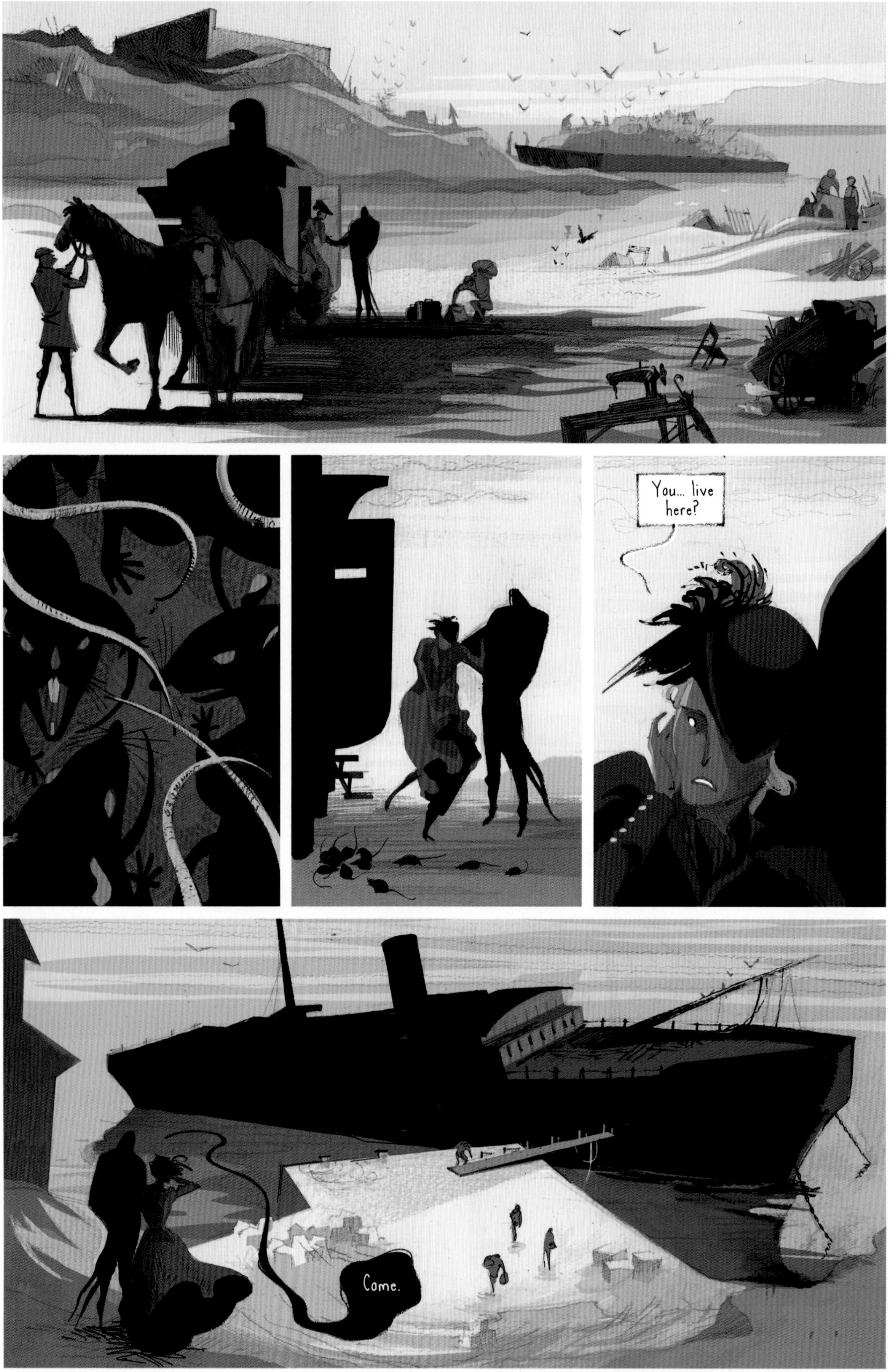
You... live here?
Come.

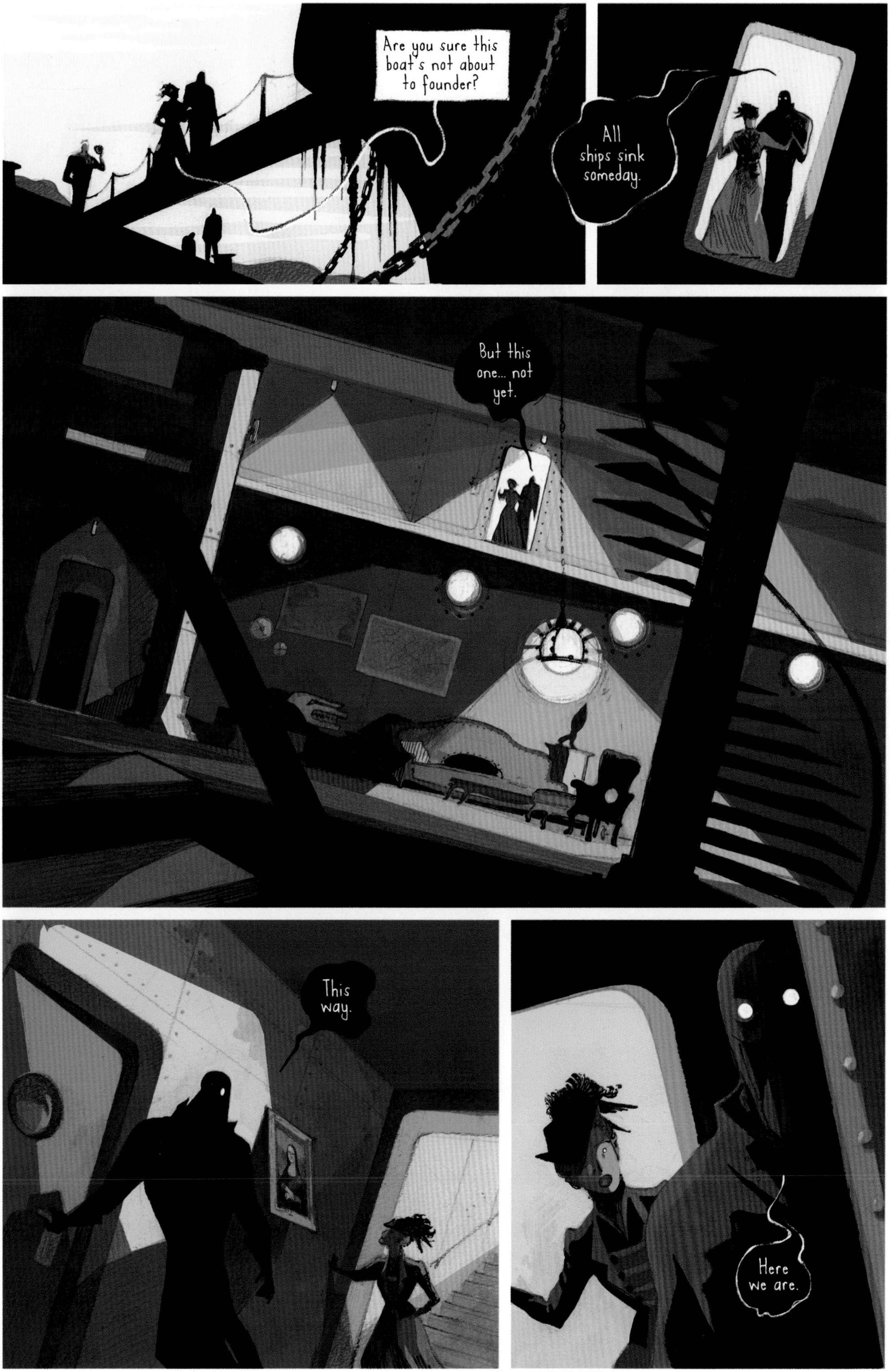
Are you sure this boat's not about to founder?
All ships sink someday.
But this one... not yet.
This way.
Here we are.

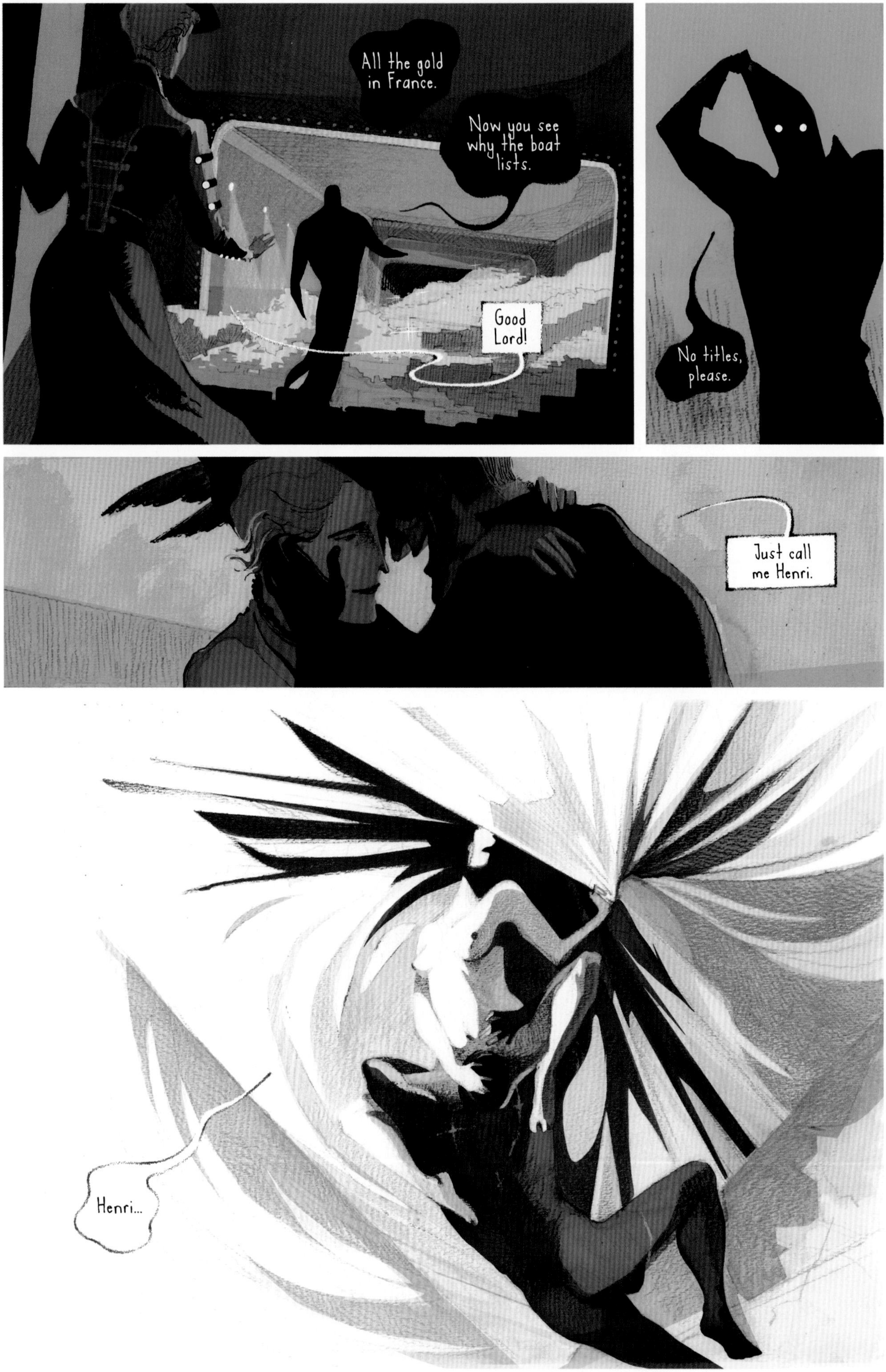
All the gold in France.
Now you see why the boat lists.
Good Lord!
No titles, please.
Just call me Henri.
Henri...

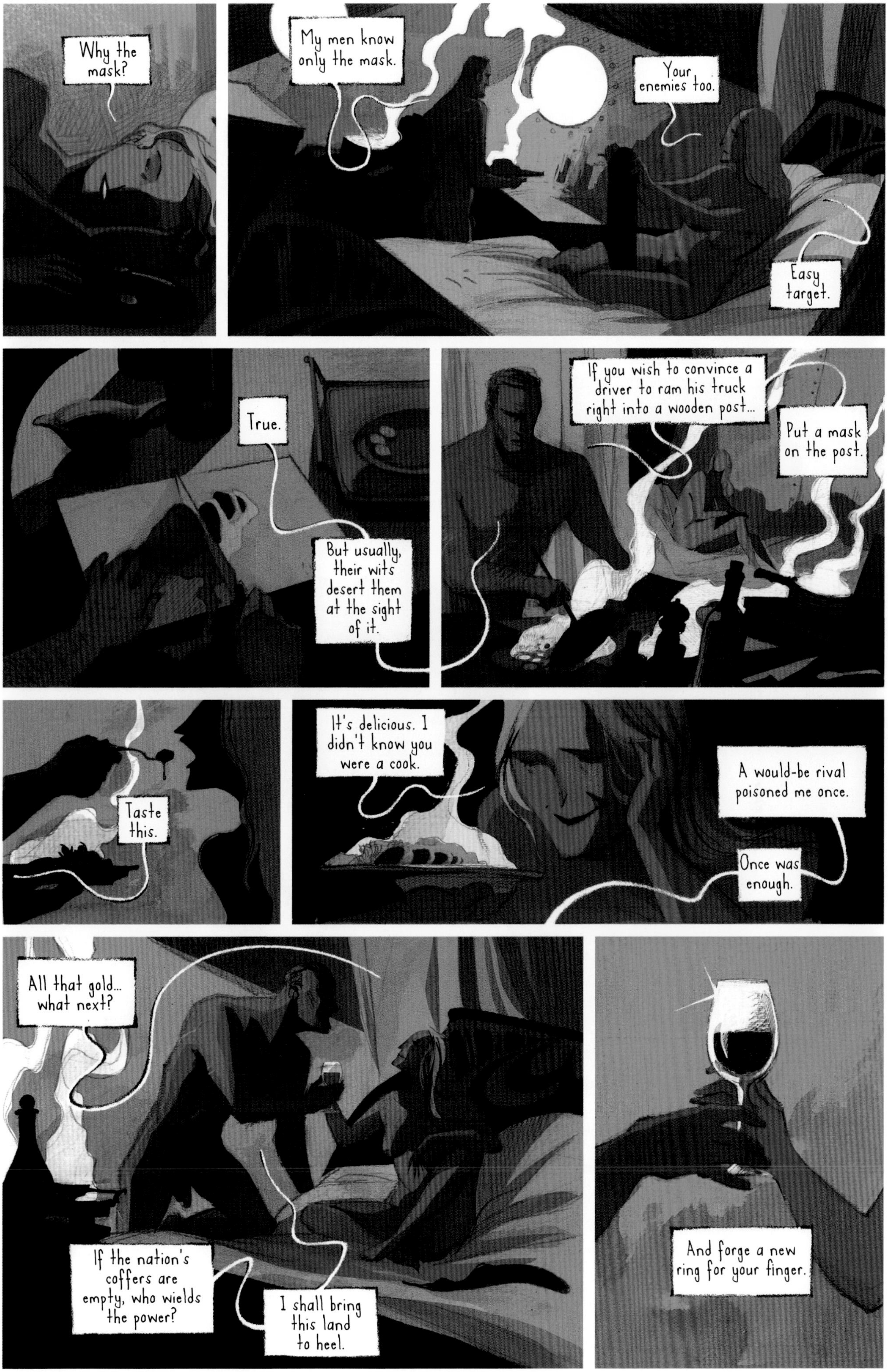
Why the mask?
My men know only the mask.
Your enemies too.
Easy target.
True.
But usually, their wits desert them at the sight of it.
If you wish to convince a driver to ram his truck right into a wooden post...
Put a mask on the post.
Taste this.
It's delicious. I didn't know you were a cook.
A would-be rival poisoned me once.
Once was enough.
All that gold... what next?
If the nation's coffers are empty, who wields the power?
I shall bring this land to heel.
And forge a new ring for your finger.

Thursday, September 14, 1911

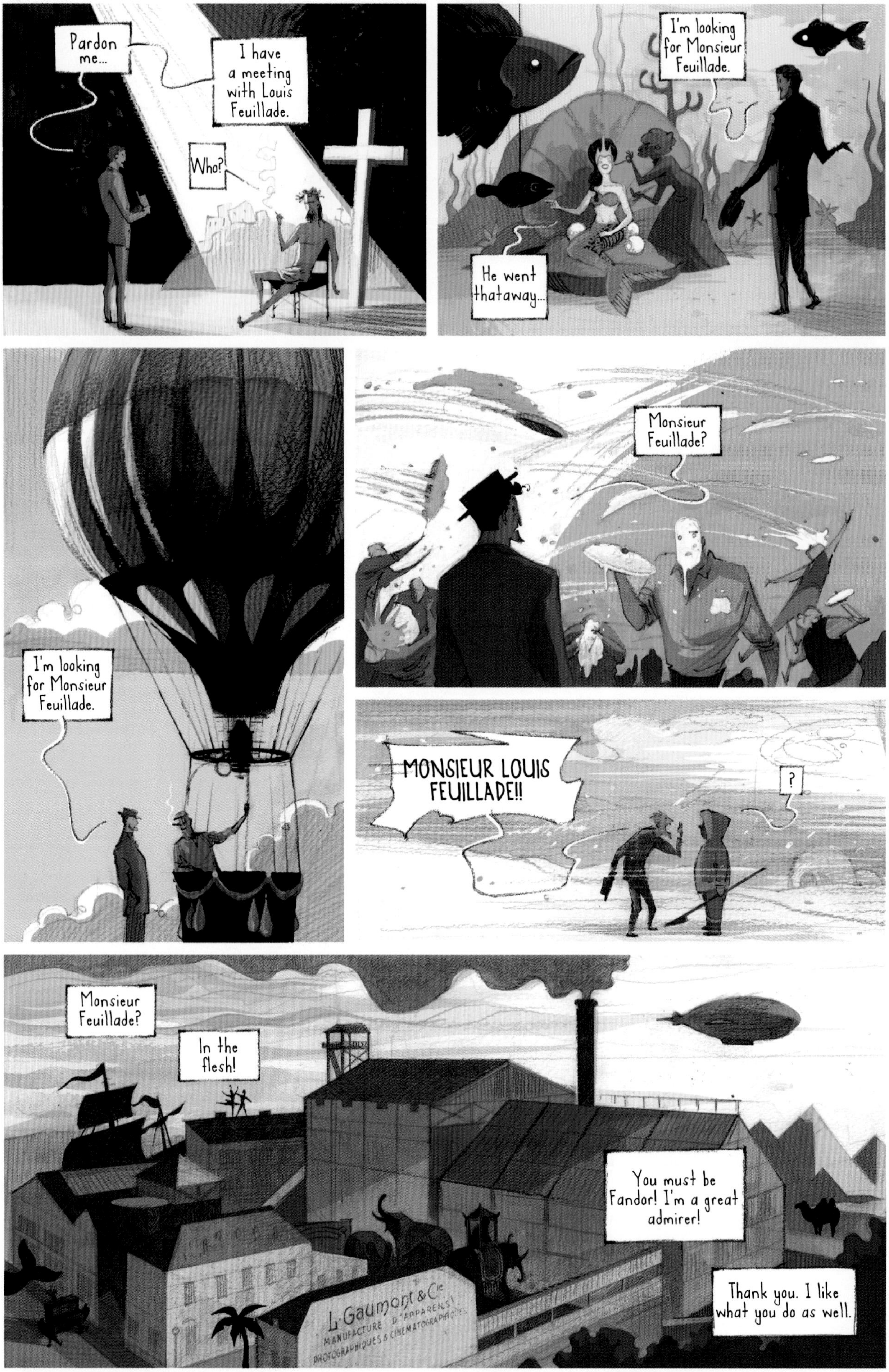
Pardon me...
I have a meeting with Louis Feuillade.
Who?
I'm looking for Monsieur Feuillade.
He went thataway...
I'm looking for Monsieur Feuillade.
Monsieur Feuillade?
MONSIEUR LOUIS FEUILLADE!!
?
Monsieur Feuillade?
In the flesh!
You must be Fandor! I'm a great admirer!
Thank you. I like what you do as well.
L. Gaumont & Cie

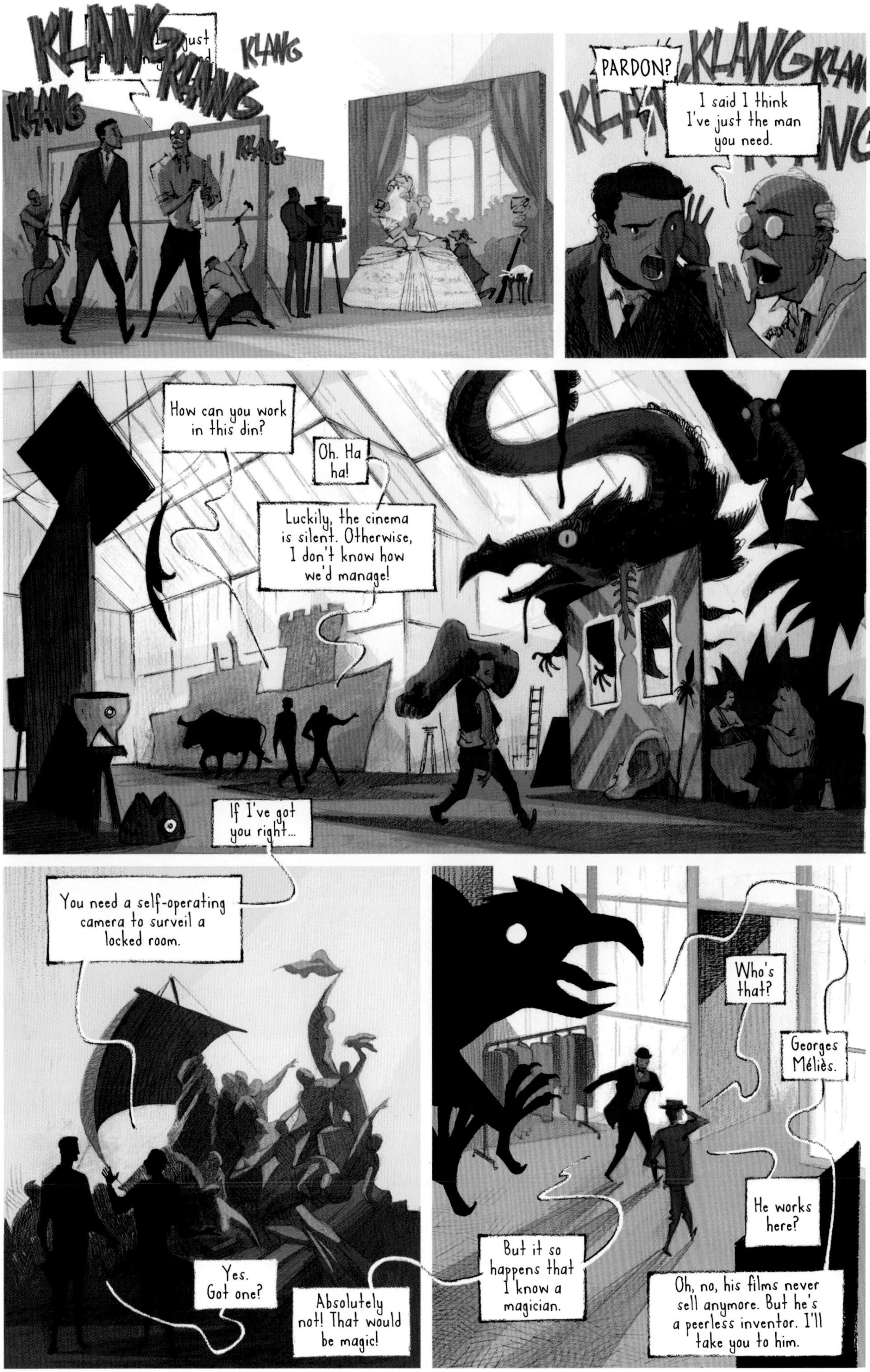
KLANG
KLANG
KLANG
KLANG
KLANG
PARDON?
I said I think I've just the man you need.
KLANG
KLANG
KLANG
How can you work in this din?
Oh. Ha ha!
Luckily, the cinema is silent. Otherwise, I don't know how we'd manage!
If I've got you right...
You need a self-operating camera to surveil a locked room.
Yes. Got one?
Absolutely not! That would be magic!
But it so happens that I know a magician.
Who's that?
Georges Méliès.
He works here?
Oh, no, his films never sell anymore. But he's a peerless inventor. I'll take you to him.

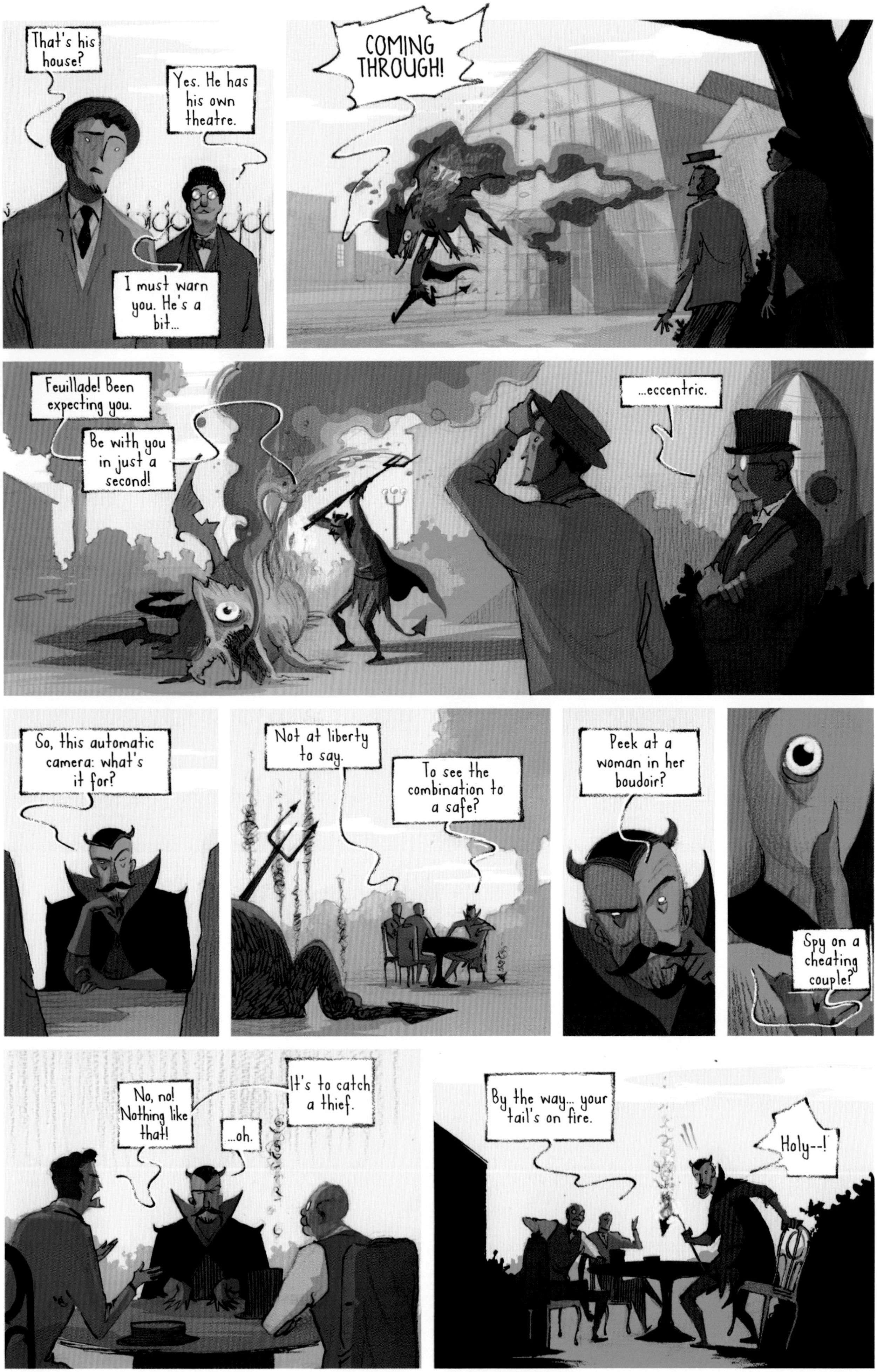
That's his house?
Yes. He has his own theatre.
I must warn you. He's a bit...
COMING THROUGH!
Feuillade! Been expecting you.
Be with you in just a second!
...eccentric.
So, this automatic camera: what's it for?
Not at liberty to say.
To see the combination to a safe?
Peek at a woman in her boudoir?
Spy on a cheating couple?
No, no! Nothing like that!
It's to catch a thief.
...oh.
By the way... your tail's on fire.
Holy--!

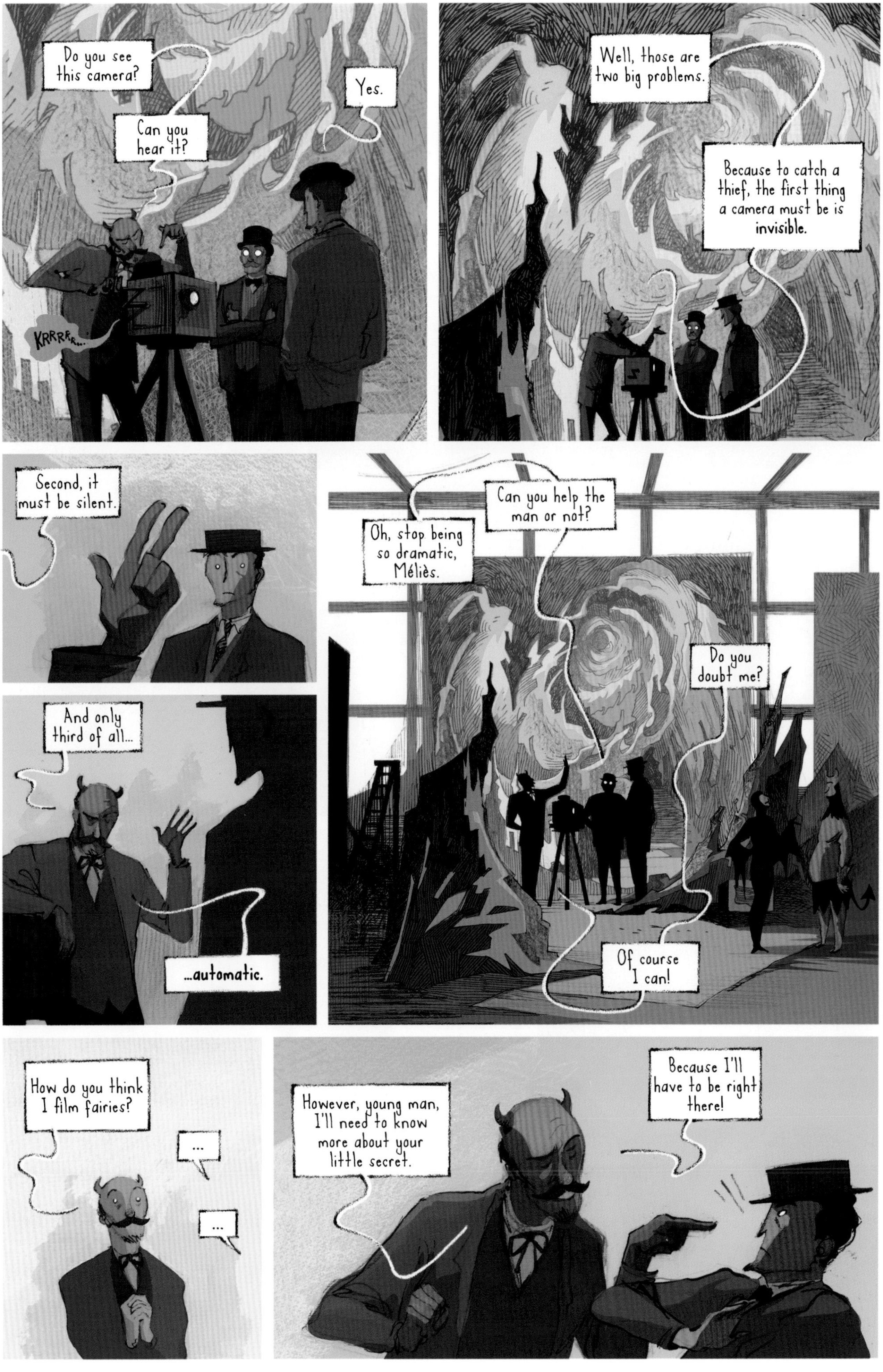
Do you see this camera?
Can you hear it?
Yes.
KRRRRR...
Well, those are two big problems.
Because to catch a thief, the first thing a camera must be is invisible.
Second, it must be silent.
And only third of all...
...automatic.
Oh, stop being so dramatic, Méliès.
Can you help the man or not?
Do you doubt me?
Of course I can!
How do you think I film fairies?
...
...
However, young man, I'll need to know more about your little secret.
Because I'll have to be right there!

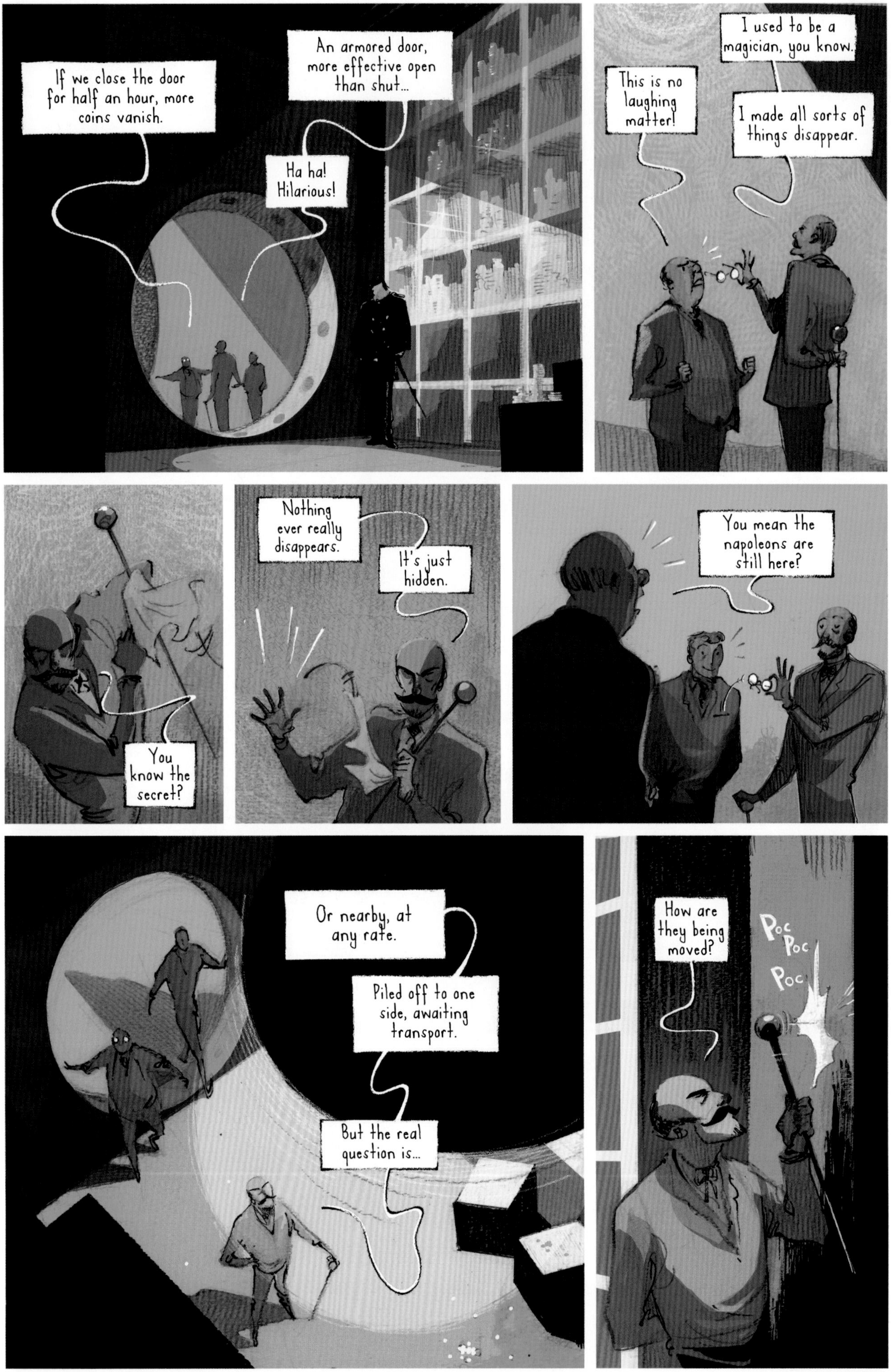
If we close the door for half an hour, more coins vanish.
An armored door, more effective open than shut...
Ha ha! Hilarious!
I used to be a magician, you know.
This is no laughing matter!
I made all sorts of things disappear.
You know the secret?
Nothing ever really disappears.
It's just hidden.
You mean the napoleons are still here?
Or nearby, at any rate.
Piled off to one side, awaiting transport.
But the real question is...
How are they being moved?
Poc Poc Poc

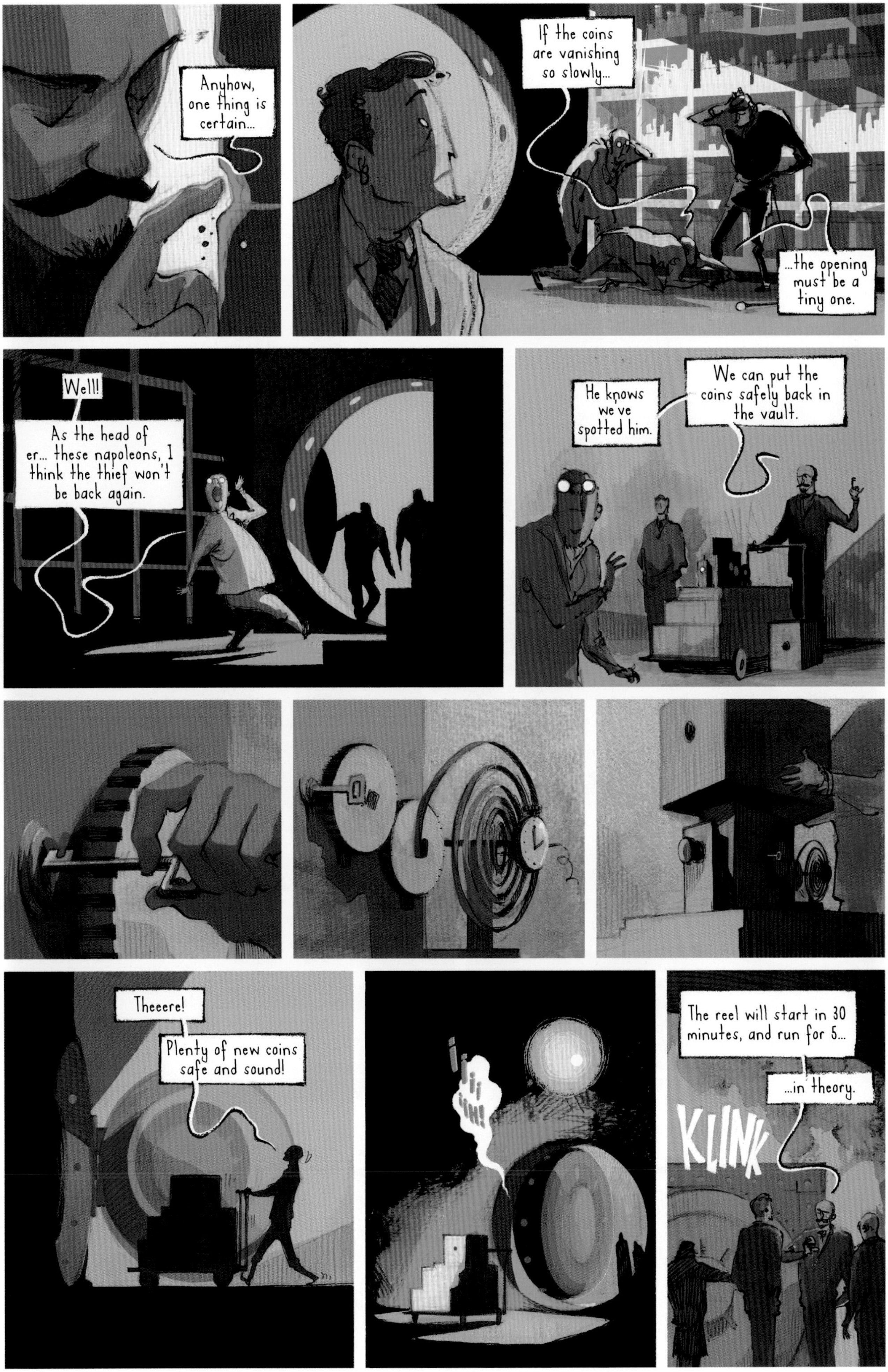

Anyhow, one thing is certain...
If the coins are vanishing so slowly...
...the opening must be a tiny one.
Well!
As the head of er... these napoleons, I think the thief won't be back again.
He knows we've spotted him.
We can put the coins safely back in the vault.
Theeere!
Plenty of new coins safe and sound!
The reel will start in 30 minutes, and run for 5...
...in theory.
KLINK

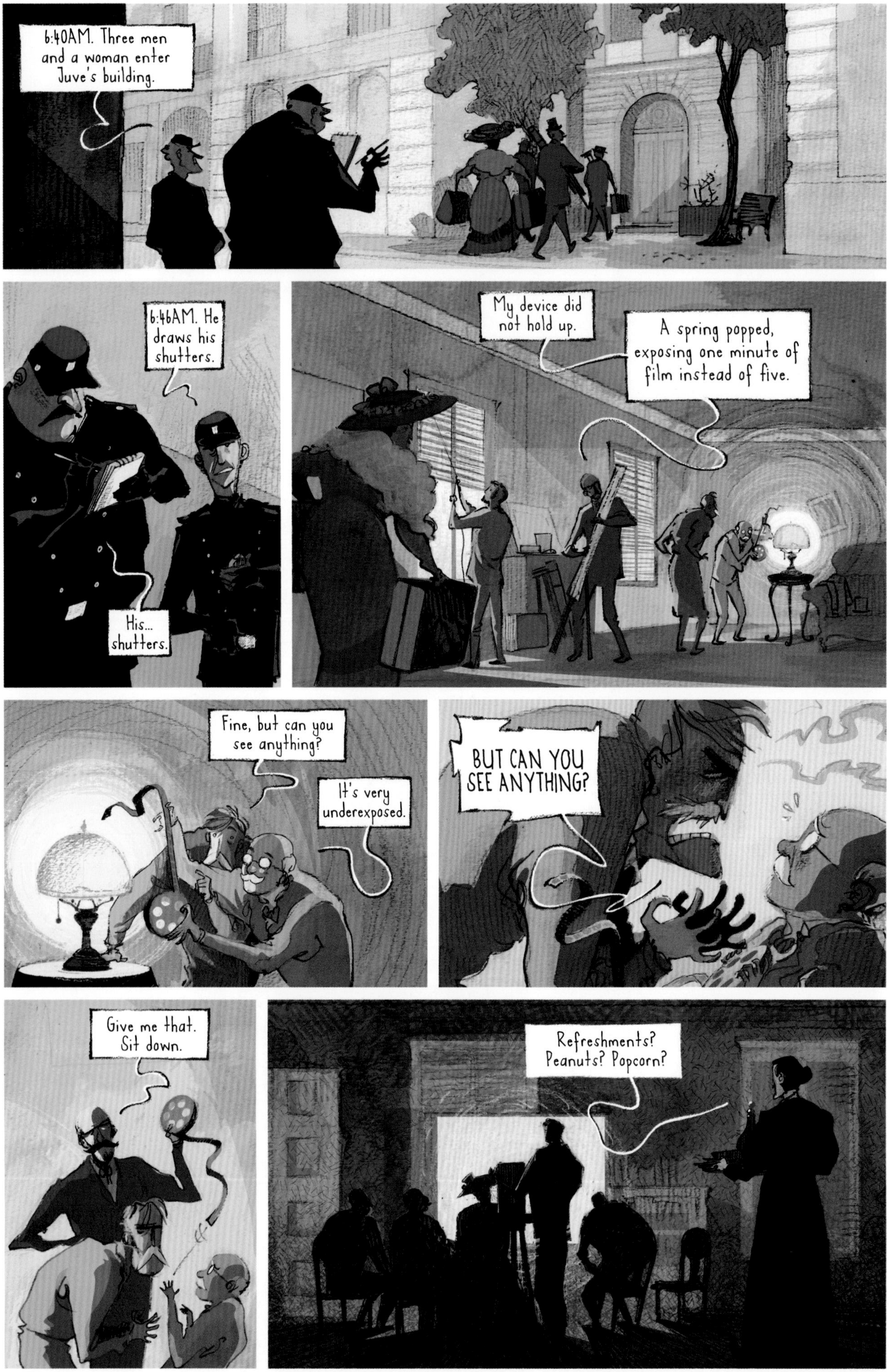
6:40AM. Three men and a woman enter Juve's building.
6:46AM. He draws his shutters.
His... shutters.
My device did not hold up.
A spring popped, exposing one minute of film instead of five.
Fine, but can you see anything?
It's very underexposed.
BUT CAN YOU SEE ANYTHING?
Give me that. Sit down.
Refreshments? Peanuts? Popcorn?

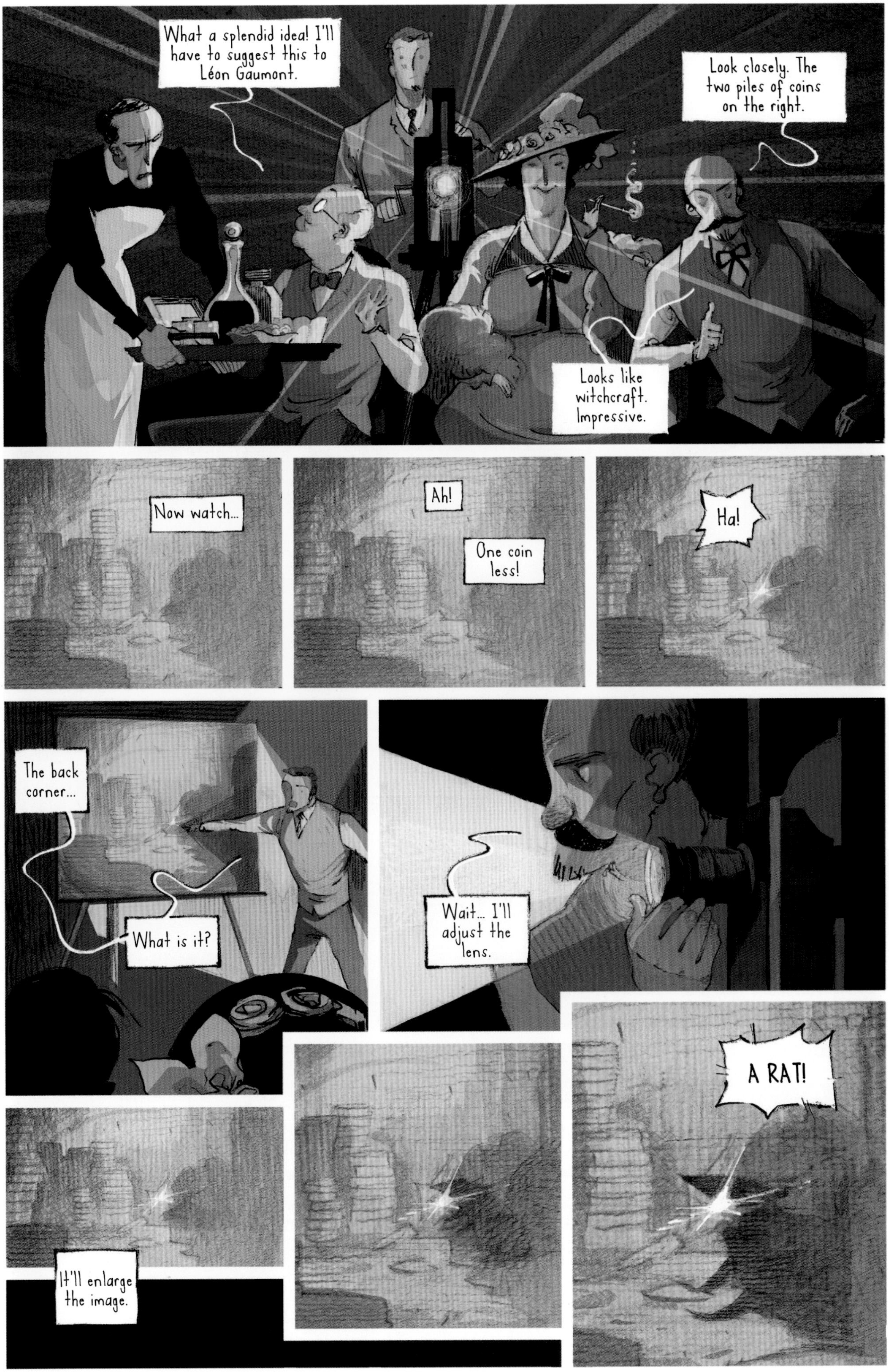
What a splendid idea! I'll have to suggest this to Léon Gaumont.
Look closely. The two piles of coins on the right.
Looks like witchcraft. Impressive.
Now watch...
Ah!
One coin less!
Ha!
The back corner...
What is it?
Wait... I'll adjust the lens.
It'll enlarge the image.
A RAT!

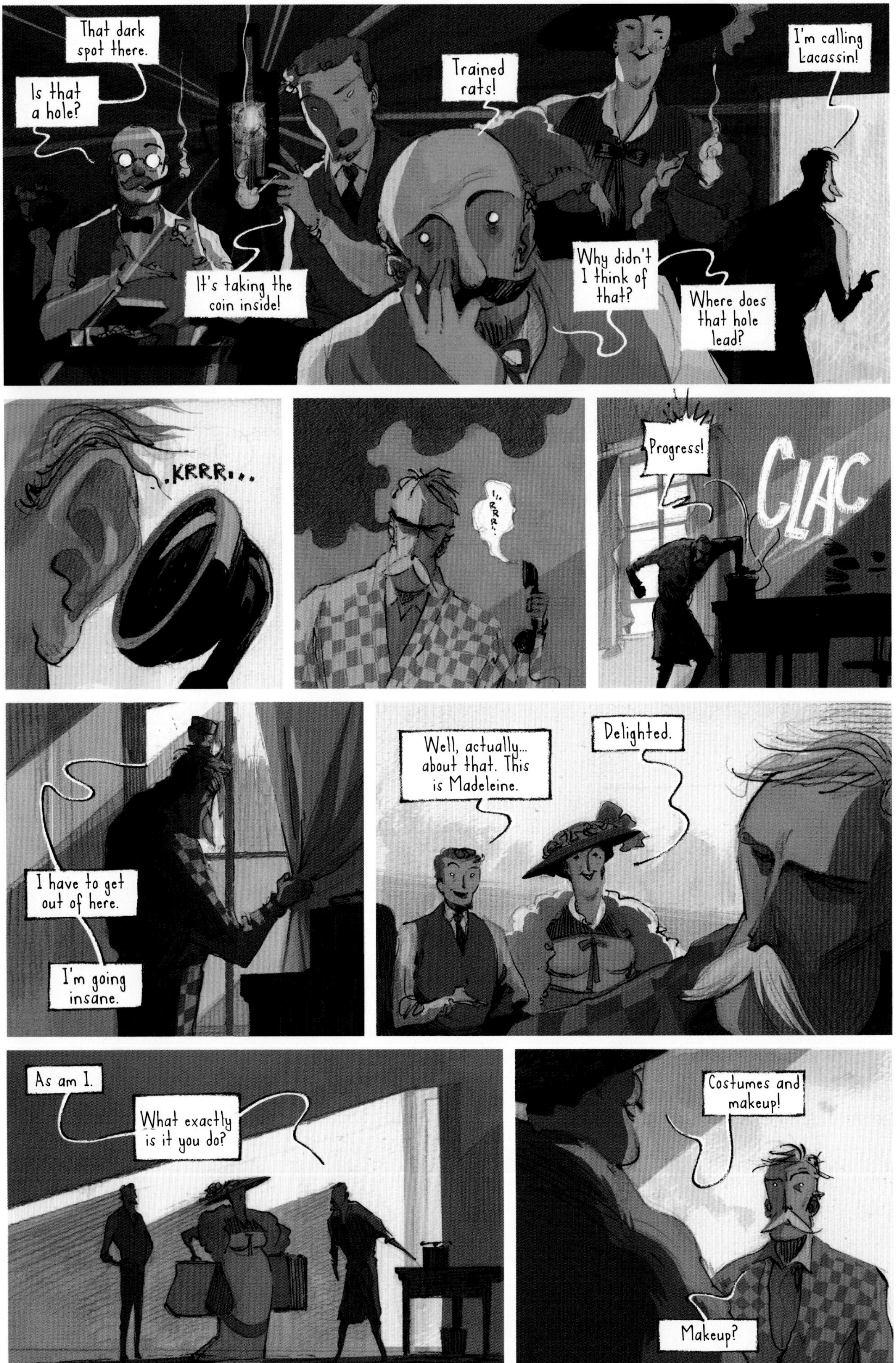
That dark spot there.
Is that a hole?
It's taking the coin inside!
Trained rats!
Why didn't I think of that?
I'm calling Lacassin!
Where does that hole lead?
.KRRR...
RRR.
Progress!
CLAC
I have to get out of here.
I'm going insane.
Well, actually... about that. This is Madeleine.
Delighted.
As am I.
What exactly is it you do?
Costumes and makeup!
Makeup?

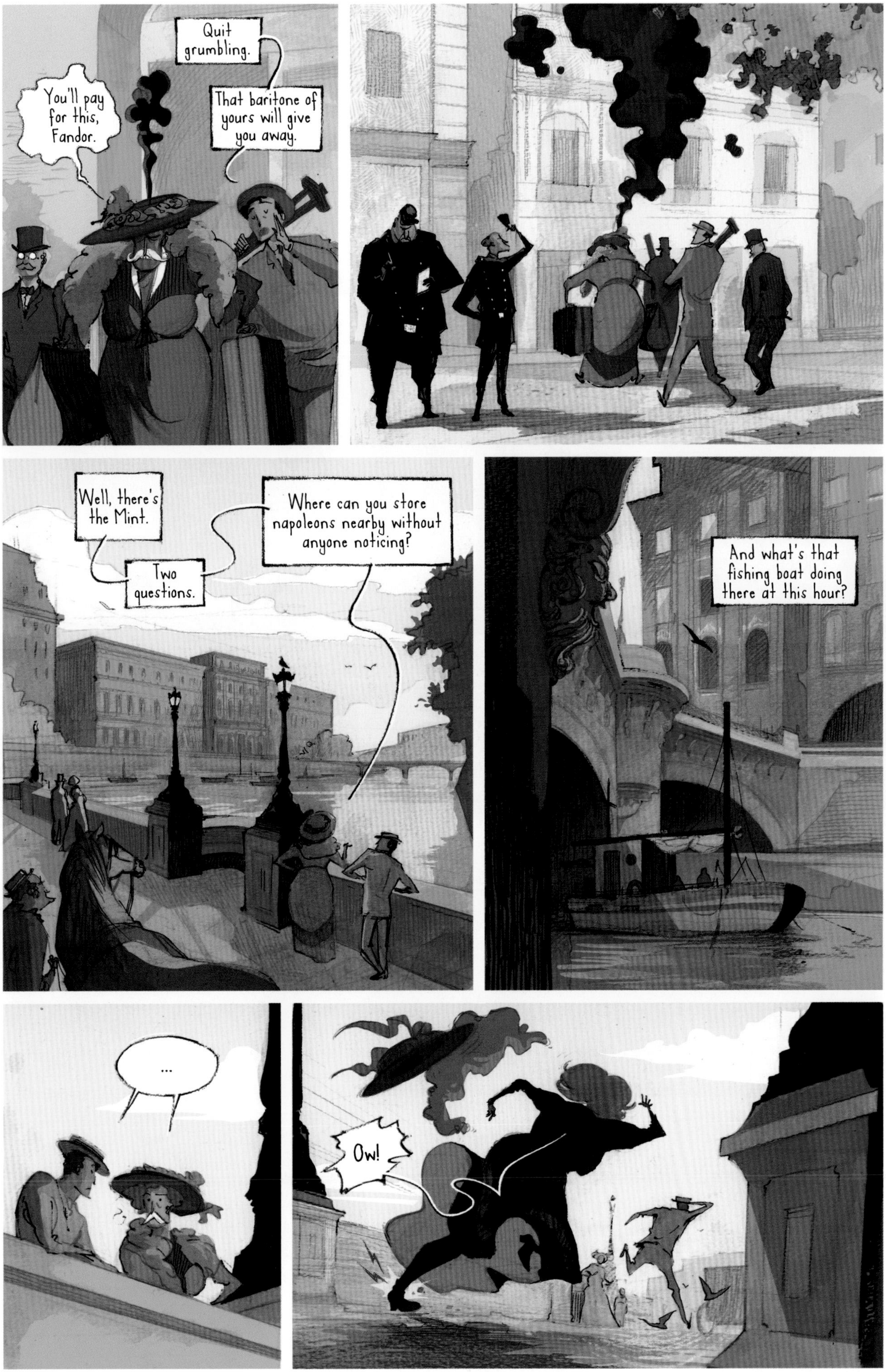
You'll pay for this, Fandor.
Quit grumbling.
That baritone of yours will give you away.
Well, there's the Mint.
Two questions.
Where can you store napoleons nearby without anyone noticing?
And what's that fishing boat doing there at this hour?
...
Ow!

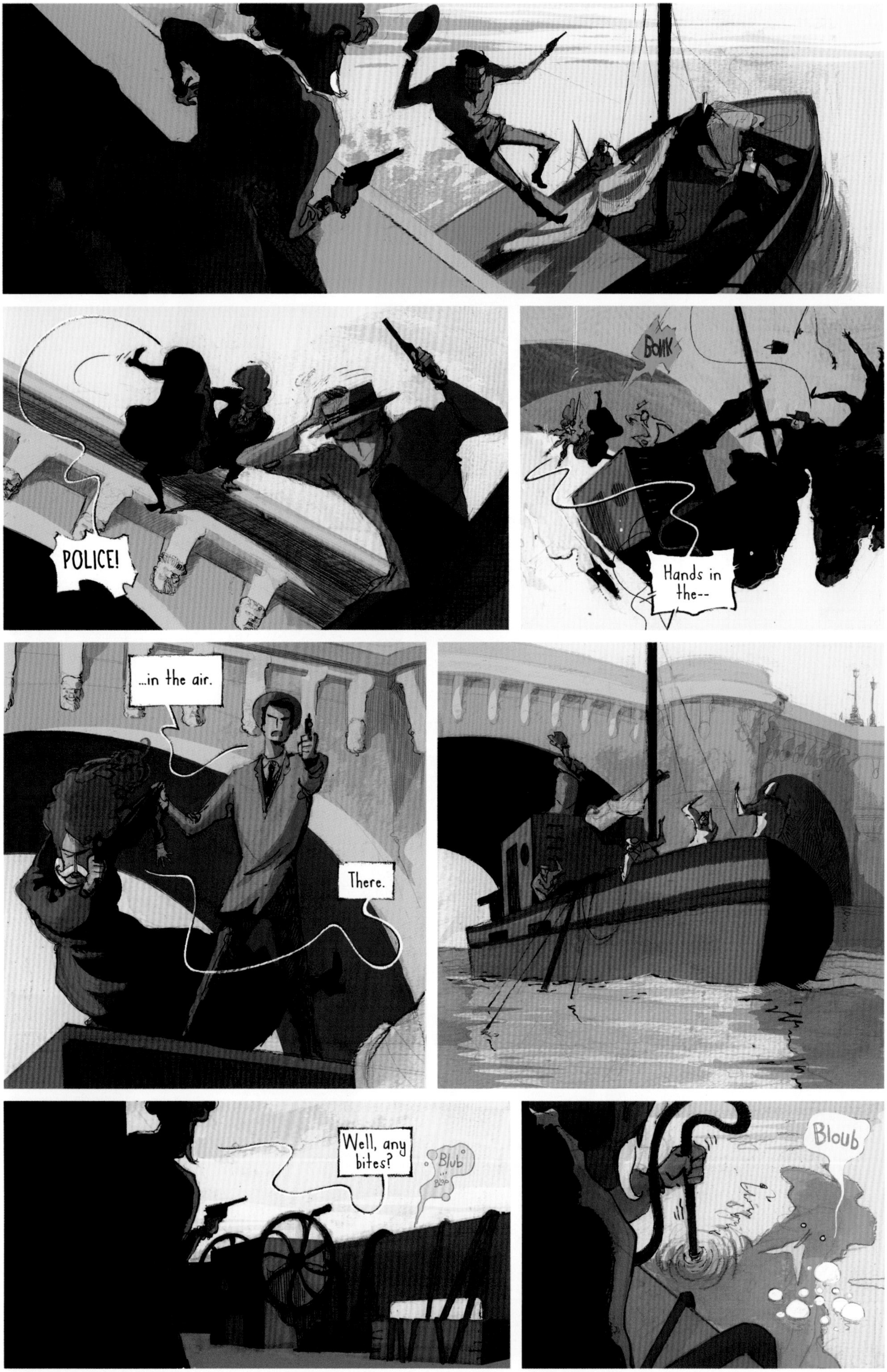
POLICE!
BONK
Hands in the--
...in the air.
There.
Well, any bites?
Blub
...
Blop
Bloub

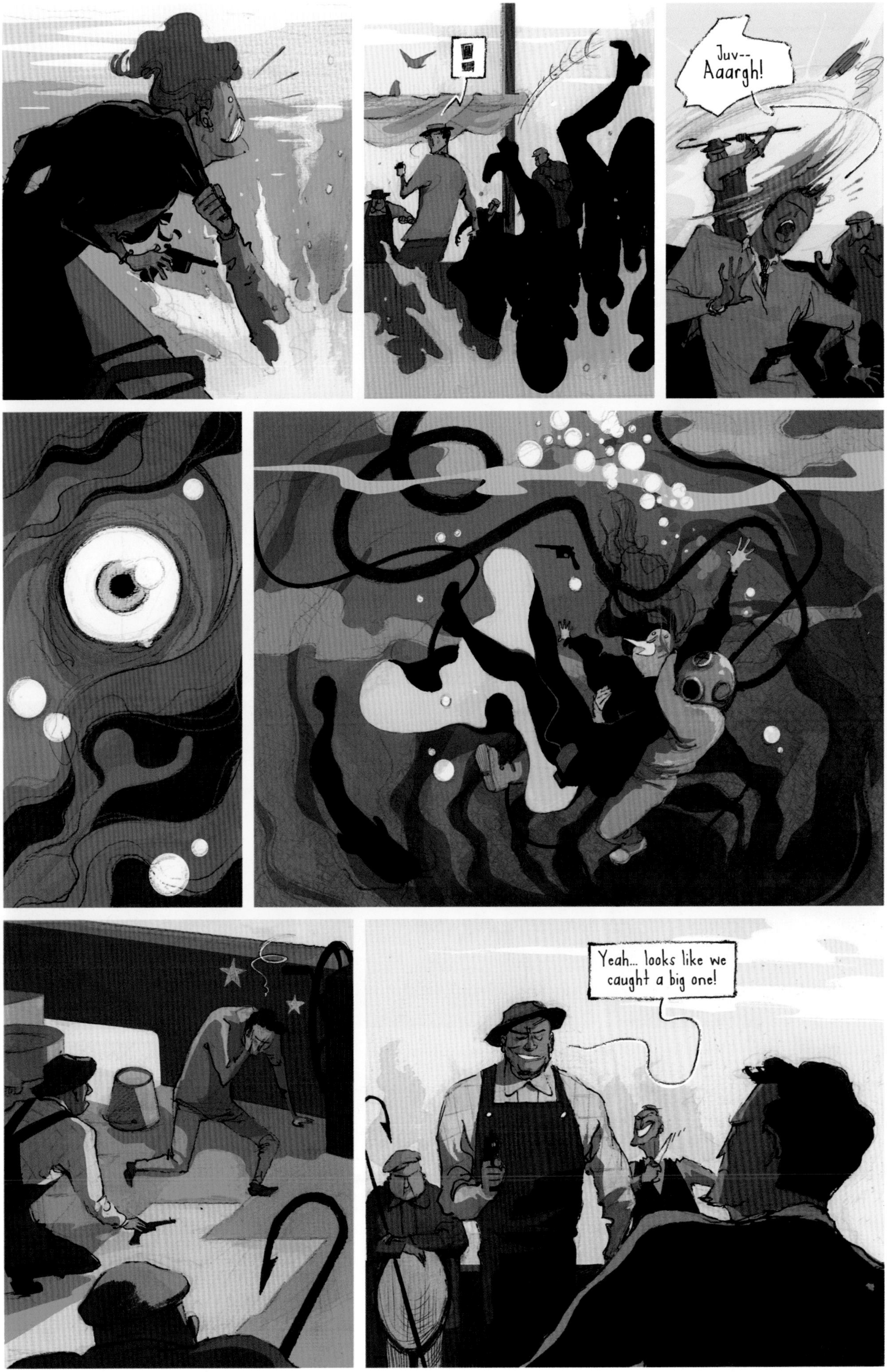
Juv--
Aaargh!
Yeah... looks like we caught a big one!

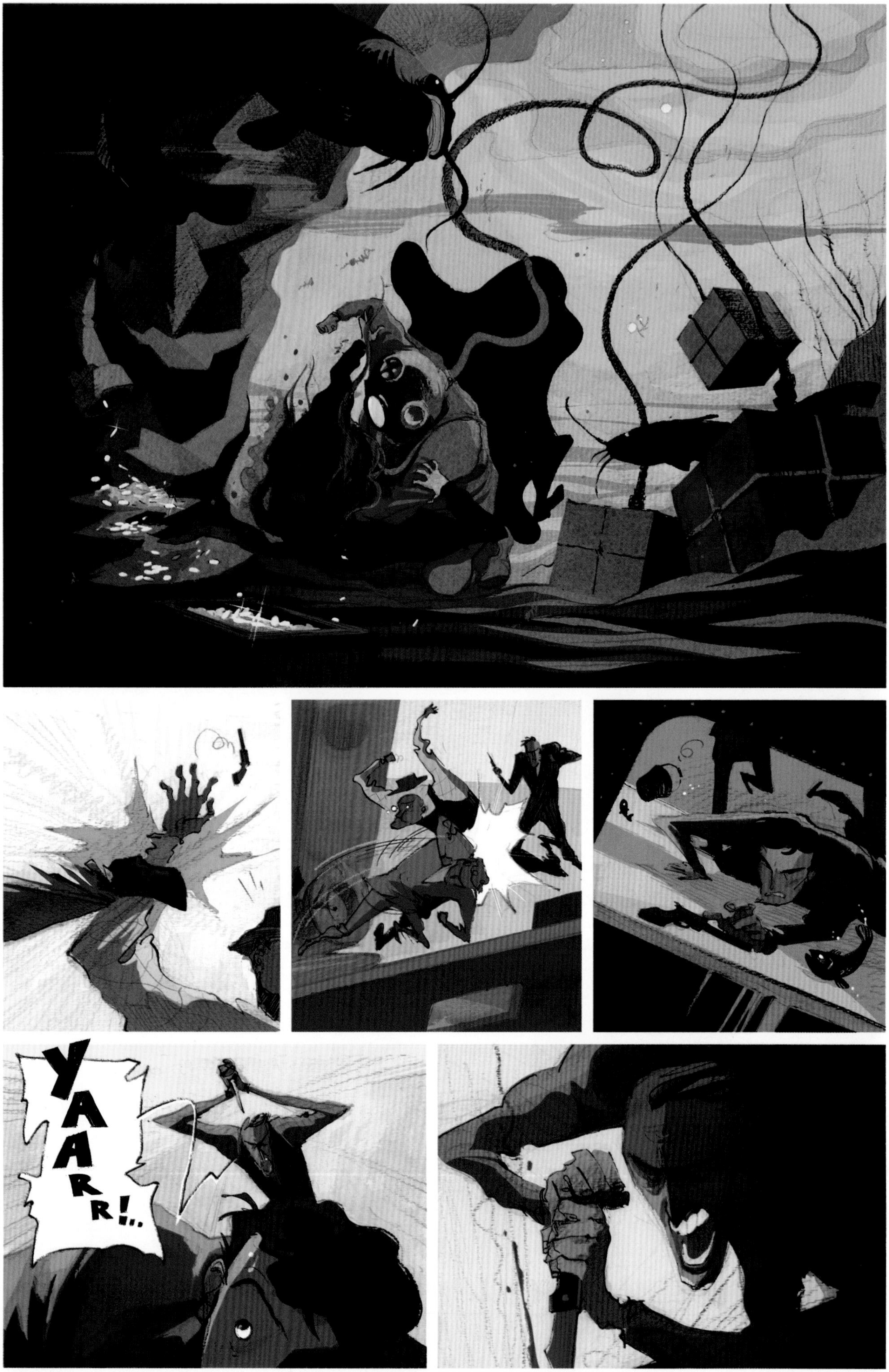
YAARR!..

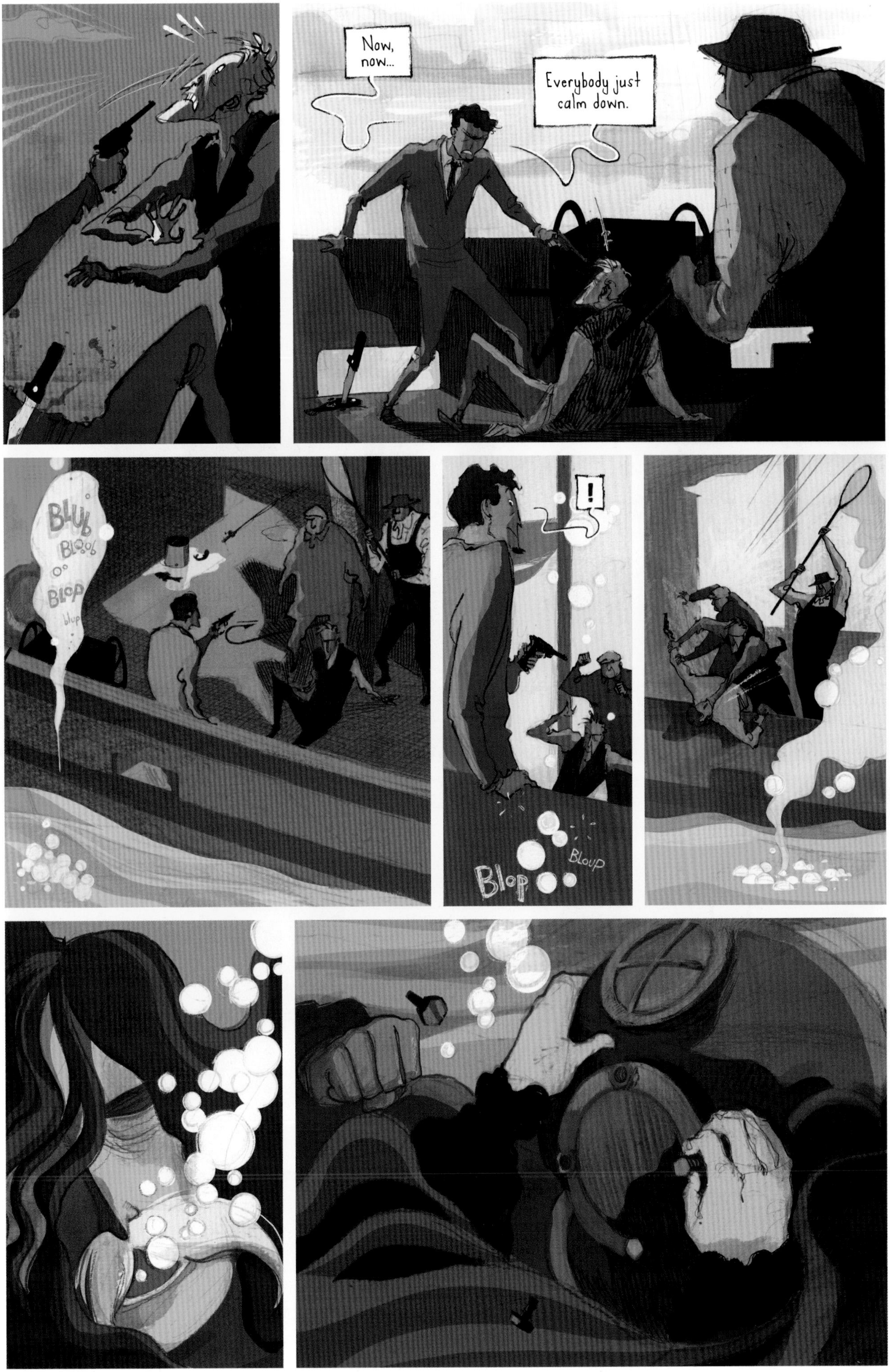
Now, now...
Everybody just calm down.
BLUB
BLOOB
BLOP
bloup
!
Blop
Bloup

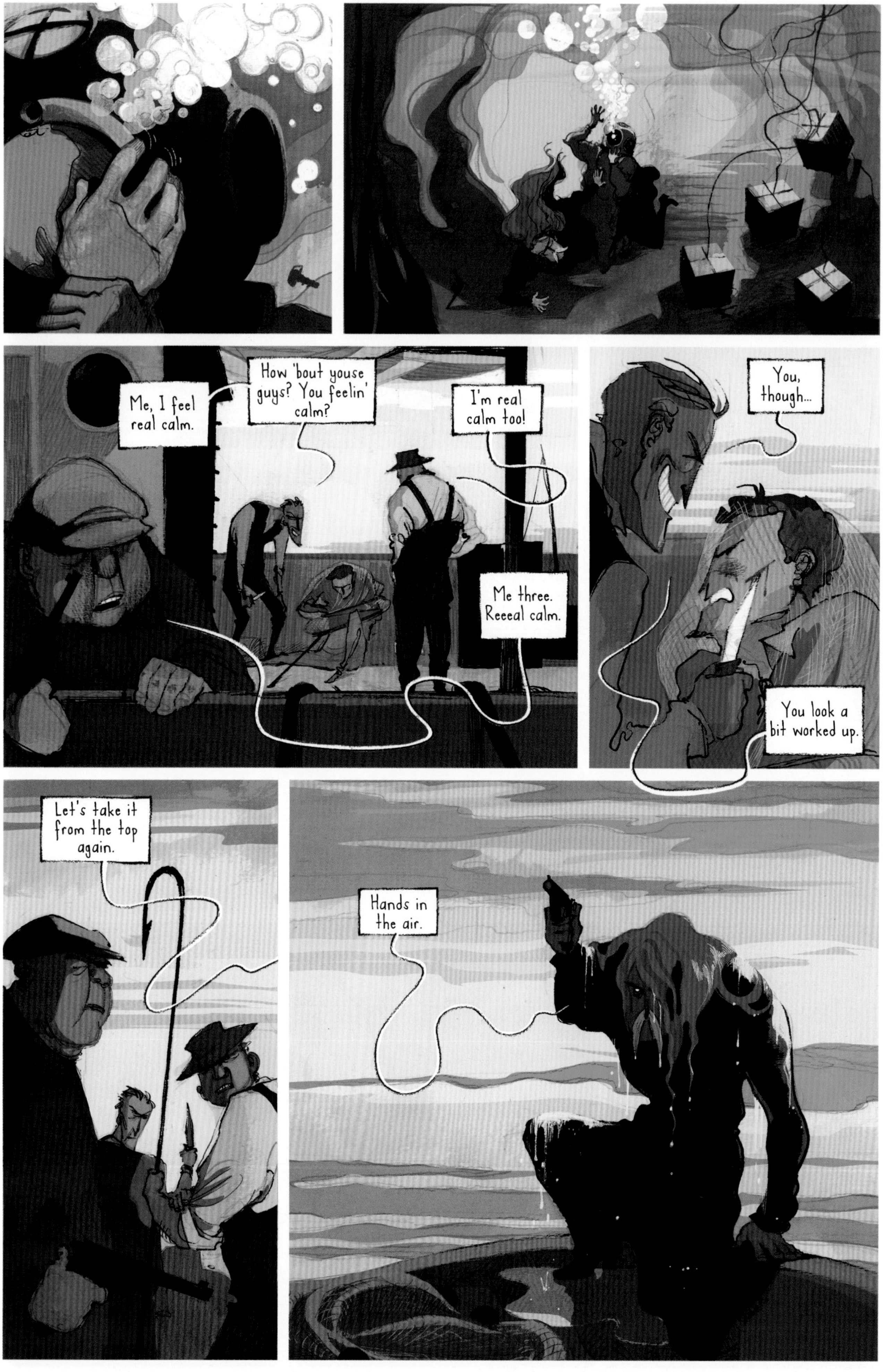
Me, I feel real calm.
How 'bout youse guys? You feelin' calm?
I'm real calm too!
Me three. Reeeal calm.
You, though...
You look a bit worked up.
Let's take it from the top again.
Hands in the air.

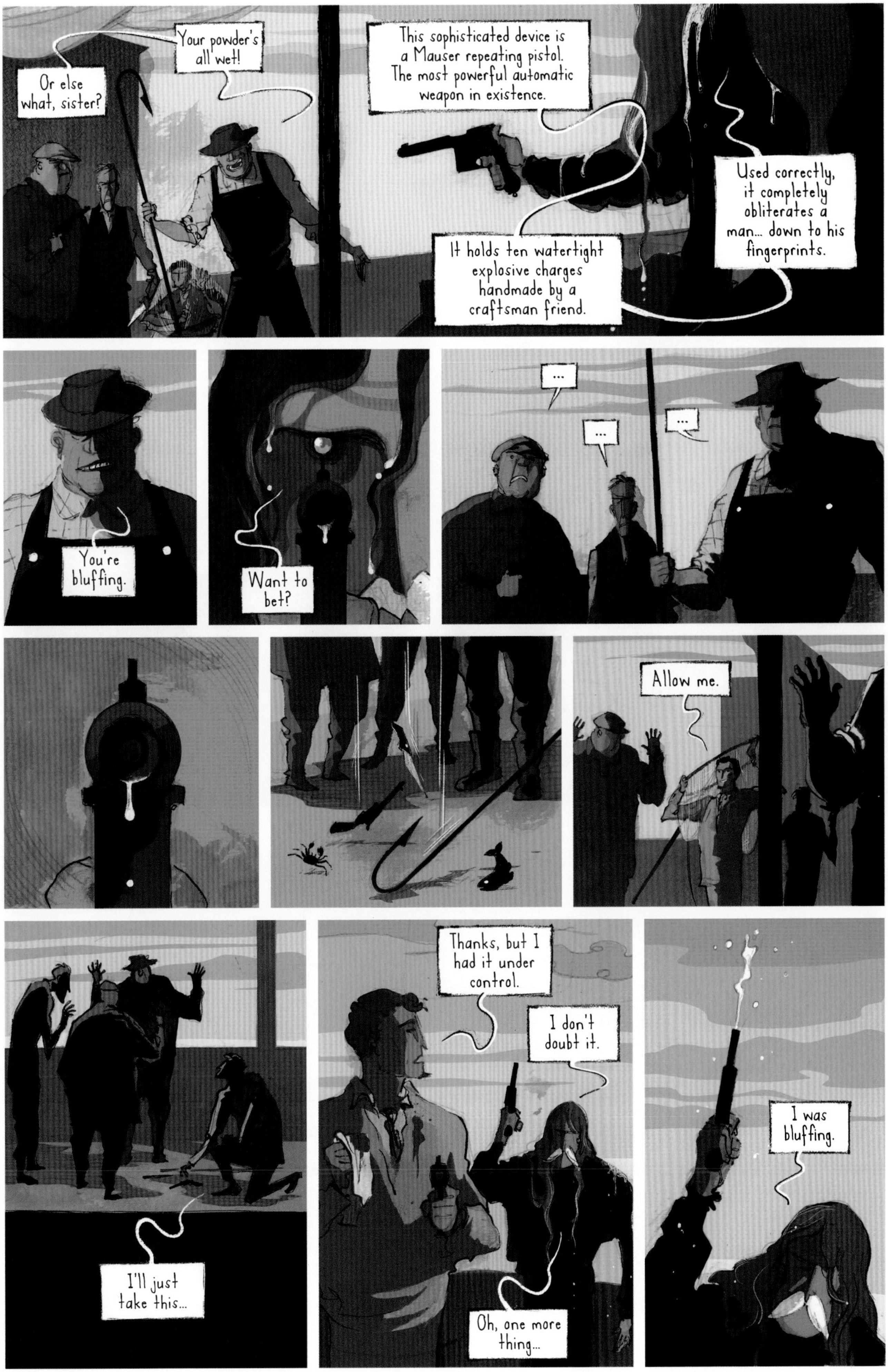

Or else what, sister?
Your powder's all wet!
This sophisticated device is a Mauser repeating pistol. The most powerful automatic weapon in existence.
It holds ten watertight explosive charges handmade by a craftsman friend.
Used correctly, it completely obliterates a man... down to his fingerprints.
You're bluffing.
Want to bet?
...
...
...
Allow me.
I'll just take this...
Thanks, but I had it under control.
I don't doubt it.
Oh, one more thing...
I was bluffing.

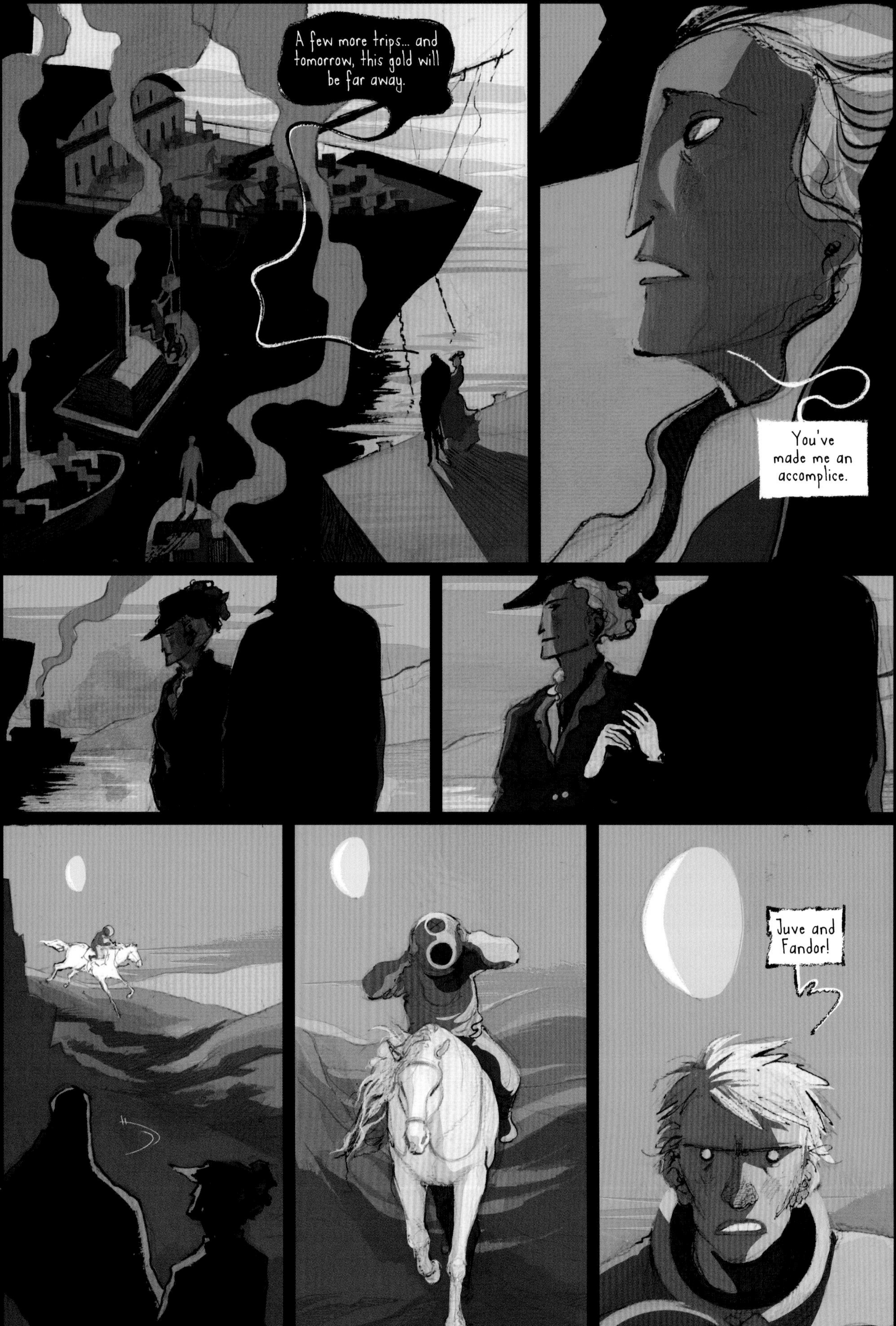
A few more trips... and tomorrow, this gold will be far away.
You've made me an accomplice.
Juve and Fandor!

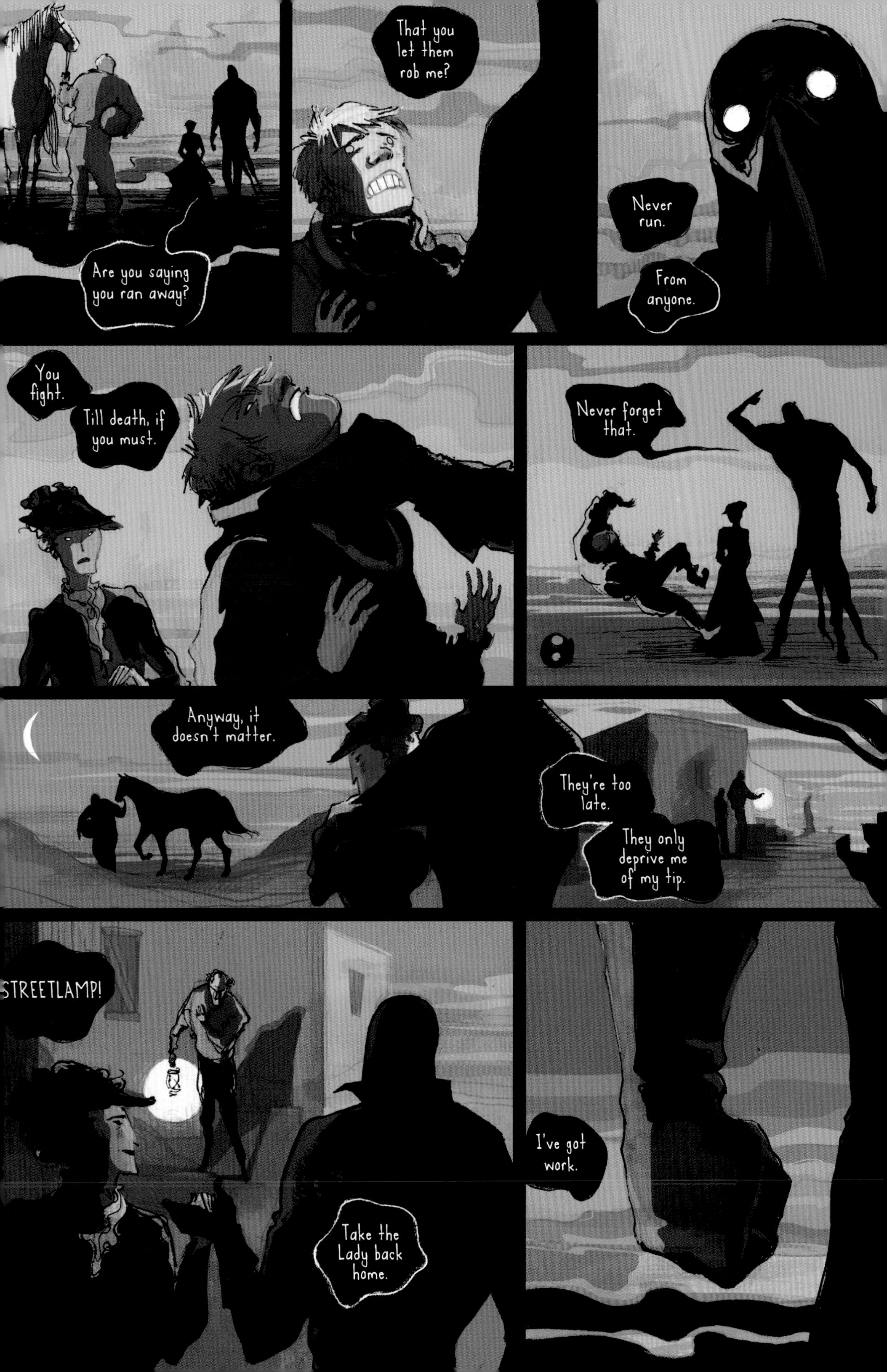
Are you saying you ran away?
That you let them rob me?
Never run.
From anyone.
You fight.
Till death, if you must.
Never forget that.
Anyway, it doesn't matter.
They're too late.
They only deprive me of my tip.
STREETLAMP!
Take the Lady back home.
I've got work.

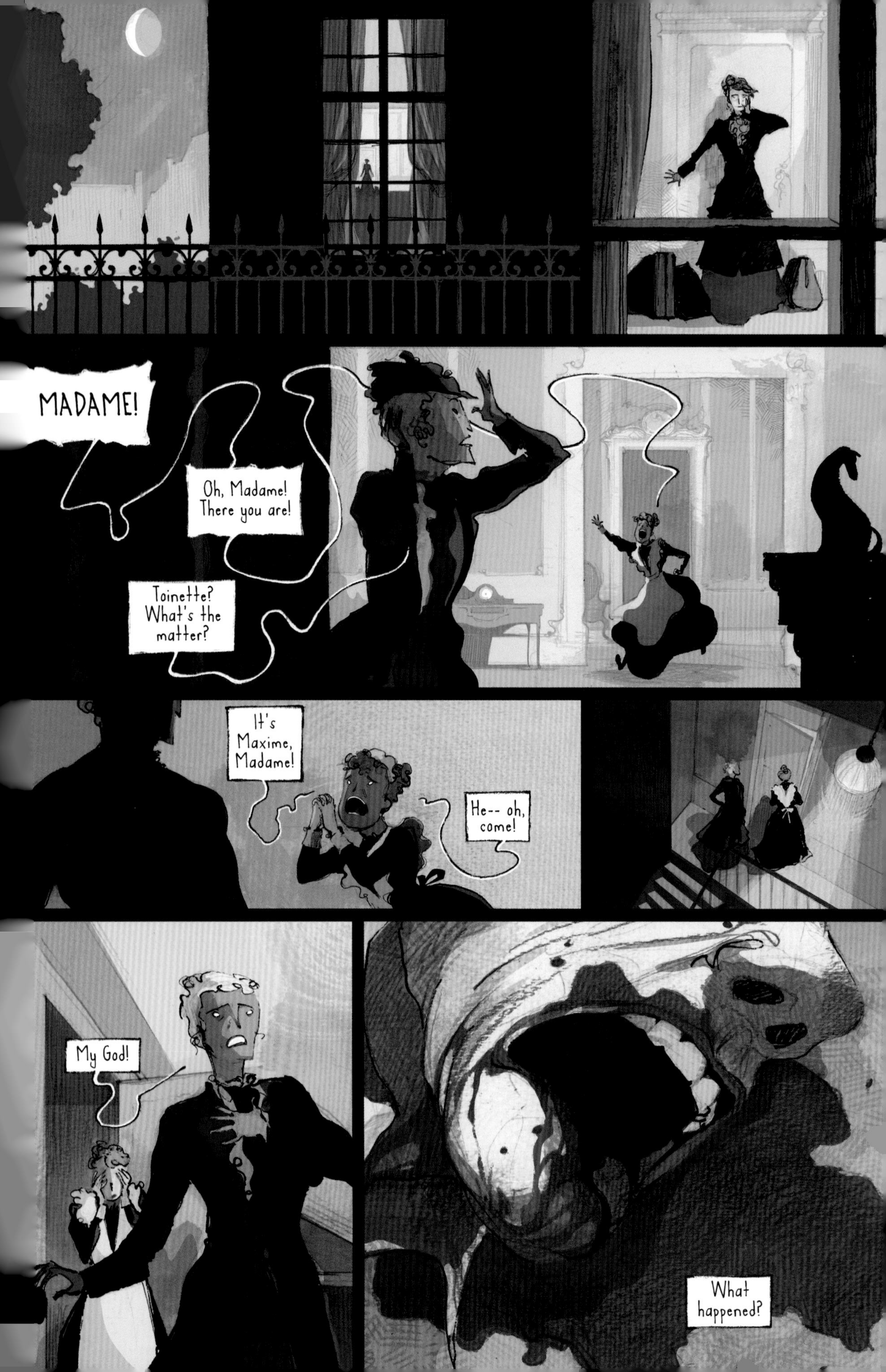

MADAME!
Oh, Madame! There you are!
Toinette? What's the matter?
It's Maxime, Madame!
He-- oh, come!
My God!
What happened?

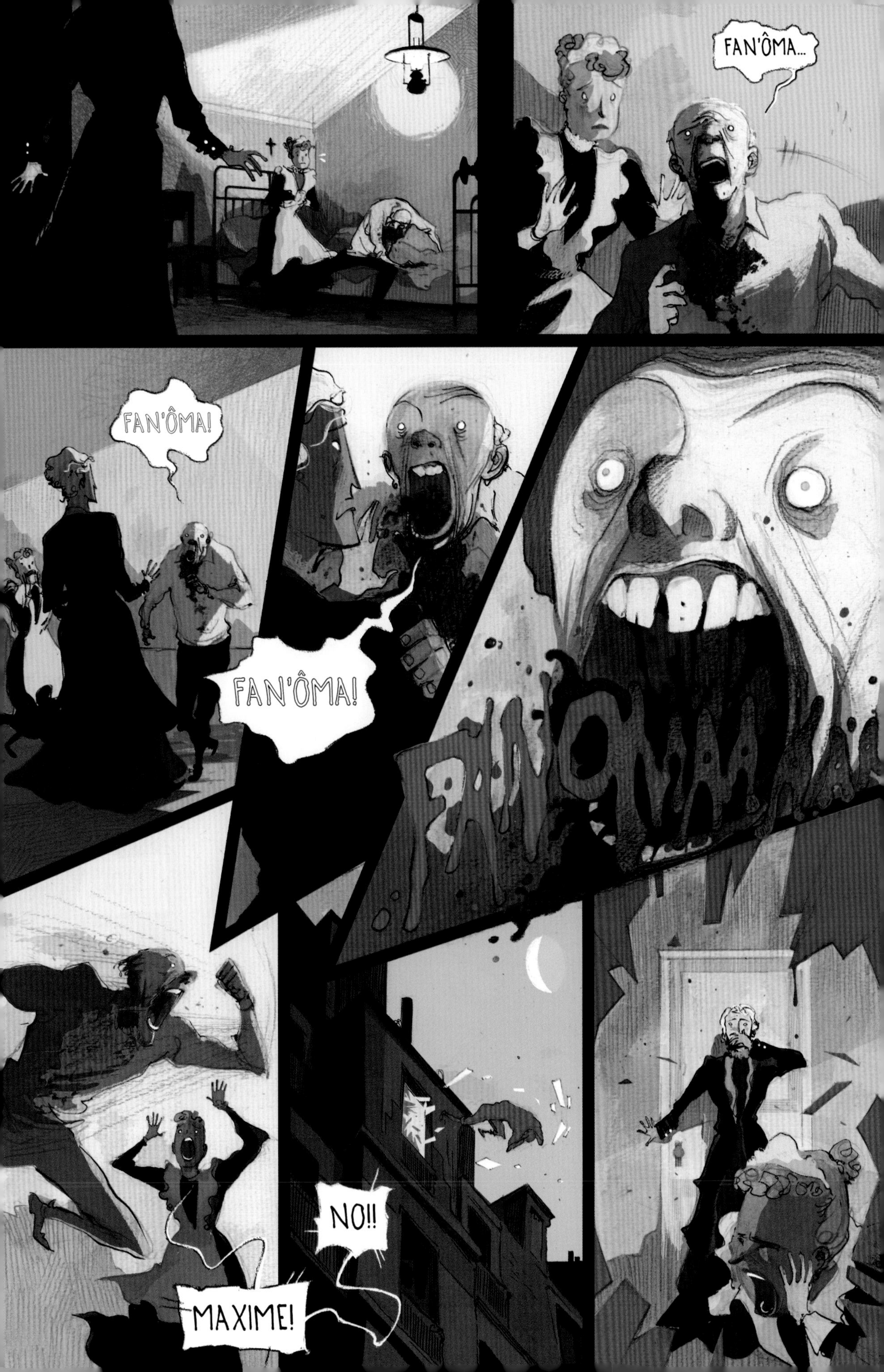
FAN'ÔMA...
FAN'ÔMA!
FAN'ÔMA!
FAN'ÔMA
MAXIME!
NO!!

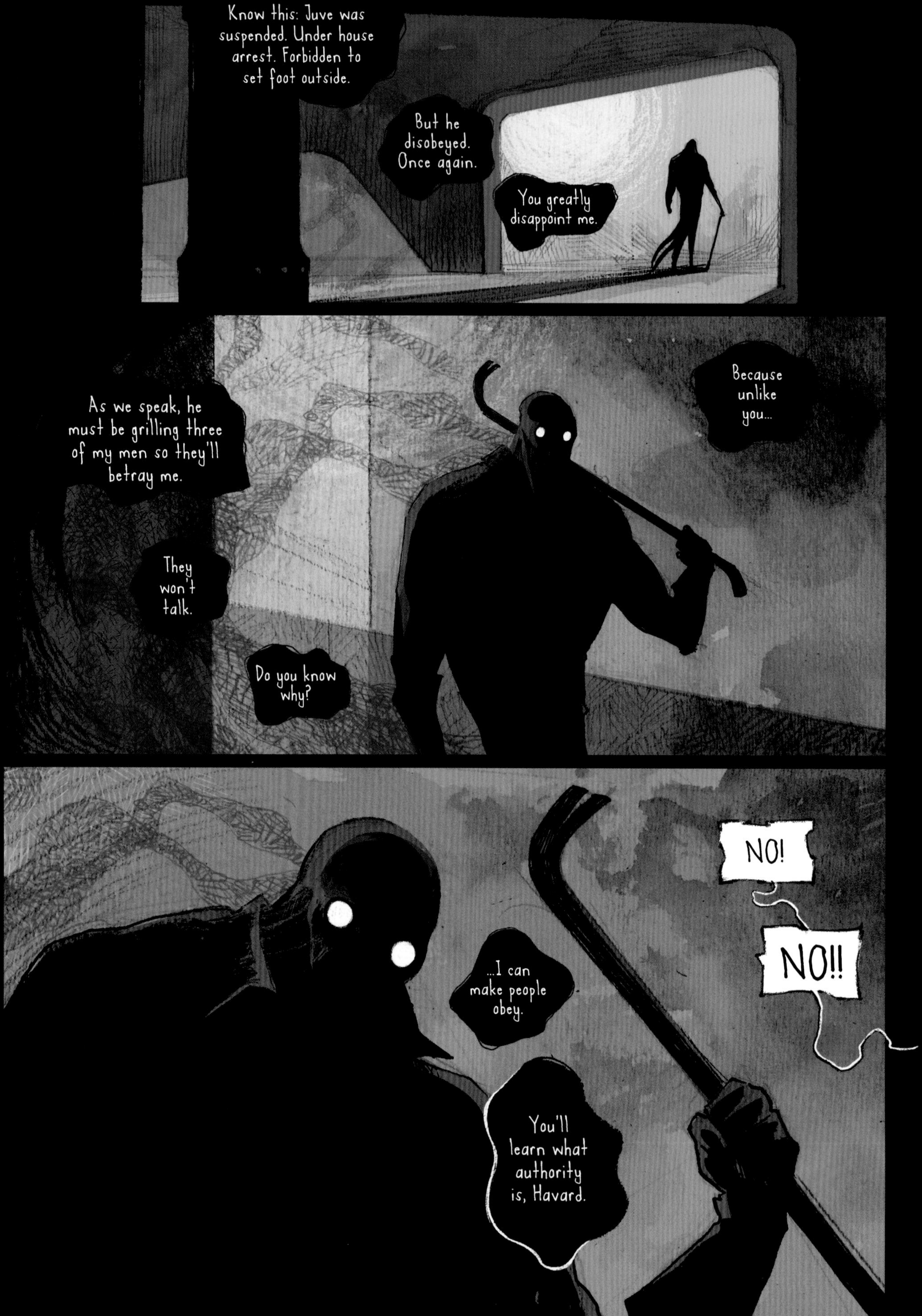
Know this: Juve was suspended. Under house arrest. Forbidden to set foot outside.
But he disobeyed. Once again.
You greatly disappoint me.
As we speak, he must be grilling three of my men so they'll betray me.
They won't talk.
Do you know why?
Because unlike you...
...I can make people obey.
You'll learn what authority is, Havard.
NO!
NO!!

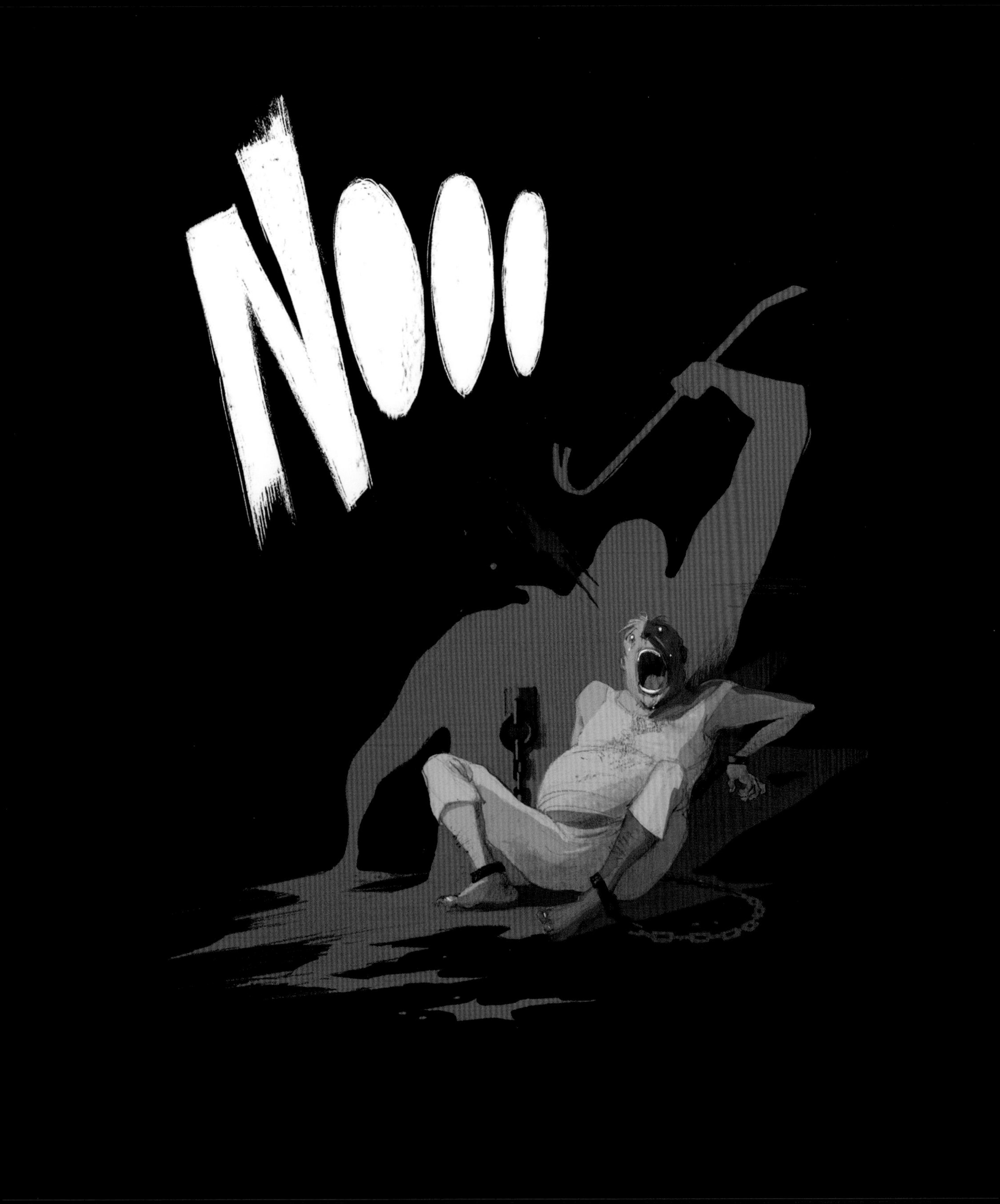
NOOO

# BOOK III

# HEADLONG

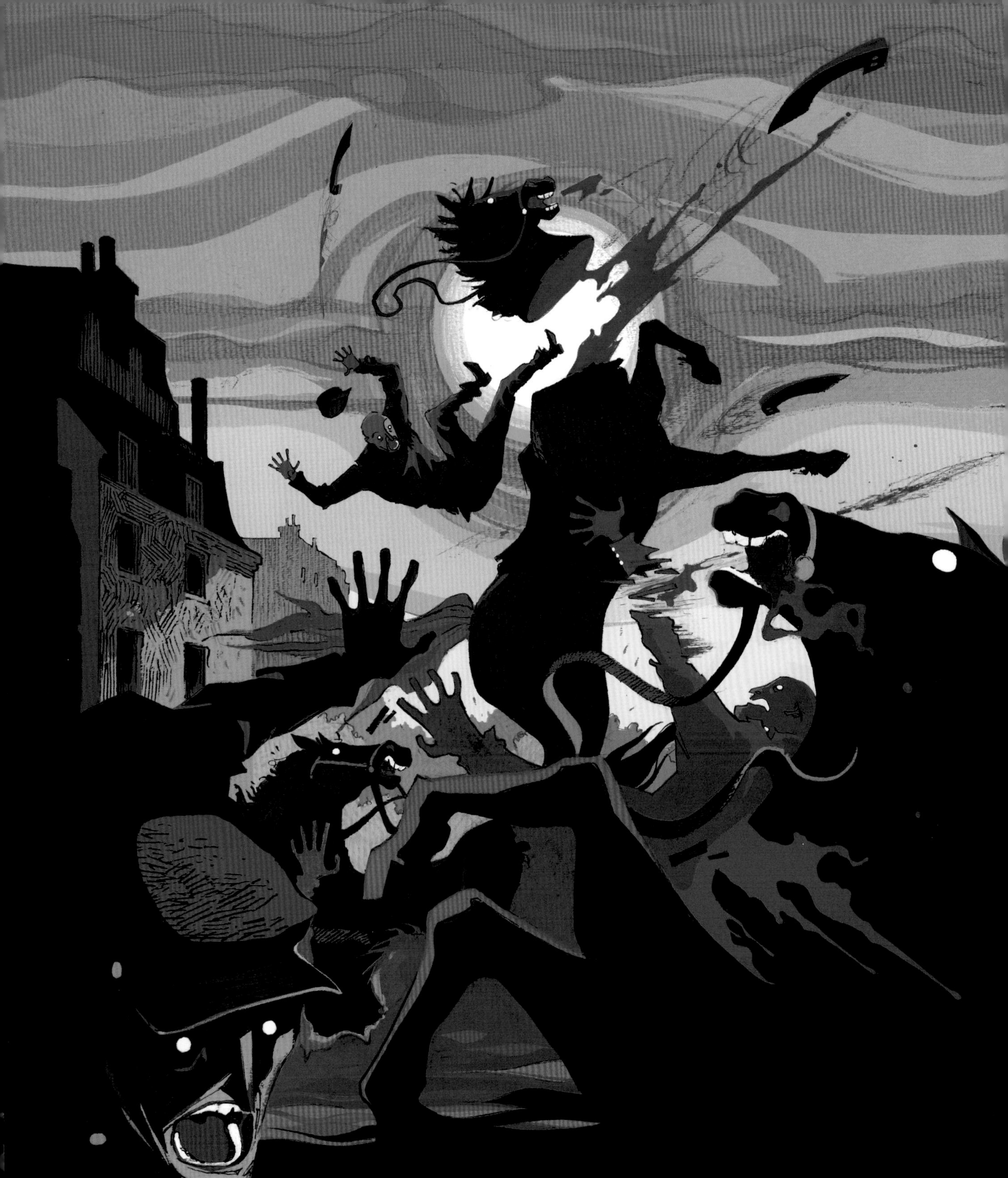

# HEADLONG

In which
an attempt to board a ship goes wrong,
Paris is crossed at a gallop,
a bolt changes the course of history,
and a love story comes to an end.

Friday, September 15, 1911

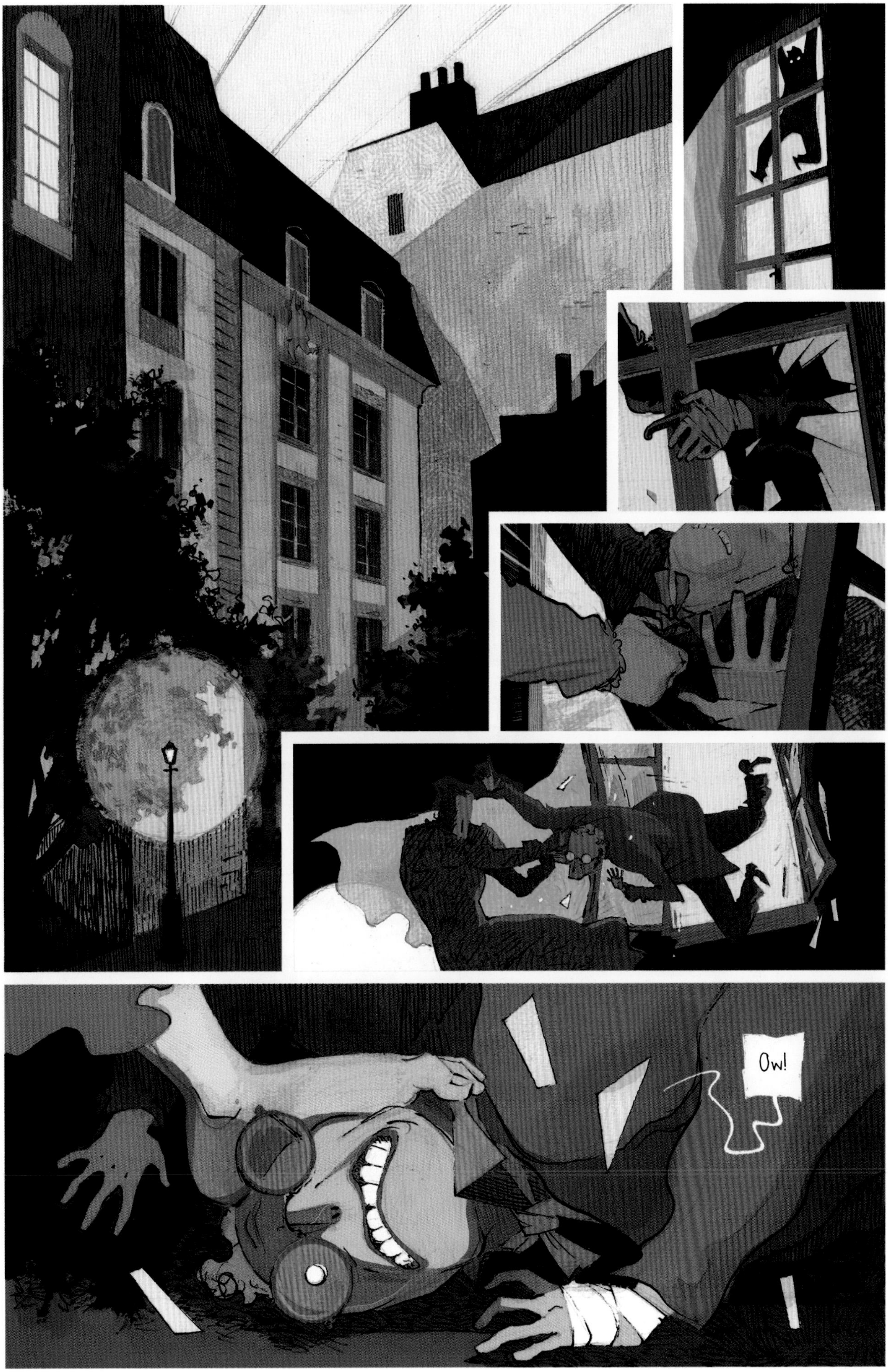
Ow!

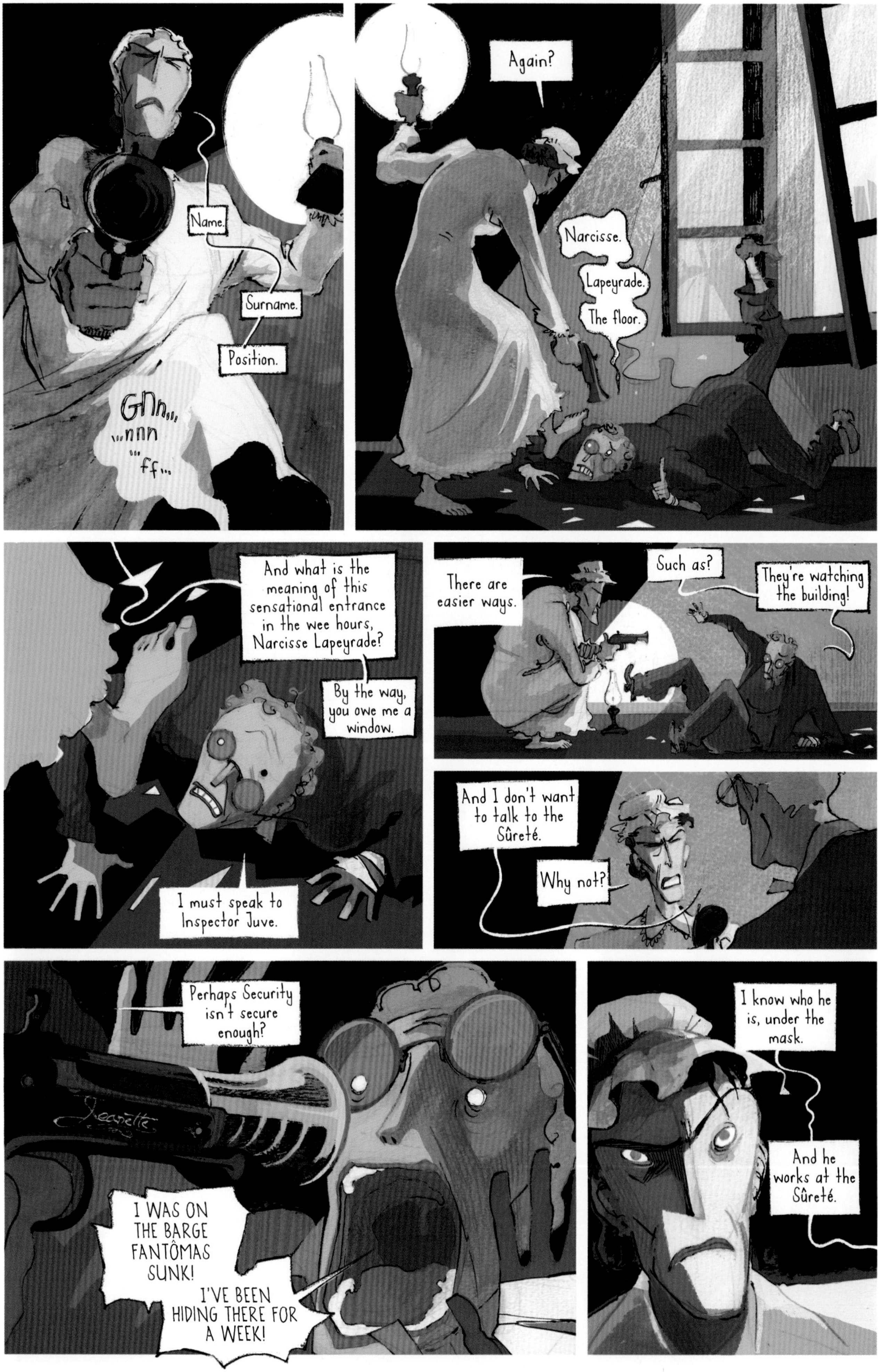
Name.
Surname.
Position.
GNn... ...nnn ...ff...
Again?
Narcisse.
Lapeyrade.
The floor.
And what is the meaning of this sensational entrance in the wee hours, Narcisse Lapeyrade?
By the way, you owe me a window.
I must speak to Inspector Juve.
There are easier ways.
Such as?
They're watching the building!
And I don't want to talk to the Sûreté.
Why not?
Perhaps Security isn't secure enough?
I WAS ON THE BARGE FANTÔMAS SUNK!
I'VE BEEN HIDING THERE FOR A WEEK!
I know who he is, under the mask.
And he works at the Sûreté.

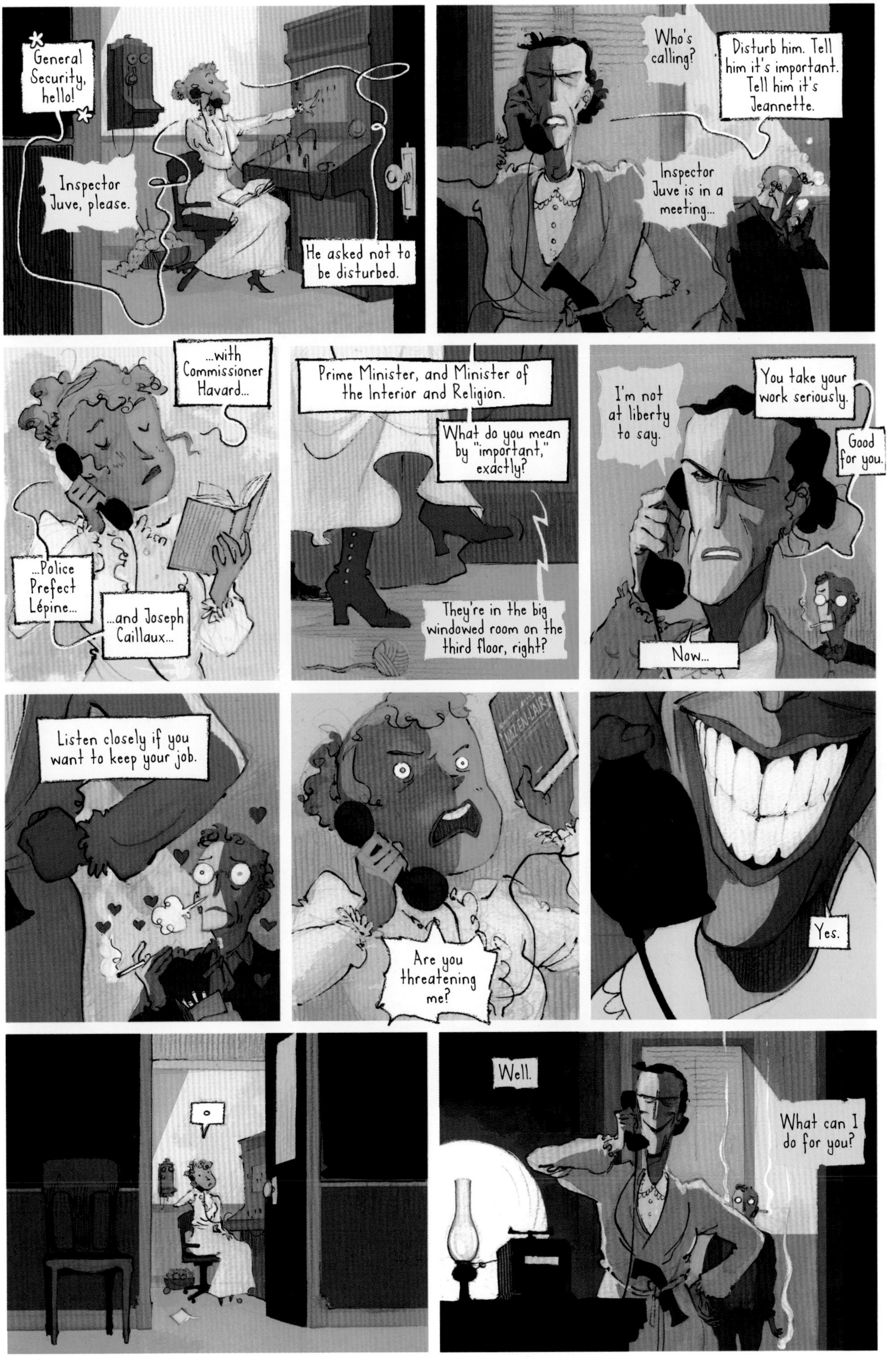
General Security, hello!
Inspector Juve, please.
He asked not to be disturbed.
Who's calling?
Disturb him. Tell him it's important. Tell him it's Jeannette.
Inspector Juve is in a meeting...
...with Commissioner Havard...
...Police Prefect Lépine...
...and Joseph Caillaux...
Prime Minister, and Minister of the Interior and Religion.
What do you mean by "important," exactly?
They're in the big windowed room on the third floor, right?
I'm not at liberty to say.
You take your work seriously.
Good for you.
Now...
Listen closely if you want to keep your job.
Are you threatening me?
Yes.
o
Well.
What can I do for you?

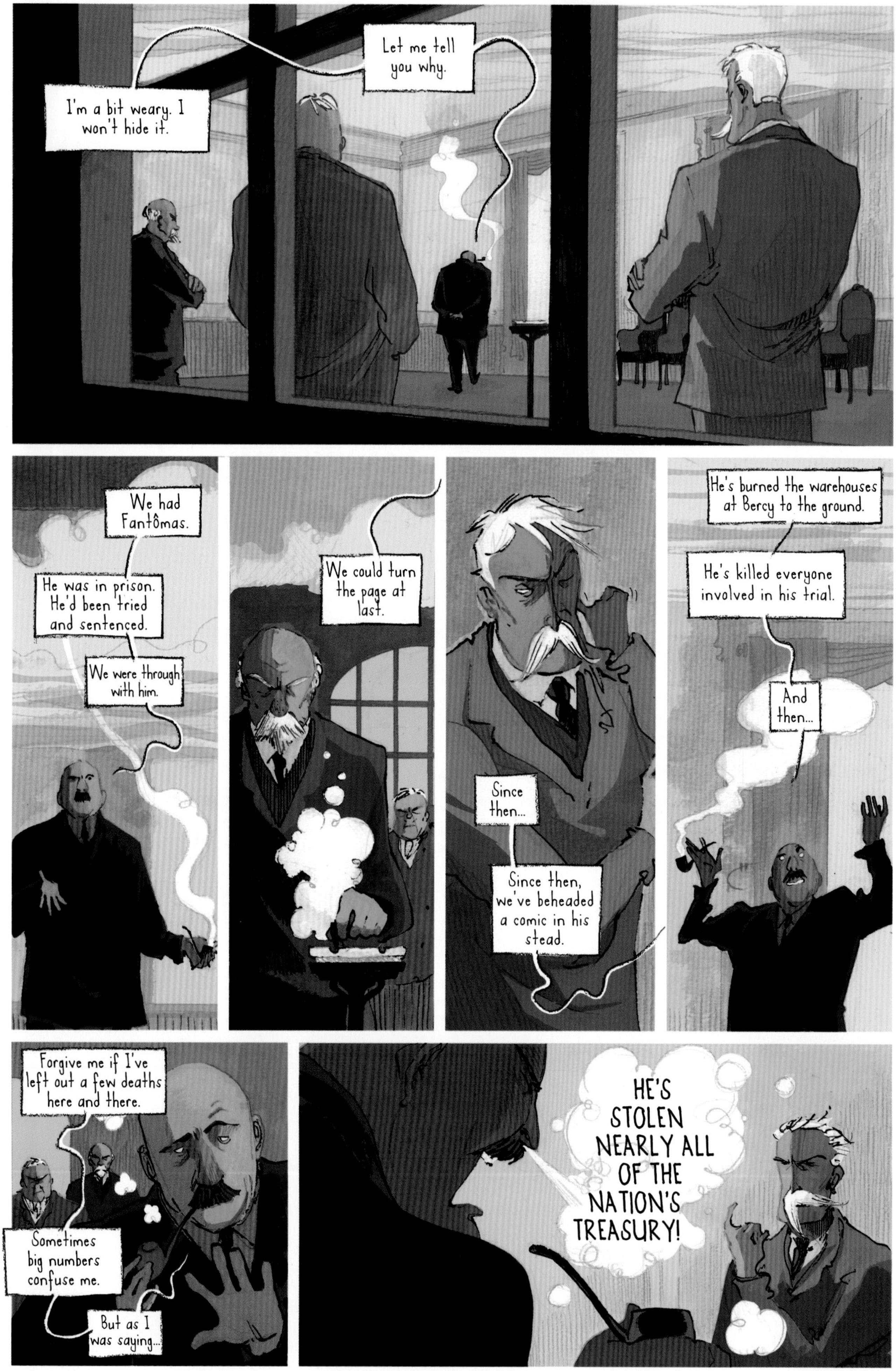
I'm a bit weary. I won't hide it.
Let me tell you why.
We had Fantômas.
He was in prison. He'd been tried and sentenced.
We were through with him.
We could turn the page at last.
Since then...
Since then, we've beheaded a comic in his stead.
He's burned the warehouses at Bercy to the ground.
He's killed everyone involved in his trial.
And then...
Forgive me if I've left out a few deaths here and there.
Sometimes big numbers confuse me.
But as I was saying...
HE'S STOLEN NEARLY ALL OF THE NATION'S TREASURY!

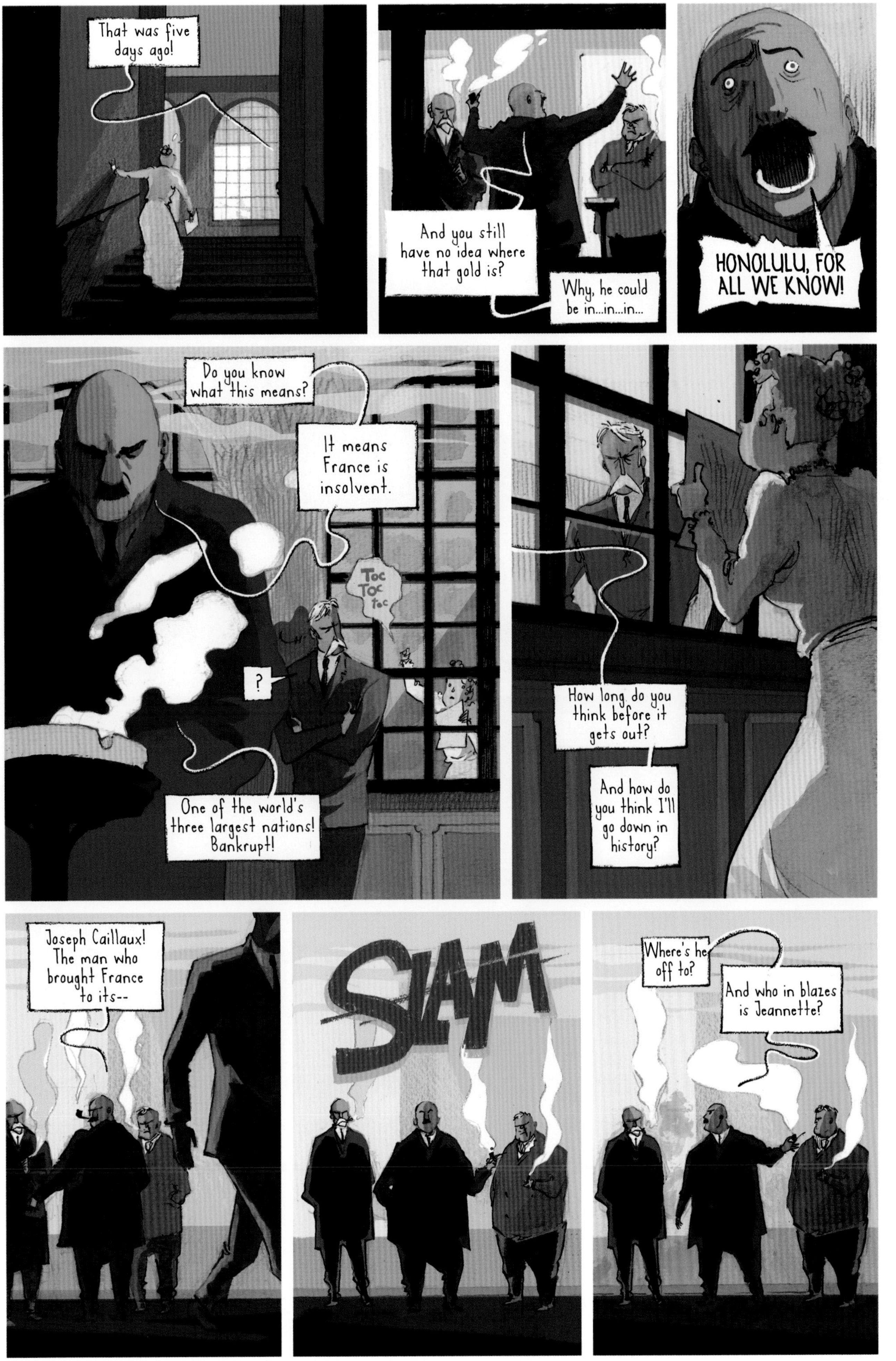

That was five days ago!
And you still have no idea where that gold is?
Why, he could be in...in...in...
HONOLULU, FOR ALL WE KNOW!
Do you know what this means?
It means France is insolvent.
TOC TOC toc
?
One of the world's three largest nations! Bankrupt!
How long do you think before it gets out?
And how do you think I'll go down in history?
Joseph Caillaux! The man who brought France to its--
SLAM
Where's he off to?
And who in blazes is Jeannette?

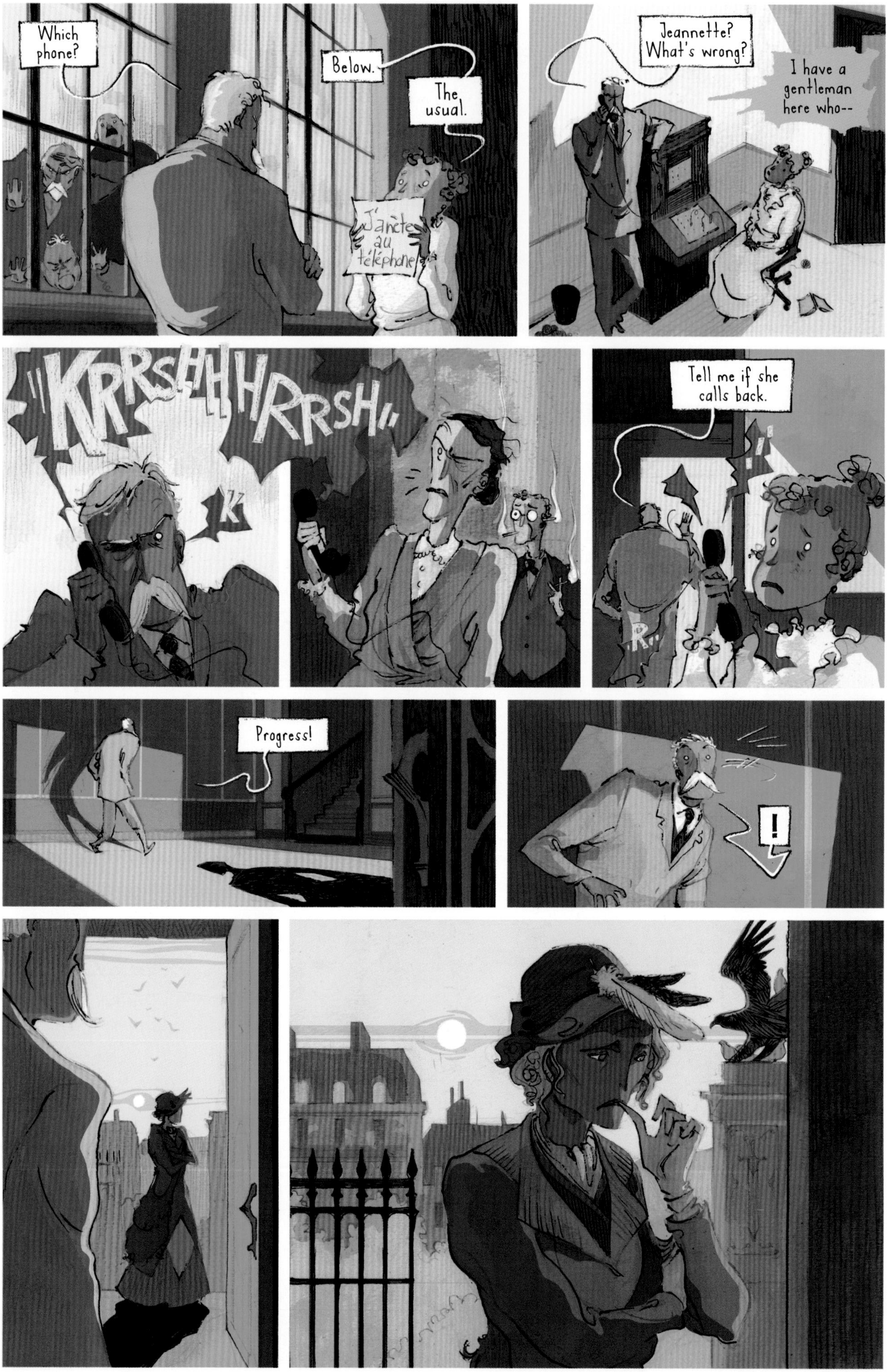

Which phone?
Below.
The usual.
J'ai ete au téléphone
Jeannette? What's wrong?
I have a gentleman here who--
KRRSHHHRRSH
K
Tell me if she calls back.
R
Progress!
!

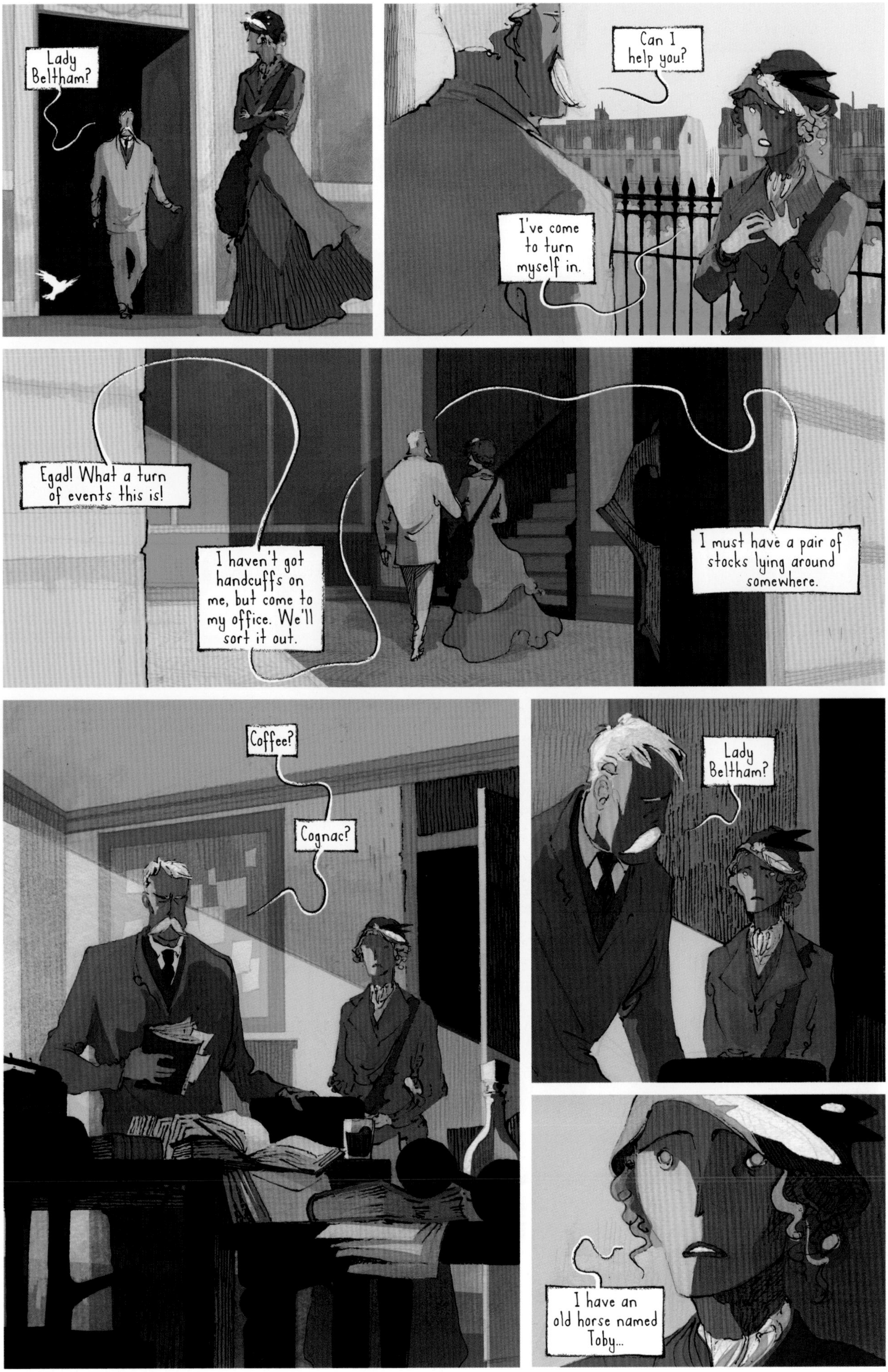
Lady Beltham?
Can I help you?
I've come to turn myself in.
Egad! What a turn of events this is!
I haven't got handcuffs on me, but come to my office. We'll sort it out.
I must have a pair of stocks lying around somewhere.
Coffee?
Cognac?
Lady Beltham?
I have an old horse named Toby...

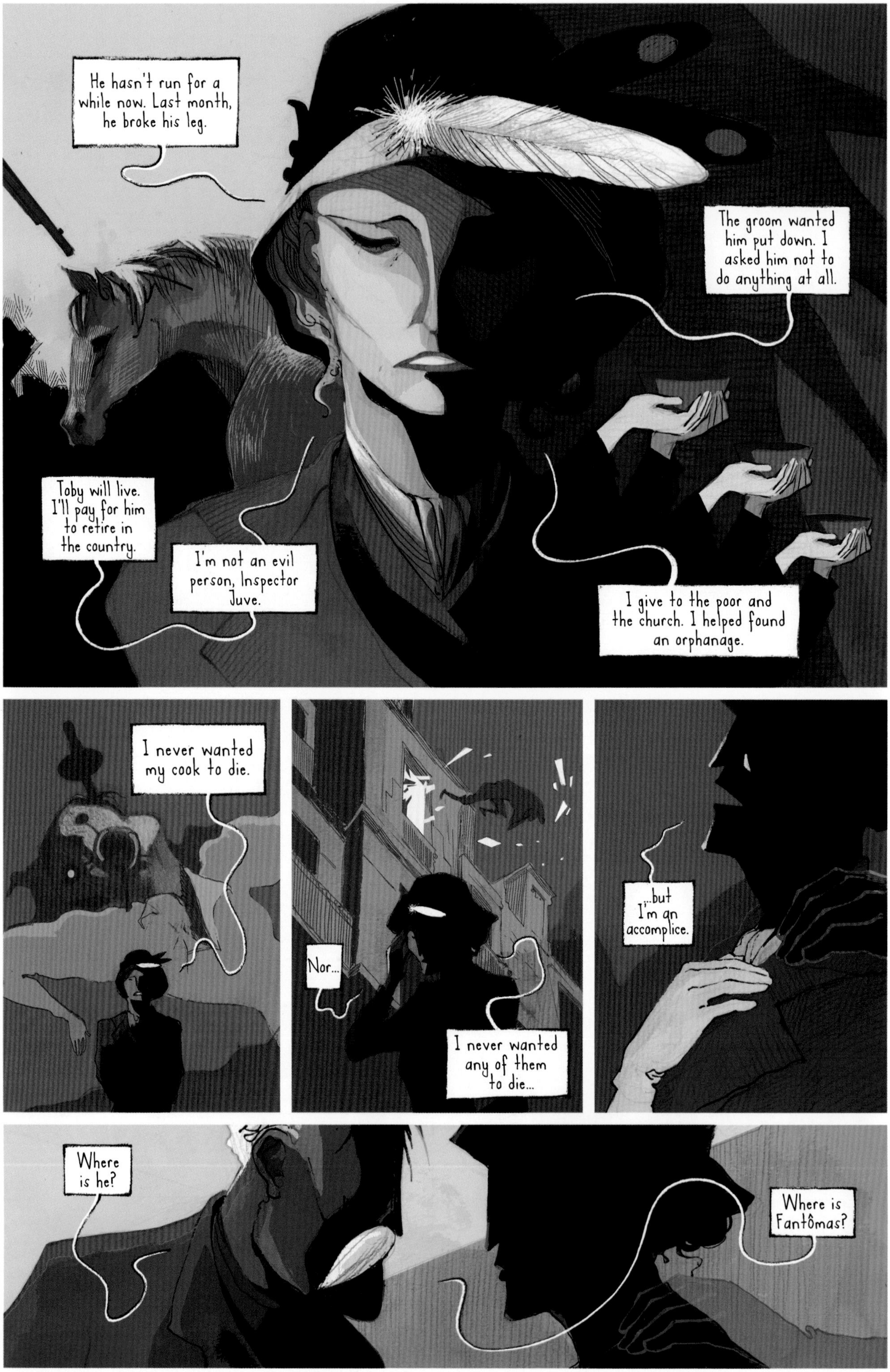
He hasn't run for a while now. Last month, he broke his leg.
The groom wanted him put down. I asked him not to do anything at all.
Toby will live. I'll pay for him to retire in the country.
I'm not an evil person, Inspector Juve.
I give to the poor and the church. I helped found an orphanage.
I never wanted my cook to die.
Nor...
I never wanted any of them to die...
...but I'm an accomplice.
Where is he?
Where is Fantômas?

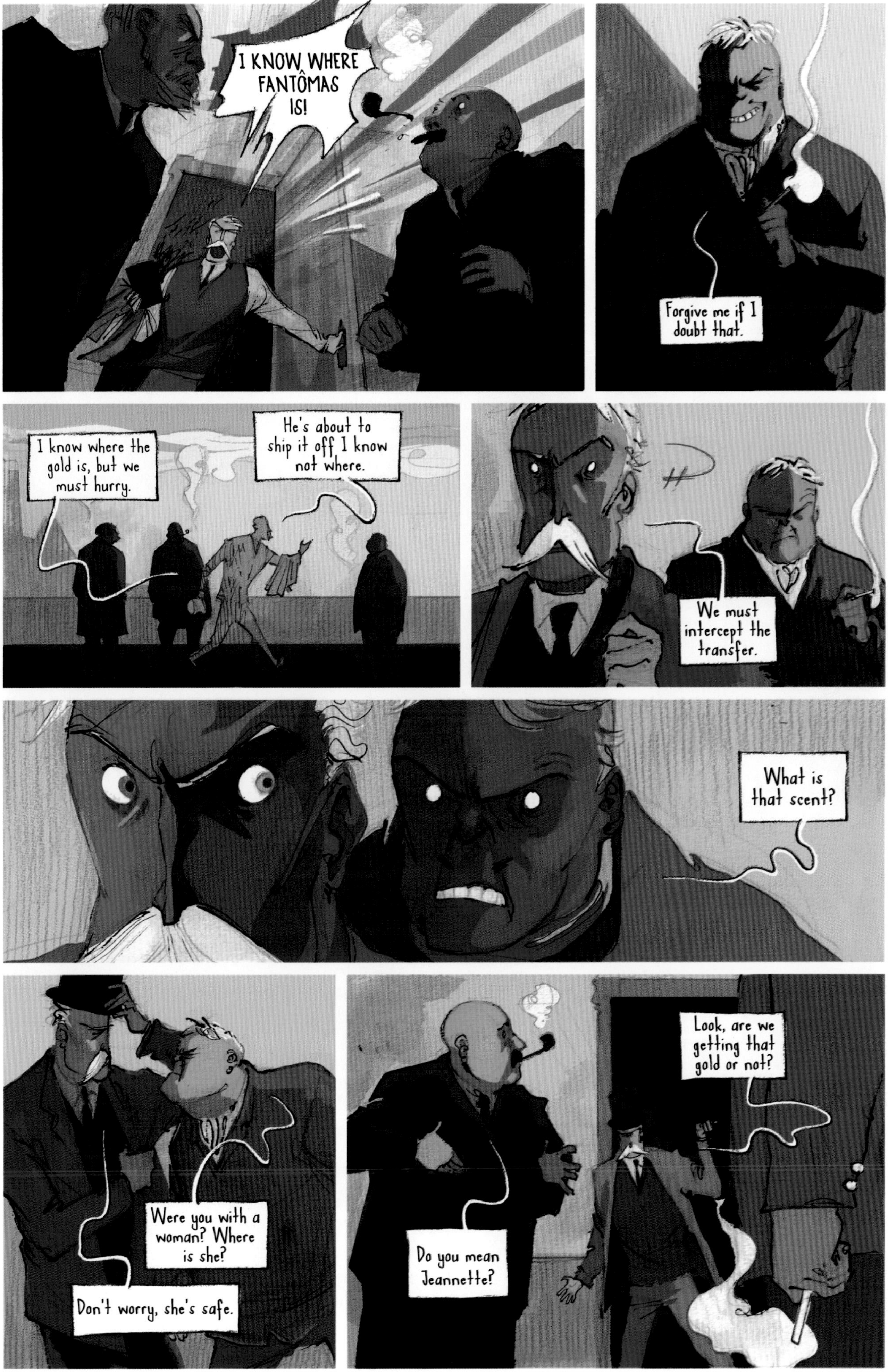
I KNOW WHERE FANTÔMAS IS!
Forgive me if I doubt that.
I know where the gold is, but we must hurry.
He's about to ship it off I know not where.
We must intercept the transfer.
What is that scent?
Were you with a woman? Where is she?
Don't worry, she's safe.
Do you mean Jeannette?
Look, are we getting that gold or not?

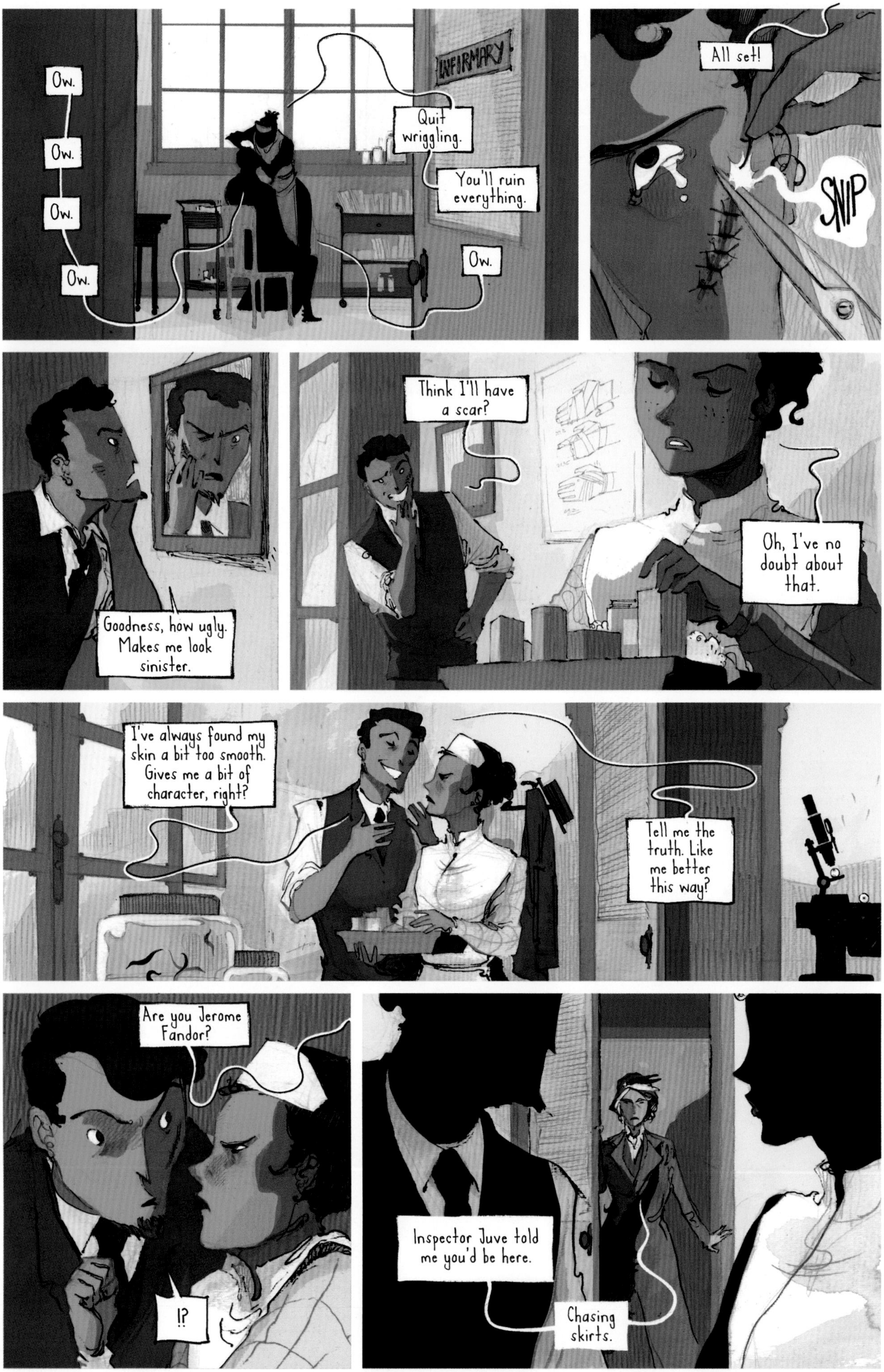
INFIRMARY
Ow.
Ow.
Ow.
Ow.
Quit wriggling.
You'll ruin everything.
Ow.
All set!
SNIP
Goodness, how ugly. Makes me look sinister.
Think I'll have a scar?
Oh, I've no doubt about that.
I've always found my skin a bit too smooth. Gives me a bit of character, right?
Tell me the truth. Like me better this way?
Are you Jerome Fandor?
!?
Inspector Juve told me you'd be here.
Chasing skirts.

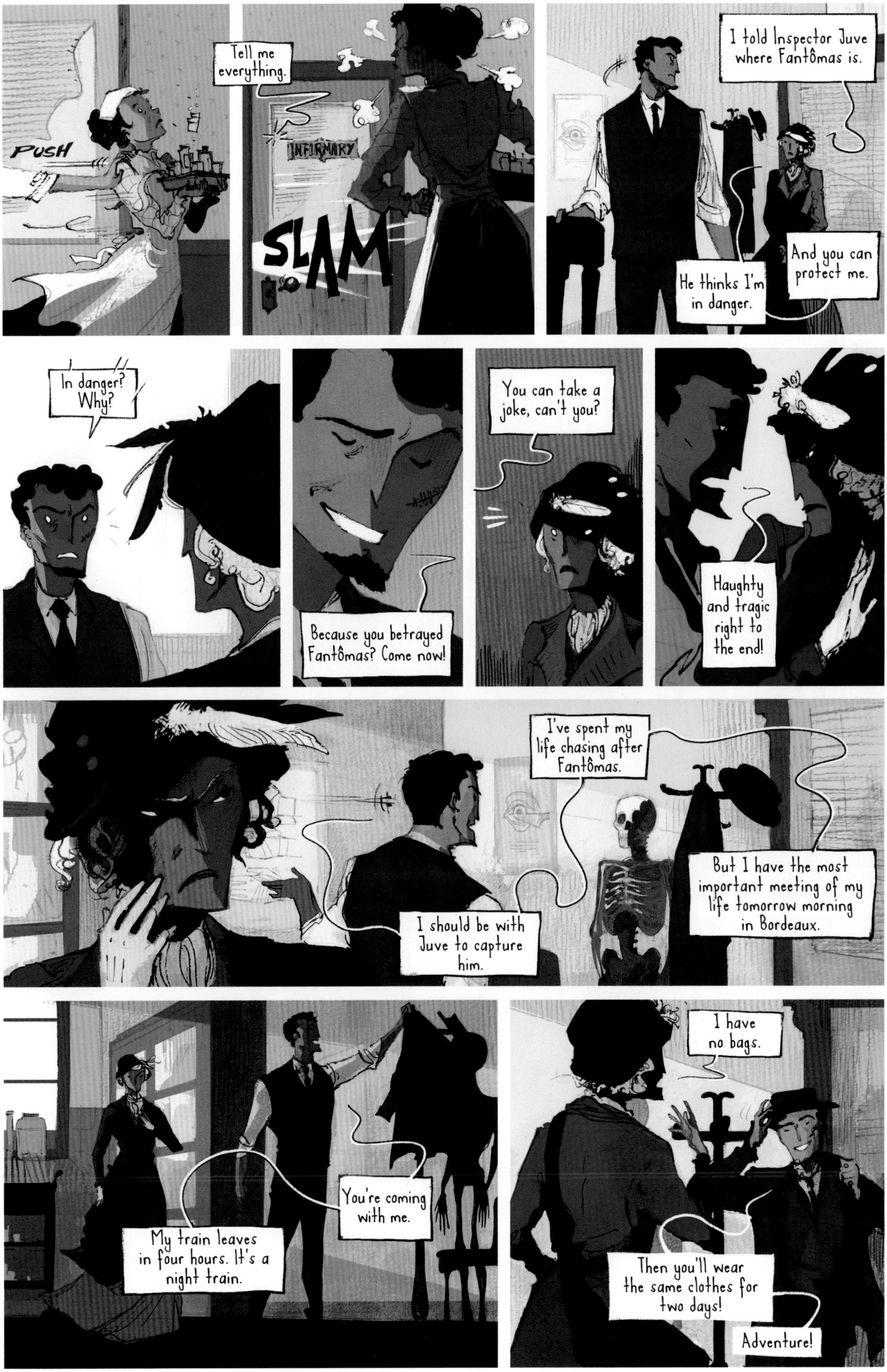
PUSH
Tell me everything.
INFIRMARY
SLAM
I told Inspector Juve where Fantômas is.
He thinks I'm in danger.
And you can protect me.
In danger? Why?
Because you betrayed Fantômas? Come now!
You can take a joke, can't you?
Haughty and tragic right to the end!
I've spent my life chasing after Fantômas.
I should be with Juve to capture him.
But I have the most important meeting of my life tomorrow morning in Bordeaux.
You're coming with me.
My train leaves in four hours. It's a night train.
I have no bags.
Then you'll wear the same clothes for two days!
Adventure!

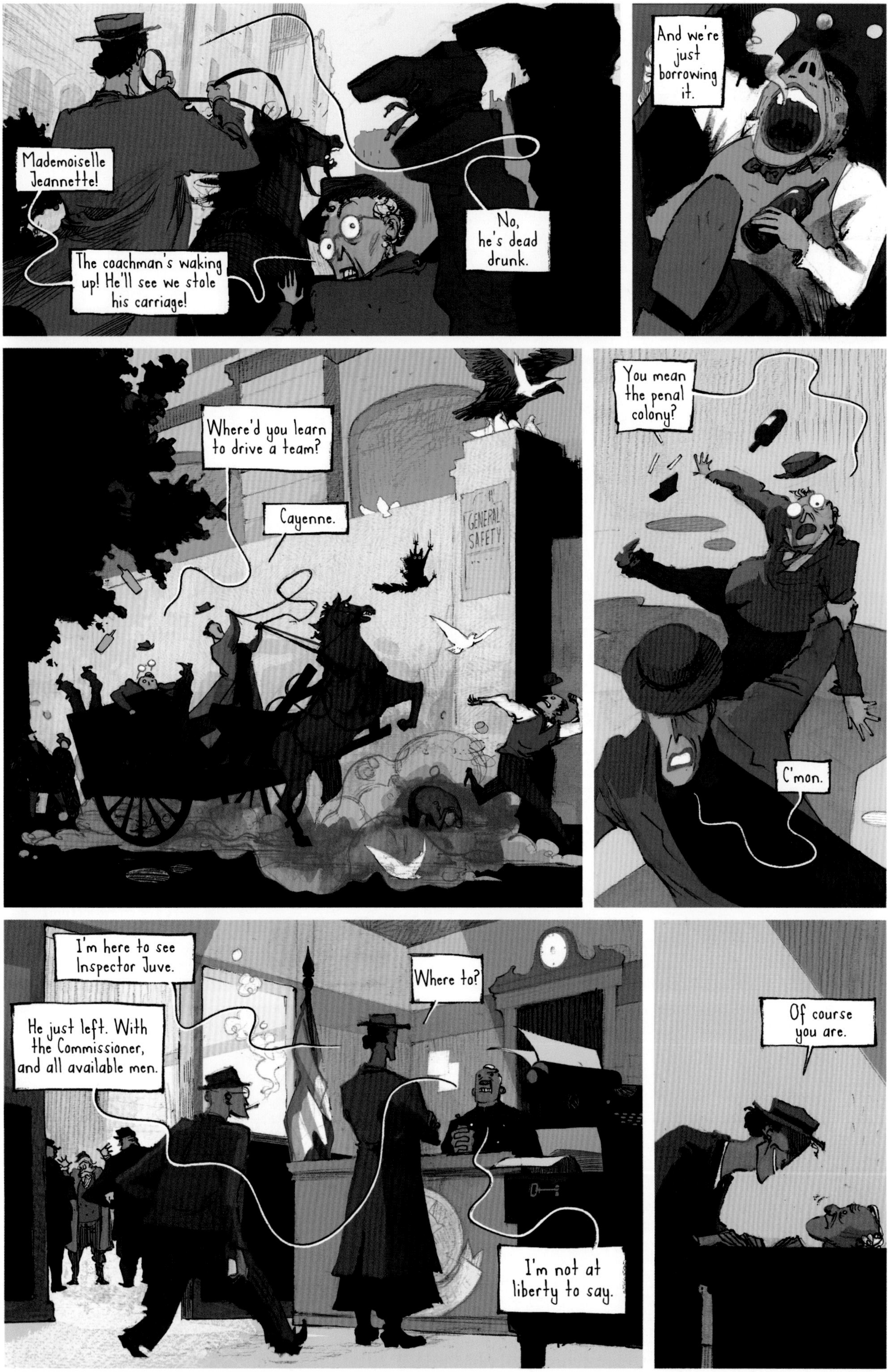
Mademoiselle Jeannette!
The coachman's waking up! He'll see we stole his carriage!
No, he's dead drunk.
And we're just borrowing it.
Where'd you learn to drive a team?
Cayenne.
GENERAL SAFETY
You mean the penal colony?
C'mon.
I'm here to see Inspector Juve.
He just left. With the Commissioner, and all available men.
Where to?
I'm not at liberty to say.
Of course you are.

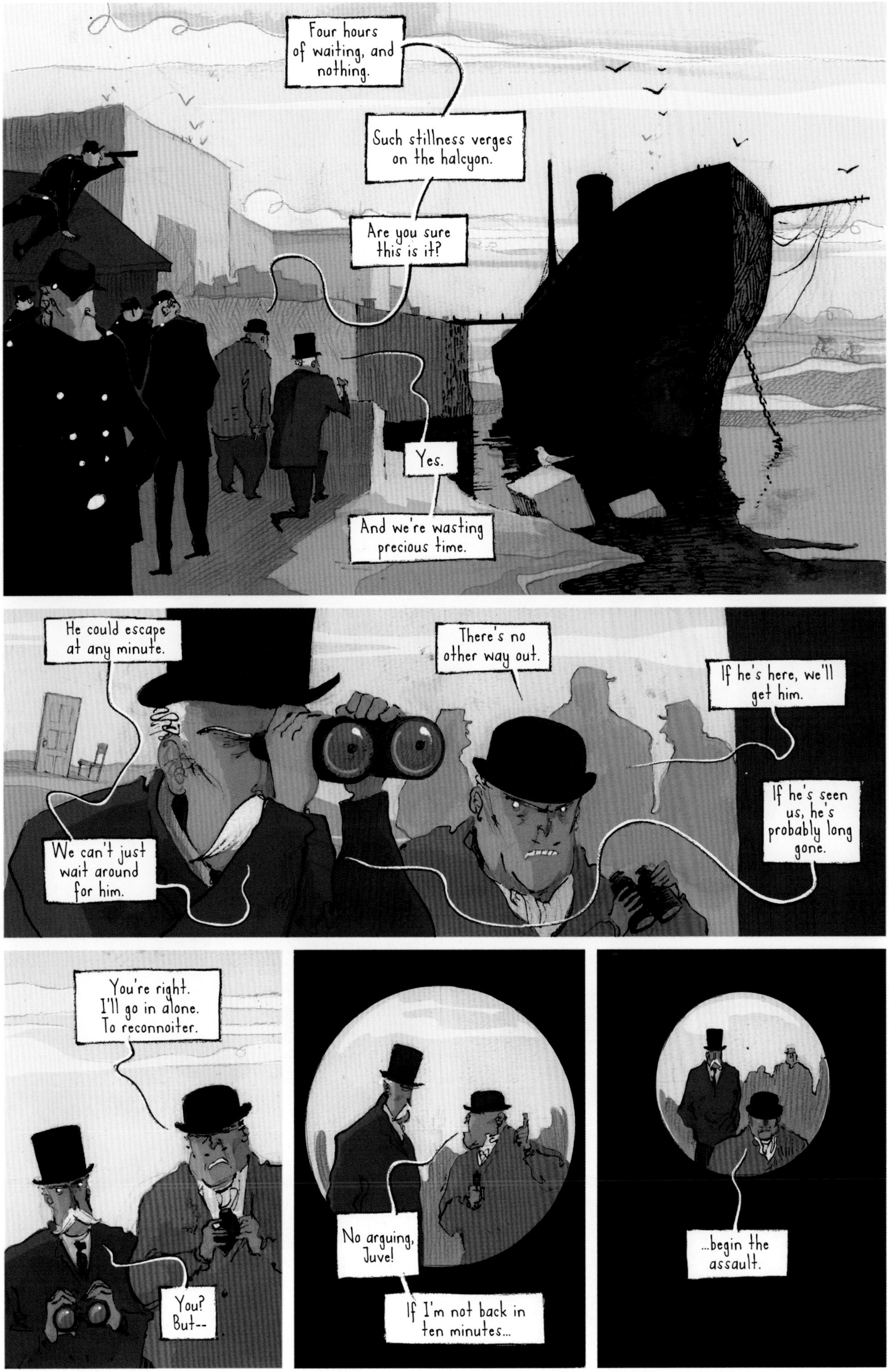
Four hours of waiting, and nothing.
Such stillness verges on the halcyon.
Are you sure this is it?
Yes.
And we're wasting precious time.
He could escape at any minute.
We can't just wait around for him.
There's no other way out.
If he's here, we'll get him.
If he's seen us, he's probably long gone.
You're right. I'll go in alone. To reconnoiter.
You? But--
No arguing, Juve!
If I'm not back in ten minutes...
...begin the assault.

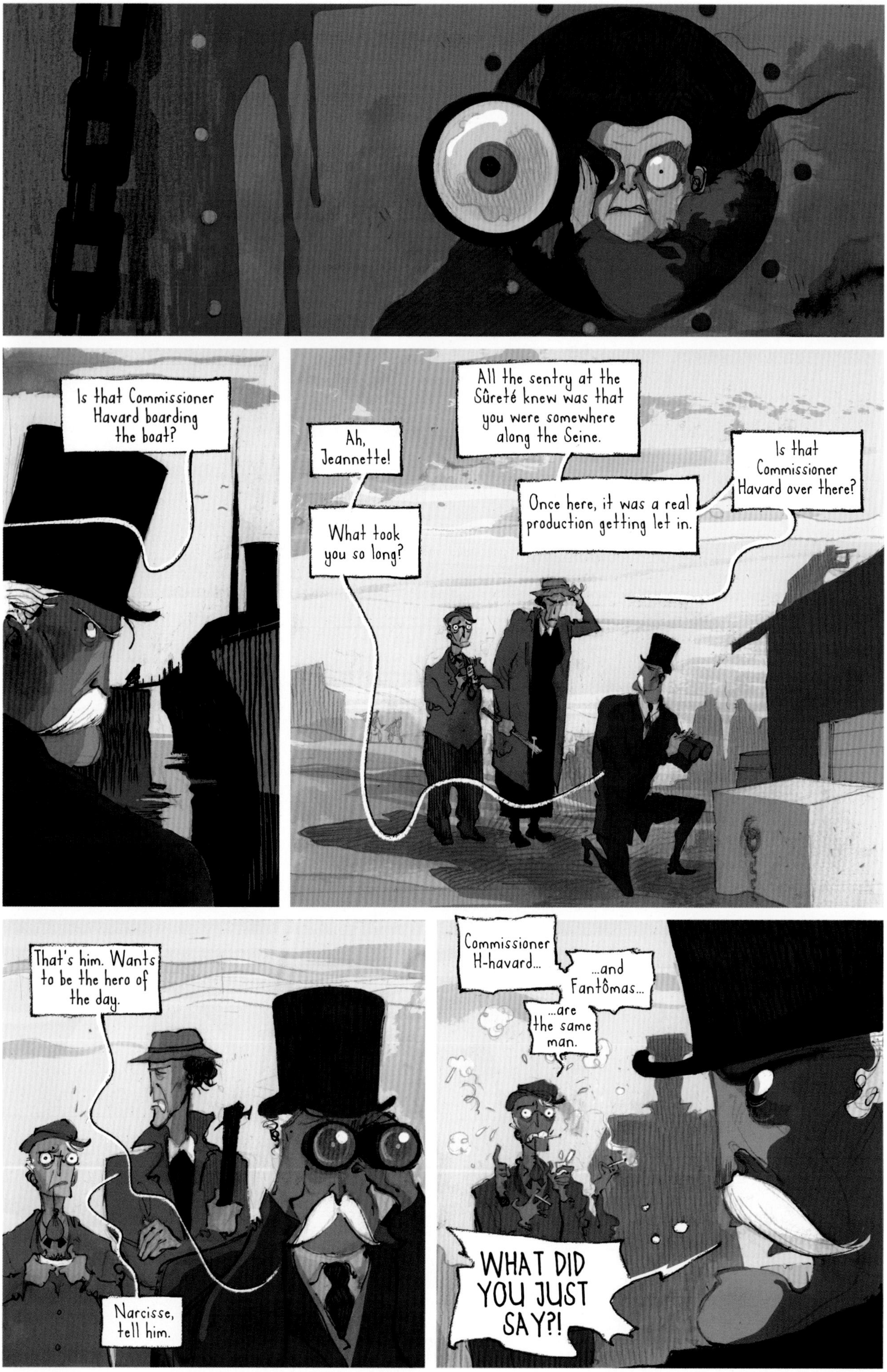
Is that Commissioner Havard boarding the boat?
Ah, Jeannette!
What took you so long?
All the sentry at the Sûreté knew was that you were somewhere along the Seine.
Once here, it was a real production getting let in.
Is that Commissioner Havard over there?
That's him. Wants to be the hero of the day.
Narcisse, tell him.
Commissioner H-havard...
...and Fantômas...
...are the same man.
WHAT DID YOU JUST SAY?!

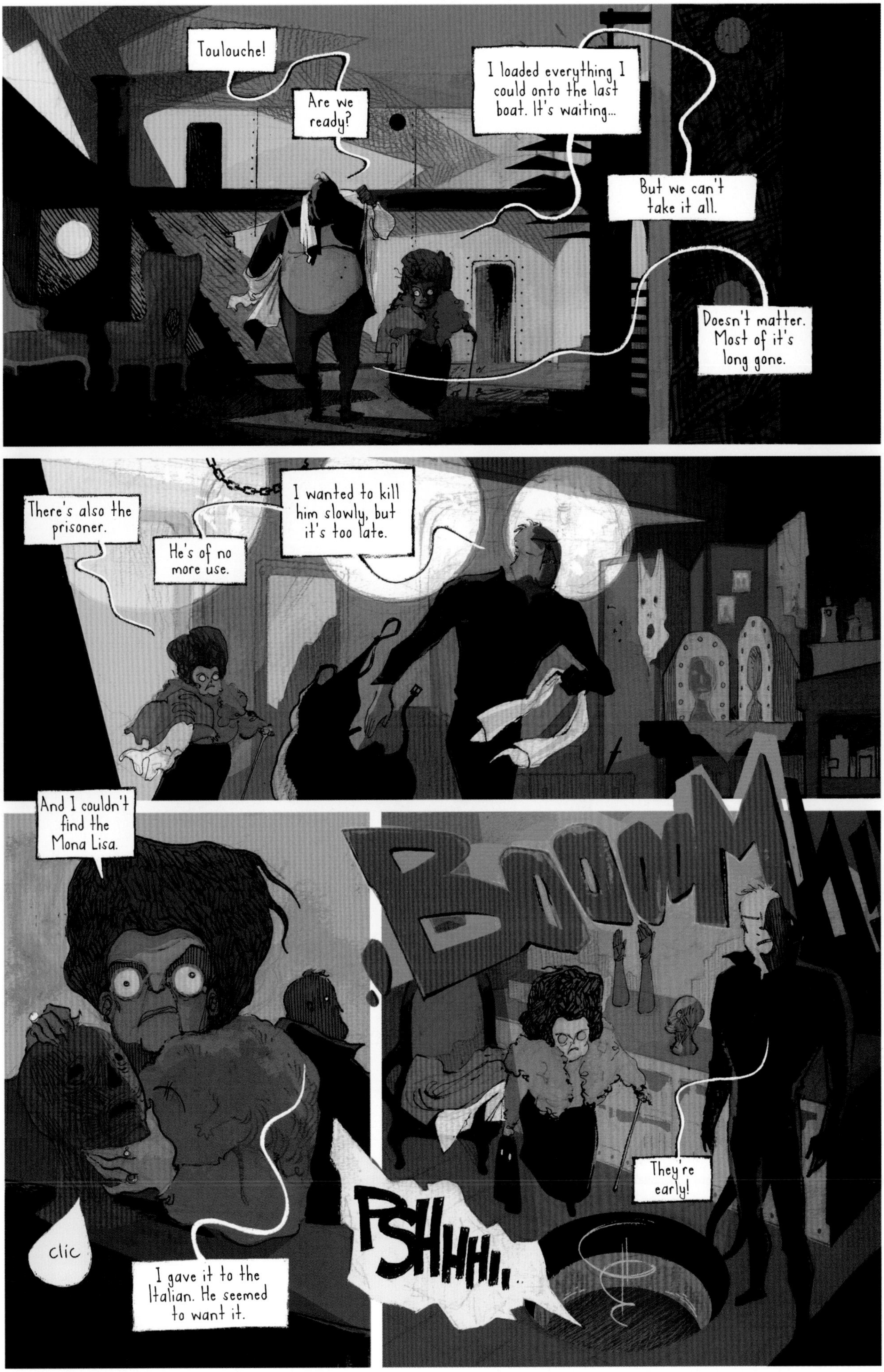
Toulouche!
Are we ready?
I loaded everything I could onto the last boat. It's waiting...
But we can't take it all.
Doesn't matter. Most of it's long gone.
There's also the prisoner.
He's of no more use.
I wanted to kill him slowly, but it's too late.
And I couldn't find the Mona Lisa.
clic
I gave it to the Italian. He seemed to want it.
BOOOM
PSHHH..
They're early!

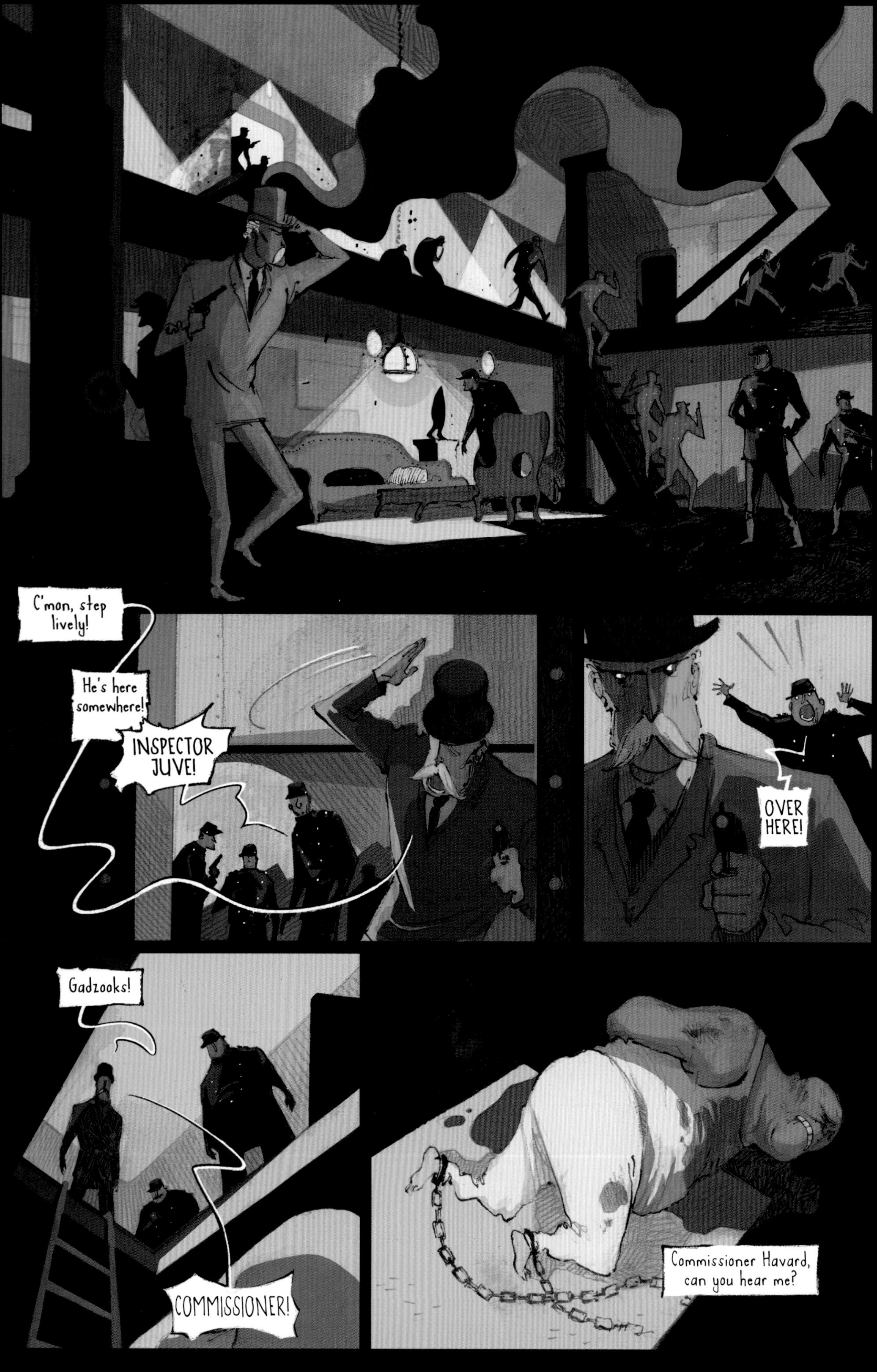
C'mon, step lively!
He's here somewhere!
INSPECTOR JUVE!
OVER HERE!
Gadzooks!
COMMISSIONER!
Commissioner Havard, can you hear me?

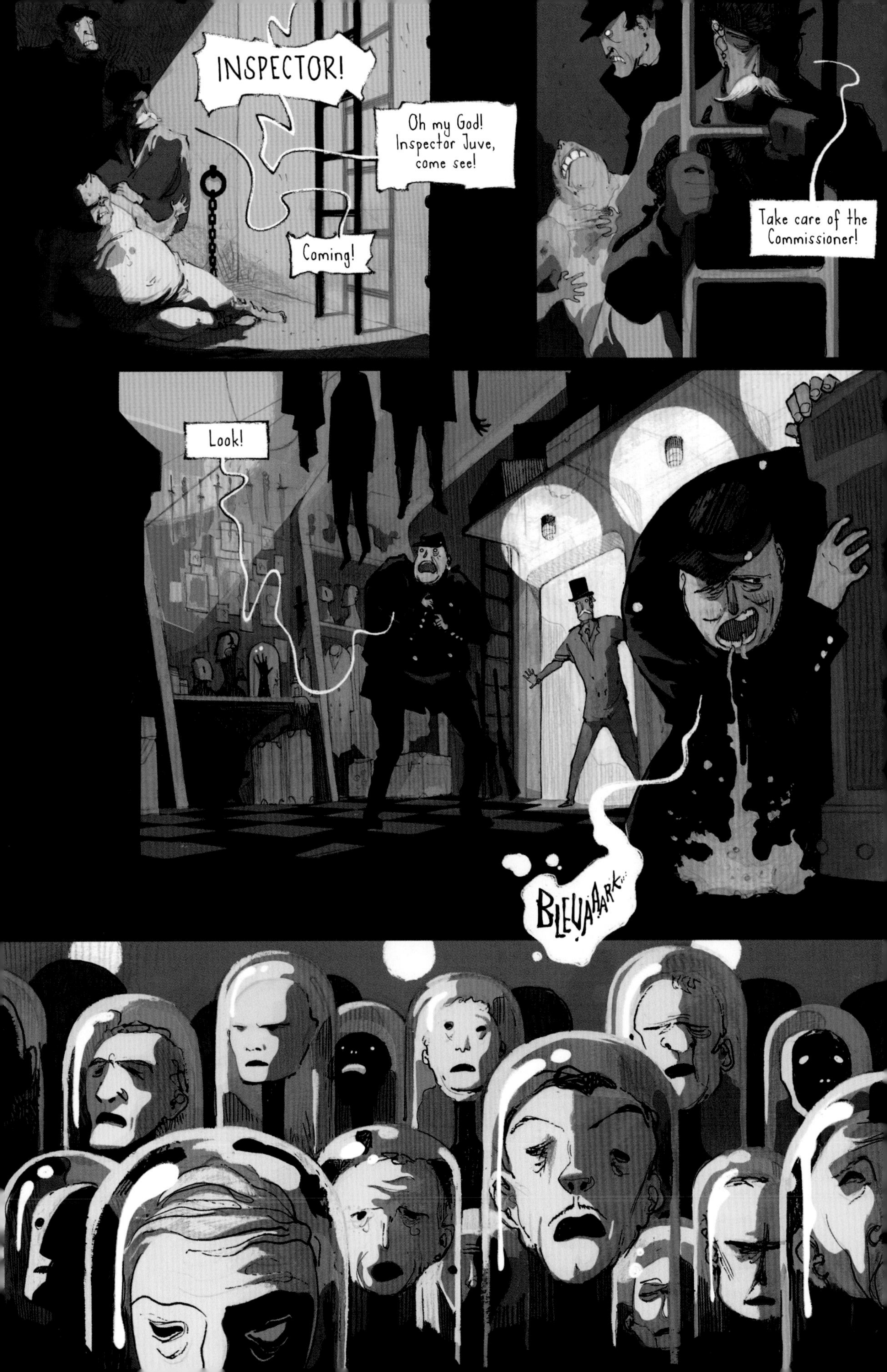
INSPECTOR!
Oh my God! Inspector Juve, come see!
Coming!
Take care of the Commissioner!
Look!
BLEUAAARK...

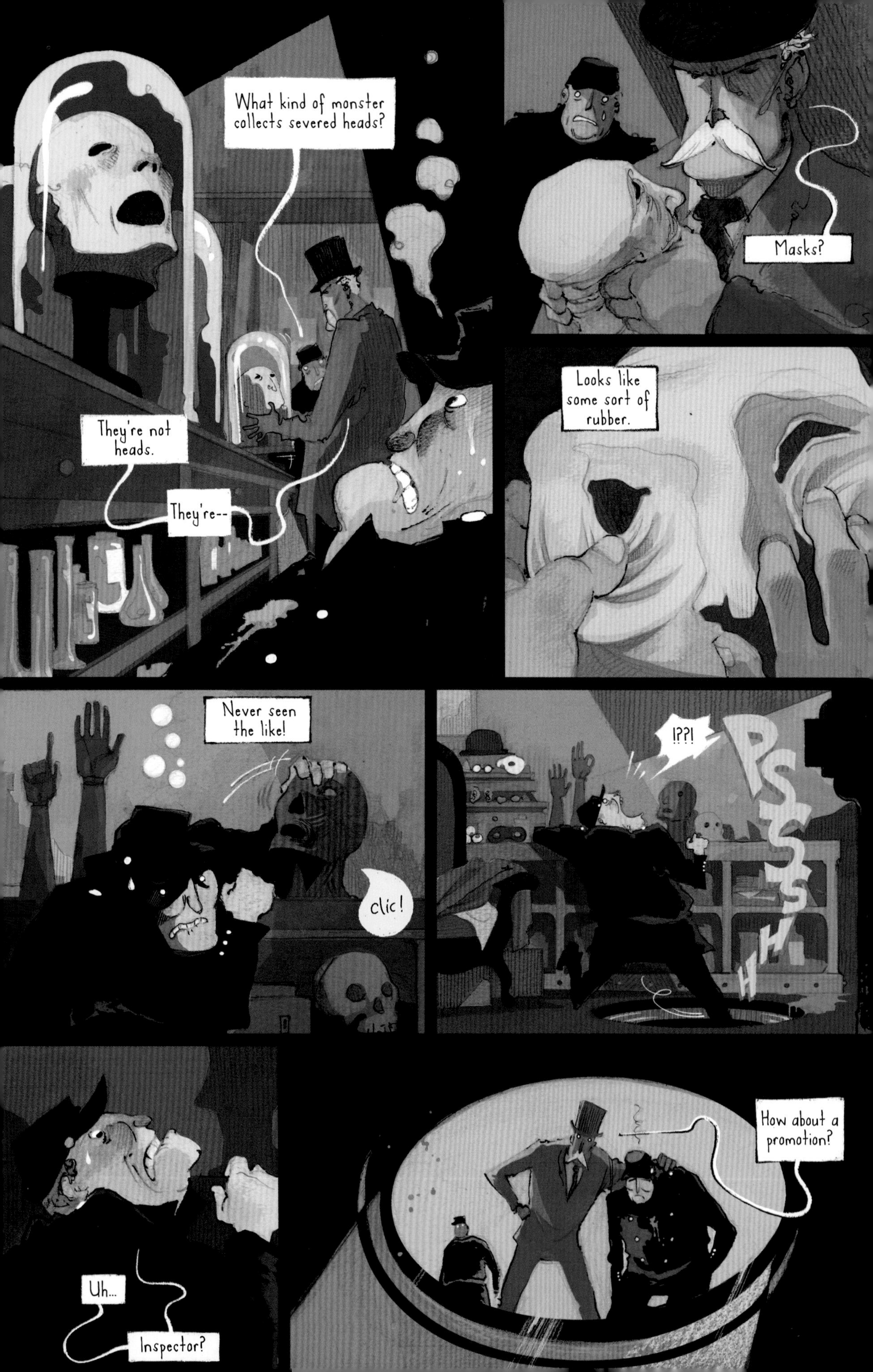
What kind of monster collects severed heads?
They're not heads.
They're--
Masks?
Looks like some sort of rubber.
Never seen the like!
clic!
!??!
PSSSHHH
Uh...
Inspector?
How about a promotion?

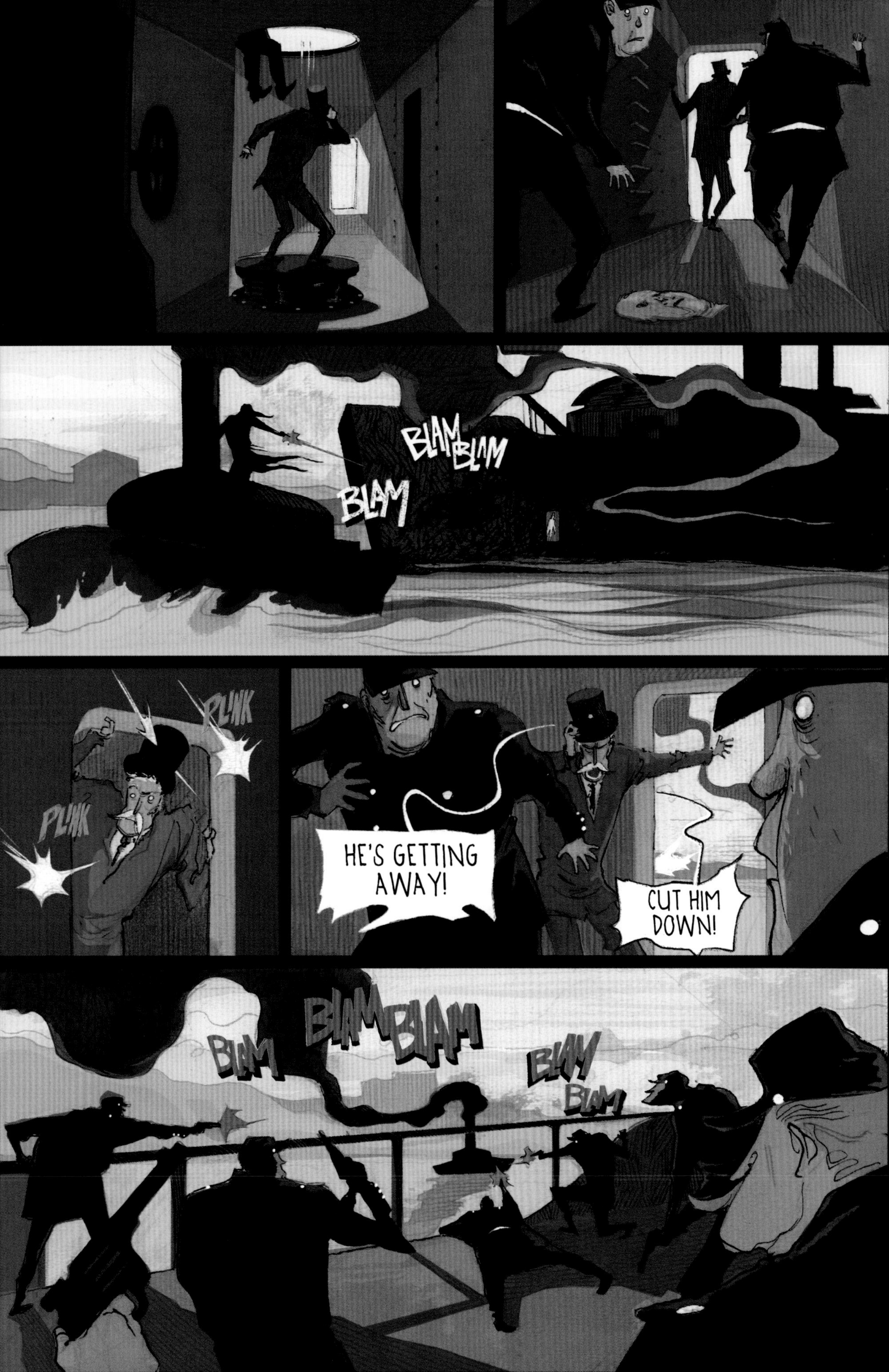
BLAM BLAM
BLAM
PLINK
PLINK
HE'S GETTING AWAY!
CUT HIM DOWN!
BLAM
BLAM BLAM
BLAM
BLAM

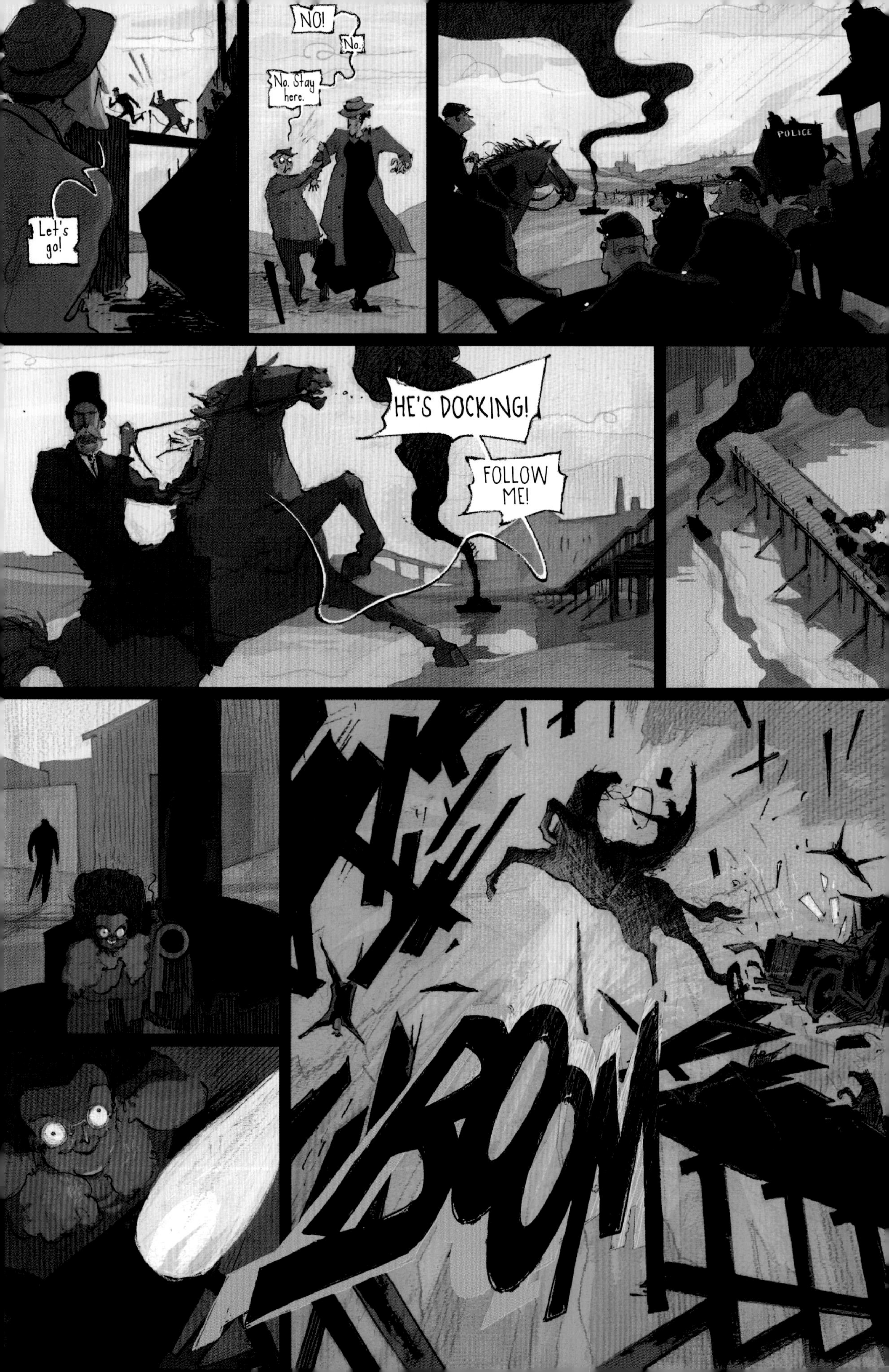
Let's go!
NO!
No.
No. Stay here.
POLICE
HE'S DOCKING!
FOLLOW ME!
BOOM

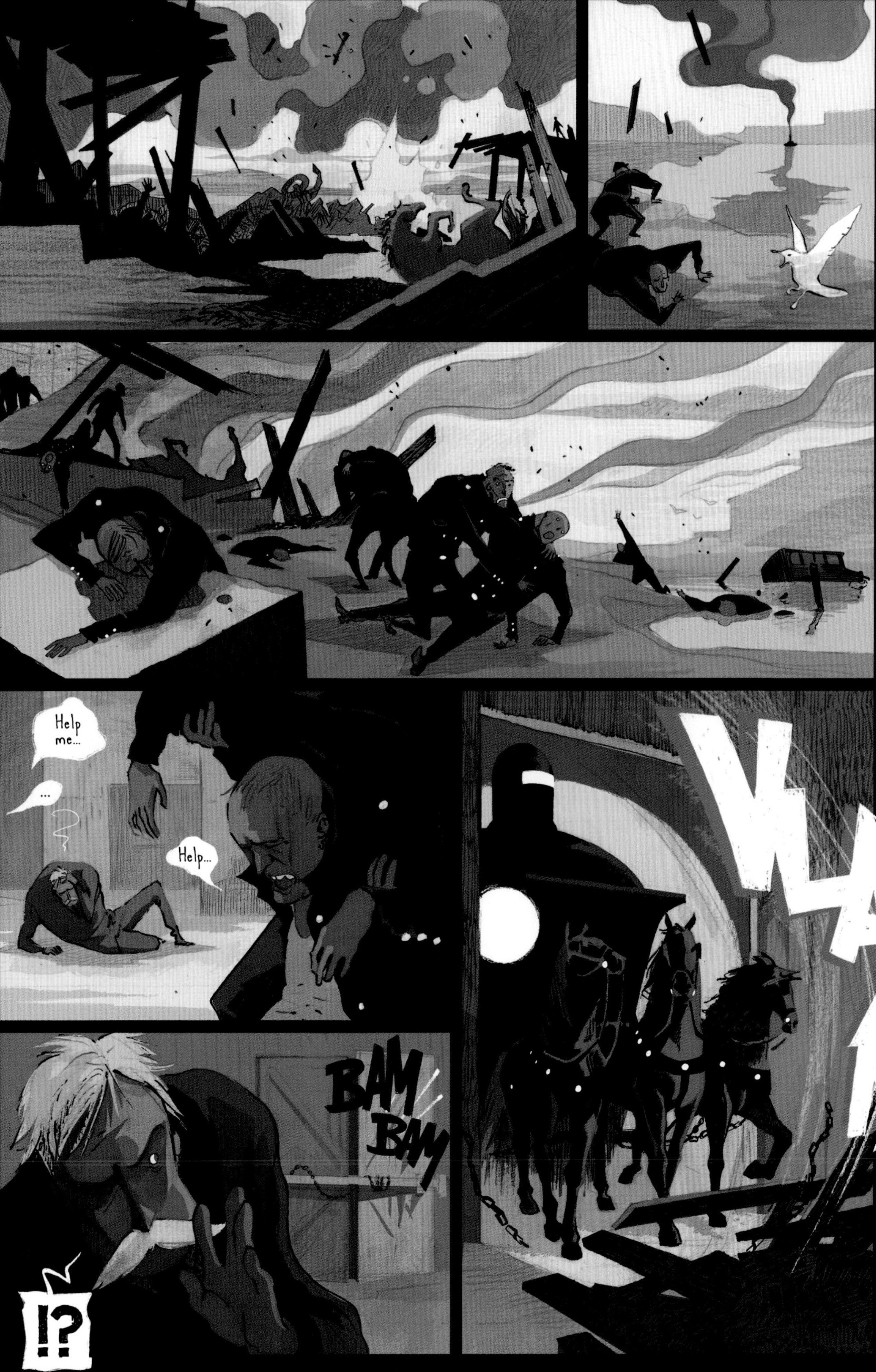
Help me...
...
Help...
VLAM
BAM
BAM
!?

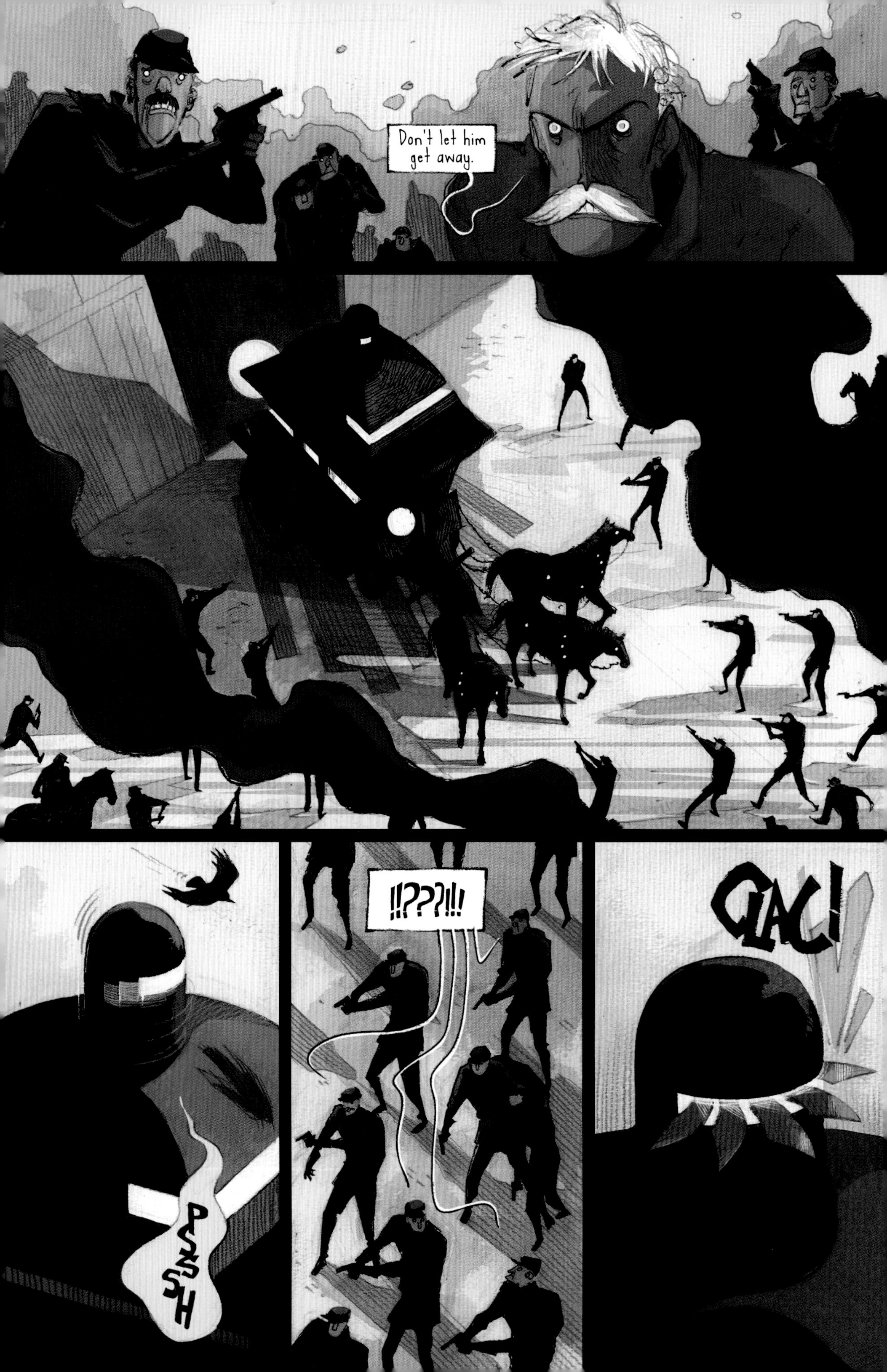

Don't let him get away.
!!???!!!
PSSSH
CLAC!

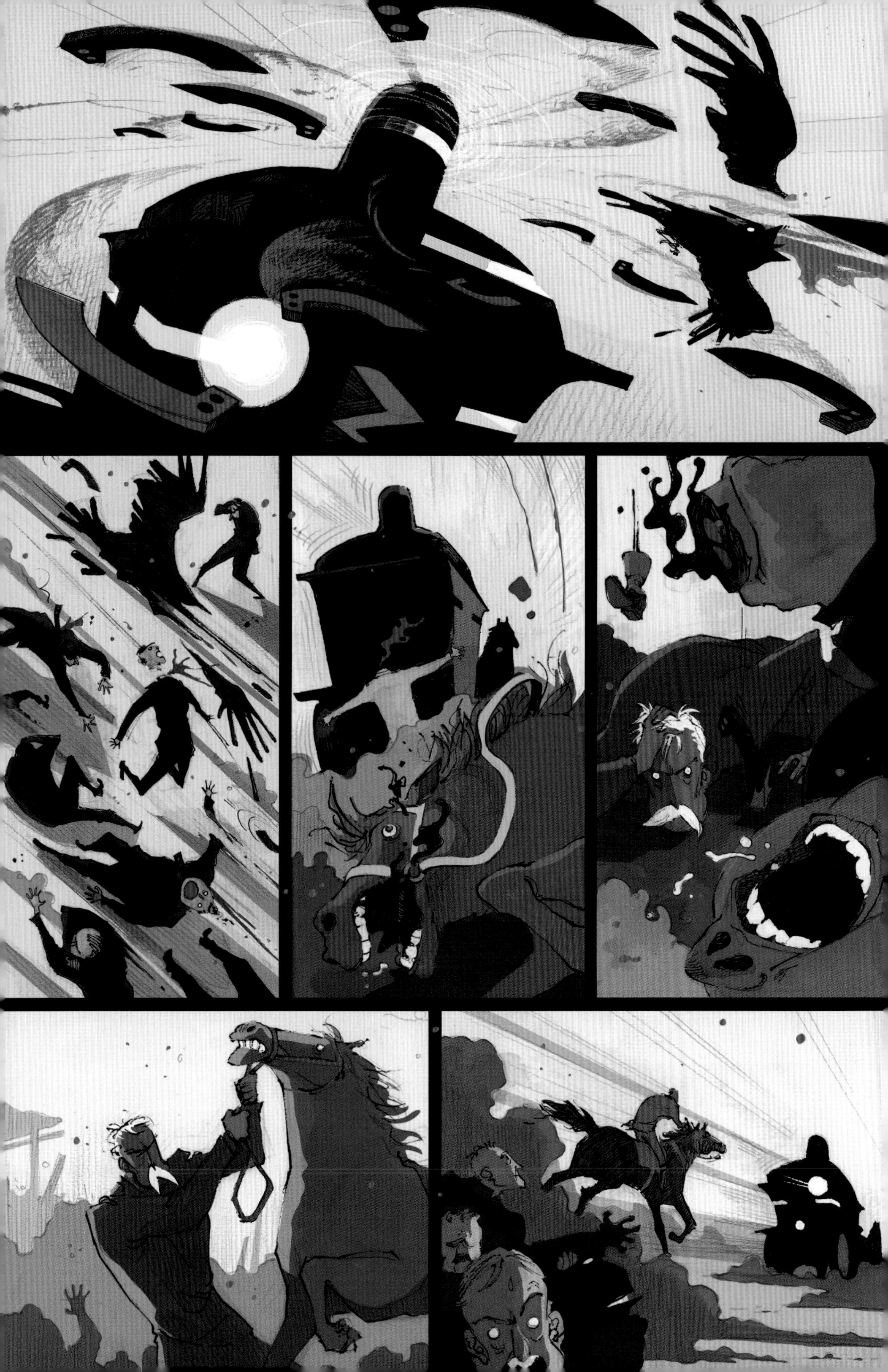

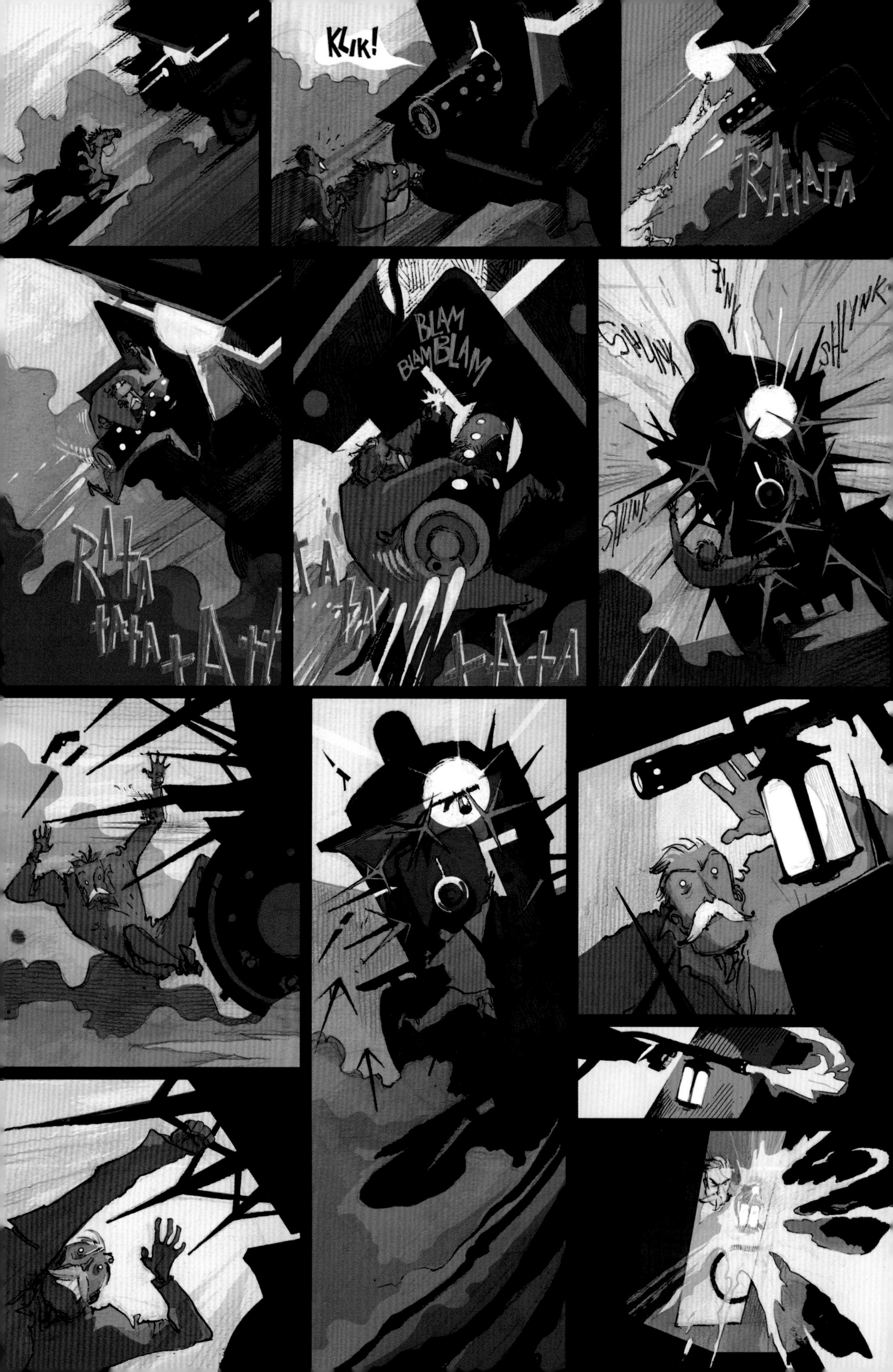
KLIK!
RATATA
RATA
BLAM
BLAMBLAM
SHLYNK
SHLINK

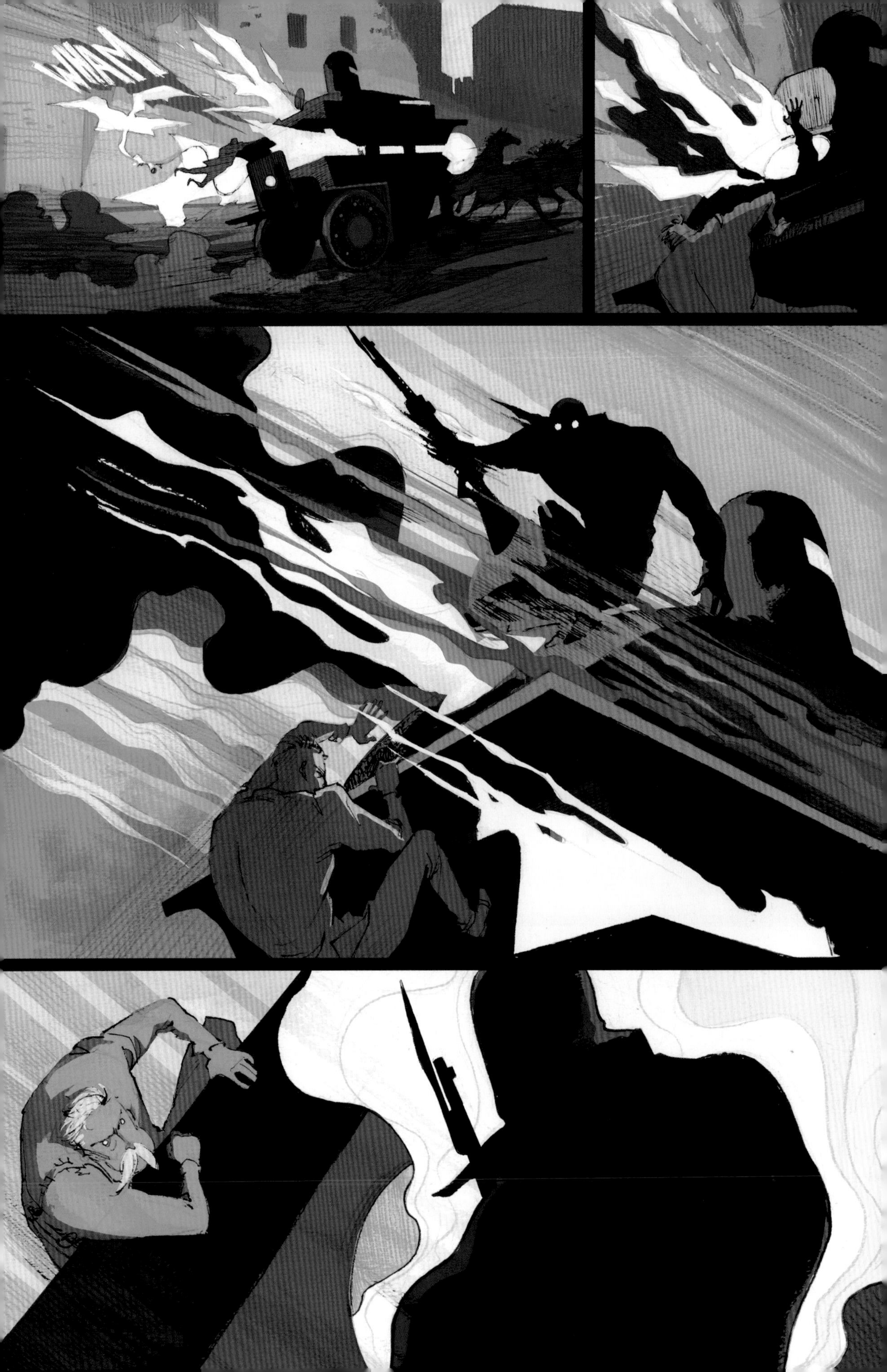
WHAM

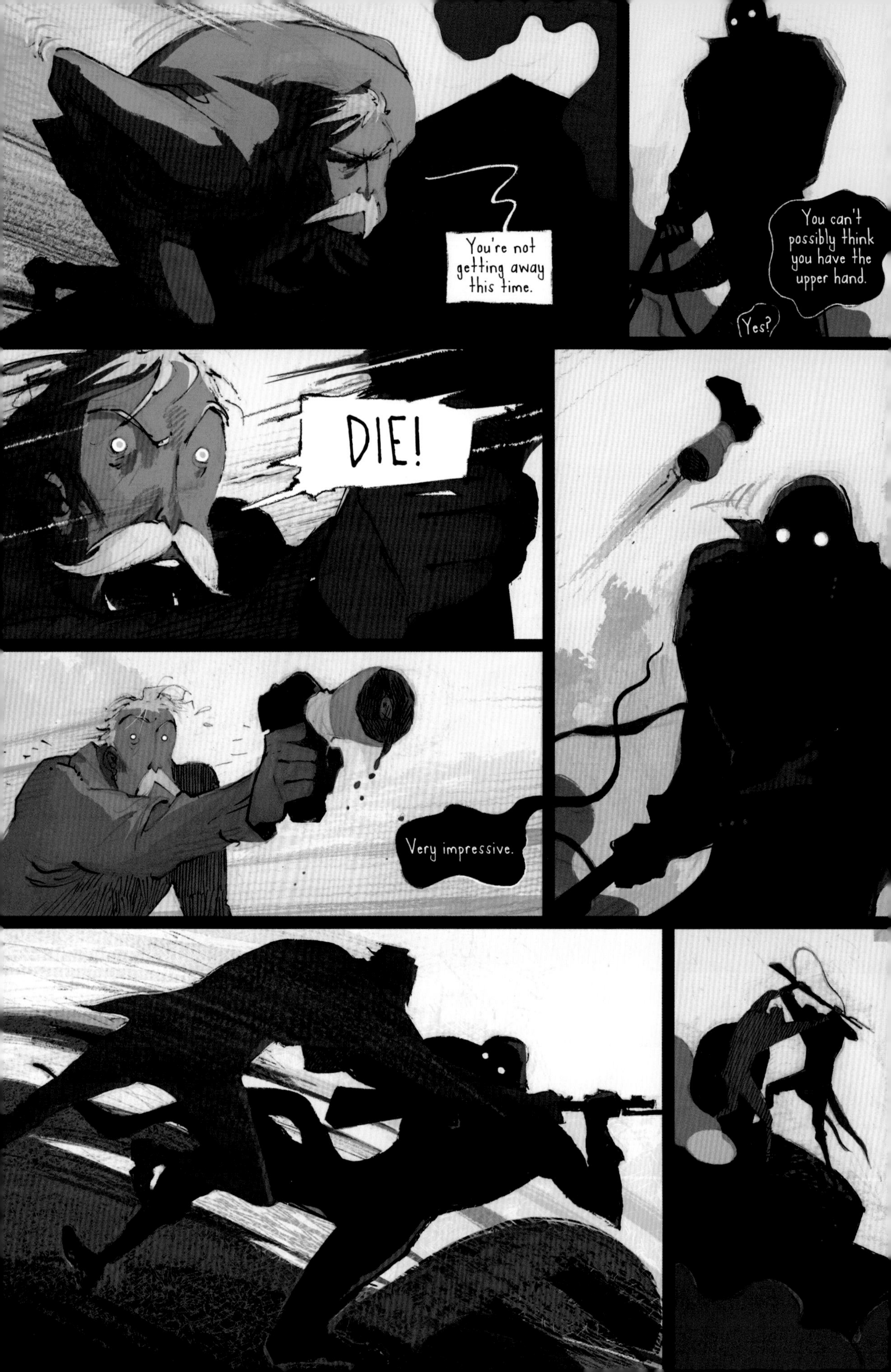
You're not getting away this time.
You can't possibly think you have the upper hand.
Yes?
DIE!
Very impressive.

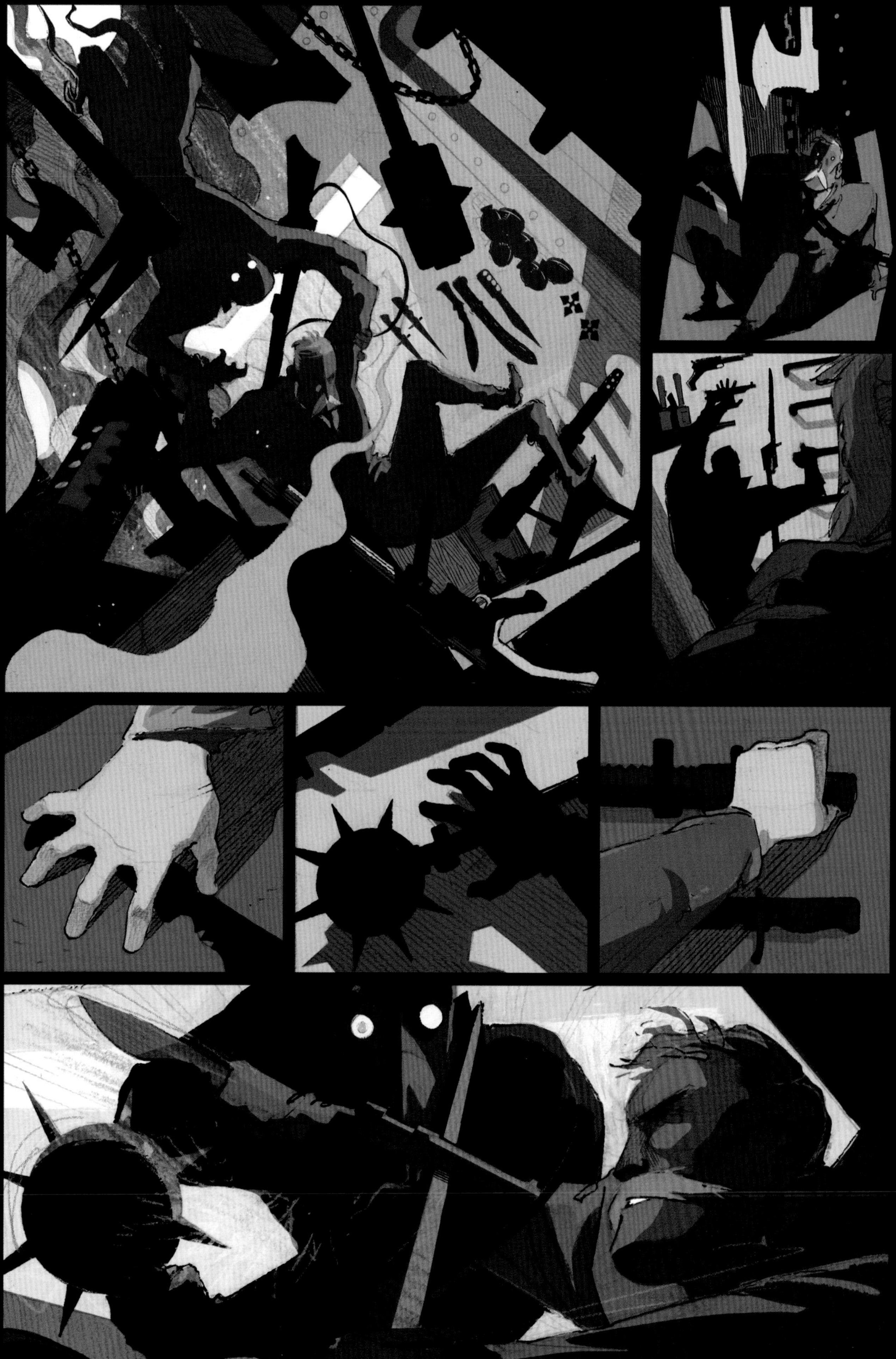

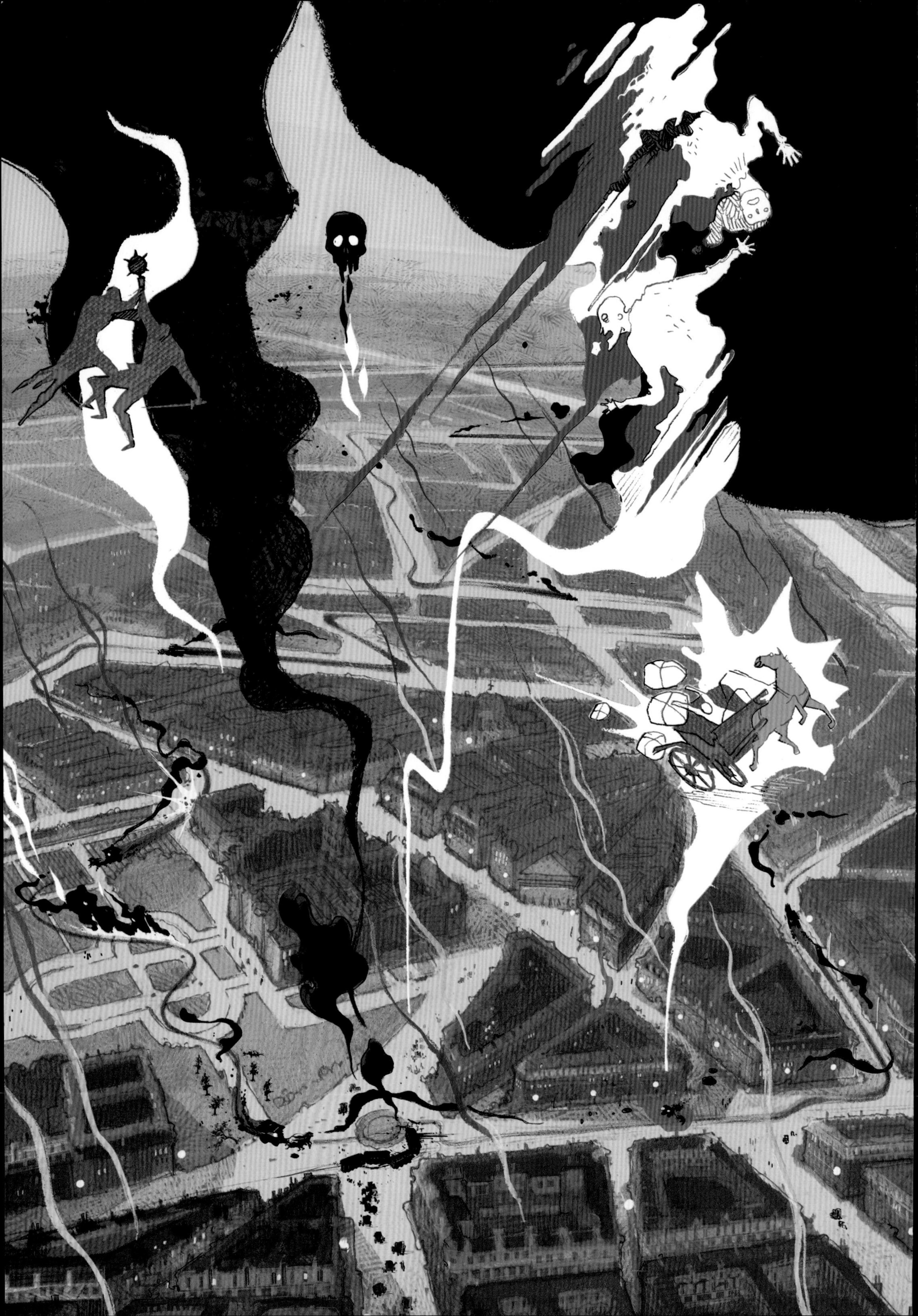

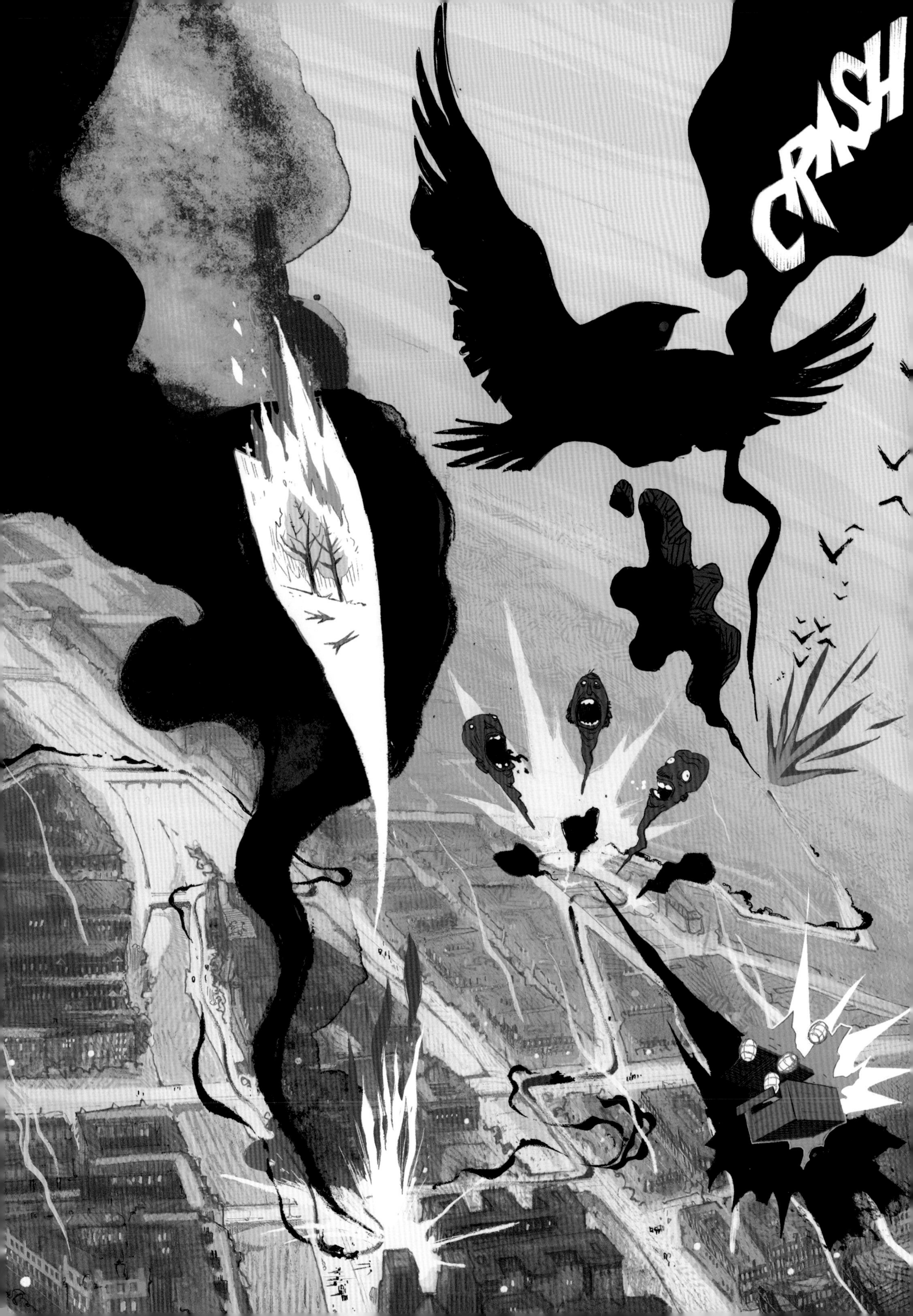
CRASH

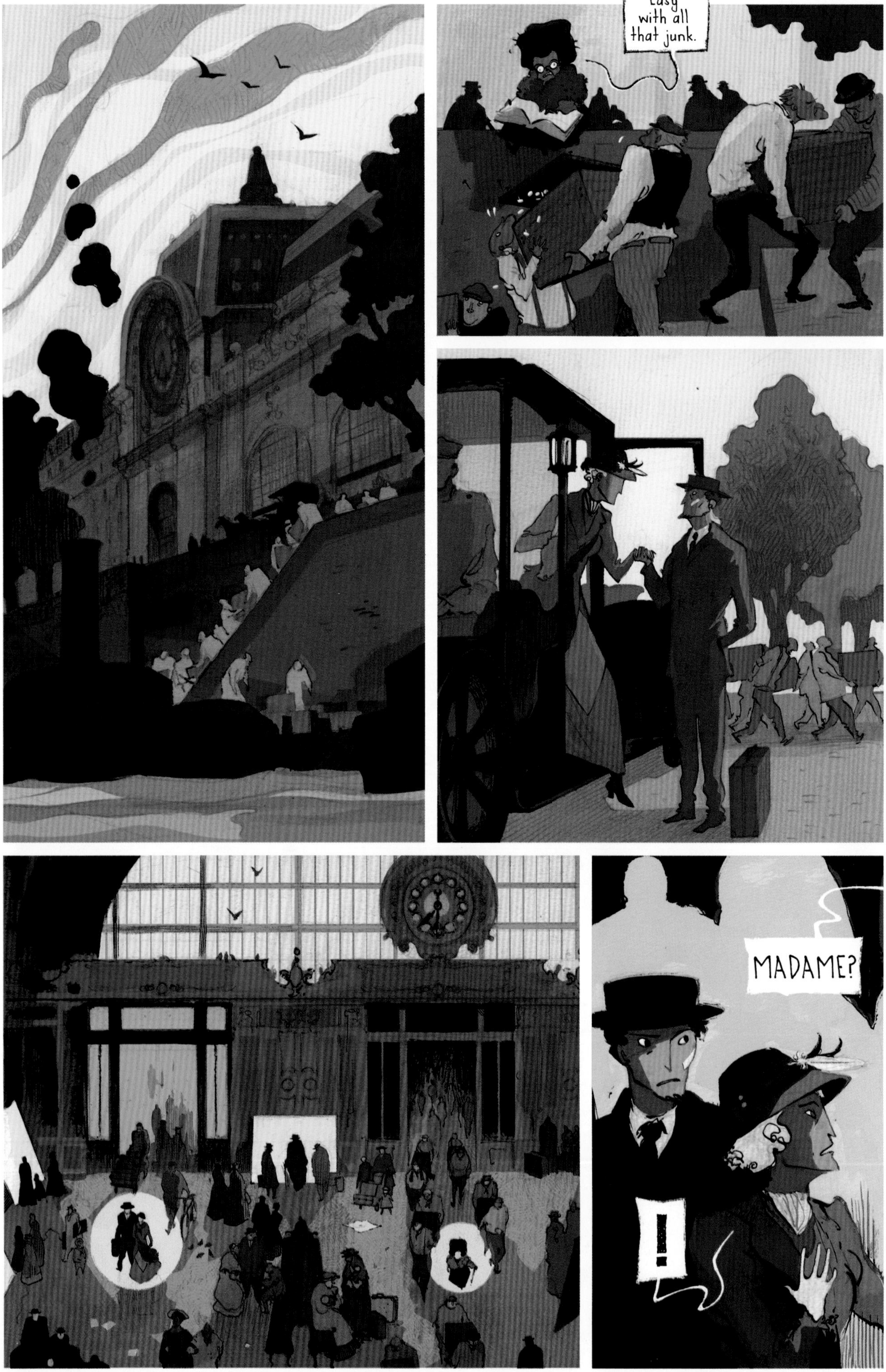
Easy with all that junk.
MADAME?
!

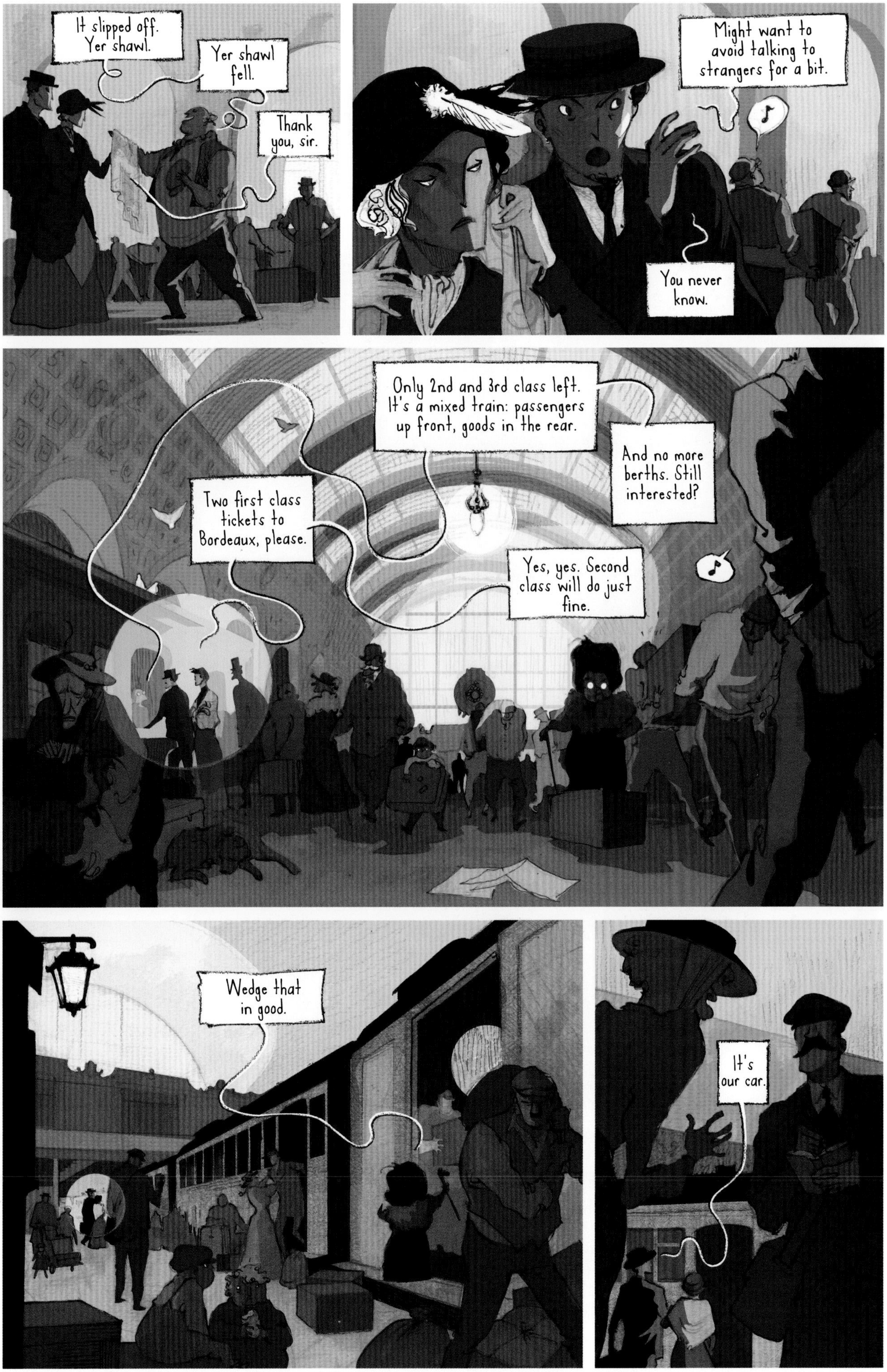
It slipped off. Yer shawl.
Yer shawl fell.
Thank you, sir.
Might want to avoid talking to strangers for a bit.
You never know.
Two first class tickets to Bordeaux, please.
Only 2nd and 3rd class left. It's a mixed train: passengers up front, goods in the rear.
And no more berths. Still interested?
Yes, yes. Second class will do just fine.
Wedge that in good.
It's our car.

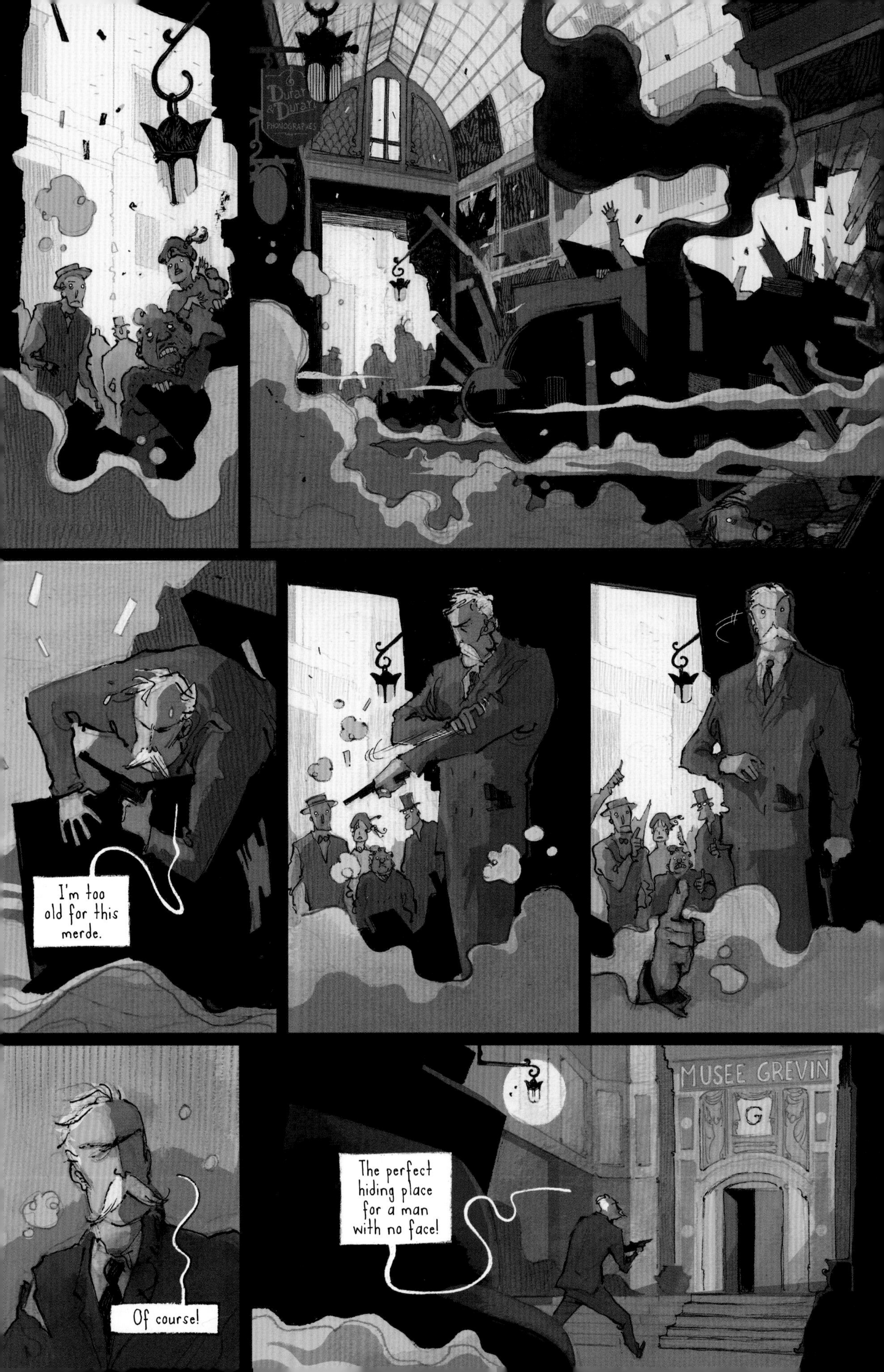
Dufay & Dufay
PHONOGRAPHES
I'm too old for this merde.
Of course!
MUSEE GREVIN
G
The perfect hiding place for a man with no face!

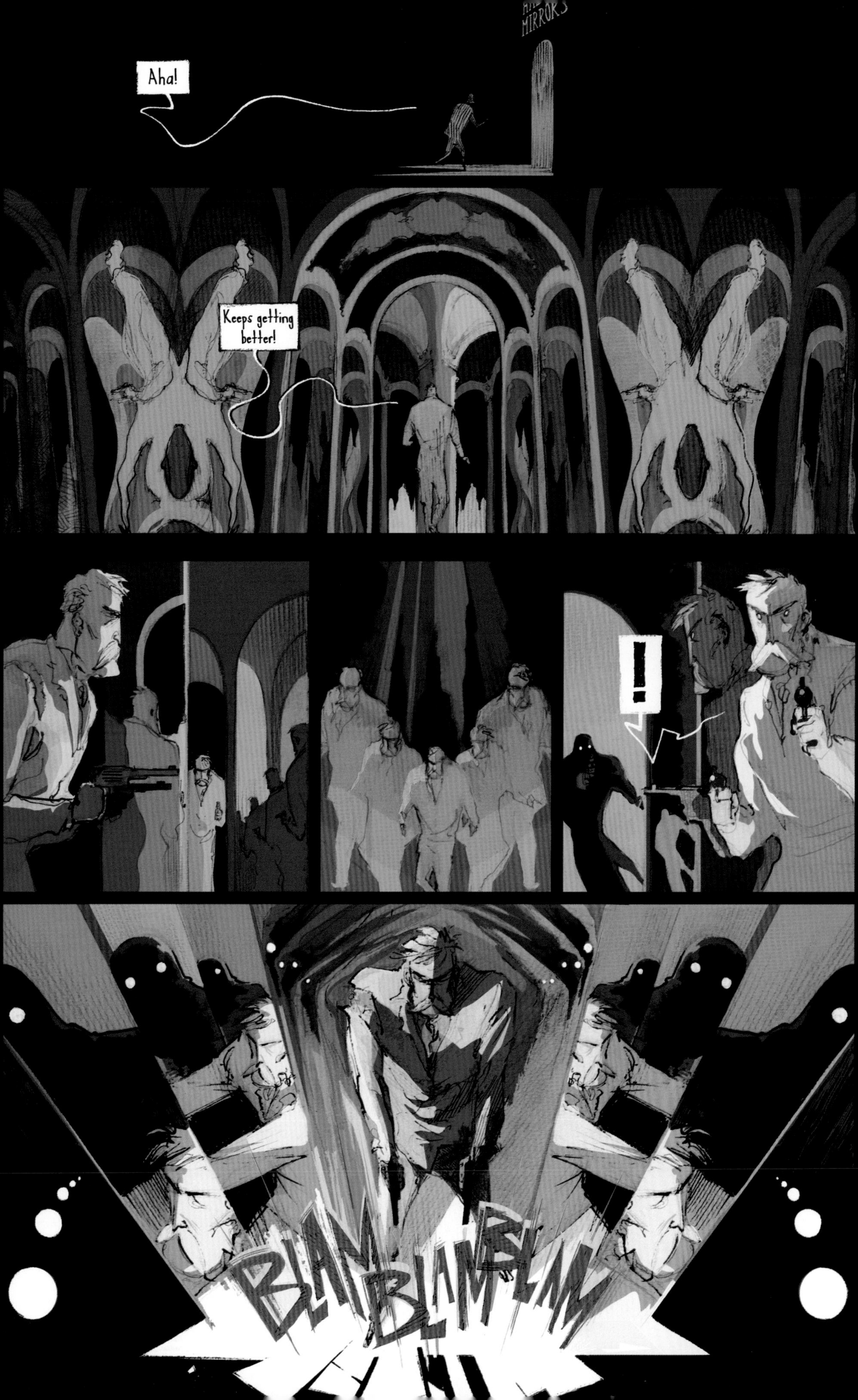
MIRRORS
Aha!
Keeps getting better!
!
BLAM BLAM BLAM

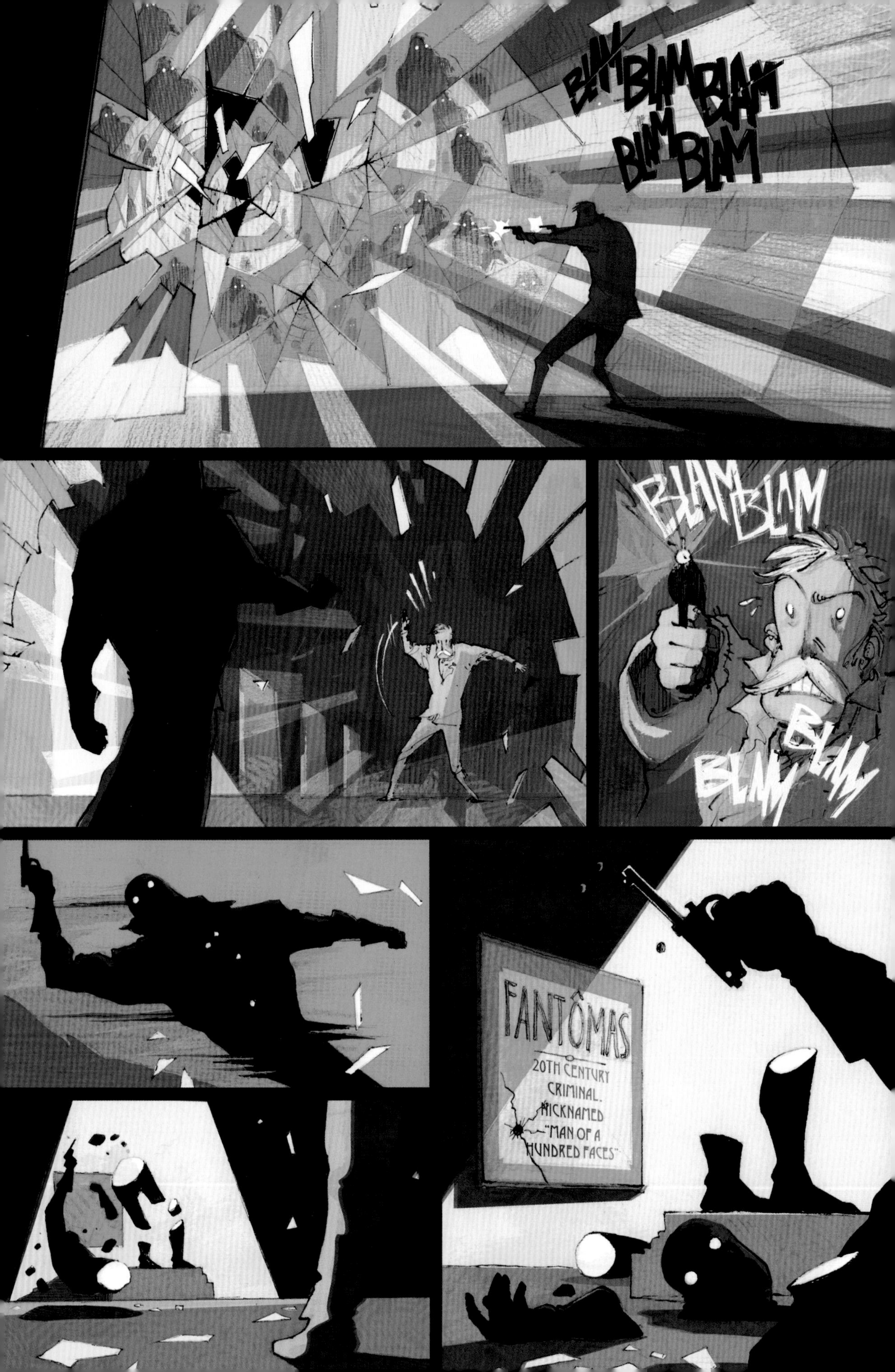
BLAM BLAM BLAM BLAM
BLAM BLAM
BLAM BLAM
BLAM
BLAM
FANTÔMAS
20TH CENTURY CRIMINAL. NICKNAMED "MAN OF A HUNDRED FACES"

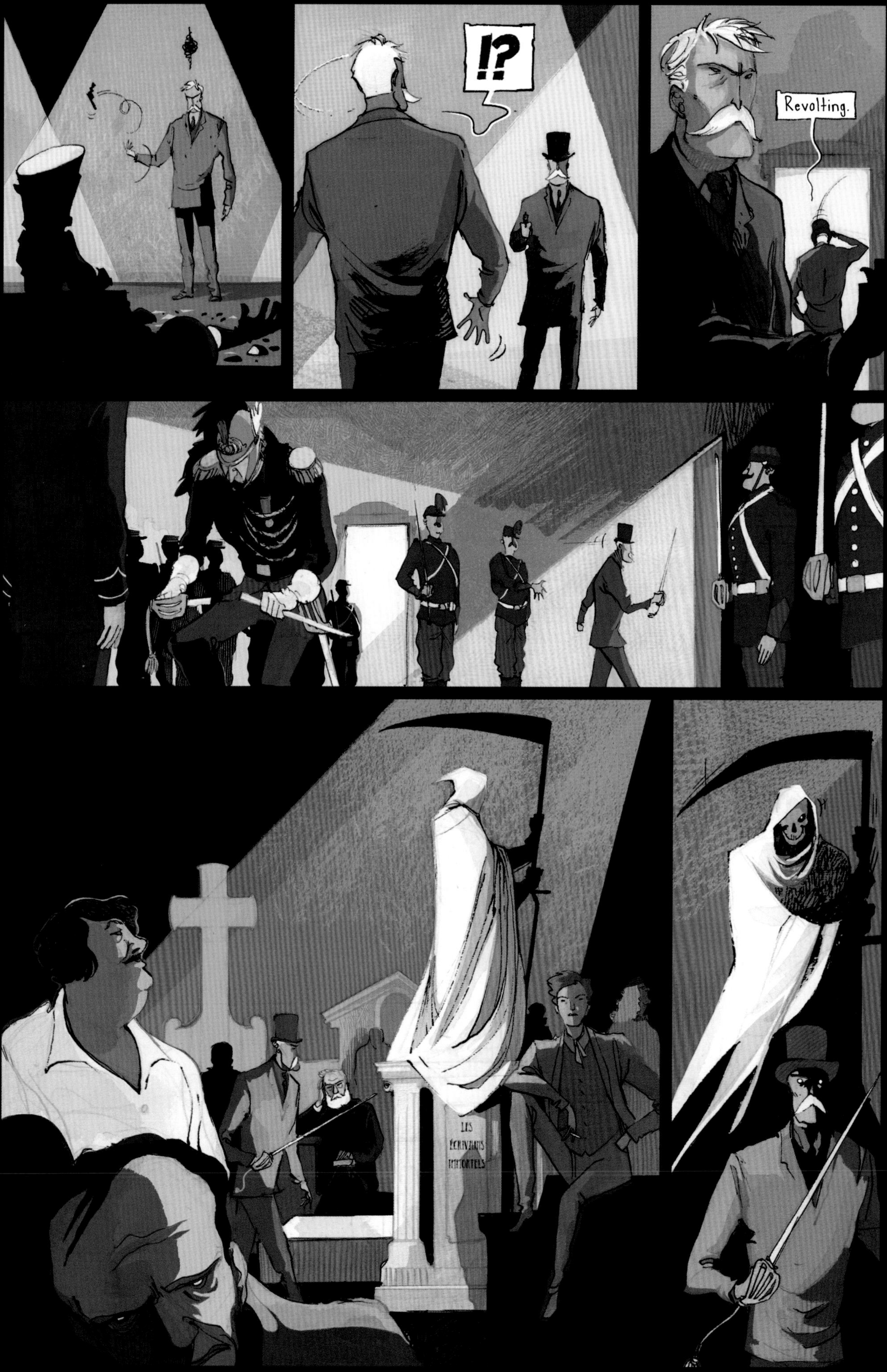
!?
Revolting.
LES ÉCRIVAINS IMMORTELS

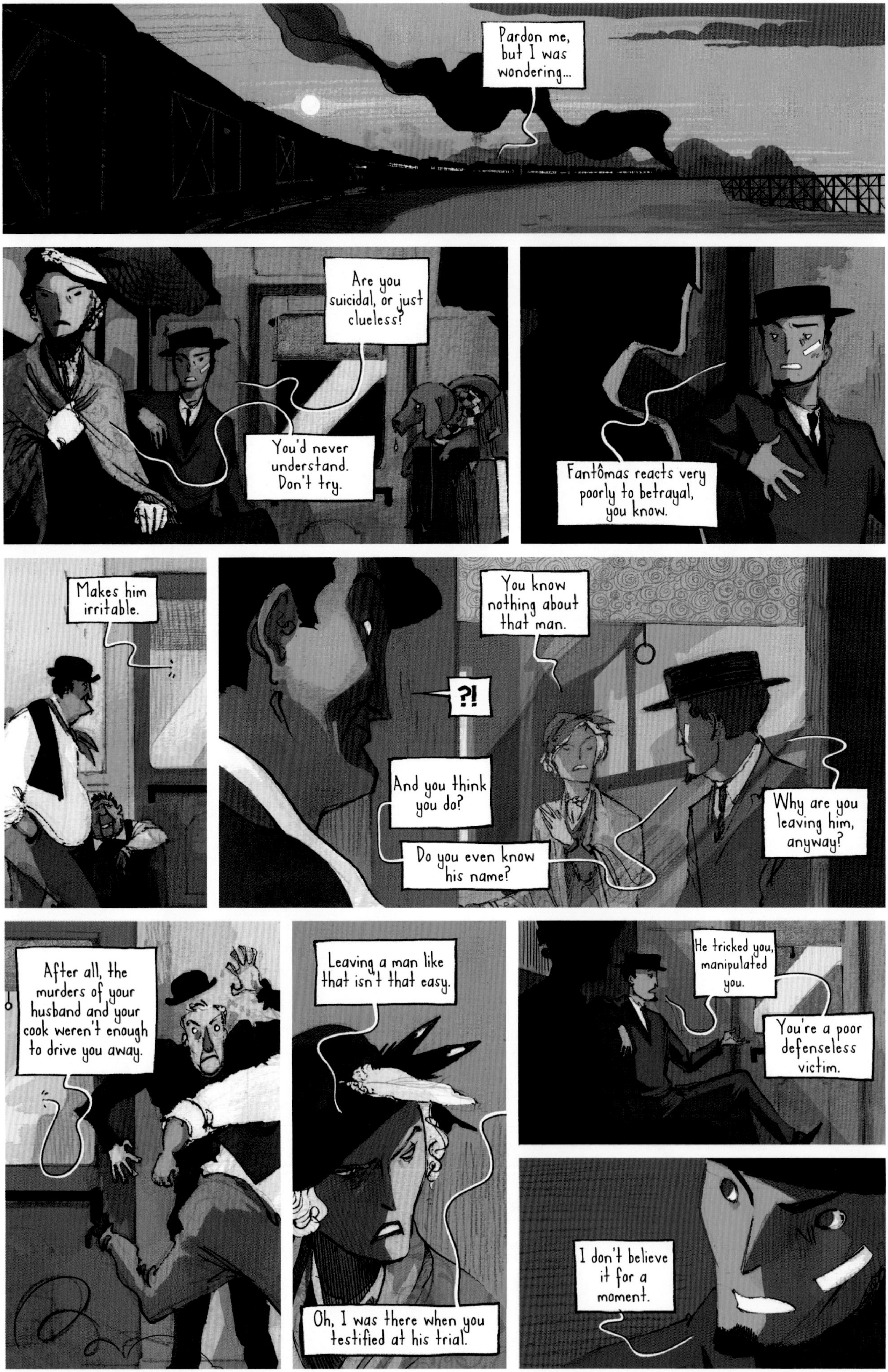
Pardon me, but I was wondering...
Are you suicidal, or just clueless?
You'd never understand. Don't try.
Fantômas reacts very poorly to betrayal, you know.
Makes him irritable.
You know nothing about that man.
?!
And you think you do?
Do you even know his name?
Why are you leaving him, anyway?
After all, the murders of your husband and your cook weren't enough to drive you away.
Leaving a man like that isn't that easy.
Oh, I was there when you testified at his trial.
He tricked you, manipulated you.
You're a poor defenseless victim.
I don't believe it for a moment.

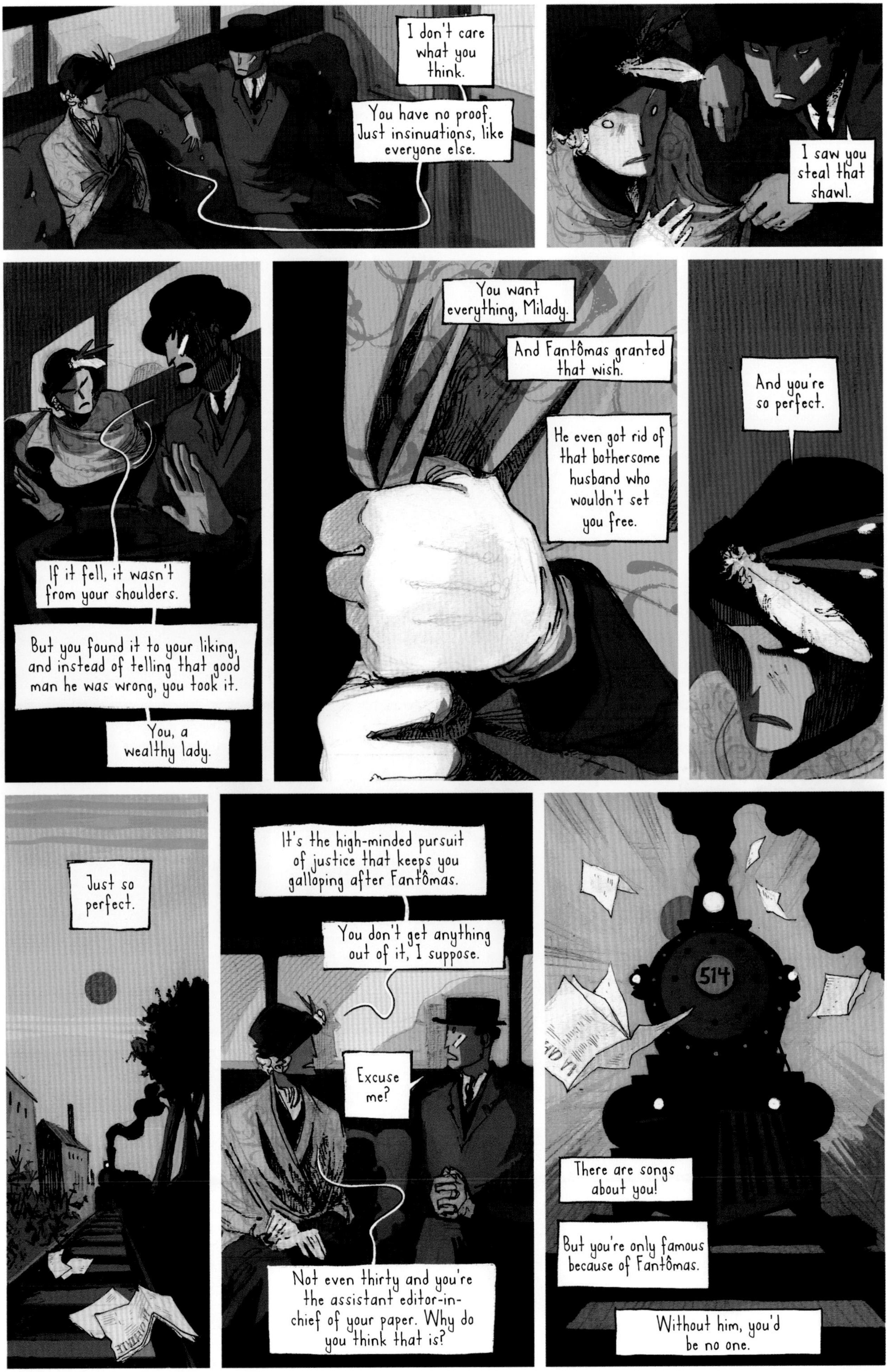
I don't care what you think.
You have no proof. Just insinuations, like everyone else.
I saw you steal that shawl.
If it fell, it wasn't from your shoulders.
But you found it to your liking, and instead of telling that good man he was wrong, you took it.
You, a wealthy lady.
You want everything, Milady.
And Fantômas granted that wish.
He even got rid of that bothersome husband who wouldn't set you free.
And you're so perfect.
Just so perfect.
It's the high-minded pursuit of justice that keeps you galloping after Fantômas.
You don't get anything out of it, I suppose.
Excuse me?
Not even thirty and you're the assistant editor-in-chief of your paper. Why do you think that is?
514
There are songs about you!
But you're only famous because of Fantômas.
Without him, you'd be no one.

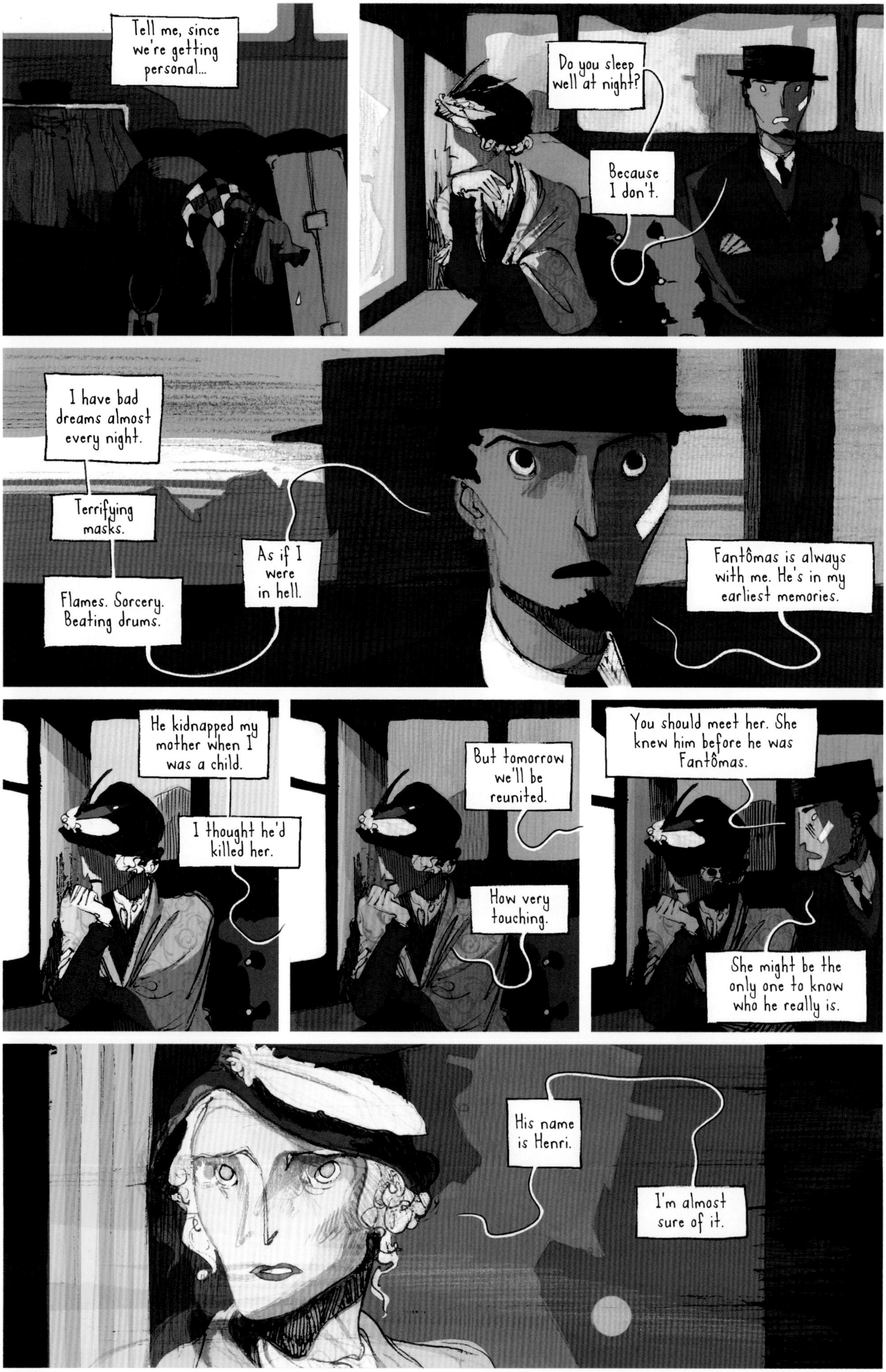

Tell me, since we're getting personal...
Do you sleep well at night?
Because I don't.
I have bad dreams almost every night.
Terrifying masks.
Flames. Sorcery. Beating drums.
As if I were in hell.
Fantômas is always with me. He's in my earliest memories.
He kidnapped my mother when I was a child.
I thought he'd killed her.
But tomorrow we'll be reunited.
How very touching.
You should meet her. She knew him before he was Fantômas.
She might be the only one to know who he really is.
His name is Henri.
I'm almost sure of it.

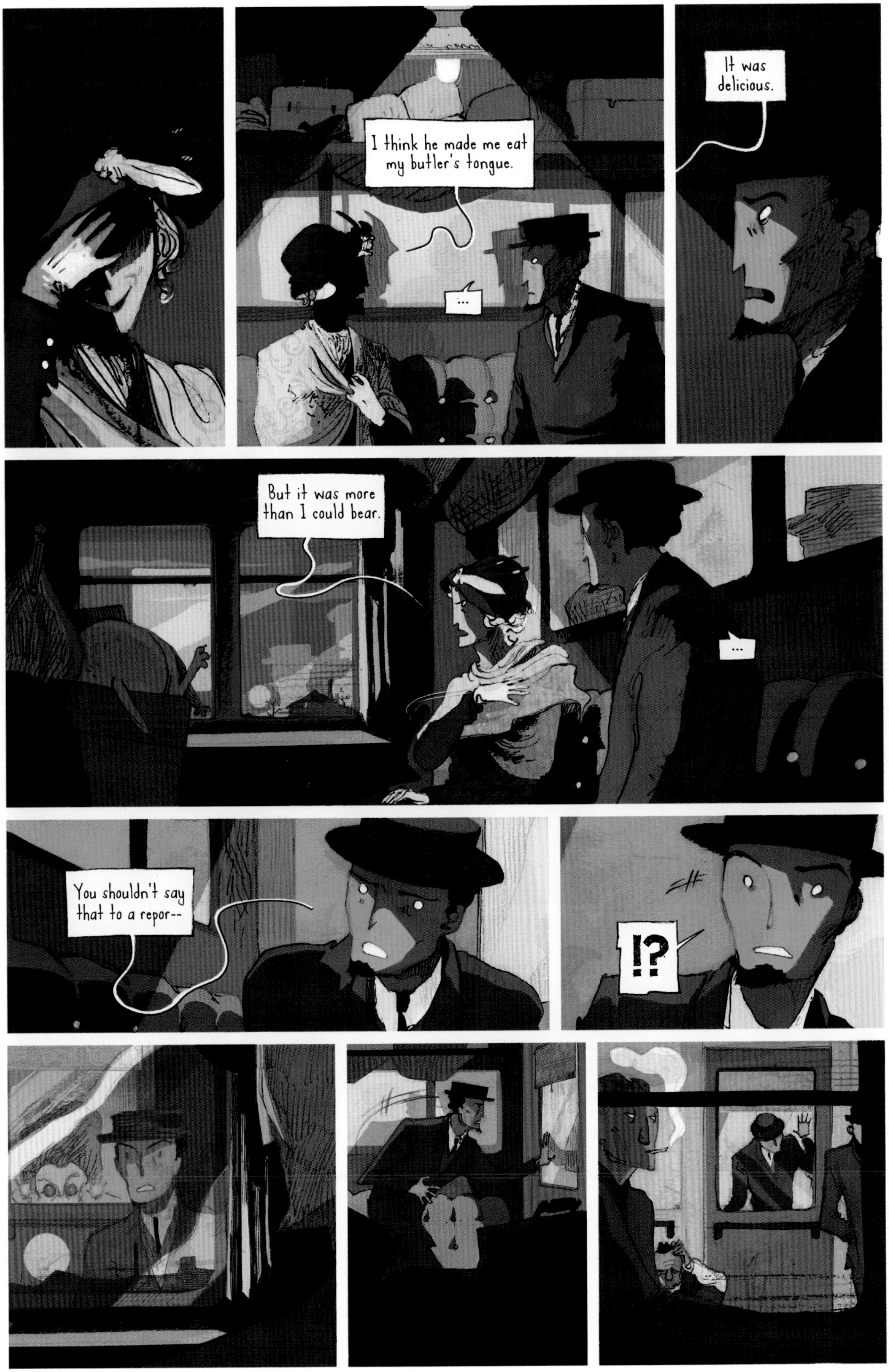
I think he made me eat my butler's tongue.
...
It was delicious.
But it was more than I could bear.
...
You shouldn't say that to a repor--
!?

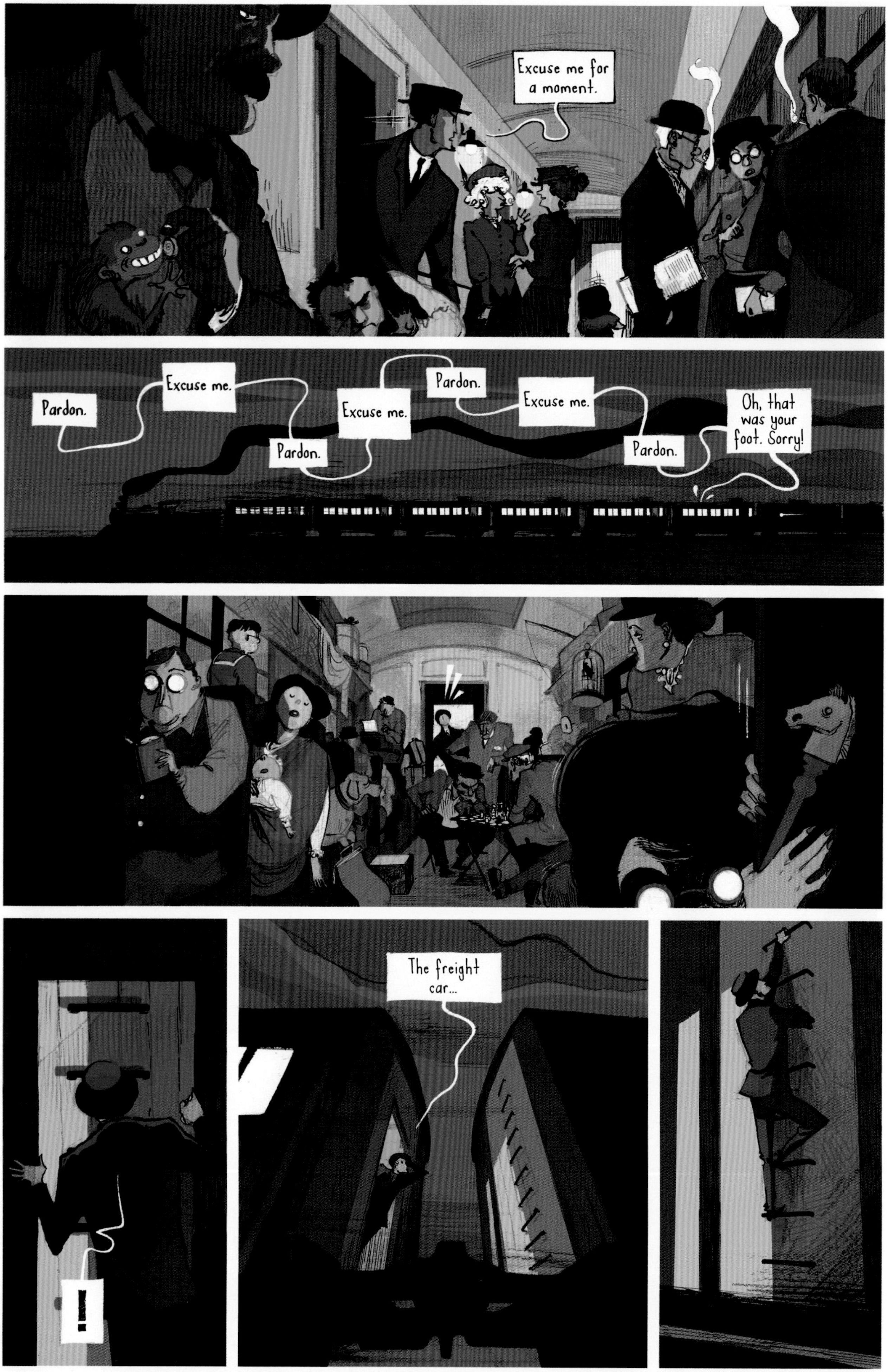
Excuse me for a moment.
Pardon.
Excuse me.
Pardon.
Excuse me.
Pardon.
Excuse me.
Pardon.
Oh, that was your foot. Sorry!
!
The freight car...

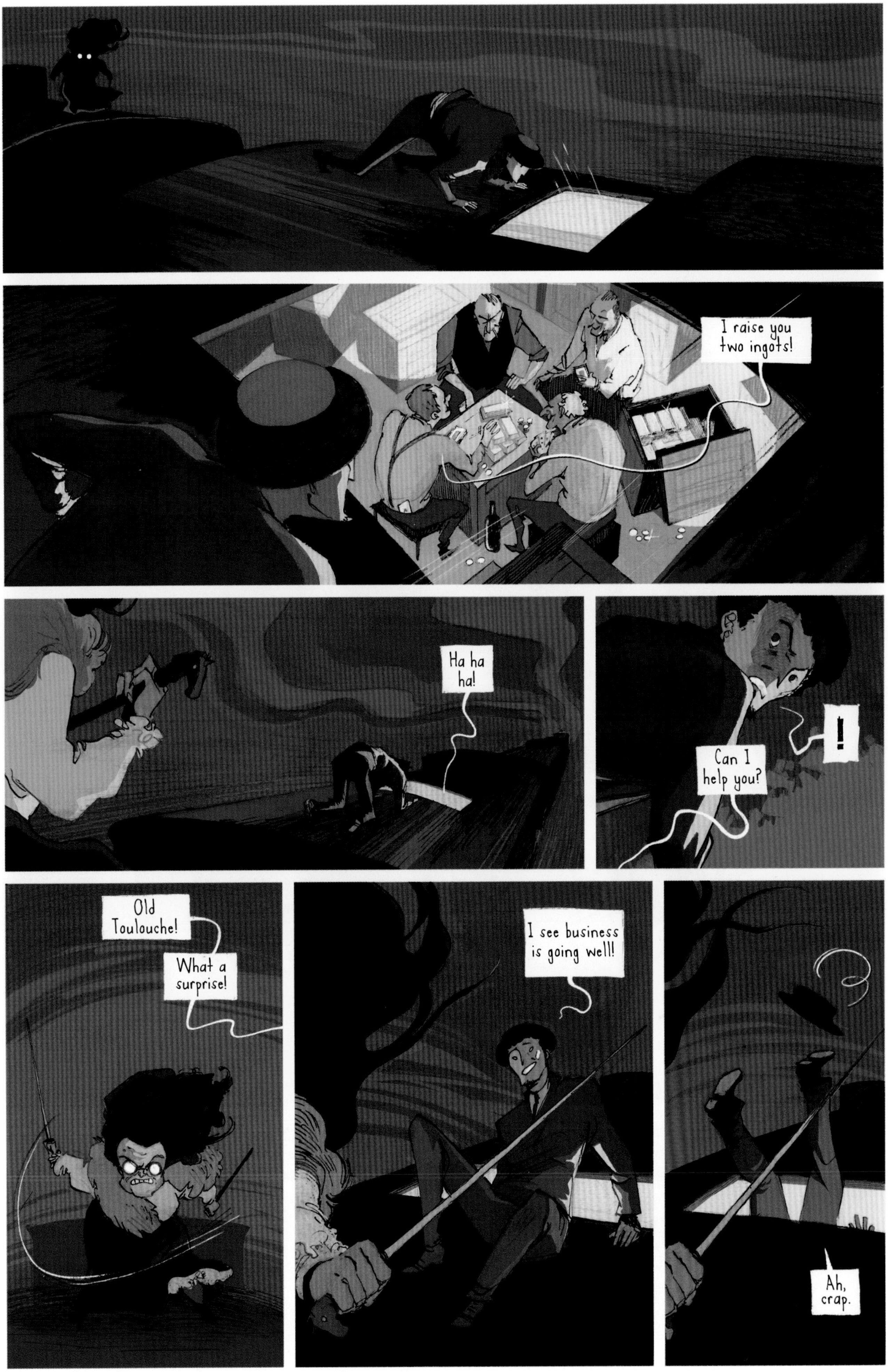
I raise you two ingots!
Ha ha ha!
!
Can I help you?
Old Toulouche!
What a surprise!
I see business is going well!
Ah, crap.

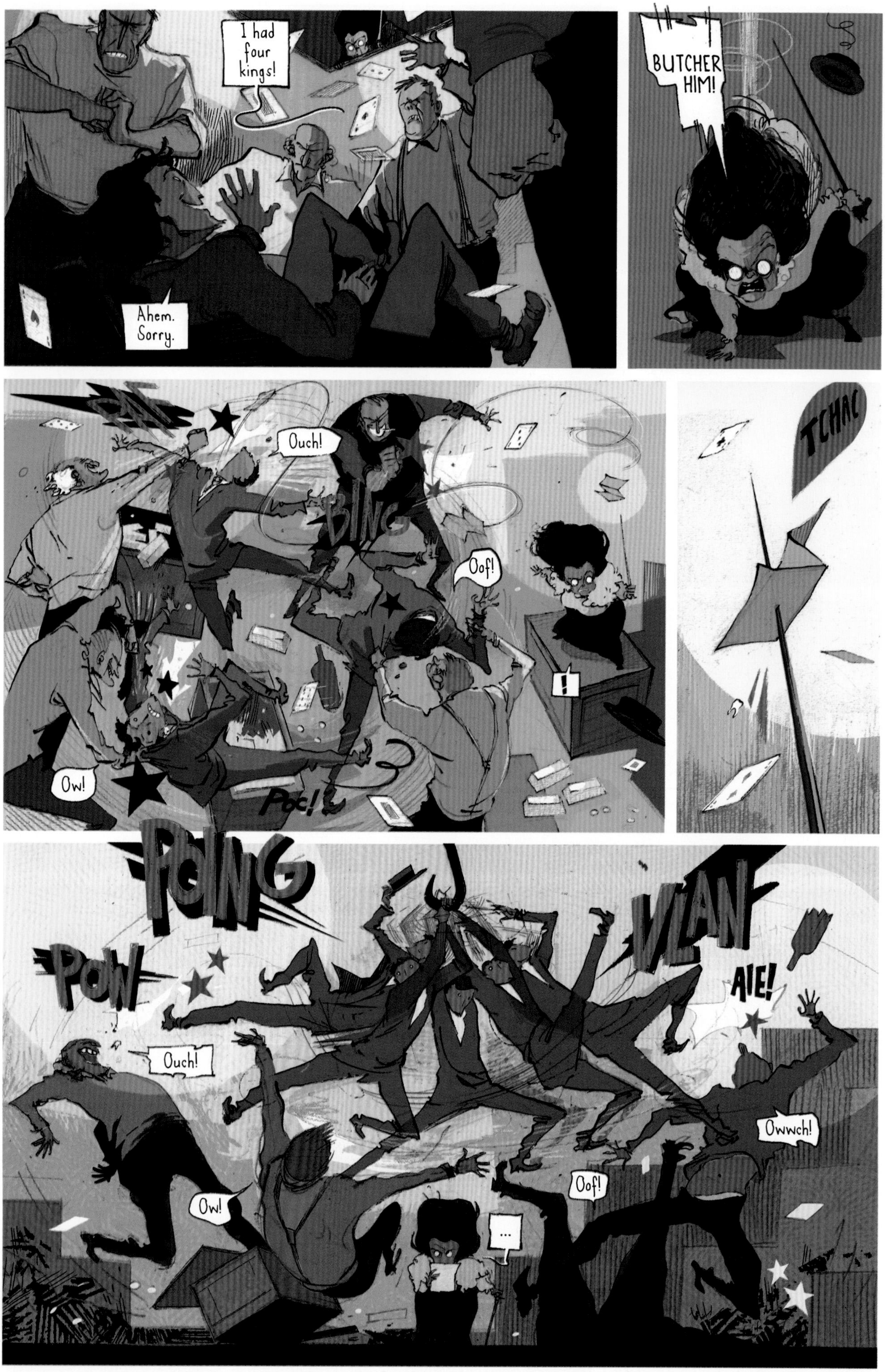
I had four kings!
Ahem. Sorry.
BUTCHER HIM!
Ouch!
BING
Oof!
!
Ow!
Poc!
TCHAC
POING
VLAN
POW
AIE!
Ouch!
Owwch!
Oof!
Ow!
...

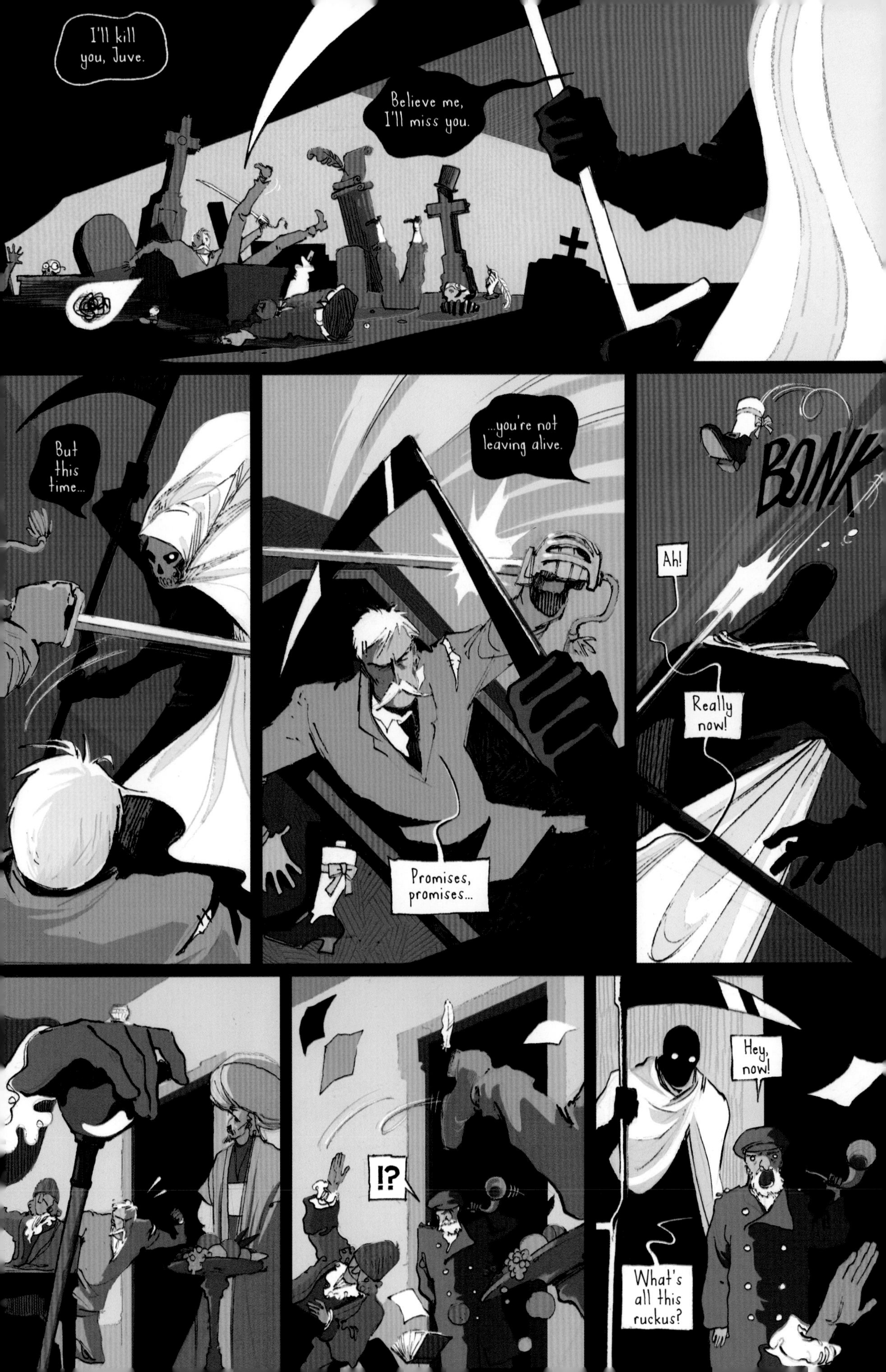
I'll kill you, Juve.
Believe me, I'll miss you.
But this time...
...you're not leaving alive.
Promises, promises...
BONK
Ah!
Really now!
!?
Hey, now!
What's all this ruckus?

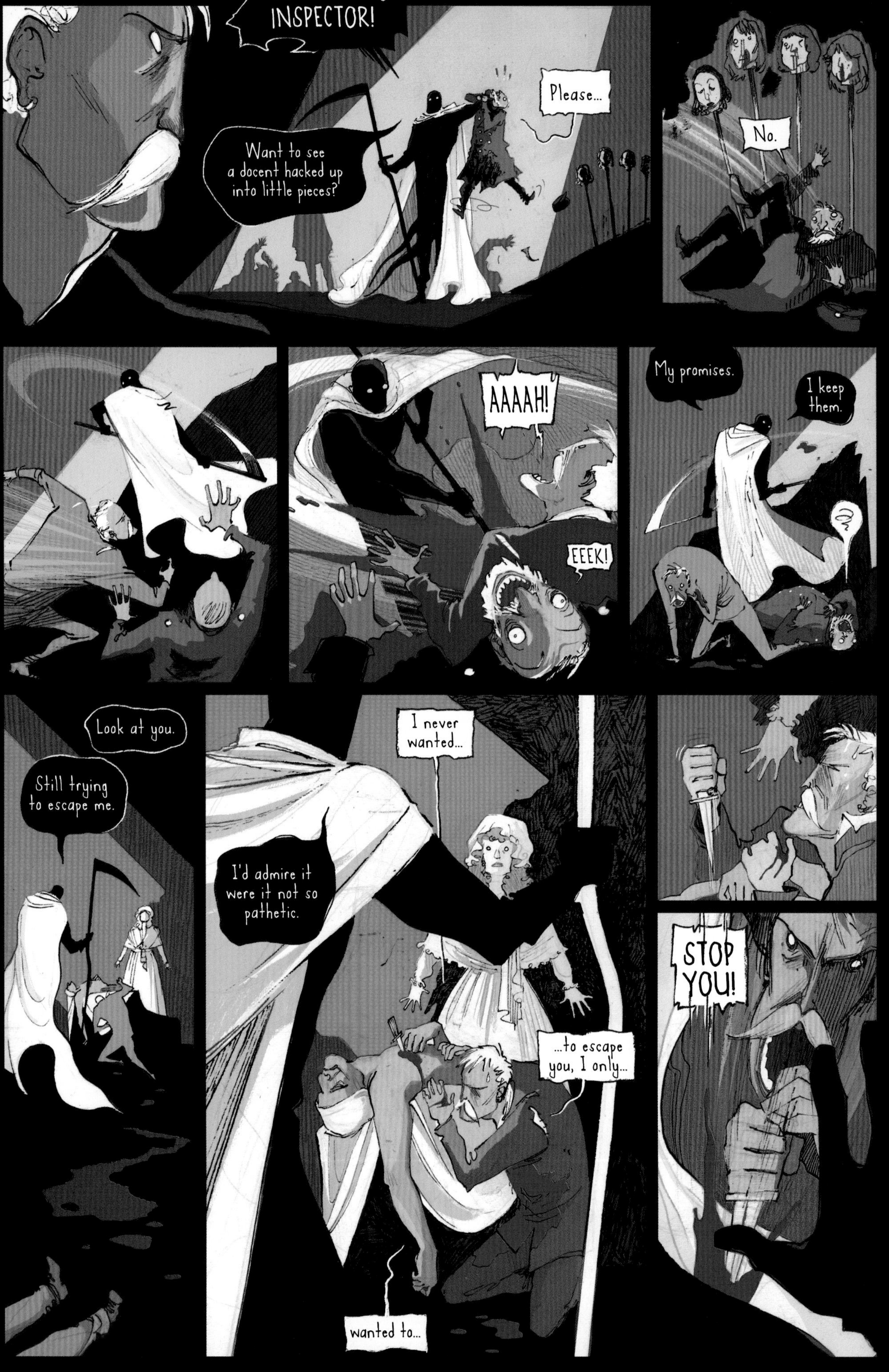

INSPECTOR!
Want to see a docent hacked up into little pieces?
Please...
No.
AAAAH!
EEEK!
My promises.
I keep them.
Look at you.
Still trying to escape me.
I'd admire it were it not so pathetic.
I never wanted...
...to escape you, I only...
wanted to...
STOP YOU!

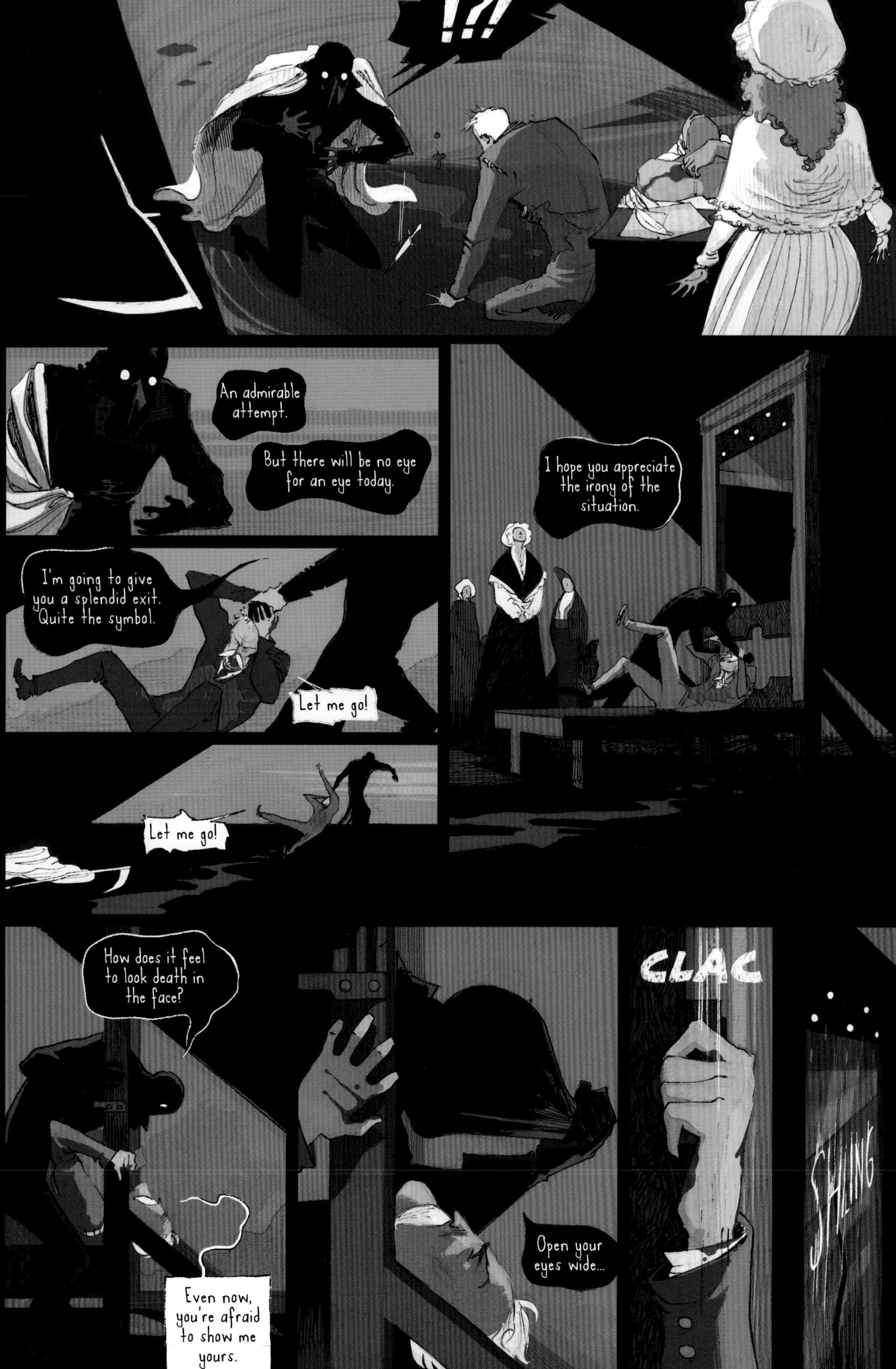
!?!
An admirable attempt.
But there will be no eye for an eye today.
I hope you appreciate the irony of the situation.
I'm going to give you a splendid exit. Quite the symbol.
Let me go!
Let me go!
How does it feel to look death in the face?
Even now, you're afraid to show me yours.
Open your eyes wide...
CLAC
SHLING

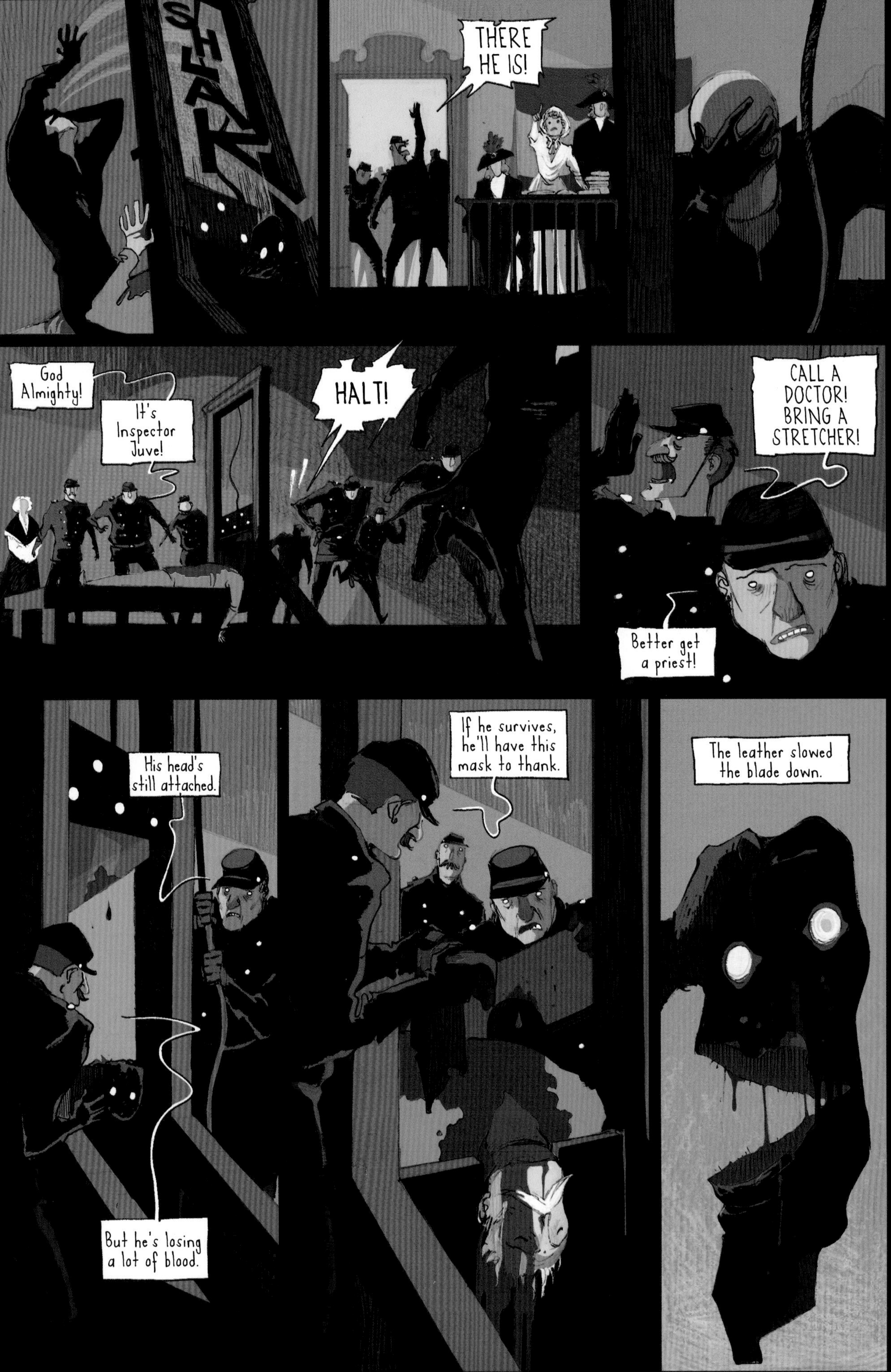
SHLANK
THERE HE IS!
God Almighty!
It's Inspector Juve!
HALT!
CALL A DOCTOR! BRING A STRETCHER!
Better get a priest!
His head's still attached.
If he survives, he'll have this mask to thank.
But he's losing a lot of blood.
The leather slowed the blade down.

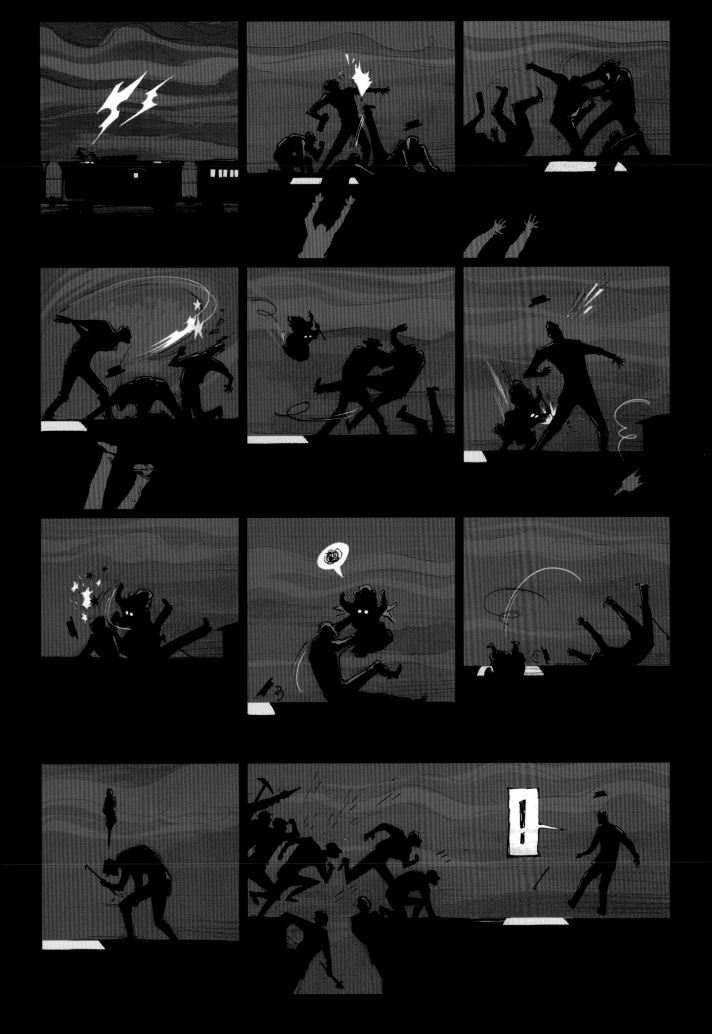

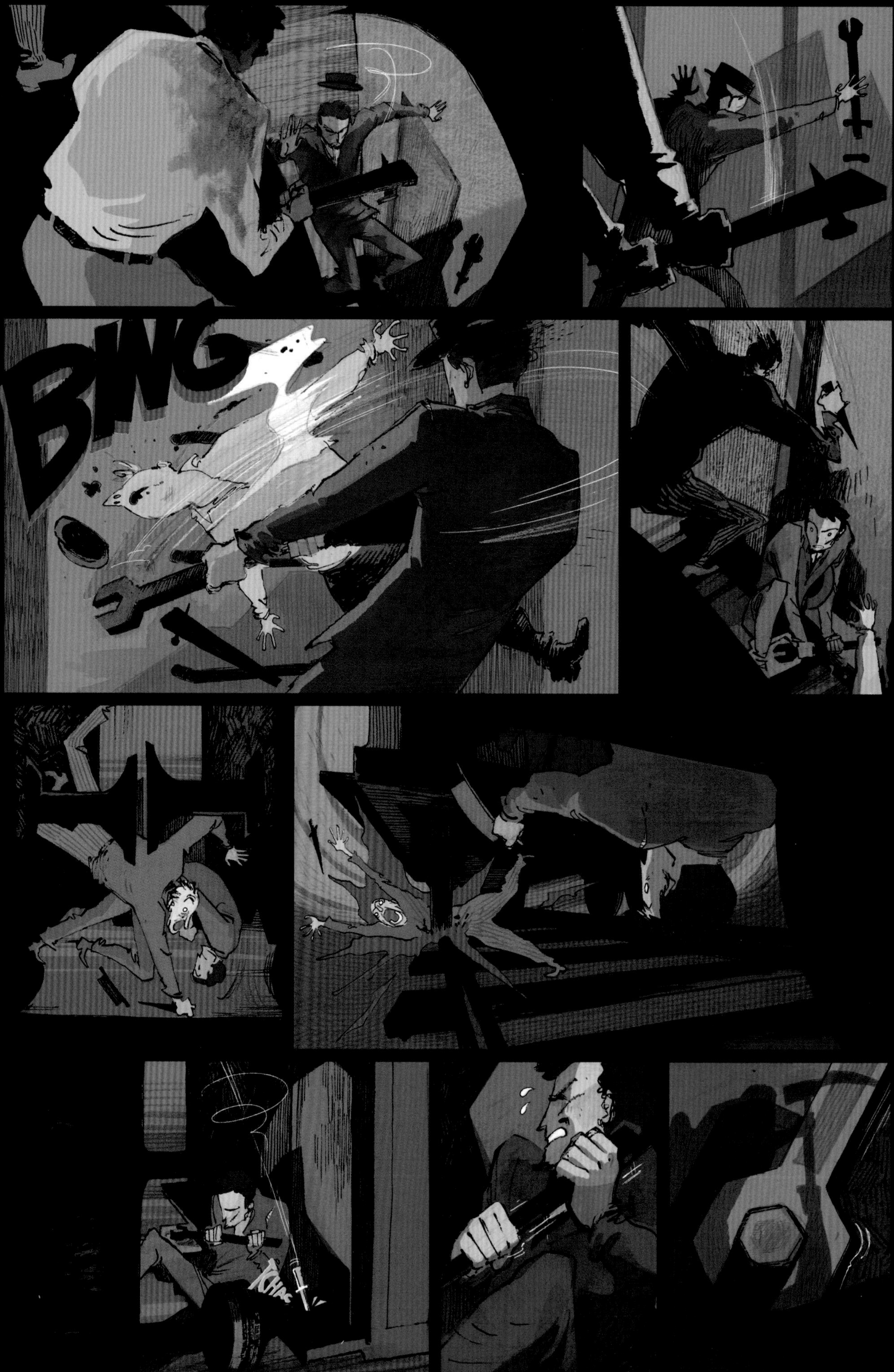
BING
TCHAC

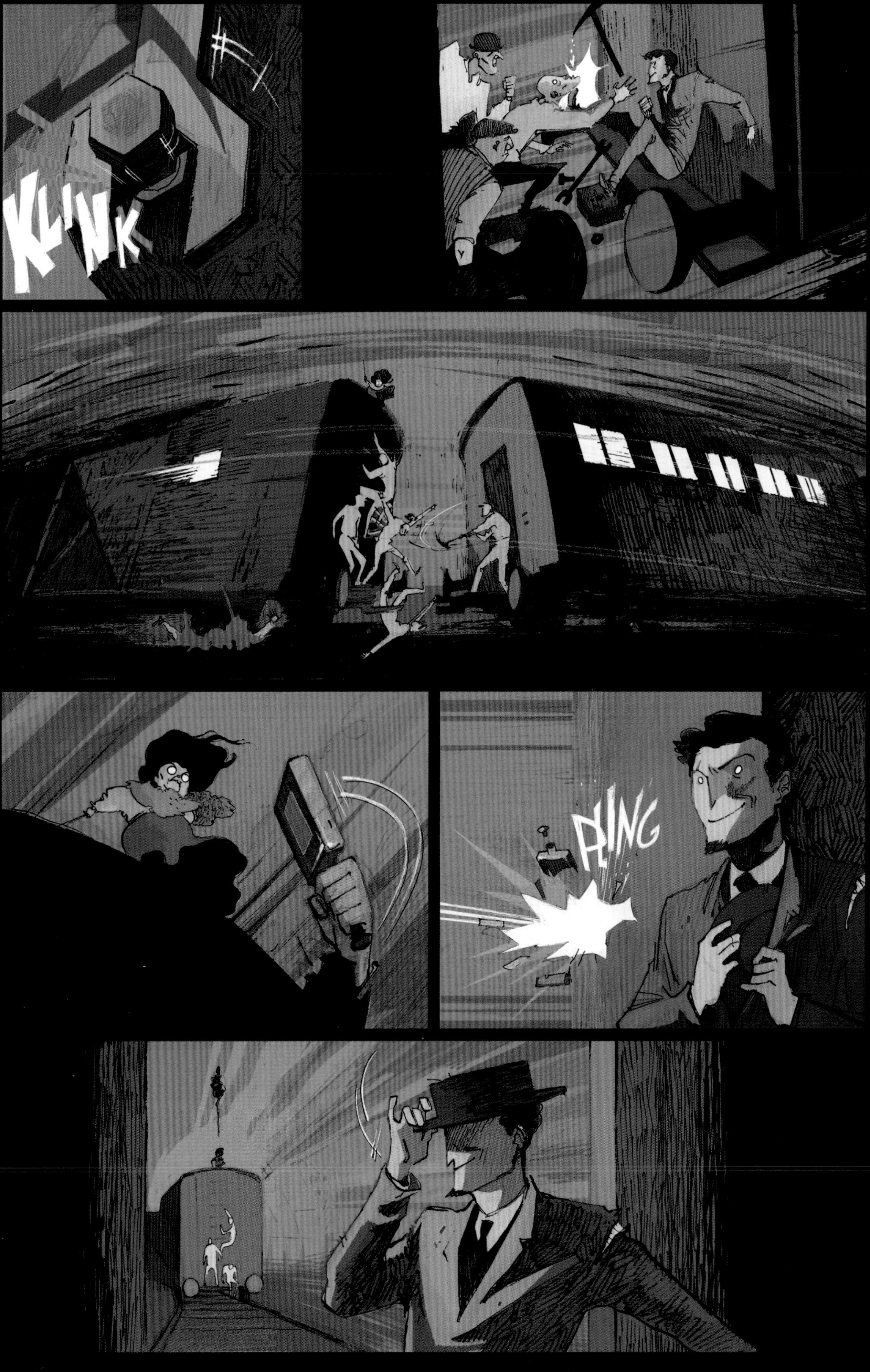
KLINK
PLING

Saturday, September 16, 1911

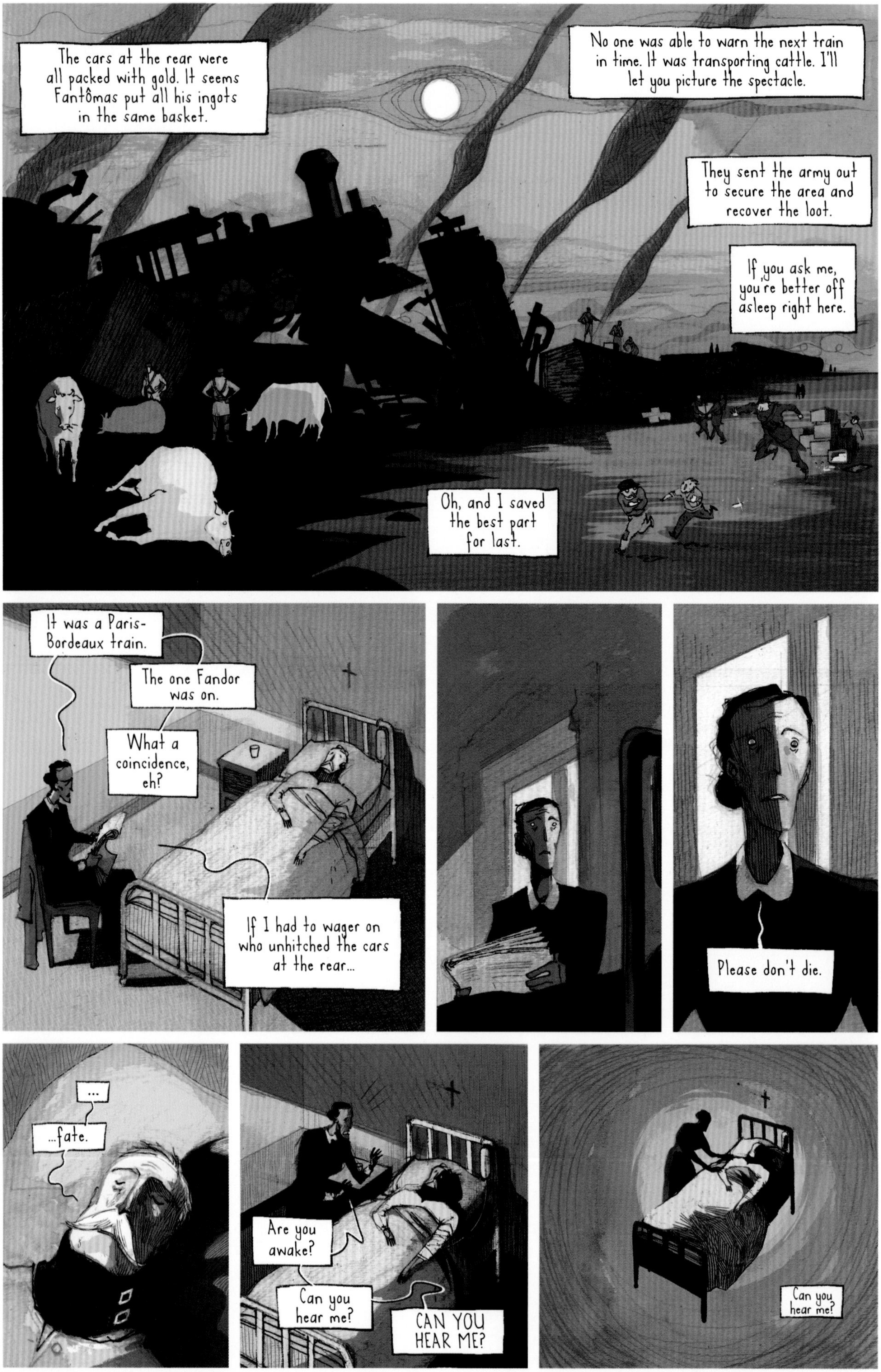
The cars at the rear were all packed with gold. It seems Fantômas put all his ingots in the same basket.
No one was able to warn the next train in time. It was transporting cattle. I'll let you picture the spectacle.
They sent the army out to secure the area and recover the loot.
If you ask me, you're better off asleep right here.
Oh, and I saved the best part for last.
It was a Paris-Bordeaux train.
The one Fandor was on.
What a coincidence, eh?
If I had to wager on who unhitched the cars at the rear...
Please don't die.
...
...fate.
Are you awake?
Can you hear me?
CAN YOU HEAR ME?
Can you hear me?

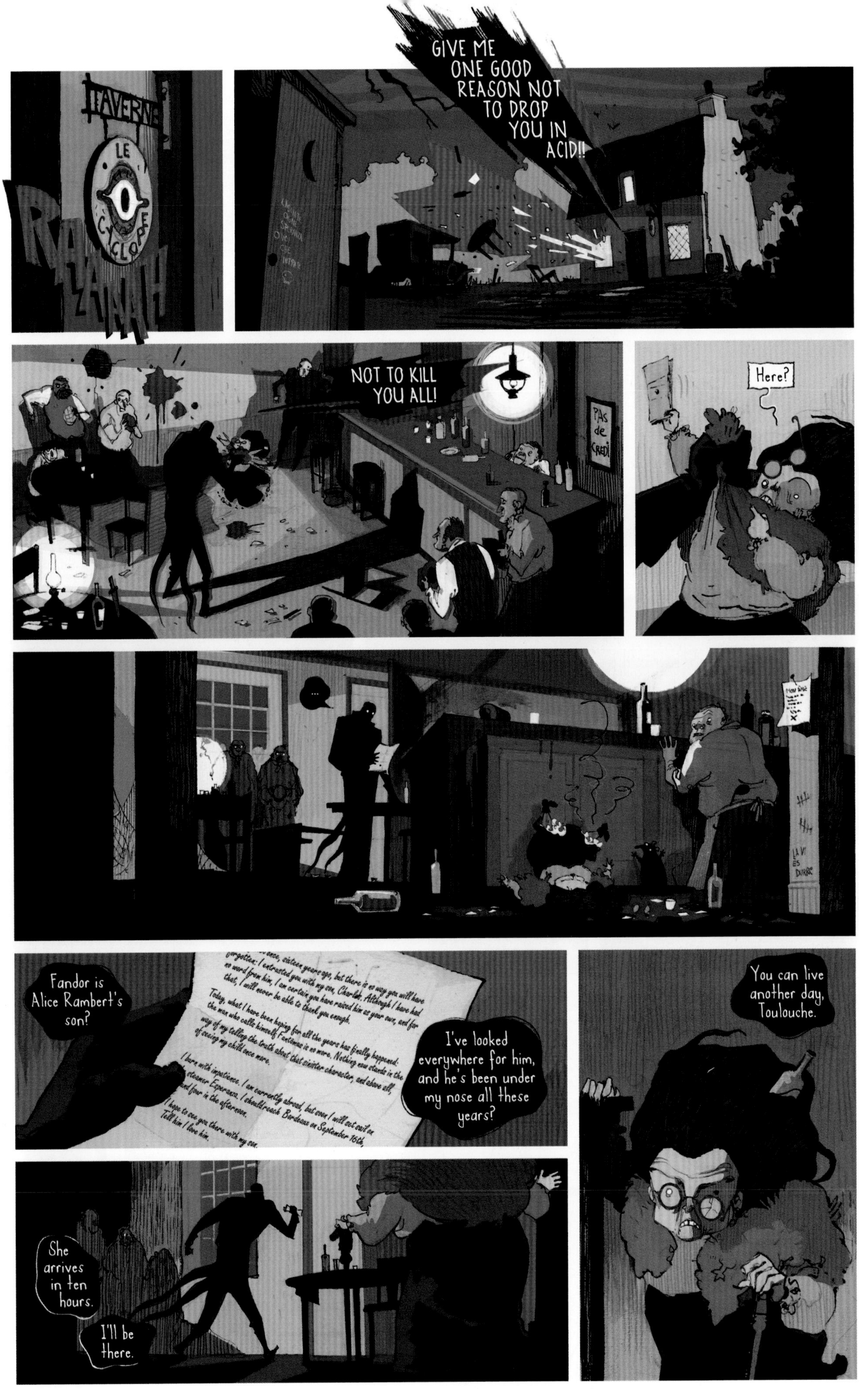
TAVERNE
LE CYCLOPE
RAAAAH
GIVE ME ONE GOOD REASON NOT TO DROP YOU IN ACID!!
NOT TO KILL YOU ALL!
PAS de CREDI
Here?
...
Fandor is Alice Rambert's son?
once, sixteen years ago, but there is no way you will have forgotten: I entrusted you with my son, Charles. Although I have had no word from him, I am certain you have raised him as your own, and for that, I will never be able to thank you enough.
Today, what I have been hoping for all the years has finally happened: the man who calls himself Fantômas is no more. Nothing now stands in the way of my telling the truth about that sinister character, and above all, of seeing my child once more.
I burn with impatience. I am currently abroad, but soon I will set sail on steamer Esperanza. I should reach Bordeaux on September 16th, and four in the afternoon.
I hope to see you there with my son.
Tell him I love him.
I've looked everywhere for him, and he's been under my nose all these years?
She arrives in ten hours.
I'll be there.
You can live another day, Toulouche.

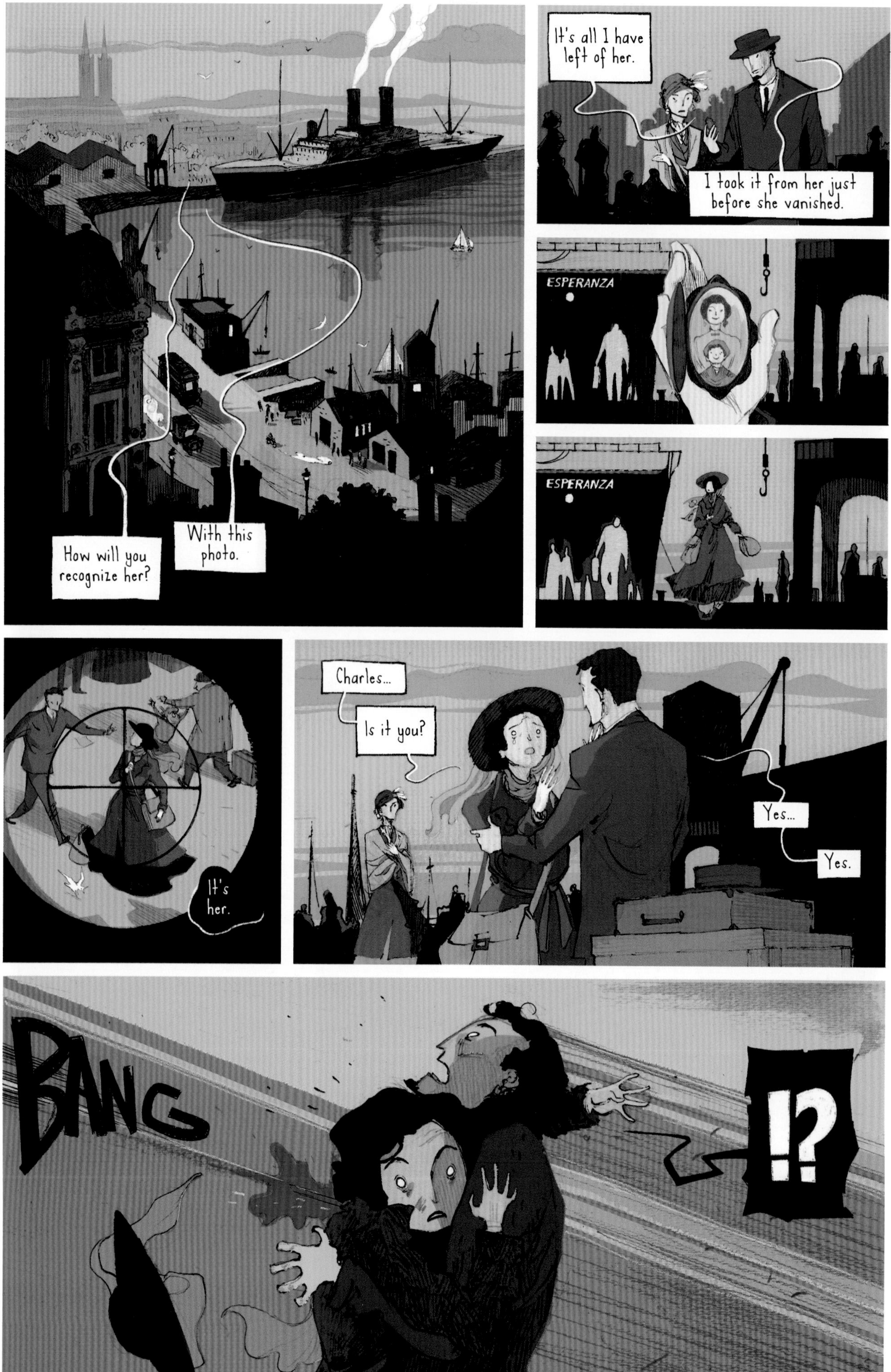
How will you recognize her?
With this photo.
It's all I have left of her.
I took it from her just before she vanished.
ESPERANZA
ESPERANZA
It's her.
Charles...
Is it you?
Yes...
Yes.
BANG
!?

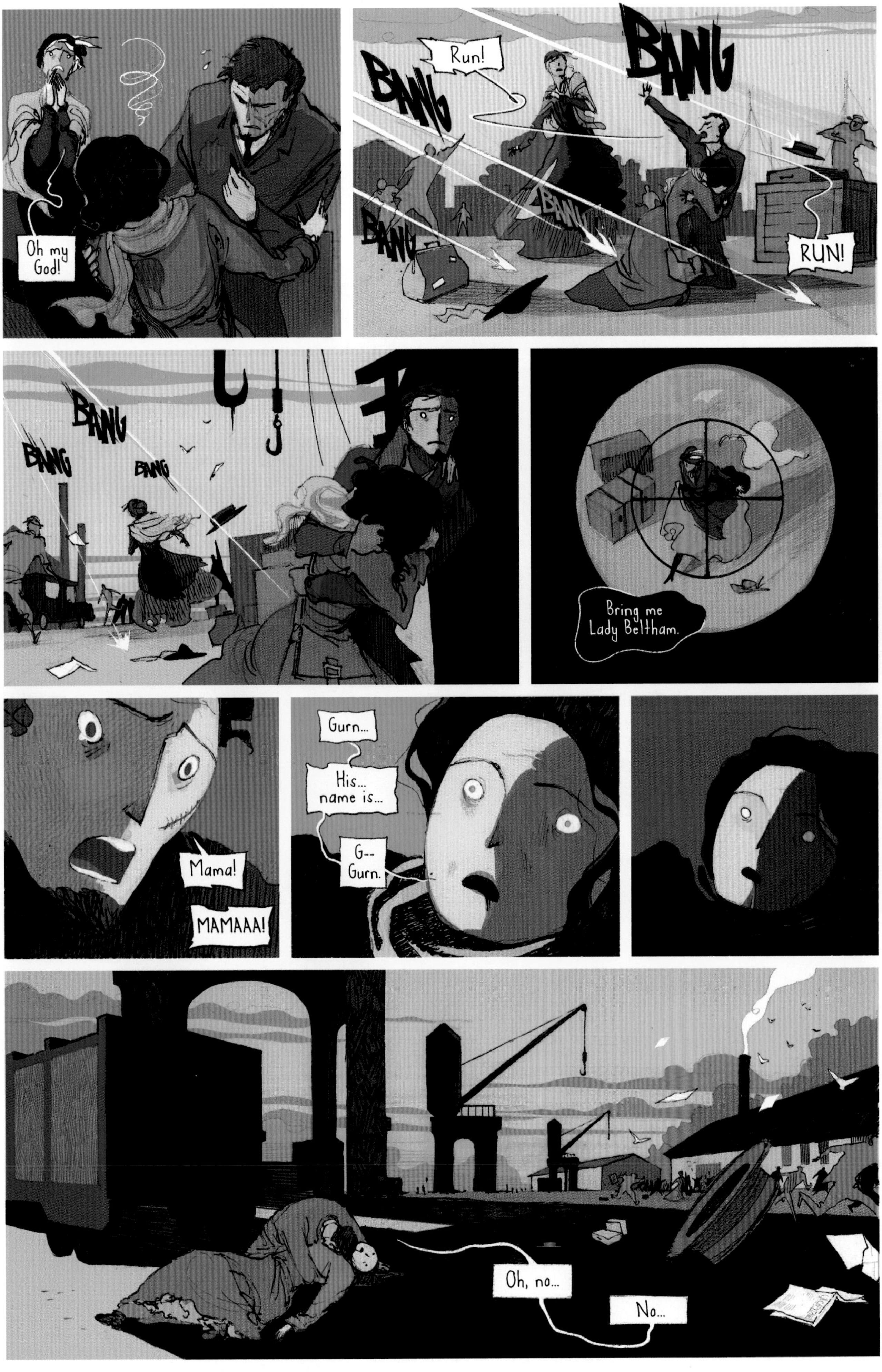
Oh my God!
Run!
BANG
BANG
BANG
BANG
RUN!
BANG
BANG
BANG
Bring me Lady Beltham.
Mama!
MAMAAA!
Gurn...
His... name is...
G-- Gurn.
Oh, no...
No...

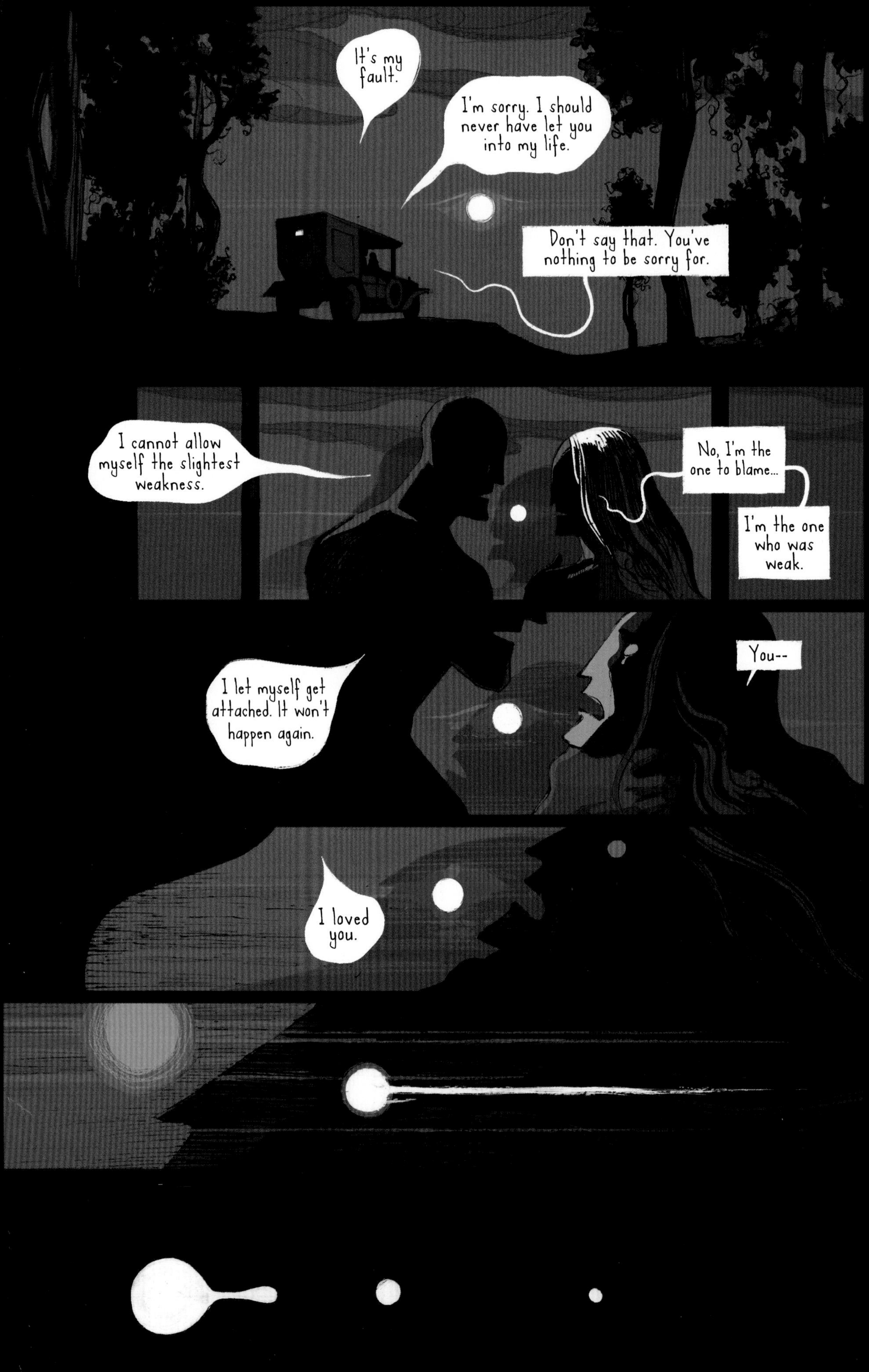

It's my fault.
I'm sorry. I should never have let you into my life.
Don't say that. You've nothing to be sorry for.
I cannot allow myself the slightest weakness.
No, I'm the one to blame...
I'm the one who was weak.
I let myself get attached. It won't happen again.
You--
I loved you.

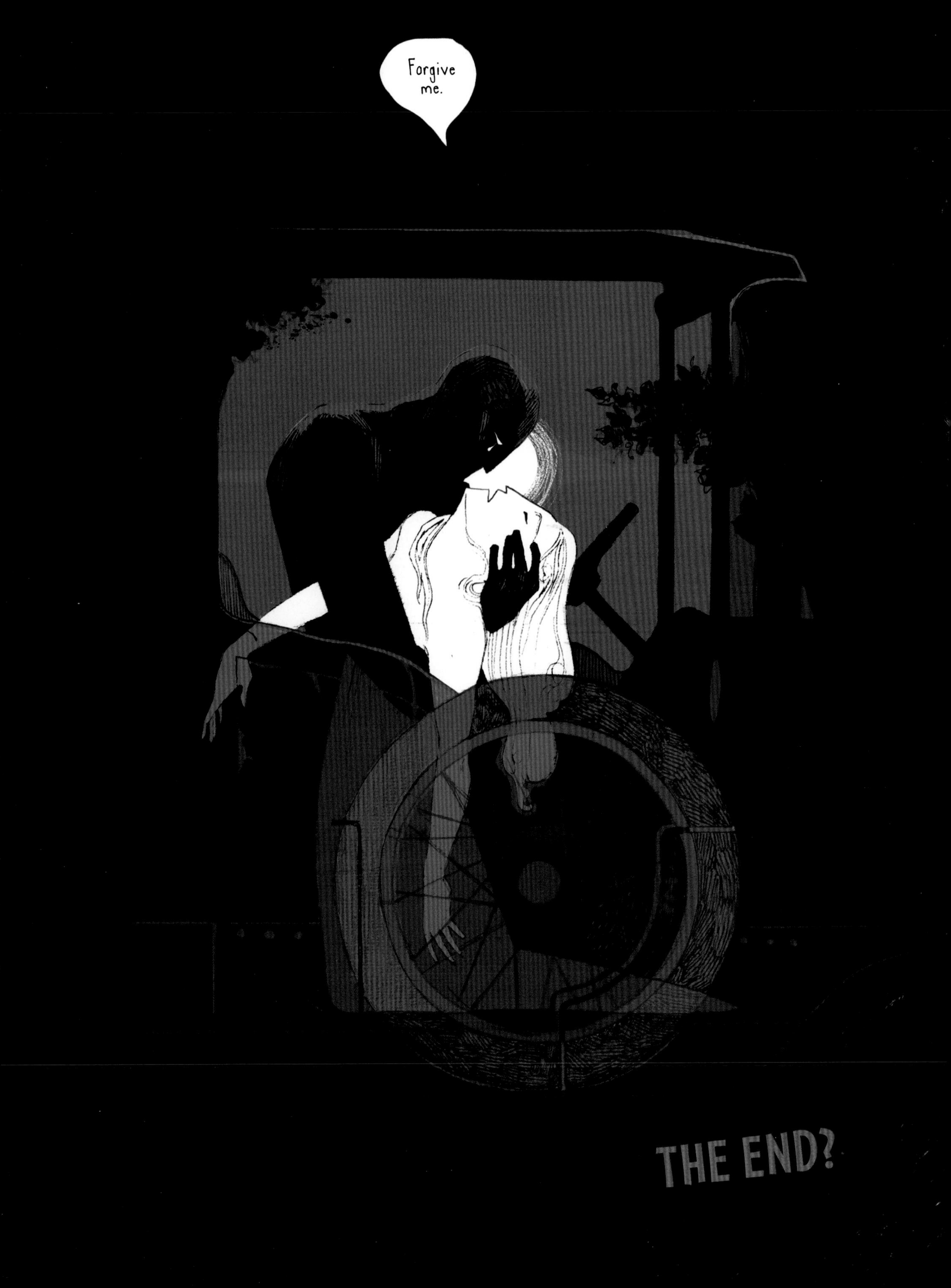
Forgive me.
THE END?

# ALSO FROM TITAN COMICS AND STATIX PRESS

**2021:** LOST CHILDREN

**ALISIK:** FALL

**ATLAS & AXIS**

**THE BEAUTIFUL DEATH**

**CENTURY'S END**

**THE CHIMERA BRIGADE** - BOOK 1

**THE CHIMERA BRIGADE** - BOOK 2

**THE CHIMERA BRIGADE** - BOOK 3

**THE CHRONICLES OF LEGION** - BOOK 1:
RISE OF THE VAMPIRES

**THE CHRONICLES OF LEGION** - BOOK 2:
THE THREE LIVES OF DRACULA

**THE CHRONICLES OF LEGION** - BOOK 3:
THE BLOOD BROTHERS

**THE CHRONICLES OF LEGION** - BOOK 4:
THE THREE FACES OF EVIL

**DEAD LIFE**

**THE DEATH OF STALIN**

**DEATH TO THE TSAR**

**DOCTOR RADAR**

**EMMA G. WILDFORD**

**EXTERMINATOR 17**

**FACTORY**

**HERCULES:** WRATH OF THE HEAVENS

**KHAAL**

**KONUNGAR:** WAR OF CROWNS

**THE 6 VOYAGES OF LONE SLOANE**

**LONE SLOANE:** DELIRIUS

**LONE SLOANE:** GAIL

**LONE SLOANE:** SALAMMBÔ

**MANCHETTE'S FATALE**

**MASKED:** RISE OF THE ROCKET

**MCCAY**

**MONIKA** - BOOK 1: MASKED BALL

**MONIKA** - BOOK 2: VANILLA DOLLS

**THE NIKOPOL TRILOGY**

**NORMAN** - VOLUME 1

**NORMAN** - VOLUME 2: TEACHER'S PET

**NORMAN** - VOLUME 3:
THE VENGEANCE OF GRACE

**NORMAN:** THE FIRST SLASH

**OSCAR MARTIN'S SOLO:** THE SURVIVORS OF
CHAOS

**PACIFIC**

**THE QUEST FOR THE TIME BIRD**

**THE RAGE** - BOOK 1: ZOMBIE GENERATION

**THE RAGE** - BOOK 2: KILL OR CURE

**RAVINA THE WITCH?**

**ROYAL BLOOD**

**SAMURAI:** THE ISLE WITH NO NAME

**SAMURAI:** BROTHERS IN ARMS

**THE SEASON OF THE SNAKE**

**SHERLOCK FOX**

**SHOWMAN KILLER** - BOOK 1:
HEARTLESS HERO

**SHOWMAN KILLER** - BOOK 2:
THE GOLDEN CHILD

**SHOWMAN KILLER** - BOOK 3:
THE INVISIBLE WOMAN

**SKY DOLL:** SPACESHIP

**SKY DOLL:** DECADE

**SKY DOLL:** SUDRA

**SNOWPIERCER:** THE ESCAPE

**SNOWPIERCER:** THE EXPLORERS

**SNOWPIERCER:** TERMINUS

**THE THIRD TESTAMENT** - BOOK 1:
THE LION AWAKES

**THE THIRD TESTAMENT** - BOOK 2:
THE ANGEL'S FACE

**THE THIRD TESTAMENT** - BOOK 3:
THE MIGHT OF THE OX

**THE THIRD TESTAMENT** - BOOK 4:
THE DAY OF THE RAVEN

**UNDER:** SCOURGE OF THE SEWER

**UNIVERSAL WAR ONE**

**VOID**

**WORLD WAR X**

**YRAGAËL / URM THE MAD**